Facebook® ALL-IN-ONE FOR DUMMIES®

by Melanie Nelson and Daniel Herndon

WILEY

John Wiley & Sons, Inc.

Facebook® All-in-One For Dummies®

Published by
John Wiley & Sons, Inc.
111 River Street
Hoboken, NJ 07030-5774

www.wiley.com

Copyright © 2012 by John Wiley & Sons, Inc., Hoboken, New Jersey

Published by John Wiley & Sons, Inc., Hoboken, New Jersey

Published simultaneously in Canada

For general information on our other products and services, please contact our Customer Care Department within the U.S. at 877-762-2974, outside the U.S. at 317-572-3993, or fax 317-572-4002.

For technical support, please visit www.wiley.com/techsupport.

Wiley publishes in a variety of print and electronic formats and by print-on-demand. Some material included with standard print versions of this book may not be included in e-books or in print-on-demand. If this book refers to media such as a CD or DVD that is not included in the version you purchased, you may download this material at http://booksupport.wiley.com. For more information about Wiley products, visit www.wiley.com.

Library of Congress Control Number: 2012937954

ISBN 978-1-118-17108-0 (pbk); ISBN 978-1-118-22783-1 (ebk); ISBN 978-1-118-23983-4 (ebk); ISBN 978-1-118-26449-2 (ebk)

Manufactured in the United States of America

10 9 8 7 6 5 4 3 2 1

WILEY

About the Authors

Melanie Nelson is a professional blogger and social media consultant who has been working with business websites since 1995 (it's true — she remembers Mosaic and Netscape). As a veteran of online publishing and marketing, Melanie has grown with changes as they happen and looks ahead to coming innovations. She owns Blogging Basics 101 (`http://BloggingBasics101.com` and `http://fb.com/BloggingBasics101`), where she shares information about using Facebook and other social media platforms to grow your business, building community, and improving search engine optimization (SEO). Hubspot.com included Blogging Basics 101 in its list of "10 Amazing Blogs About Blogging to Start Reading NOW." Melanie's presentations and workshops have inspired attendees at conferences such as Blog World & New Media Expo, Type-A Parent, BlogHer, and Blissdom.

Daniel Herndon is founder and CEO of Indianapolis-based marketing and innovation agency redwall LIVE. His firm creates campaigns, strategies, and tools for marketing, especially interactive and social marketing. He speaks often on practical social media use and integration with traditional marketing. He has been recognized for his efforts in creative philanthropy, the highlight of which was profiled in *USA Today* when he and non-profit director Darren Heil lived in a van alongside an Indianapolis highway, where they live streamed their life for 5 days while promoting their efforts to raise funds through social media. Daniel was recognized by the *Indianapolis Business Journal* in the 2011 "40 under Forty" featuring local business leaders who have achieved outstanding success in their community before the age of 40.

Dedication

Melanie Nelson: I dedicate this book to my husband Bill and my best friend Kathy Cordeiro — my loudest cheerleaders; David Cordeiro because he introduced me to HTML and technology in 1995 and sparked a passion I didn't know I had; and to Ryan, Emily, Jacob, Adam, Trevor, and Ewan because how fun is it to see your name in print?

Daniel Herndon: I dedicate this book it to the biggest dummy I know, who shall remain unnamed. You have always inspired me to look for opportunities to teach and help improve the world around me; also to my wife Carrie who is an amazing writer herself and always believes in and supports my ability; lastly to the great people of redwall LIVE that are a major resource for everything I do.

Authors' Acknowledgments

Melanie Nelson: A project's success rarely lies with a single person, and that is definitely the case with writing a book. I'd like to thank everyone who worked with us on *Facebook All-in-One For Dummies,* especially Amy Fandrei and Jean Nelson of John Wiley & Sons. In addition, I'd like to thank my blogging and social media friends who offered help and advice when asked: David Griner, Karen Lewis, Kelby Carr, Heather Solos, Melissa Culbertson, Sarah Pinnex, and Lisa Frame were invaluable resources throughout this process.

On a personal level, I must thank my husband, Bill, and our kids for their unending patience and support as I once again threw myself into an all-consuming project. I appreciate that you pulled me away from writing for pizza, game nights, and much-needed breaks. I must also thank Kathy Cordeiro for doing everything a best friend does plus one. Most importantly, Kathy listened daily as I talked through ideas and asked for input on certain passages. It's quite possible Book I, Chapter 1 in particular wouldn't have been written without her help. Thank you all.

Daniel Herndon: I'd like to take the time to thank the people that when called upon, were always willing to help. This process could have been much harder without them. First to all off my Social Media Savvy Colleagues in Indianapolis, what a great community you've built for the socially connected! I'd like to recognize Amy Fandrei for her skillful pushing to ensure we meet deadlines, and Jean Nelson and her team for catching just about everything I didn't mean to put in this book.

For me, writing *Facebook All-in-One For Dummies* was made possible by some of the most important people in my life. First of all, Corinne and Kaija, my two very smart and very dynamic daughters, your names will always go down in history as the cool kids that were willing to allow me to spend hours in front of the computer writing between homework sessions, or during our time at the bookstore on Sunday. Of course to Adam, Blaise, and Heather for committing time to make sure that we kept the lights at the office when I was less available to help. To Doug Karr and Kyle Lacy, my friends and fellow *For Dummies* authors whom I admire and enjoy talking business with. Lastly, I thank you for connecting and sharing.

Publisher's Acknowledgments

We're proud of this book; please send us your comments at `http://dummies.custhelp.com`. For other comments, please contact our Customer Care Department within the U.S. at 877-762-2974, outside the U.S. at 317-572-3993, or fax 317-572-4002.

Some of the people who helped bring this book to market include the following:

Acquisitions and Editorial

Project Editor: Jean Nelson

Acquisitions Editor: Amy Fandrei

Technical Editor: Michelle Oxman

Editorial Manager: Jodi Jensen

Editorial Assistants: Amanda Graham, Leslie Saxman

Sr. Editorial Assistant: Cherie Case

Cover Photo:
©iStockphoto.com / Laurent Davoust;
©iStockphoto.com / Andrejs Zemdega;
©iStockphoto.com / Johnny Greig;
©iStockphoto.com / Johnny Greig

Cartoons: Rich Tennant
(`www.the5thwave.com`)

Composition Services

Project Coordinators: Nikki Gee, Patrick Redmond

Layout and Graphics: Jennifer Creasey

Proofreader: Kathy Simpson

Indexer: BIM Indexing & Proofreading Services

Special Help
William Harrel

Publishing and Editorial for Technology Dummies

Richard Swadley, Vice President and Executive Group Publisher

Andy Cummings, Vice President and Publisher

Mary Bednarek, Executive Acquisitions Director

Mary C. Corder, Editorial Director

Publishing for Consumer Dummies

Kathleen Nebenhaus, Vice President and Executive Publisher

Composition Services

Debbie Stailey, Director of Composition Services

Contents at a Glance

Table of Contents

Introduction

Facebook is the most prolific social media platform so far. It has over 800 million active users as we write this book. (If Facebook were a country, it would be the third largest in the world.)

Facebook itself can be polarizing. Some people worry about their privacy, while others can't share enough. Some worry that Facebook is getting too big, while others appreciate the innovation that comes from crowdsourcing. As the authors of this book, we tend to fall on the side of loving Facebook. We love the way we can keep up with friends and family, meet new people, network with colleagues across the world, and market to our audiences. Facebook and other social platforms have given the public a larger voice in every conversation being had.

About This Book

If you picked up this book, it's probably because you're not on Facebook yet, and you're wondering about the hype. Or maybe you're on Facebook, but you have questions and need some answers. We've written this book with the beginner and intermediate social media user in mind. As you work with Facebook, we're confident you'll discover why it's so popular.

Our goal in writing this book is to introduce what Facebook is, show how you can use it personally and professionally, and show you a few tips and tricks along the way. We cover a fairly wide range of topics — this is an *All-in-One* book, after all — and you may or may not want to read everything we offer.

One thing we should point out is that social media changes almost daily, and Facebook is no exception. Although Facebook likes to change things up here and there, it generally doesn't change much more than tabs' locations and maybe make ad pictures a little bigger. Occasionally, Facebook changes some basic function — usually by making it more useful overall. As we were writing this book, Facebook unveiled a game changer: Timeline. We discuss Timeline (both for your personal profile as well as your Fan Page) throughout the book, but we're bringing it up here to make a point. We kept up with changes as they were happening, and we've documented all the new stuff that's come out of Facebook HQ since September 2011, but new features continue to roll out. Facebook itself will never be done evolving. You can keep up with the most recent changes to Facebook by checking www.facebook.com/help/whats-new-on-facebook periodically.

Conventions Used in This Book

Throughout this book, we're consistent in how we present certain information. You find these conventions throughout the book:

✦ Whenever you need to type something, we put the stuff you need to type in **bold** so it's easy to see.

✦ When we introduce a new word you may not be familiar with, we put it in *italics* and define it.

✦ When we share website addresses (URLs) with you, they look like this: www.dummies.com. (If you're reading this book as an e-book, URLs are clickable links.)

✦ If you need to select an option from a menu, we use an arrow (⇨) as shorthand. For example, "Choose Home⇨Log Out" means to click the Home menu and then click the Log Out option.

Facebook is a website, so it's not specific to PCs or Macs. If you can surf the web, you can get on Facebook. However, if we share instructions for tasks that are specific to a Windows PC or Mac, we tell you. For example, if you need to copy text, press Ctrl+C (Windows) or ⌘+C (Mac).

What You Don't Have to Read

You're certainly welcome to read this book cover to cover, but you don't have to. Like in all *For Dummies* books, you can skip around to the sections you need without reading everything in between. In fact, you'll notice that we frequently point you to another chapter or section where we discuss the topic in more detail.

If you already have a Facebook account and/or have been using Facebook for a while, you can skip most of Book I, because those chapters focus mostly on why you would decide to join Facebook and on setting up your account. On the other hand, if you're new to Facebook, you may not be ready to dive into our chapters on creating apps or using Facebook ads. But we know you'll be ready soon enough.

Sidebars — you'll notice them because they have a gray background — are extra information we thought you'd find useful but aren't necessarily integral to your Facebook experience.

The bottom line? Use this book as you will. Highlight the important stuff, make notes in the margins, plaster it with sticky-note bookmarks. Our goal was to make this book as useful as possible, and we want you to use it any way that makes sense to you.

Foolish Assumptions

It would be impossible to consider every single type of reader for this book, so we've had to make some foolish assumptions. These assumptions allowed us to write a consistent book and, we hope, allow you to follow along without too much trouble. Here's what we assumed:

✦ You have a computer and know how to use it.

✦ You know what a web browser is and can surf the web.

✦ You have an e-mail address and know how to use it.

How This Book Is Organized

We divided this *All-in-One* into minibooks, which are organized by topic. The minibooks point out the most important aspects of Facebook. If you're looking for information on a specific Facebook topic, check the headings in the Table of Contents, or skim the Index.

Book 1: Creating a Personal Timeline

As you decide to join Facebook, there are some important things to consider, such as privacy and how to share things. We explain the personal and professional benefits of joining Facebook and walk you through how to set up your personal Timeline (that is, your Facebook profile). And, of course, we explain how privacy works on Facebook and give you tips about how to best protect yourself and others, and still share as openly as possible (but with the right people).

Book II: Connecting with Others

After you create your personal Timeline, you'll probably want to know how to start sharing content. Book II discusses your online persona and how you can put your best foot forward when interacting with others. We also explain how to share photos, video, and basic updates with your circle of Facebook friends. And we start to widen your circle by introducing you to Groups, Places, Fan Page Timeliness, and games.

Because almost everyone these days is mobile, we explain how you can take your Facebook show on the road and check your account with smartphone apps.

Book III: Connecting Facebook and Other Social Media

Book III is all about helping you understand what social media is, how Facebook fits in, and what other platforms you can use to go with the social media flow. Social media works best when it's integrated with all aspects of your marketing strategy. Find out why linking your website and your Fan Page Timeline is important (and how to do it).

Book IV: Building a Fan Page Timeline

If you own a small business, Facebook offers an excellent marketing opportunity for you to grow your customer base. Find out how to create a Fan Page Timeline, how to use it for marketing and customer service, and how to encourage word-of-mouth marketing with things like check ins and Deals. We even give you important pointers on growing your Facebook community.

Book V: Marketing Your Business on Facebook

Facebook is one of the most amazing marketing platforms available right now, with 800 million users. You're bound to find new customers here! In Book V, we tell you how to build your online influence, how to set up and track Facebook ads, how to run a proper giveaway on Facebook, and how to use Insights (Facebook's analytics program). This minibook is chock full of information that will take your business from meh to amazing.

Book VI: Developing Facebook Apps

If you really want to get going with Facebook, you want to delve into *apps* (short for applications). Apps are what make Facebook so incredibly useful — you use apps for everything from sharing news articles you've read to playing games to listening to music. Apps are particularly useful as you work on your Fan Page Timeline. We explain the basics of apps and take you through building your own, if you want to give it a try.

Icons Used in This Book

To make your experience with the book easier, we use various icons in the margins of the book to indicate particular points of interest.

When we share something we think is useful or will make life easier for you, we use the Tip icon.

If we want to reinforce a point or concepts, we use the Remember icon. This stuff is worth committing to memory.

If we need to warn you about something that could give you problems, we use the Warning icon. Pay close attention when you see a Warning, because when we use it, we mean it!

Information tagged with the Technical Stuff icon gets, well, technical. Technical Stuff isn't essential to your understanding of Facebook, so you can skip these paragraphs if you're not interested.

Where to Go from Here

You can always start by turning the page and reading the first chapter (Book I, Chapter 1). Or look over the Table of Contents and find something that catches your attention or a topic that you think can help you solve a problem. Or peruse the Index to find a specific item or topic you need help with.

We encourage you to Like our Fan Pages on Facebook:

✦ **Blogging Basics 101:** `http://fb.com/BloggingBasics101`

✦ **redwallLIVE:** `http://fb.com/redwallLIVE`

Book I

Creating a Personal Timeline

The 5th Wave   By Rich Tennant

"I know it's a short profile, but I thought
'King of the Jungle' sort of said it all."

Contents at a Glance

Chapter 1: Deciding to Join Facebook

In This Chapter

✔ Weighing the pros and cons of joining a social media platform

✔ Understanding the benefits of being part of the crowd

✔ Finding the limitations of Facebook

*I*f you're considering whether or not to join Facebook, you probably want to know what it is, how you use it, and whether it's going to be invasive in your life. Those are all fair concerns, and the purpose of this chapter is to address them. First, we explain what Facebook is and how it fits into the scheme of social media. Then we discuss the benefits of joining Facebook and the basic rules of doing so, and how you can customize your experience.

Explaining What Facebook Is

Facebook is a social networking platform where people share their thoughts, actions, photos, and videos with friends, family, and (in some cases) the public at large.

By setting up a personal Timeline, you can create status updates and keep others up to date on what you're doing. Facebook is where you can hang out with friends, even when you're not in the same location. Through status updates and shared applications, you can listen to the same music your friend is listening to or see where your friend had lunch if she checked in.

In fact, Facebook is becoming more than just a way to keep up with friends or family, it's a new way of marketing as well. Brands create Fan Page Timelines to connect with their customers on a more personal level and may offer marketing campaigns, coupons, or special deals to Facebook fans. Some brands have gone so far as to launch new products or services to their Facebook fans first.

Enjoying the Benefits of Joining Facebook

We're just going to put this out there: We love Facebook. When we tell people that we love Facebook, we get all kinds of reactions. Some people don't get it because they are Twitter diehards. Others don't get it because they think Facebook is fine, *thankyouverymuch,* but they're not passionate about it. And luckily, there are others who completely understand what we mean. They understand that when we say we love Facebook, we mean we love the opportunity it brings. Facebook is not just a way to share photos of the new baby, your lunch, or Saturday's party. It's an integral way of interacting with others — personal friends, colleagues, businesses, and even celebrities. It's a way to research your interests and learn new things. Facebook offers you a new way to broaden your social circle with people you've never even met before (indeed, they could be a world away). Of course, you can start by finding and reconnecting with old friends (say, friends from high school, college, or even old workplaces).

Customizing Your Experience

A benefit of being on Facebook is that you have the opportunity to be heard. Until social media truly became mainstream, we were broadcast to as a whole. News outlets, businesses, and celebrities all shouted their information to you to further their interests. The crux of social media is that broadcasting is frowned upon, and conversations are encouraged. You have a chair at the table and an opportunity to have your say. We don't mean to imply that all voices are equal. There are still obstacles, but social media has opened new avenues that make it more likely for your voice to have an impact if you use it wisely.

When you join Facebook, you have the opportunity to customize how you interact, who you interact with, and how often you interact overall. Your Facebook Timeline is a record of your voice. As you interact with other users, brands, Fan Page Timelines, and so on, you build your online persona. Others begin to create a perception of you, based on what you share on Facebook. Throughout Books I and II, we emphasize how you can bring your personality into your online persona by choosing your friends, sharing photos and video, controlling your privacy settings, and creating a stellar cover photo for your Timeline. (Your *Timeline* is your profile, and it allows you to share all the milestones of your life in one place.)

Avoiding the Timesuck — Using Facebook as a Tool

What we often hear as a reason to avoid Facebook is that Facebook is a timesuck. We get that. You could easily waste hours of your time sifting through the shared content on Facebook. You could log on to Facebook during your morning coffee, and easily turn around and realize it's noon. Your coffee's cold, and it's time to get some real work done, not just play around on Facebook with online friends and ideas. And that's where we try to help people see the bigger picture. Facebook can be so much more than a timesuck. It can be an incredible way to connect with others.

When you use Facebook efficiently, it becomes less of a detriment and more of a tool. Using Facebook as a tool doesn't come naturally to everyone. We can attest that even we have spent hours following a rabbit trail. Melanie's habit when she's killing time is what she calls the Trifecta of Timesuck: switching from e-mail to Twitter to Facebook to see what's new in the five minutes since she last checked. It's true that part of using Facebook as a tool requires some self-control (and dude, we're not judging — we've been there).

You can do several things to help you get the most out of Facebook without wasting time:

✦ **Use lists.** Facebook allows you to group your connections based on criteria that you determine. Melanie created lists for local friends, blogging buddies, family, and so on. With lists, you can easily check out what everyone's doing without missing updates that may have slid by in your News Feed. See Book I, Chapter 3 to find out how to set up lists.

✦ **Use your navigation wisely.** Your main Facebook page shows your navigation options in the left sidebar. You can move list and groups you visit most frequently to your Favorites at the top of that bar so you can easily access them. See Book I, Chapter 4 to find out how to organize your navigation sidebar.

✦ **Subscribe to Fan Page Timelines you like.** Just about every website out there has a link to its Fan Page Timeline. The next time you visit your favorite website, check for a Facebook link. Clicking the Facebook link takes you to the Fan Page Timeline for that site, and from there, you can click the Like button to subscribe to the Fan Page Timeline. Many people use Facebook as a *feed reader* (a way to know when a website publishes new content). When you Like a Fan Page Timeline, any time it updates, you can see it in your News Feed (though you need to interact regularly with those posts to continue seeing them; see Book V, Chapter 3 to find out how that works).

✦ **Subscribe to public figures you like.** Public figures can be athletes, celebrities, or even social causes. Now, granted, your choice of public figure is going to weigh on how useful this tip is. We're not just talking about subscribing to Lady Gaga's Facebook updates, though she's included. When we say *public figure,* we're also talking about people like Neil deGrasse Tyson (an astrophysicist who makes science accessible to lay people: https://www.facebook.com/neiltyson) and George Takei (the actor who played Sulu in the original *Star Trek* series:

https://www.facebook.com/georgehtakei) — both of whom update their Facebook statuses regularly in interesting ways. As well, you can find just about any bigwig from any industry on Facebook. See Book II, Chapter 2 to find out how to use the Subscribe feature.

✦ **Create a group and invite people you like to interact with.** We're in a few groups on Facebook, and we've made some incredible personal and professional connections with people because of them. Groups start out with a common thread. That thread may be that you know all these people, or it may be that you're all passionate about video games. You invite people, and those people suggest adding people they know. Before you know it, you're meeting new people who share your interests. See Book II, Chapter 5 for more instruction on how to start or find a group.

As you hone your time on Facebook, it helps to ask yourself why you're using it. It's perfectly fine to be on Facebook because you want to keep up with your grandkids. (Hi, Grandma Patsy! Yes, that's right. Melanie's grandma is on Facebook.) It's okay if you want to be on Facebook because you like to see what others are doing. And it's just dandy if you're using Facebook as a networking tool. More likely than not, your reasons are a little bit of everything, and as you start using Facebook, you'll start to see where your real interests lie when you visit.

Embracing Facebook as an Extension of Your World, Not a Replacement

You may have seen the commercials or comics poking fun at Facebook. The message is similar to this: "All my friends live in my computer." It's funny because there's a grain of truth to it, but it's really an exaggeration.

If you're using Facebook as a tool, it's unlikely to take the place of your "real" life, where you're out and about doing things. Rather than thinking of Facebook as a *zero-sum game* (that is, you're either in or out), we think of Facebook as a way to extend relationships. So much of "real" life is mimicked on Facebook. When you connect with people at a conference, you can keep the networking going on Facebook. If you meet someone at a party, you can keep the social relationship going on Facebook. And if you go to a family reunion and catch up with everyone, but try to avoid that one weird cousin (you know we all have them), you can still do all of that on Facebook. You can still catch up with the family you love, and you can filter out the crazy cousin. And, to celebrate someone's life, you can even create a memorial on Facebook. Many times when you say goodbye to a loved one, the grieving process can be lonely. Facebook provides a way for you to connect with others who miss someone, share photos and stories, and help one another through the grief.

When you meet new people at a conference or a party and hit it off, you don't have to wait until you run into them again to continue getting to know them. Instead, you can connect with them on Facebook. From there, you can see what else you have in common, and you may find that you're even more *simpatico* than you originally thought! Think of Facebook as a way to keep the conversation going. Read the rest of Book I for advice on how to use lists and subscribe features to help filter your News Feed and control what you hear from certain friends.

Another way Facebook is an extension of your daily life is that it's always available to you. Apps on your smartphone or tablet device (such as an iPad) allow you to quickly check for breaking news, updates from friends, and so on. Flipboard is one of our favorite apps because it provides a nice overview (with lots of pictures) of what's going on without your having to spend a lot of time sifting through content. You can also use your mobile device to check in with friends to let them know where you are or what you're doing. You can even check in to a specific venue and redeem coupons! Book II, Chapter 5 and Book IV, Chapter 4 discuss check ins and Deals more thoroughly.

Finding Your Community on Facebook

Generally speaking, when most people start their Facebook accounts, they're doing it to keep tabs on what everyone else is doing. You start by connecting with people you actually know (this is called *friending* in the world of Facebook). Then you start connecting with people you meet around town, at work, or at conferences. Your circle of friends starts to grow. And as it does, you start to find your groove. You may notice that friends of friends share your interests, so you either friend them or subscribe to their updates. Or you may find a group that shares your passion for whatever it is you're passionate about. Your News Feed becomes fine-tuned to your interests and interactions.

Each community you join provides a ripple effect. Those communities build other communities (and when those communities grow too large, they splinter into more specialized groups, and you're once again interacting with people who share your philosophies). Suddenly, Facebook isn't an anonymous place with too much information; it's your customized News Feed that gives you the scoop on the things that matter to you most.

Using Facebook for News and Marketing

When news breaks, people don't flock to their TVs to see what's happening anymore; they turn to Twitter and Facebook for real-time information from the people who are already there. You don't have to wait for the news crew to get there; someone on the ground is already reporting what's happening. When the Occupy Wall Street protest movement started in 2011, you could immediately find them on Facebook, and follow their progress and growth all over the nation. And because news stories aren't filtered through a news agency, the information you gather may or may not be more accurate. At the very least, you can see varying points of view and piece together a more complete picture of what's happening.

If you're a small business owner, Facebook can open an entirely new marketing option for you. We're sure you're aware of how critical it is to be able to tap into targeted communities — Facebook is where you'll find those communities. If you're considering using Facebook as part of your marketing strategy, be sure you read Book IV to get the scoop on building your Fan Page Timeline. We explain the importance of understanding social media before jumping in and broadcasting your message, and we give you pointers on how to build your community from the ground up. Then flip over to Book V to discover how Facebook ads and Insights (the Facebook analytics software) can help you further target your audience and position yourself as an authority in your niche.

An interesting benefit of using Facebook is the ability to reach a wide audience for little or no money. You can spread the word about a cause, a movement, or a memoriam, and reach hundreds or thousands of people. Looking for an answer about something? Ask the crowd on Facebook (this is called *crowdsourcing*). People have posed questions or posted pictures on Facebook to crowdsource an answer and have had amazing results. If you want to know what your audience wants from you, just ask them.

Agreeing to Facebook's Terms of Service

So you decided to try out Facebook (yay!). Before you begin, you must agree to or meet the following requirements (you can find a complete list of the terms of service at `https://www.facebook.com/legal/terms`):

+ You're 13 years old or older.

+ You use your real information (name, e-mail, birthday, and so on).

+ You maintain a single account.

Facebook's goal is to "make the world more open and transparent, which we believe will create greater understanding and connection" (`www.facebook.com/principles.php`). To do that, Facebook relies on each user to create an account based on real information. Besides, how can people find you if you make a fake account? Two important parts of social media are authenticity and trust. You can set the foundation for them with your Facebook account.

Facebook is an interesting beast. On the one hand, it's a place where you can send out messages and updates to others when and how you choose. On the other hand, other users can choose how they receive your updates. Facebook allows everyone to control their own privacy and customize their interactions — as long as you adhere to the terms of service.

Facebook have developed a set of principles they use as a basis for all other Facebook rules, terms, and guidelines. You can find those principles spelled out here: www.facebook.com/principles.php. Generally speaking, Facebook strives to provide a free platform where people can connect and share information and experiences while owning their personal space and content. You can share what you want, with whomever you want, as long as both parties consent — which means don't bother, bully, or harass someone. The principles also support the following:

✦ **You own your content, and you control your privacy settings.** You can remove your content from Facebook any time you like, and you can set your privacy settings to reflect how you want to share your content and/or protect it from others.

You do own your content on Facebook. However, should you lose access to your account (for a violation of terms, for instance), you no longer have access to that content. Although it's unlikely that you'll run into that issue, we highly recommend backing up your content (especially photos and video) weekly or even monthly so you truly own and control your content by having a separate copy. See Book I, Chapter 2 for instructions on downloading your Facebook data.

✦ **Everyone's equal on Facebook.** We all follow the same rules, whether we're using Facebook for fun or business. Each Facebook user can build his own reputation on Facebook and won't be excluded unless he violates the terms of service. In other words, Facebook has to have a good reason to lock you out.

The Facebook Terms of Service (https://www.facebook.com/legal/terms) are based on the Facebook principles. When you create your Facebook account, you agree to those terms. The following list highlights a few of those agreements (again, we encourage you to read the terms yourself for a full understanding of what Facebook expects):

✦ You're in charge of your privacy on Facebook.

✦ You own your original content on Facebook.

✦ You won't spam other users or collect their information without their consent.

✦ You won't promote pyramid schemes, upload malicious code or viruses, or post hateful content.

When you agree to the Facebook terms of use, you agree that you will not (remember this is just overview, this list is not exact or inclusive)

✦ Engage in bullying, harassment, or hate speech.

✦ Sell your status updates.

✦ Post pornographic content.

Facebook has guidelines and terms of service for every aspect of the platform. We encourage you to read each set for yourself so you know exactly what the expectations are. Here's a list for your reference:

✦ **Facebook Principles:** www.facebook.com/principles.php

✦ **Statement of Rights & Responsibilities:** https://www.facebook.com/legal/terms

✦ **Family Safety Center:** https://www.facebook.com/help/safety

✦ **Terms of Service for Pages:** www.facebook.com/terms_pages.php

✦ **Data Use Policy:** https://www.facebook.com/about/privacy

✦ **Fan Page Guidelines:** www.facebook.com/page_guidelines.php

✦ **Community Standards:** https://www.facebook.com/community standards

✦ **Promotions Guidelines:** www.facebook.com/promotions_guidelines.php

✦ **Facebook Brand Permissions:** www.facebook.com/brandpermissions

✦ **Facebook Ad Guidelines:** https://www.facebook.com/ad_guidelines.php

✦ **Nonprofits on Facebook:** www.facebook.com/nonprofits

Chapter 2: Creating Your Facebook Account

*C*reating your Facebook account is a fairly easy affair. You just fill out a short form, and you're on your way. In fact, Facebook walks you through the three most important steps in customizing your account: finding friends, filling out your profile information, and uploading a profile picture. But there are a few other things you want to know about, like where to find your Account Settings dashboard so you can manage things like your password, username, and security options. This chapter discusses all those things, as well as how to connect your mobile phone to your account and how to deactivate or delete your Facebook account.

Starting Your Account

It's easy to create a new Facebook account! Just point your browser to www.facebook.com to get started. You begin by completing the form on the front page. You need to provide your first and last name, your e-mail address, the password you want to use, your sex, and your date of birth. Facebook then sends you an e-mail with a confirmation link. When you receive the e-mail, click the link to complete your Facebook sign-up. Facebook has this step to ensure that the e-mail account you're using is real.

You can have only one Facebook account, and you should be at least 13 years old to create an account. Be sure to use real information (including your birth date — which you can hide from the public later).

When you've completed the form, click the Sign Up button. Type the CAPTCHA words in the text box to prove you're a real person, and click the Sign Up button. At this point, Facebook wants to walk you through some steps to get you started.

Completing Step 1: Finding friends

You begin by finding your friends who are already on Facebook by using your e-mail account contacts list. Facebook offers options for Windows Live Hotmail, Gmail, AOL, Yahoo!, and other e-mail services. Click the Find Friends link next to the type of e-mail account you have, type your e-mail address in the text box, and click the Find Friends button. A dialog box may appear, asking your permission for Facebook to access your e-mail account and contact list. You need to grant this access in order for Facebook to cross-check the e-mail addresses in your contact book with those already registered on Facebook.

You can find friends associated with multiple e-mail accounts. For instance, if you have three different Gmail accounts, you can type in any of those addresses to find friends who are already on Facebook. Or if you have a Gmail account and a Yahoo! account, find your Gmail friends and then repeat the process for your Yahoo! account.

After you allow Facebook to access your e-mail account, depending on which type of e-mail account you're working with, you're presented with a list of friends who are currently on Facebook or, if you're a Gmail user, instructions for uploading your contacts.

If you see a list of friends, select the check box next to each friend you'd like to connect with on Facebook. If you want to connect with all of your contacts, you can select the Select All Friends check box. When you've selected your friends, click the Add Friends button to continue.

If Facebook finds e-mail addresses for people who are not on Facebook yet, you're asked if you'd like to invite those people to connect on Facebook. If you choose to do that, Facebook sends a message to those people on your behalf, asking them to join Facebook.

Completing Step 2: Filling in profile information

Step 2 allows you to start filling out your personal profile information, beginning with the name of your high school, college/university, and current place of employment. When you type in the names of your high school and college/university, you have the chance to include the year you graduated as well. When you're done, click Save & Continue.

Based on the information you've shared so far, Facebook pulls a list of recommended friends for you. These are generally people who may be in your address book or attended the same high school, college, or university while you were there. You can choose to add any of these people as a friend on Facebook simply by clicking the Add Friend link under the person's name. When you do, Facebook sends a friend request to that user and alerts you if he or she accepts your friend request.

You don't have to complete this information right now. You can click the Skip link to move directly to Step 3.

Completing Step 3: Uploading a profile picture

Your profile picture is one of the most important aspects of your Facebook account because it's what people come to associate with your updates. Facebook offers you the option of uploading an existing image from your computer or taking a new photo with your computer's webcam. (See Book II, Chapter 3 for tips on taking pictures with your webcam.) After you choose your photo, click Save & Continue. Your personal Timeline appears, and you can start using Facebook.

It's best to choose a picture that clearly shows your face so friends and family will recognize you immediately. (This is *Face*book, after all!) We suggest using a picture of yourself, not a picture of your child, pet, favorite team, and so on. Because so many people scan their Facebook News Feed quickly, it's easier for them to spot your updates if they can clearly see *your* picture. In addition, using logos or other found pictures you don't own yourself may be in violation of copyright. Contrary to what you may have heard, just because you find something interesting on the Internet doesn't mean it's free to use.

Finding Friends

Because Facebook is all about being social, it makes sense that you'll want to connect with your friends, family, and colleagues. In fact, as you become more comfortable with Facebook, you may interact with friends of friends, see that they're good fits, and send friend requests to them. Facebook says the average number of friends is 130, but just about everyone we know has many, many more. The following sections aim to help you understand what it means to be friends on Facebook and how to find people you want to connect with.

Understanding what it means to be friends on Facebook

In the real world, the term *friend* has different meanings to different people. If you ask an extrovert how many friends she has, she may say hundreds, because to her, everyone she meets is a friend. If you ask an introvert how many she has, she may say three, because her definition of a friend is much different from her extrovert counterpart's. Neither answer is wrong, but you can see how perspective can change what it means to be friends. Along those same lines, the term *friend* is a little different in the world of social media than in the real world. Online, you may find that you're friends with people you've never even met in person but have interacted with online via the comments on a mutual friend's status updates or through other social media (such as Twitter or blogs). Or maybe someone you met at a party sends you a friend request on Facebook, and you accept. Your circle is widening in a way it may not in the real world.

> *Melanie notes:* I'm an introvert. If you ask me how many friends I have, I'll tell you I have three or four, maybe five friends. Now, I know and interact with many more people than that in person. In fact, I know quite a few people in real life. But only three of them know my jeans size. Online I know thousands more people than I do in my everyday life. I'm connected to over 3,000 people on Twitter and hundreds of people on Pinterest, and I have over 500 friends on Facebook. My Fan Page has over 1,700 fans. My intention in sharing those numbers is to show that my online and offline friends are quite different, and so are their expectations and the way I interact with them. Online, a *friend* can be someone you just met or haven't met at all. A friend may be someone you're interested in following just because you have a common interest.

It's important to consider how you want to connect with others and what your criteria are for requesting and accepting Facebook friend requests — and respect how others deal with online friends. Understand that some people like to keep their Facebook Timelines private and limited to real-life friends and family. Others are an open book and accept requests from friends of friends or just about anyone. The key is not to take it personally if someone doesn't accept your friend request (sometimes easier said than done). Social media is interesting because on one hand, it's a very public forum where you can be heard by thousands. On the other hand, it's a very private place where you can establish your own place and determine who you interact with. It's a balancing act. We suspect your idea of how to relate with others will change as you become more comfortable interacting on Facebook and other social media platforms. We suggest starting slowly and building a group of Facebook friends you know and are comfortable with, and then expanding your community as you become more familiar with Facebook (and possibly other social media). In particular, pay attention to your privacy settings (see Book I, Chapter 3) and how and what you share in your status updates (see Book II, Chapter 2).

Searching for people you know

When you first set up your account with Facebook, it walks you through finding friends who may already be on Facebook. The platform allows you to use your existing e-mail contacts to see if any of those e-mail addresses are registered with accounts on Facebook and then lets you send a friend request to people you know. (See the earlier section "Completing Step 1: Finding friends.") If you skipped that step or decided to wait to find friends later, that's not a problem. You can find friends in several ways:

✦ **Check out Facebook's suggestions.** When you visit your personal Timeline, click the Friends link. At the top of the resulting page, click the +Find Friends button to see a list of people Facebook thinks you may know. Facebook draws this list from other accounts that have shared similar information to your own (for example, hometown, education, mutual friends, and so on). When you click the +Find Friends button, the Friends from Different Parts of Your Life page appears, as shown in Figure 2-1.

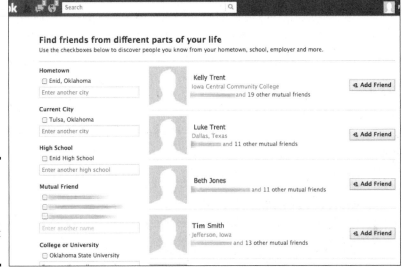

Figure 2-1:
Facebook suggests friends you can connect with.

You can filter the list using the list and check boxes in the left column. For example, if you want to only see a list of potential Facebook friends from your hometown, select that check box. If you see someone you'd like to connect with, you can click the +1 Add Friend button.

You may also see friend suggestions from Facebook on the right side of your News Feed page.

✦ **Use Facebook's list features.** Lists are a handy way to keep groups of friends together so you can see their updates any time you like. Facebook has a few lists it creates for you based on information you shared when you created your account (like where you live or where you went to school). Facebook takes that information, tries to find other Facebook accounts that have similar information, and adds them to your lists (you can remove anyone from those lists if you like). See Book I, Chapter 3 for further information on creating and managing friend lists.

✦ **Use the Search text box.** At the top of every Facebook page is a blue toolbar that has a Search text box. Start typing a name in the text box, and see if you can find who you're looking for. The name may not come up in the initial list, so be sure to click the See More Results option to see a longer list of possible matches. You can also search previous companies you worked for, your hometown, alma maters, and so on.

✦ **Look at friends of friends.** As you build your friend list, you can click over to someone's Timeline and view her friends. If you spot someone you know, you can click over to his Timeline and send him a friend request.

✦ **Search for topic pages.** Do a search for your high school, college/university, favorite sports team or hobby, and so on. If you see someone you know, send her a friend request, or see if she has subscriptions enabled and connect with her that way. (See Book II, Chapter 2 for more information on the Subscribe feature and how it works.)

✦ **Look on the sidebar of a website or blog.** Many businesses and bloggers would love to have you connect with them on Facebook. See if your favorite websites have a Facebook logo that links to their Fan Page Timeline.

Sending, receiving, and responding to friend requests

In order to connect with someone on Facebook, you need to send him a friend request. When you visit his personal Timeline, you can click the +1 Add Friend button to send him a request.

If you don't see the +1 Add Friend button or any option to send a friend request, that person may have her privacy set in a way that doesn't allow people she doesn't know to send a request. For example, Melanie's personal privacy settings allow only friends of friends to request a connection with her. If you don't know her or her friends, you can't send her a friend request; you can, however, subscribe to her public updates.

If you don't actually know someone but would like to follow his public updates, you can click the Subscribe button on his personal Timeline (if he's enabled it). When you subscribe to someone, you aren't actually Facebook friends with that person, but you can see any public updates he shares. Subscriptions are a good way to follow leaders in your line of work or something you're really interested it. For example, Melanie isn't Facebook friends with Mignon Fogarty (Grammar Girl), but she subscribed to her public updates. (It would be awkward for Melanie to try to friend her because they've never met and Melanie is a fangirl. Rather than submitting a random friend request, Melanie settled for subscribing to her public updates.)

When you receive a friend request, Facebook alerts you by highlighting a number next to the friends icon in the blue toolbar at the top of the page (look in the top-left corner next to the Facebook logo). If you aren't sure if you have pending friend requests, click the friends icon to see a list similar to the one in Figure 2-2.

Figure 2-2:
Your
pending
friend
requests
are under
the friends
icon.

You can see from Figure 2-2 that you have two choices: Confirm or Not Now. When you confirm a friend, Facebook immediately adds him to your Friends list. In Figure 2-3, you can see the Friends button, which shows the person was added to that list. Facebook also suggests a list of other people you may want to connect with, based on your new friendship.

Figure 2-3:
When you
confirm a
Facebook
friend, he
goes into
your Friends
list.

If you click the Friends button, you can add that person to any of your lists (see Figure 2-4).

Figure 2-4:
You can add
your new
Facebook
friend to
any list
for easier
access.

If you choose to ignore a friend request or click the Not Now button, Facebook wants to know if you know the person or not, as shown in Figure 2-5.

Figure 2-5:
Do you
know the
person who
tried to
friend you?

Facebook asks if you know the person to help cut down on spam and unwanted requests. If you click Yes, Facebook thanks you for your feedback, and that person can send another friend request. If you click No, Facebook won't allow that person to send any more friend requests to you.

If you don't accept a friend request, Facebook doesn't tell the person who sent the request. However, there are a few ways she can figure it out. For instance, if she looks at her own list of friends and you aren't there, or if she looks at your personal Timeline and sees the +1 Add Friend button instead of the Friend Request Pending button, she'll realize you didn't accept her request.

If you choose to ignore a friend request or clicked the Not Now button, that person can still see any public updates you post. If you're the one who initiated the friend request, you can see public posts by the person you sent the request to. As we mentioned, the Subscribe feature is a great alternative if you aren't quite ready to be Facebook friends with someone. The Subscribe feature is a good way to stay connected to people because you can subscribe to an account (if that person turned on subscriptions) and see public updates without bothering the person with a friend request.

Finding and Customizing Your Account Settings

Your Account Settings is one of three options for controlling the information you share on Facebook (the other two being your Privacy Settings and Timeline — see Book I, Chapters 3 and 4, respectively). You can find your Account Settings page by clicking the down arrow at the far-right end of the blue Facebook toolbar at the top of any Facebook page and choosing Account Settings from the menu. On the main Account Settings page, you have the option to customize your General Settings, Security, Notifications, the Applications (or apps) associated with your account, Mobile Settings, Facebook Payments (usually used for games and/or advertisements), and Facebook Ads. It's entirely possible you may not use some of these features (for example, payments). If that's the case, you don't need to worry about those options. The next few sections explain what you can expect to find with each option and how you can control the options to suit your Facebook needs.

General Account Settings

Your General Account Settings page lists the basics of your account and allows you to edit that information. You see options for editing your Name, Username, E-Mail, Password, Networks, Linked Accounts, and Primary Language. You also have the option to download a copy of your Facebook data. We explain each of these options in the following sections.

Name

The Name row shows the name you registered when you created your Facebook account. This name is what others see when you share content via Facebook. When you click the Edit link, you have the option to change your first and last names, and add your middle name if you like. You can also use the drop-down list to choose how your name appears on your Timeline (First, Last or Last, First). Most people have their names appear as First, Last. The alternative-name option lets you include a nickname or maiden name to help others find you. If you make any changes here, you need to confirm them by typing your Facebook password in the Password text box and then clicking the Save Changes button.

Username

A *username* is a customized URL for your Facebook account and is sometimes referred to as a *vanity URL*. Facebook assigns a unique number to all new accounts and uses that number in the address for your personal Timeline. For example, when you click over to your personal Timeline, look in the address bar of your browser, and you probably see something like this: `www.facebook.com/profile.php?id=100003296325790`. The long string of numbers following `id=` is your account ID. That would be pretty hard to remember, not to mention a little inconvenient to include on a business card. When you choose a username, it replaces the numbers in the URL for your Timeline and looks something like this: `https://www.facebook.com/MelanieMNelson`.

To set your username, follow these steps:

1. **Navigate to your General Account Settings page and click the Edit link next to Username.**

2. **Verify your account via your mobile phone (if it's not already verified).**

   If you've just established your Facebook account, it may not be verified yet (even if you clicked the link in the e-mail Facebook sent you when you signed up). If that's the case, you can wait a little longer until Facebook confirms your verification, or you can click the Verify via Mobile Phone option. To verify via your phone, do this:

   1. *Click the Verify via Mobile Phone link.*

   2. *Use the drop-down list to choose the correct country code for your cellphone's number.*

   3. *Type your cellphone number in the Phone Number text box.*

   4. *Select whether you prefer to receive a text or an automated phone call.*

   5. *Click Continue.*

      The We Texted You dialog box appears.

   6. *After you receive your verification code via text, type the code into the text box, and click Continue.*

      A dialog box appears.

   7. *Select the check boxes next to the options you want to enable, and click Submit.*

      If you activate text messages, Facebook texts your notifications to you. Normal text messaging charges apply, so be sure you know what your phone's data plan is — you could be receiving a lot of texts.

      When your account is verified, the Username option changes to look like Figure 2-6.

      If the Username option doesn't change right away, click another option (for example, Name) and then click back to Username.

Figure 2-6:
The
Username
option looks
like this
if you've
verified your
account.

3. **Type your desired username into the text box behind** `http://www.` `facebook.com/.`

   If your username isn't available, Facebook lets you know so you can try another username.

   You can change your username only one time. It's best to use your real name if you can. (You may have to include your middle name or at least your initial if you have a fairly common name.) Choosing something like PartyBill may be fun now but probably won't be quite as impressive if work colleagues are looking you up.

4. **Type your Facebook password in the Password text box and click Save Changes.**

E-mail

The E-mail row shows the e-mail address you used when you created your Facebook account. When you click the Edit link, you have these options:

✦ **Add another e-mail addresses to your account.** If you have multiple addresses associated with your account, you must choose one to be your primary address. Facebook uses your primary e-mail to send notifications to you. You can remove an address from your account by clicking the Remove link.

✦ **Activate your Facebook e-mail.** You need to have a username associated with your account in order to activate your Facebook e-mail. Your username is your Facebook e-mail address (for example, `MelanieMNelson@facebook.com`). Any messages sent to that address appear in your Facebook Messages. You can check for new messages by clicking the Messages icon in the blue toolbar at the top of all Facebook pages.

To activate your Facebook e-mail, navigate to your General Account Settings page and click the Edit link beside E-mail. Click the Activate Facebook E-mail link.

You may not have e-mail available if your account is fairly new. Wait a few days and try again.

✦ **Allow friends to include your e-mail in the information that's downloaded when they back up their accounts.** When a Facebook user downloads a copy of his Facebook data (explained in a moment), all sorts of information is included: status updates, comments, pictures, video, and even contact information for his Facebook friends. If you don't want your e-mail address to be included in that download, be sure to deselect the check box next to this option.

If you make any changes to your e-mail settings, be sure to type your Facebook password into the text box and click the Save Changes button for those to take effect.

Password

It's a good idea to periodically change your account password. You can do that by typing your current password in the Current text box, and then typing and retyping your new password in the appropriate boxes. When you click the Save Changes button, your password is updated, and you'll need to use the new password the next time you log into Facebook.

Good passwords are an important part of protecting your privacy online. Lucretia Pruitt of The Social Joint (`http://thesocialjoint.com/`) gave us an excellent suggestion for choosing a password. Take a line from your favorite song and then use the first letter from each word in that line. For example, if your favorite song is "New York, New York" by Frank Sinatra, you could choose the line "It's up to you, New York, New York!", and it would look like this: `Iuty,Ny,Ny!`. Now add a number associated with someone else (like a good friend's birthday) to the end of it. Your new password would be something like this: `Iuty,Ny,Ny!530`, which looks like it would be impossible to remember, but it's actually easy because you know the song and friend's birthday. We provide more tips on choosing a password and protecting your privacy in Book I, Chapter 3.

Networks

Facebook has networks associated with high school, college, and some supported companies. In order to join a specific network, you need to have an official e-mail address associated with the college or work network you're trying to join so you can confirm your affiliation. If you are trying to join a high school network, a classmate in the network must approve you.

You can join up to five networks. If you join more than one, you're prompted to choose your primary network. Your primary network appears next to your name and is public. Your primary network also affects your search results in Facebook. If you do a search, results associated with your network appear at the top of the results.

To join a network, type the name of the network into the Network name text box and then type your associated e-mail address in the Network E-mail text box. Click Save Changes. You need to check that e-mail for your confirmation message and follow the instructions to join the network.

To remove a network from your account, click the Remove link beside the network you want to leave. Click Save Changes.

Facebook no longer accepts requests for new networks, so if your work doesn't have an approved network, you can create a group and invite people to join that way.

Linked Accounts

You can link your Facebook account to another account (for example, Google), and any time you're logged into that second account, you're also logged into Facebook. Use the drop-down list to choose the account you want to use.

Language

Because Facebook is an international social media platform, it's available in myriad languages. Use the drop-down list to change your primary language, and click Save Changes.

Download a copy of your Facebook data

You should always remember that you don't own your space at Facebook. Although it's rare, you can find yourself locked out of your account for violation of Facebook's terms of service. If that were to happen, you'd lose access to all the content you've added to Facebook: status updates, pictures, video, comments, friends and their contact information, and so on. Facebook makes it so easy to use your smartphone to upload pictures and updates that many people use their phones to record and share important life events directly to Facebook. We suggest making a habit of backing up your data on a regular basis if you're consistently keeping important content (for example, vacation photos) on Facebook rather than somewhere else. Your download will include everything you've uploaded to Facebook, including status updates, pictures, video, private messages, chats, and a list of Facebook friends and their contact information (if they've enabled that on their account).

To back up your data, follow these steps:

1. **Navigate to your General Account Settings page and click the Download a Copy of your Facebook Data link.**

   The Download Your Information page appears.

2. **Click the green Start My Archive button.**

   The Request My Download dialog box appears and explains that it will take some time to create the backup file.

3. **Click the Start My Archive button.**

   Facebook shows a message that it will send a message to the primary e-mail associated with your account when your archive is ready.

4. **Click Okay.**

5. **When you receive the e-mail stating your archive is ready, click the link to download the file to your computer.**

When you open the archive file, you find the following information:

✦ Your biographical Timeline information (for example, your contact information, interests, work history, and so on)

✦ All your status updates and comments by you and your friends

✦ All your photos and video you uploaded to your account (and the comments associated with them)

✦ Your friend list

✦ All the Notes you wrote and shared

✦ All your sent and received private messages

It's great that you've backed up your Facebook information, but we encourage you to go a step further and save the file to your computer as well as another source (for example, Dropbox or an external hard drive). That way, if something happens to your computer, you'll still have your content.

Security

Facebook states that it takes your personal privacy very seriously. To that end, Facebook provides many options so you can control how and what you share (see Book I, Chapter 3 for more information on privacy). The Security tab in your Account Settings dashboard is where you find many of the options for securing your account. From here, you can set up secure browsing, set your login notifications and approvals, change your application passwords, monitor your recognized devices (such as your phone), active Facebook sessions, or even deactivate your account. We explain each option in the next few sections.

Secure browsing

Facebook offers the opt-in feature of using secure browsing on your laptop or desktop computer while you're logged into Facebook. We highly recommend turning on this feature. What secure browsing does is encrypt your

Facebook activity so it's harder for others to access it without your permission (you grant permission via your share settings, tags, and so on). You may notice that some Facebook Welcome pages or other custom tabs on Fan Page Timelines don't work with the secure browsing feature. You can turn off secure browsing temporarily to access those pages, or you can choose to skip them. Facebook is working to require custom tabs to be housed on secure servers, so this issue may be resolved soon, and you won't notice any anomalies with Fan Page Timelines and custom tabs.

To turn on secure browsing, select the check box next to Browse Facebook on a Secure Connection (https) When Possible. Then click the Save Changes button. When you look in the address bar of your browser, the URL shows `https://www.facebook.com` — that means you're using secure browsing. If you notice that the URL reverts to `http://` instead of `https://`, revisit your settings to be sure you still have this option enabled. It's possible you turned off secure browsing to access a noncompliant Fan Page Timeline and forgot to turn it back on.

Secure browsing is not currently available for mobile devices, so even if you opt to turn on secure browsing, your phone and iPad can't take advantage of the feature. Read more about your privacy and mobile devices in Book I, Chapter 3.

Login notifications

If you're concerned that someone may access your account without your consent, we suggest enabling the login notifications option. This option notifies you via e-mail or text message when your account is accessed from a device that you haven't used before. So if you usually use your desktop computer to access your account, but one afternoon you use your laptop, Facebook sends you a note (either an e-mail or text message) letting you know that your account was accessed from a new device. If you were the one logging in from the new device, no problem. If you weren't, you can investigate.

To turn on login notifications, select the E-mail and/or Text Message/Push Notification check box — whichever is more convenient for you to receive. Keep in mind that charges for text messages apply here. Click Save Changes to complete the process.

Login approvals

The login-approvals option adds another layer of protection to the login notifications. Each time you (or someone else) logs into your account from a device you haven't used before, Facebook sends you a text message with a code you have to use to complete your Facebook login. For example, if you usually log into your Facebook account with your desktop computer but decide to log in with your laptop, Facebook texts you a code that you must type in when prompted in order to access your account. Obviously, to use this option, you need to be sure you have a cellphone number associated with your account. You can associate a cellphone number with your account via the Mobile tab on your Account Setting page dashboard or when you verify your account via your phone (see the "Username" section, earlier in this chapter).

To turn on login approvals, follow these instructions:

1. **Navigate to your Account Settings page, and click the Security link in the left navigation pane.**

2. **Click the Edit link next to Login Approvals.**

3. **Select the Require Me to Enter a Security Code Each Time an Unrecognized Computer or Device Tries to Access My Account check box.**

   The Set Up Login Approvals dialog box appears, with an explanation of how login approvals work.

4. **Read the overview of login approvals, grab your cellphone, and then click Set Up Now.**

   Facebook sends you a text with a confirmation code.

5. **Type the confirmation code into the text box, and click Submit.**

   The Name This Computer window appears.

6. **In the text box, type a name for the device you're using (for example,** home computer) **and click Next.**

   The Success dialog box appears, with information about what to do if you get a new phone, lose your phone, or use Facebook apps.

7. **Click the Close button to complete the process.**

Now that login approvals are set up, every time you log in from a new device, Facebook texts a login code to your phone. You see the message shown in Figure 2-7.

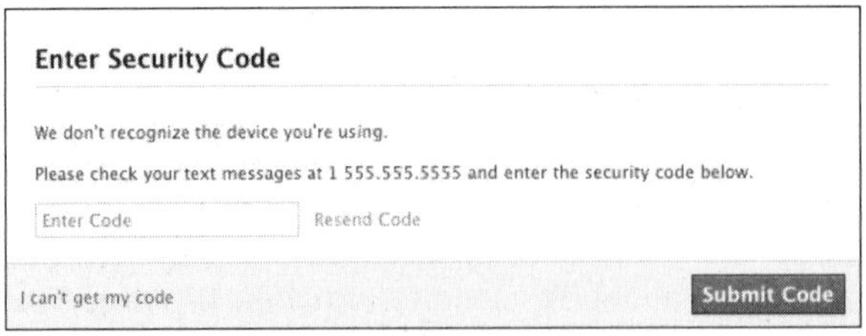

Figure 2-7:
Use the
security
code
Facebook
texts you
to log in
to your
account.

Enter Security Code

We don't recognize the device you're using.

Please check your text messages at 1 555.555.5555 and enter the security code below.

Enter Code   Resend Code

I can't get my code   Submit Code

Type the login code into the text box and click Submit Code to start using Facebook.

App passwords

Some Facebook applications don't work with Facebook login approval codes, so if you have that option enabled, you may not be able to use all of your apps. Facebook has fixed it so you can use app passwords instead of your account password to log in to certain apps (for example, Skype). According to Facebook's Help section, "when you use an app password you won't have to wait to receive a [login approval] code. Instead, you can skip login approvals and log in immediately." You can read more about app passwords at http://on.fb.me/FBAppPasswords.

To generate an app password, follow these instructions:

1. **Go to Account Settings; click the Security link; and in the App Passwords row, click Edit.**

2. **Click the Generate App Passwords link.**

   The Generate App Passwords dialog box appears and explains that some apps don't work with login approvals.

3. **Click the Generate App Passwords button.**

4. **In the text box, type the name of the app you want to approve and click Generate Password.**

   A window appears, with the choice of creating another password (click Next Password) or finishing (click Finish).

5. **Click the appropriate button.**

You can remove a password by clicking App Passwords and then clicking the Remove link next to the password you want to delete.

Recognized Devices

Recognized Devices are those you've used to log into your Facebook account. For instance, if you activated the Login Notifications option discussed earlier, you named your primary device. That device is listed under Recognized Devices. As you use other devices to log in, and they are confirmed as belonging to you, you can name those devices as well, and they appear in Recognized Devices too. Any device listed under Recognized Devices doesn't require secure login confirmation. You can remove a device from this section simply by clicking the Remove link next to the name of the device. Be sure to click Save Changes to complete the removal process.

Active Sessions

This section shows you a list of your recent active sessions on Facebook. You can see the name and type of device used to log in and where the login occurred. If you see a location that doesn't look familiar, be sure to check to see if the session is linked to your smartphone, because those sessions don't always reflect an accurate location.

If you see an active session, and you think someone may be accessing your account without permission, click the End Activity link next to the questionable active session. Facebook suggests you also change your account password, as well as your e-mail password, as an added measure to ensure no one can access your account at this point.

Want to find the IP address of the device used to log in to Facebook? Mouse over the location, and a black box appears with that information.

Deactivate your account

Deactivating your account is not the same as deleting your account. When you deactivate your account, it's still around; it's just not in use. People can't find your personal Timeline or view previous content you've shared, but friends can still tag you and invite you to events and groups. You also lose your admin status in groups, Events, and Fan Page Timelines. You can choose to reinstate your account at any time, and Facebook will restore your Timeline to the way it looked before you deactivated your account.

Deleting your account will completely erase your information and content from Facebook. At the end of this chapter, we explain how you can delete your Facebook account.

To deactivate your Facebook account, follow these steps:

1. **Go to Account Settings, click the Security link on the left, and click the Deactivate Your Account link at the bottom of the Security Settings list.**

   A new page appears, asking if you're sure you want to deactivate your account.

2. **Select a reason for leaving.**

3. **In the text box, type an extended explanation of why you're deactivating your account (this is optional, but it helps Facebook pinpoint areas that may need work).**

4. **Select the Opt Out of Receiving Further E-mails from Facebook check box.**

   When you deactivate your account, your friends can still tag you in updates, photos, and videos, and invite you to Events and groups. If you choose to opt out of further e-mails from Facebook, you won't receive notifications about those tags and invitations.

If you've created any apps, and you're the only developer, Facebook gives you the option to edit or delete those apps before you deactivate your account.

5. **Click Confirm.**

   A password confirmation window appears.

6. **Type your password in the text bo and click the Deactivate Now button.**

   Another security check window appears. (Facebook really wants you to think about your decision!)

7. **Type the CAPTCHA in the text box and click the Submit button.**

   Your account is deactivated.

To reinstate your account, go to www.facebook.com and log in with your e-mail and password. Facebook sends you a confirmation e-mail (so be sure you can access the e-mail address you originally used to set up your Facebook account). After you've confirmed you own your account, Facebook reinstates your Timeline as it was before you left. However, you still won't have any admin privileges for groups, Events, or Fan Page Timelines you had before you left. You need to have someone add you as an admin if that's something you're interested in.

If you're the only administrator for a Fan Page Timeline, we urge you to add another administrator to the Fan Page before you deactivate your account. If you don't, you lose all administrative rights to your Fan Page Timeline. You won't be able to access your dashboard, and you won't be able to regain your administrative status. When you add another person as an admin, if you decide to reinstate your Fan Page Timeline, the other admin can grant you admin capabilities again.

Notifications

Notifications are e-mails messages that alert you when someone tags you in an update, photo, or video, or comments on one your posts (or comments on someone else's post that you commented on). Some people like to enable notifications because they remind them to visit Facebook and respond to what's happening. On the other hand, if you're on Facebook quite a bit, the notifications may be overkill for you. The Facebook team understands that everyone uses the platform a little differently, so Facebook allows you to determine how you receive notifications.

When you first create your account, your Notifications Settings page looks similar to the one shown in Figure 2-8.

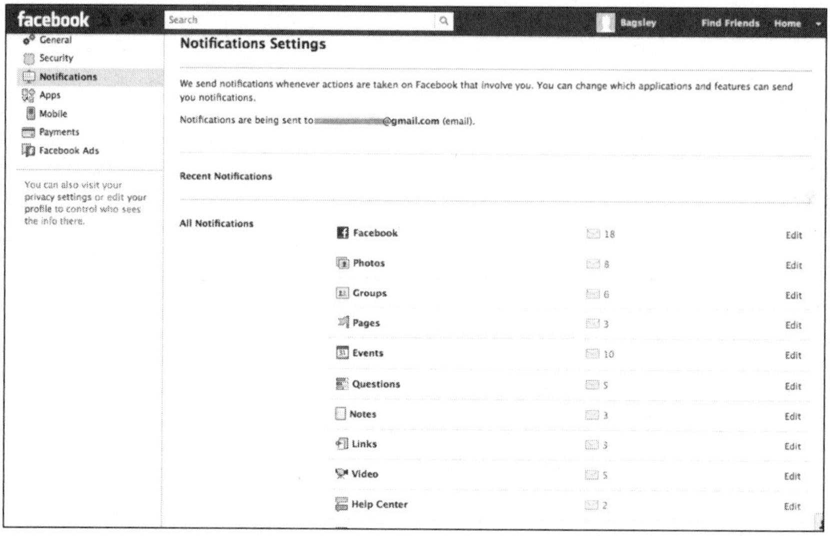

Figure 2-8:
Your Notifications Settings page allows you to choose how you receive updates.

The Notifications Settings page lists all the different types of notifications you can set. To determine which notifications you receive, click the Edit link next to each option. That option expands to show a list of further options. You can select or deselect the items you want a notification about. Remember to click Save Changes for each category so your changes will take effect.

As you use Facebook regularly, you'll receive more notifications, because people will be interacting with your regularly as you grow your friend base and share content. If you find that you receive too many e-mail notifications from Facebook regarding updates and comments, return to Notifications Settings. You see an alert at the top of the page that looks similar to Figure 2-9.

Figure 2-9:
The Notifications Settings page.

You can select (or deselect) the check box beside Email Frequency. This switches your settings so you receive fewer e-mails alerting you to what people are doing on Facebook. This is a handy setting if you frequent Facebook and don't need alerts to know when others are interacting with you. On the other hand, if you rely on those updates to know when to respond to others, deselect this check box to ensure you'll continue to receive alerts.

Consider setting up an e-mail address that you use solely for Facebook. That way, all your Facebook correspondence is in one place, and you can check as you like without cluttering your primary e-mail inbox. As an added bonus, if your Facebook account is ever hacked or you click a bad link, you have a single e-mail address to deal with (and it doesn't affect your other accounts).

Apps

As you interact on Facebook, you'll find that it's nearly impossible to avoid Facebook applications. (We explain applications and how they work in Book VI.) Apps allow you to interact more fully on Facebook. When you play a game, share photos via Instagram (`http://instagr.am`), update your status via HootSuite (`https://hootsuite.com`), or even enter a giveaway, you utilize a Facebook application. With the release of Timeline for personal profiles in late 2011, Facebook applications are becoming even more prevalent because they're a primary way people choose to share activity (for example, listening to music via Spotify or watching a movie via Netflix).

Each time you click an activity related to an application, Facebook checks to see if your account is already associated with that app. If it is, you move forward and complete the action. If your account isn't associated with the app, you get an alert asking if you'd like to allow the app to have access to your account. And that's where people new to Facebook start to get concerned (rightfully so; your privacy and protecting your account are important!). By their nature, apps must have access to your account in order to function properly. For instance, when you play Words With Friends (it's like mobile Scrabble), you probably want to find out if any of your other Facebook friends are playing so you can start a game with them. By allowing Words With Friends to access your account, the app can look at your list of Facebook friends and compare it with the people who have Words With Friends accounts and let you know who is already playing. Then, after you play Words With Friends, you can choose post your wins to your Timeline and let people know you are the king or queen of word strategy (or not). If you don't want to use applications or are uncomfortable allowing them to access your account information, you don't have to install or allow the application on your account. You'll miss out on some functionality of Facebook and interacting with your friends on a different level, but it's all a trade-off. If you decide to allow an app, you can always remove it later.

To see which apps you currently have associated with your account, click the down arrow in the top-right corner of any Facebook page, choose Account Settings, and click Apps to see a list of what's working on your account. The list is similar to Figure 2-10 and shows you the name of the application, when you last accessed or used the application, the option to edit the application, and the option to remove the application completely.

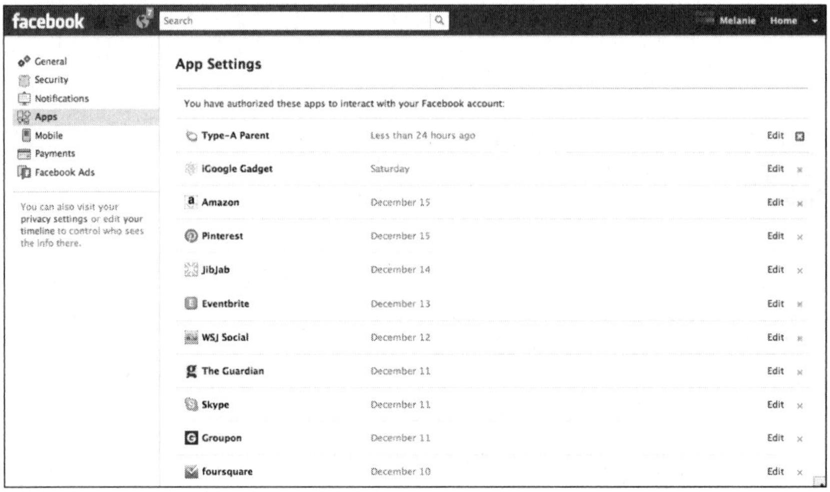

App Settings

You have authorized these apps to interact with your Facebook account:

Type-A Parent	Less than 24 hours ago	Edit	☒
iGoogle Gadget	Saturday	Edit	×
Amazon	December 15	Edit	×
Pinterest	December 15	Edit	×
JibJab	December 14	Edit	×
Eventbrite	December 13	Edit	×
WSJ Social	December 12	Edit	×
The Guardian	December 11	Edit	×
Skype	December 11	Edit	×
Groupon	December 11	Edit	×
foursquare	December 10	Edit	×

Figure 2-10: Your App Settings page lists the apps associated with your Facebook account.

We recommend checking your App Settings page periodically just to clean out apps you no longer use. There's no use having extra apps hanging around.

If you want to see what permissions a particular app has for your account, click the Edit button next to the application name. The app window expands, as shown in Figure 2-11.

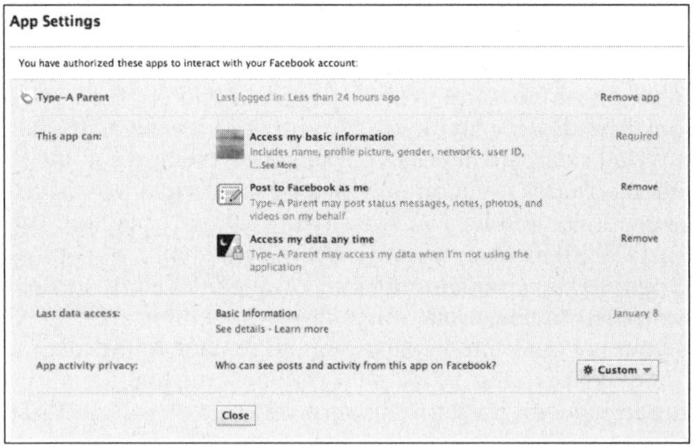

App Settings

You have authorized these apps to interact with your Facebook account:

Type-A Parent — Last logged in: Less than 24 hours ago — Remove app

This app can: Access my basic information — Includes name, profile picture, gender, networks, user ID, ... See More — Required

Post to Facebook as me — Type-A Parent may post status messages, notes, photos, and videos on my behalf — Remove

Access my data any time — Type-A Parent may access my data when I'm not using the application — Remove

Last data access: Basic Information — See details · Learn more — January 8

App activity privacy: Who can see posts and activity from this app on Facebook? — ⚙ Custom ▾

Close

Figure 2-11: Check to see what permissions an app has for your account (and customize as necessary).

Figure 2-11 shows several options for working with this app:

✦ Remove the app by clicking the Remove App link at the top.

✦ Remove nonessential functions such as Post to Facebook as Me or Access My Data Any Time.

✦ Check to see when the app last accessed you data.

✦ Customize which of your friends or lists can see when and how you use the application.

TIP

If you choose to remove an application for whatever reason, you can always add it back to your account later.

Applications are going to become much more integral to Facebook than they already are. In general, people don't like to leave Facebook to complete other actions. That's why you can watch video in your News Feed instead of clicking over to YouTube, or click a photo, and a lightbox appears with a larger version of the image. As we move forward, people are going to want to interact even more on Facebook, and we suspect we'll be doing quite a bit of shopping within Facebook rather than clicking over to a website. Because Facebook offers secure browsing and applications that allow PayPal payments via an application, it's not unreasonable to think F-commerce will soon catch on. If that's the case, as products sales on Facebook grow, so will the use of applications that can connect third-party websites to Facebook and share inventory.

Mobile

Enabling your mobile settings allows Facebook to text you when you have friend requests or other notifications. Additionally, you can text updates (including photos and video) from your phone directly to your Facebook Timeline.

However, if you have a smartphone, you can do all of these things directly from the Facebook app for your phone. We explain mobile Facebook options more thoroughly in Book II, Chapter 6; you can also point your browser to `https://www.facebook.com/mobile` to find out more.

To set up your Facebook mobile settings, follow these instructions:

1. **Click the down arrow in the top-right corner of any Facebook page and choose Account Settings; click Mobile in the left navigation pane.**

The Mobile Settings page appears.

2. **Click the green +Add a Phone button.**

The Add Mobile Phone dialog box appears.

3. **Type your password into the text box and click Confirm.**

The Activate Facebook Texts (Step 1 of 2) dialog box appears.

4. **Select your country and mobile carrier from the drop-down lists and click Next.**

The Activate Facebook Texts (Step 2 or 2) dialog box appears.

5. **Text the letter F to 32665.**

   You receive a text from Facebook with a confirmation code.

6. **Type the confirmation code into the text box.**

7. **Select whether you want to share your phone number with your friends and whether you want to allow friends to text you from Facebook.**

   If you activate text messages, Facebook texts your notifications to your mobile phone. Normal text messaging charges apply, so be sure you know what your phone's data plan is — you could be receiving a lot of texts if you're very active on Facebook.

8. **Click Next to complete the process.**

   The Facebook for Mobile page appears, and you can read more about your mobile options.

   The Confirm a Phone Number dialog box appears.

To remove a phone number from your account, simply click the Remove link beside the number.

The Mobile Settings page has additional options as well. The following list explains them:

✦ **Text Messaging:** If you have more than one mobile phone associated with your profile, you can click Edit and choose which phone receives text messages. Although Facebook doesn't charge you for texting, your mobile carrier may. Be sure to understand your data plan.

✦ **Notifications:** If you don't want to receive text notifications about Facebook activity, you can turn them off. Click Edit and choose which notifications and settings you want to enable (or disable). Remember to click Save Changes when you're done.

✦ **Facebook Messages:** This option enables you to control when Facebook can text you. Click Edit and use the drop-down list to choose the option that works for you.

✦ **Daily Text Limit:** This option lets you control how many texts you receive from Facebook each day. You can choose 1, 5, 100, all the way to Unlimited. But again, remember that your mobile carrier's text rates apply.

Payments

Your Facebook Payments page allows you to keep track of the credits and payments. Facebook defines *credits* as "virtual currency you can use to buy virtual goods in any games or apps of the Facebook platform that accept payments." You can buy credits with your credit card or another option (for example, PayPal) just as you'd buy anything else online. When you buy credits, you can spend them on virtual goods in games and apps. It's sort of like buying tokens at the local arcade.

To check your credits balance, navigate to your Payment Settings page by clicking the down arrow at the top-right corner of any Facebook page, choosing Account Settings, and clicking Payments in the left navigation pane. On this page, you can check your credits balance, view your credits purchase history, manage your payment methods, and choose your preferred currency. We explain each of those options in the following sections. You can read more about Facebook credits at `http://on.fb.me/FBCreditsInfo`.

Credits Balance

On the Credits Balance row, you can see how many credits you currently have, and you can buy more by clicking the Buy More link.

Before you buy Facebook credits, be sure you've read, understand, and agree to Facebook's Payments Terms at `https://www.facebook.com/payments_terms`.

To buy more credits, follow these instructions:

1. Click the down arrow at the top-right corner of any Facebook page, choose Account Settings, and click Payments in the left navigation pane.

   In the Credits Balance row, Facebook lists how many credits you currently have.

2. Click the Buy More link.

   The Get Facebook Credits dialog box appears, as shown in Figure 2-12.

Figure 2-12:
You have several payment options when buying Facebook credits.

3. **Select the radio button next to your preferred method of payment.**

    A dialog box appears, asking you how many credits you'd like to purchase. You choices vary depending on your payment method.

4. **Select the number of credits you want to buy and click Continue.**

5. **Complete the transaction as instructed (options vary, depending on how you're paying).**

Credits Purchase History

If you've ever purchased Facebook credits or do so regularly, you can find a record of your purchase history by clicking the View link in the Credits Purchase History row. This is a handy resource, especially if you have others at home who use your account to purchase Facebook credits. You can keep track of how much you're spending.

Payment Methods

Facebook offers many payment method options. You can use your cellphone, credit card, PayPal, or even a Facebook gift card. To create a payment method, you must first purchase credits (as explained in the earlier section, "Credits Balance"). The method you use to purchase credits is saved in the Payment Methods row. For example, if you use PayPal to pay for your credits, your PayPal information is saved, and you can edit it in the Payment Methods row. You also have the option to add another credit card to your payment methods. To add a new credit card, follow these instructions:

1. **Click the down arrow at the top-right corner of any Facebook page, choose Account Settings, and click Payments in the left navigation pane.**

2. **Click the Manage link in the Payment Methods row.**

    A new page appears, asking for your Facebook account password.

3. **Type your password into the text box and click Continue.**

    The Payment Methods box expands and lists payment options, as shown in Figure 2-13.

4. **Complete the form with the necessary information and click the Add button.**

    Facebook saves your information so you don't have to resubmit the same information each time you want to buy credits.

You can remove credit card or payment information any time by clicking the Manage link next to Payment Methods, and then clicking Remove for the information you want to delete.

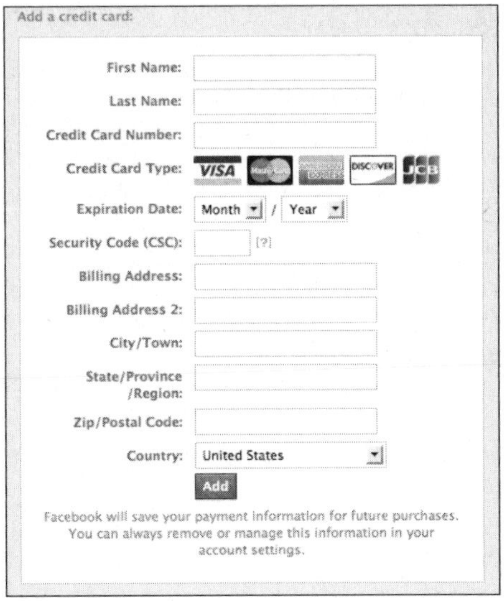

Figure 2-13:
Choose your
payment
method.

Preferred Currency

Preferred Currency is pretty much what it sounds like. You can choose the currency that you use the most from the drop-down list. The currency you choose determines how Facebook displays pricing to you (for example, either in American dollars or euros). If you make changes to your preferred currency, remember to click Save Changes for those to take effect.

Facebook Ads

The Facebook Ads option on your Account Settings page isn't referring to how to create Facebook ads (which we discuss in Book V, Chapter 5). Instead, this option explains how Facebook ads work with your personal Timeline account, what the ads can and can't do, and how your information and your friends' information is (or isn't) used with ads.

Take a moment to read Facebook's explanation and familiarize yourself with how ads work. In a nutshell, Facebook is reminding you that third-party apps and networks don't have the legal right to use your information (including your picture) in their advertisements. You can control third-party ad settings by clicking the Edit Third Party Ad Settings link and using the drop-down list to choose who can see your information if Facebook makes changes to its ad policies in the future. Be sure to click the Save Changes button to ensure your preference is saved.

Deleting Your Facebook Account

If you decide to delete your Facebook account, your information becomes irretrievable. Unless you've made a copy of your Facebook data and saved that file somewhere other than Facebook, you'll lose your photos, videos, status updates, comments, friends lists, and private messages.

We give step-by-step instructions for archiving your Facebook data earlier in this chapter, in the "Download a copy of your Facebook data" section. We firmly suggest you archive your Facebook data before you delete your account so you don't lose anything of value.

When you delete your account, there's no going back. You can't reinstate your account. If you choose to return to Facebook, you have to create a brand-new account and start from scratch.

To delete your account, follow these instructions:

1. **Log in to your Facebook account, and then visit** `https://www.facebook.com/help/contact.php?show_form=delete_account`.

   The Delete My Account page appears, with a strict warning that you will not be able to retrieve any of your data after your Facebook account is deleted.

2. **Click Submit if you're sure you'd like to delete your Facebook account.**

   The Permanently Delete Account dialog box appears.

3. **Provide your Facebook account password and type the CAPTCHA phrase in the correct text boxes.**

4. **Click Okay.**

   One more warning appears, explaining that at this point, your account has been deactivated but not deleted. If you log in to Facebook within 14 days, you have the option to cancel your deletion request.

5. **Click Okay again to confirm you want to delete your account.**

   You still have 14 days to change your mind. If you don't log in to your account within 14 days, your Facebook account is permanently deleted.

Chapter 3: Customizing Your Facebook Privacy Settings

In This Chapter

✔ **Knowing how to protect your privacy online**

✔ **Managing your privacy settings**

✔ **Understanding how privacy options change what others see**

✔ **Using Facebook lists**

✔ **Discovering Interest lists**

*O*nline privacy is a topic we're passionate about. The way you interact online is trackable and findable (and yes, Google, Facebook, Amazon, and others are tracking your interactions and behavior). You're constantly creating your digital footprint by purchasing items online, using Google to find something, creating a Facebook account, interacting with blogs and websites, and so on. There's nothing wrong with that — in fact, it's almost impossible to *not* have a digital footprint these days.

The important thing is that you understand that you, and you alone, are responsible for your privacy. Don't rely on the sites you visit to protect your information. While it's reasonable to expect a site not to compromise your credit card information, it's up to you to decide what information to share, who to share it with, and how you'll share other information you find. You must take the time to review your privacy options and understand how they work. This chapter helps you navigate Facebook's privacy options and explains how you can take control of how you share your information on the Facebook platform.

Understanding Online Privacy

You are always in charge of your privacy — online and offline. Although it isn't popular to say, the platform isn't responsible for protecting you — it's your responsibility to protect yourself. Would it be easier if the tool, in this case Facebook, started out with your privacy set to the highest level instead of the most open level? Perhaps. But consider two things:

1. Facebook's mission isn't to provide a personal space for you. Facebook wants to create an open community whose members constantly share their lives and milestones with others. It makes sense that Facebook encourages that by setting default privacy to be more open rather than closed.

2. No matter what the default settings for privacy are, you will most likely have to visit your dashboard and tweak those settings for your own needs. Whether Facebook sets those privacy settings high or low, you still have to tweak them to your satisfaction.

In September 2011, Facebook announced that it would be introducing a new way to share called *frictionless sharing.* The idea behind frictionless sharing is that when you install an application, the default setting will be to allow the application to automatically share updates. For example, when you play a game like Bejeweled on your smartphone, each time you make a high score, a window pops up and asks if you'd like to share with your Facebook friends. Facebook calls that interruption in play *friction* and believes that eliminating that step allows for a smoother interaction between you and the application and allows for more opportunities for sharing on Facebook. Many applications default to the frictionless sharing (that is, they automatically share your actions with the News Feed), but you can change that setting by visiting your application's dashboard (which we explain later in this chapter, in the "Apps and Websites settings" section).

The new apps and sharing Facebook introduced at the end of 2011 allow you to have full control over what you share. If you don't want to share your actions with people, you don't have to install the application (or if you want the application, at least check to be sure the application offers the option to customize how you share). If you don't want everyone to see your Timeline updates, change your share settings to Friends Only. If you want to share your updates with select people, you can customize your updates by clicking the Public button below your Status Update text box and choosing who can and can't see your update. Your privacy lies with you as much as it ever did. These new changes are not taking it away. There may or may not be instances where you need to think twice about what you share and with whom, but you should be doing that anyway.

Consider this: Do you use the free Wi-Fi at your local coffee shop or library or *anywhere?* Are you concerned that whoever is supplying the Wi-Fi isn't covering your privacy? Why not? When you're on public Wi-Fi, someone could easily hijack your passwords and make purchases on sites that you've logged in to, so it's best to change your working and browsing habits when you aren't using a secure Wi-Fi connection. That's your responsibility.

Taking Responsibility for Your Own Privacy

The way Facebook works is that you share information with friends. Some of that information is considered public (that is, your name, user ID, and profile picture), and some of it is considered private, and you can elect not to share it with others (via the privacy settings we discuss throughout this chapter). As we mention previously, Facebook relies on you to customize your settings and actively participate in protecting your privacy. Check your privacy settings regularly, and adjust them as necessary. Facebook doesn't always alert you to changes.

An important first step in protecting your online privacy, whether with Facebook or another website, is to ensure that you have a strong password in place so your account is much less likely to be compromised. Here are a few tips for taking charge of your privacy on Facebook:

✦ **Turn on Facebook's secure browsing option.** Facebook has an option that allows you to browse the site using a secure connection. You'll know you're using the secure connection because the address bar will show `https://` instead of `http://`. To turn on this option, click the down arrow at the top right of any Facebook page and choose Account Settings; click the Security link on the left navigation pane, and click the Edit link in the Secure Browsing row. Select the Browse Facebook on a Secure Connection (https) When Possible check box, and click the Save Changes button.

✦ **Enable Facebook login notifications.** If you're concerned that someone may try to access your Facebook account, login notifications will send you an alert when your account is accessed from a device (for example, computer or phone) that you haven't used before. To turn on login notifications, click the down arrow at the top right of any Facebook page and choose Account Settings. Click the Security link on the left navigation pane, and click the Edit link in the Login Notifications row. Select the Email check box or the Text Message/Push Notification check box (or both, if you want) to receive alerts, and then click the Save Changes button.

✦ **Assign more than one admin to your Fan Page Timeline.** If you should ever find your Facebook account compromised or locked for some reason, it would be a shame to lose your Fan Page Timeline access as well. It makes sense to make a trusted friend or employee a co-administrator of your Fan Page Timeline. Choose a person you trust to act as admin for you (and give you access to the Fan Page Timeline if necessary). It's a little like giving your neighbor your house key in case you lock yourself out of the house.

General online privacy do's and don'ts

While this chapter focuses on Facebook security and privacy, we have a few general online security tips to share. Keep these do's and don'ts in mind to increase your online security and privacy:

✔ **Do choose a strong password.** Use a mix of uppercase and lowercase letters, numbers, and symbols. We've heard it said that if you can remember your password, it may not be strong enough. Check how strong your password is at www.howsecureismy password.net.

✔ **Don't share your password or write it down anywhere someone could easily find it.** If you have trouble keeping track of your passwords, you may want to consider using a service such as www.roboform.com or www.lastpass.com.

✔ **Do create an e-mail address specifically for signing up for things.** Don't use this e-mail address for everyday interactions. Instead, just use it when you're signing up for e-newsletters, placing orders online, or signing up for website memberships (for example, signing up for Facebook). That way, any spam related to those interactions won't fill up your main e-mail address.

✔ **Do be careful when using public Wi-Fi.** Your local coffee shop, bookstore, and library probably all offer free Wi-Fi, and that's pretty handy. But public Wi-Fi makes it very easy for others to spy on your digital comings and goings. If you're going to log on in a public space on an unsecured wireless network, don't make purchases online or do your banking.

Tip: If you want to log on to a website such as Facebook while using pubic Wi-Fi, see if the website offers the option to get a single-use password. Facebook offers this option. Just text **otp** to 32665 to receive a temporary password. That password expires after 20 minutes. Note that it doesn't mean your session expires after 20 minutes; it just means that you need to use the one-time password to log in within 20 minutes of receiving it.

✔ **Do assume everything you post online is public.** Even when you customize your privacy settings, it's important to realize that privacy online is an illusion. Private messages can be copied. Friends can take screen shots of your status updates and share them with others. You may forget to set your share settings for a specific update, or you may accidentally Reply All when you just wanted to e-mail one person with a response that was maybe better left unsaid. It happens to everyone at some point. There's no need to stop interacting online; just be vigilant in how you interact with others.

Managing and Customizing Your Privacy Settings

We explain how you can control the privacy of individual status updates in Book II, Chapter 2. This chapter explains how you can control your account privacy in general. To access your general Facebook privacy options, click the down arrow in the top-right corner (next to the Home link), and choose Privacy Settings from the menu. The Privacy Settings page appears and explains how you can manage your privacy settings.

When you scroll down the Privacy Settings page, you see the heading Control Your Default Privacy and three options: Public, Friends, and Custom. The option you choose determines how people can find you, who can see your updates and images, and so on:

✦ **Public:** If you choose to make your account public, everyone on Facebook (whether you've friended them or not) can see what you post, who you tag, and any photos or videos you post. As the name states, everything is public. In other words, you've essentially turned off any privacy settings.

✦ **Friends:** This option allows you to automatically share all of your updates and uploads with people you have specifically connected with (that is, your Facebook friends) rather than the public at large.

✦ **Custom:** The Custom option allows you to use lists to include and/or exclude specific people or groups of people when you post an update, photo, or video. (We explain what lists are and how to use them later in this chapter.) When you select the Custom option, the Custom Privacy dialog box appears. From there, you can choose to make your account (all your updates and uploads) visible to the following:

  • *Friends:* People you are personally connected to on Facebook.

  • *Friends of Friends:* People connected to your connections; you may or may not know those people.

  • *Specific People or Lists:* You can choose from your list of friends or lists you created.

  • *Only Me:* You're the only person who can see your updates.

  You can also hide your status updates from specific people or lists by typing a name or list name in the Hide This From text box.

Under the default privacy settings, you see the following options:

✦ How You Connect

✦ How Tags Work

✦ Apps and Websites

✦ Limit the Audience for Past Posts

✦ Blocked People and Apps

Each of these options allows you to determine further privacy settings for your account. We explain them more thoroughly in the following sections.

For more information on privacy and security, visit `https://www.facebook.com/security` and `https://www.facebook.com/help/privacy`.

How You Connect settings

You can determine how you connect with others via your choices for the How You Connect options. Click the Edit Settings link in the How You Connect row; in the dialog box that appears (shown in Figure 3-1), you determine who can

✦ Search for you on Facebook

✦ Try to connect with you via friend requests or private messages

✦ Post to your Timeline (formerly called your Wall)

✦ See posts by others on your Timeline

Figure 3-1:
You can control how you connect with others.

Each option is self-explanatory; you use the drop-down lists to choose how you would like to interact with each option.

How Tags Work settings

Tagging is when someone names a friend in a status update or check in, or wants to label a photo or video as including a friend. When someone is tagged, Facebook notifies them, and, depending on that person's settings, they can approve or deny the tag.

When you click the Edit Settings link in the How Tags Work row, a dialog box appears with options you can turn on or off:

✦ **Timeline Review:** When someone tags you in a post, that post will show up in your Timeline if this setting is Off. If you turn this setting On, you can review tagged posts and approve or deny the tag. If you deny the tag, the post doesn't show up on your Timeline, but it may still show you as tagged in other places (such as the Timeline of the person who tagged you).

✦ **Tag Review:** Turn on this option if you'd like to review tags your friends add to your content before it appears on your Timeline (for example, tags in photos). When you approve a tag, the tagged person and their friends can see that content (for example, your photo that the person was tagged in).

✦ **Maximum Timeline Visibility:** This option determines the default sharing of your content. Use the drop-down list to choose who can see your content when it's posted.

REMEMBER

Any time you change your sharing settings on your Timeline, that setting becomes your default. So, for instance, if you choose Friends in the How Tags Work dialog box, only people you're friends with on Facebook can see your updates. But if you create a new status update on your Timeline and change your share settings to Public, Public will be your new default sharing setting for updates. You can change your settings again on your next status update, or you can return to the Privacy Settings page and reset your default.

✦ **Tag Suggestions:** This is a photo-recognition option. Facebook uses software to determine if friends upload pictures of people who look like you, and then suggests to them that they tag you in the photo. If you disable this option, friends won't be prompted to tag you, but they may decide to tag you on their own.

✦ **Friends Can Check You into Places:** In Book II, Chapter 5, we explain how you can check into a Place and tag people with you. If you enable the Friends Can Check You into Places privacy option, Facebook alerts you when you've been checked in/tagged and lets you remove the tag from your Timeline if you like. If you turned on Timeline Review, you'll have to approve the tag before it appears in your Timeline.

Apps and Websites settings

Facebook has this policy in place: "On Facebook, your name, profile picture, gender, networks, username, and user ID (account number) are always publicly available, including to apps. Also, by default, apps have access to your friends list and any information you choose to make public."

There are reasons why applications and games need access to your information. For example, when you play a game, it's more fun to play it with friends. Game apps can look at your Facebook friend list and tell you who else is playing the game, so you can invite them to start a game with you. Or for example, if you use Spotify (a music app), your Facebook friends can share playlists with you so you can try out new music or listen to what your friends like. These are just some of the social aspects of Facebook that require applications to have access to some of your public information.

However, you can change your settings to better control how you share information with apps, games, and websites. Click the Edit Settings link in the Apps and Websites row. The Apps, Games, and Website page appears (similar to the page shown in Figure 3-2). You can change the settings for the following options:

✦ **Apps You Use:** Click the Edit Settings button to see the App Settings page.

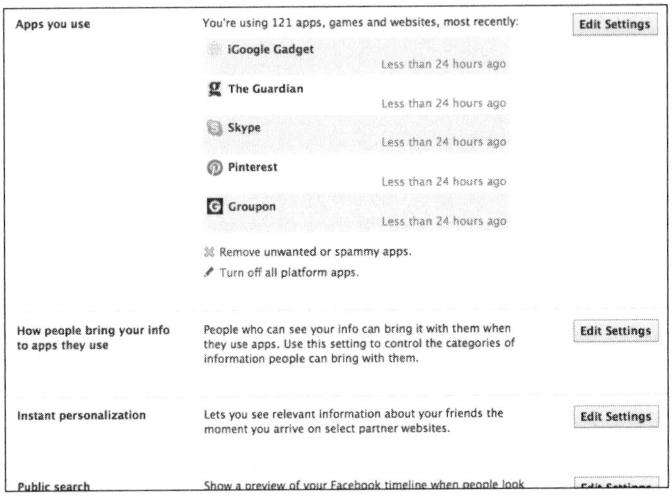

| Apps you use | You're using 121 apps, games and websites, most recently: | Edit Settings |

iGoogle Gadget — Less than 24 hours ago
The Guardian — Less than 24 hours ago
Skype — Less than 24 hours ago
Pinterest — Less than 24 hours ago
Groupon — Less than 24 hours ago

✖ Remove unwanted or spammy apps.
✐ Turn off all platform apps.

How people bring your info to apps they use — People who can see your info can bring it with them when they use apps. Use this setting to control the categories of information people can bring with them. — Edit Settings

Instant personalization — Lets you see relevant information about your friends the moment you arrive on select partner websites. — Edit Settings

Public search — Show a preview of your Facebook timeline when people look — Edit Settings

Figure 3-2: The App Settings page shows you the apps associated with your account.

The App Settings page lists the applications you have granted account access to, how often you've used that app, an option to edit the settings for each app, and the option to delete the app (click the X on the far right to delete an app).

To see what privileges an application has for your account, click the Edit link. The app listing expands to show more information. Each application has its own settings and options. Figure 3-3 shows an example of these settings for Pinterest.

Most apps have similar options that may include the option to remove the app, control what the app can do (for example, post your activity on the app to your Timeline), and assign default privacy settings (you can determine who sees your activity related to an app). For instance, if you install the *Washington Post* Social Reader Facebook app, any articles you read from the *Post* appear with a link in your Timeline and are visible in your friends' News Feeds. If you don't want to share your reading habits with specific people or lists, you can customize those privacy settings.

✦ **How People Bring Your Info to Apps They Use:** Facebook is, by definition, a social sharing site. Any information you share — whether completely publicly or just with friends — can be shared by others. If you share an interesting link or video, your friends may want to share that content too, and they can do that. Apps and games also have a heavy social component — it's interesting to see how your friends compare. If you're playing a game, you may want to find other Facebook friends who also play that game and start a new game with them. Facebook allows you to have some control over what information friends and apps can share about you. When you click the Edit Settings button, a dialog box appears, with a list of categories. You can select the check boxes next to which information you're willing to share. For example, Melanie selected only My Website and My App Activity. You can select all the categories you're comfortable sharing.

Figure 3-3: Pinterest application settings and options.

Your friend lists, gender, and other public information are shared with applications. The only way to prevent that is to turn off all applications. But doing so means you can't use apps or games. You can read more about how Facebook and apps work with your privacy settings, as well as how to disable all applications, at `https://www.facebook.com/about/privacy/your-info-on-other#friendsapps`.

✦ **Instant Personalization:** Facebook partners with some sites to share information about you and your friends so that when you visit the partner site, you see reviews or recommendations from people you know. You can find out more about how Facebook handles this feature at `https://www.facebook.com/instantpersonalization`.

To turn off instant personalization, click the Edit Settings button. The Understanding Instant Personalization dialog box appears with a video that further explains how this feature works. Click the Close button. On the Instant Personalization page, deselect the Enable Instant Personalization on Partner Websites check box to turn off instant personalization.

✦ **Public Search:** You can control whether strangers and/or friends can search for your Timeline in Facebook. If you'd like people to find you, enable public search by clicking the Edit Settings button, and then selecting the Enable Public Search check box.

Limit the Audience for Past Posts settings

When you create a status update or share content, you have the option to set customized sharing (see Book II, Chapter 2). If you'd like to change the customization of any update after it's posted, you can do that. The Limit the Audience for Past Posts tool allows you to change the share settings from public to friends. This tool is inclusive. That means any previous posts you shared as public will be changed to being shared only with friends. The exception is people you've tagged — they and their friends can see the content, regardless of whether they're connected to you. If you don't want to make a change to all your updates, you can simply find individual updates you'd like to change (see Activity Log on your Timeline) and edit the audience for those posts as needed.

Blocked People and Apps settings

Facebook provides several ways for you to control how you interact with others (and how they interact with you). Click the Manage Blocking link on the Blocked People and Apps row. The Manage Blocking page appears and provides options for the following:

✦ **Add Friends to Your Restricted List:** We explain lists a little later in this chapter. One of the lists Facebook provides for you is the Restricted list. When you add someone to this list, she can't see any of your updates unless those updates are marked Public. Luckily, Facebook doesn't notify people when you add them to your Restricted list. To add people to your Restricted list, click the Edit List link.

✦ **Block Users:** If you don't want to interact with someone on Facebook, you can block him from connecting with you. He can't see your updates, and you can't see his. The exception is Groups you both belong to and apps or games you both use. To block someone, type his name or e-mail address into the appropriate text box, and click the Block button. A list of people you have blocked appears under the text boxes. You can unblock someone by clicking the Unblock link next to his name.

✦ **Block App Invites:** Sometimes, you may have a friend who *really* likes Facebook apps and games and constantly invites you to join them by installing those apps and games. Those invites can clutter up your stream and get annoying. Facebook allows you to block app invites from specific people so your account will ignore future invites. In the text box, start typing the name of the friend whose app requests you want to ignore, and Facebook provides a list of matching names. Choose the correct name from the list, and future requests are ignored. To unblock the requests, just click the Unblock link next to the person's name.

✦ **Block Event Invites:** This option is similar to Block App Invites. If you're receiving too many event invitations from someone, you can set your account to ignore future invites from her. In the text box, start typing the name of the friend whose event invites you want to ignore, and

Facebook provides a list of matching names. Choose the correct name from the list, and future requests are ignored. To unblock the requests, just click the Unblock link next to the person's name.

✦ **List Blocked Apps:** This section lists all Facebook applications you have blocked. To block an application, you can visit its Fan Page Timeline (use the Search text box to find the app's Fan Page Timeline) and then click the Block App link on the left navigation list. To unblock an app, just click the Unblock link next to the name of the application.

Understanding How Privacy Settings Affect What Others See

When you customize your privacy settings, it's helpful to know how those settings affect how you and others see things on Facebook. Want to see how your personal Timeline looks to others? Just follow these steps:

1. **Go to your Timeline and click the gear icon under your main profile picture (the gear is next to the links for Update Info and Activity Log); choose View As.**

   An alert appears at the top of the page that says `This is how your timeline looks to the public.`

2. **(Optional) type a specific person's name in the text box to see how your Timeline looks to her.**

3. **Click the Back to Timeline button when you're finished.**

The next few sections explain how people can find you on Facebook, how friend requests work, and how you can control how you share your status updates.

How people can find you

We've said before that the crux of Facebook is social sharing. Generally, Facebook would love to have everyone's information accessible to all others because it believes that an open exchange is the wave of the future. Facebook may be right. However, most of us haven't quite caught up to that vision, and we still value our privacy, *thankyouverymuch.*

If you'd like to exert some control over how you're contacted by others on Facebook, the first thing you need to consider is whether you want people to be able to find you on Facebook. To control your privacy settings, click the down arrow in the upper-right corner and choose Privacy Settings. In the How You Connect row, click the Edit Settings link. The first option is Who Can Look Up Your Timeline by Name or Contact Info. Whatever you choose from the drop-down list determines how visible you are to others via Facebook search. Your choices are as follows:

✦ **Everyone:** If you want anyone to find you on Facebook, choose this option. If you really want an open experience on Facebook, this is the way to go.

✦ **Friends of Friends:** If you know you're not quite ready to friend everyone out there, consider choosing the Friends of Friends option.

✦ **Friends:** Don't want anyone finding you that you haven't already found and connected with first? This is your option. It's the most closed and private option available for personal Timeline search.

Your personal Timeline is searchable only within Facebook, but Fan Page Timelines are searchable outside Facebook via Google, Bing, Yahoo!, and so on. The settings you choose in the How You Connect dialog box apply only to your personal Timeline. For more information about Fan Page Timelines, see Book IV.

How friend requests work

When you want to connect with someone on Facebook, you send a friend request. Sometimes, you receive a friend request you don't want to approve for one reason or another. Maybe the request is from someone you don't know. Or maybe you know her, but you don't want to connect with her on Facebook for whatever reason. (See Book I, Chapter 2 for more information and advice about choosing Facebook friends.) You have a few options:

✦ You can choose to accept the friend request and share your Timeline freely. If that's the case, remember that you can exclude individuals from specific content by clicking the Share Settings wheel under your status updates.

✦ You can choose to ignore the request (click the Not Now button next to the request) — essentially putting the friendship on hold in the ether by neither accepting nor declining the invitation. However, you should be aware that anyone you ignore can still see any status updates that are shared with the public rather than specific people or lists, but he or she can't comment.

✦ You can always accept the friend request and assign the person to a specific list. We love lists because they allow you to control how you share things across the board. We explain lists later in this chapter.

How your updates are shared

Earlier in this chapter, we show you how to set your default privacy for status updates and photos, and we mention that you can set the privacy individually for each status update you share. When you set your privacy to Public, you are essentially allowing anyone on Facebook to see your update — but only friends can comment on those updates. The exceptions to that are as follows:

✦ If you post a status update that tags someone, anyone who is friends with the person you tagged can comment on your status update — even if you're not friends with them.

✦ If you turn on the subscription option for your Facebook account (see Book II, Chapter 2), anyone who subscribes to your updates can see and comment on any public updates.

On a related note, when Facebook released the Timeline version of personal Timelines, your updates from previous months and years became more readily available. This may or may not be a problem for you, depending on what you've shared over the years. Luckily, Facebook recognized the issue and included a way for you to change the share settings for individual pieces of content. As you set up your Timeline (see Book I, Chapter 4), you may choose to customize how you share certain things. To change the share settings for previously shared content, follow these instructions:

1. **Visit your personal Timeline and click the Activity Log button directly below your main Timeline picture.**

Your Activity Log page appears.

2. **Find the status update you want to change the sharing preferences for.**

If you hover over the Share icon, you can see what the original share settings were for a status update, as shown in Figure 3-4.

3. **Click the Share Settings icon and choose a sharing option from the list, as shown in Figure 3-5.**

Figure 3-4:
Original share settings for any status update.

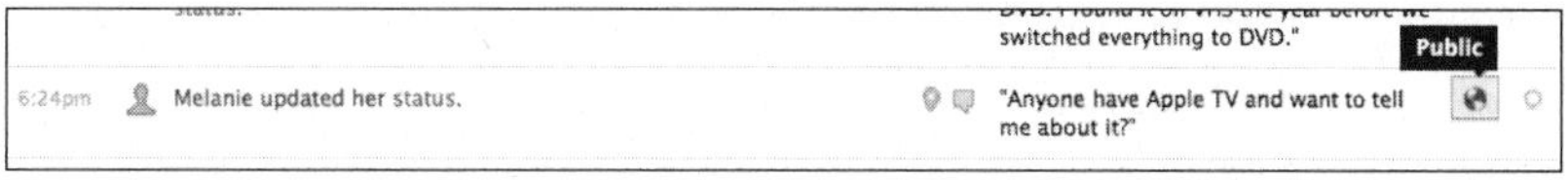

Figure 3-5:
Change who
can see
previous
status
updates.

Utilizing Lists So You Don't Miss a Thing

One of the biggest complaints about Facebook is that the News Feed doesn't always show what users want to see. Facebook uses an algorithm called EdgeRank (see Book V, Chapter 3) to track what content you interact with most, and then tries to determine what updates you want to see. The problem is that it's not a perfect system, and sometimes you can miss updates from people you're interested in keeping up with, but you may not comment on or Like their updates regularly. To keep track of people easily, we suggest using the Lists feature. You can create multiple lists for various groups of people. For instance, Melanie created lists for family, high school friends, local friends, blogging friends, and so on. Each list includes specific people (and yes, there's some overlap because some friends are included in more than one list). When you click a list name, your News Feed shows only the recent updates from the people included in the list, so you're less likely to miss an update you're interested in.

You can also use lists to conceal your chat availability. To do that, just click the gear icon at the bottom of your Facebook chat window (it's on the right side of your page). From the menu, choose Advanced Settings. In the dialog box that appears, you can customize who can and can't see you on Chat. Click to select one of these options:

✦ **All Your Friends See You Except:** This option allows you to type specific Facebook friend names or list names in the text box. Those individuals (or those on a list) won't see you as available to chat.

✦ **Only Some Friends See You:** Type the names of Facebook friends or lists you want to be able to see you. This is handy if you want only a few people to know you're available to chat.

✦ **No One Sees You (Go Offline):** If you don't want to be available to chat, select this option. None of your Facebook friends or lists will see you as available.

Facebook creates several Smart Lists to help you organize your friends, family, and colleagues so you can better track their status updates. These lists compare your shared information about work, education, family, and city with the shared information of your Facebook connections. When there's a match, Facebook adds that person to your Smart List. Facebook continues to update these lists as you add or remove friends from your contacts or as your friends update their information. The Smart Lists Facebook creates are as follows:

✦ **Family:** Facebook populates this list with people you have said you're related to or vice versa. You can add or remove people as appropriate.

✦ **School:** Facebook creates a list for both high school and college/university (if you share that information), and then autopopulates those lists with people from your friend list who have indicated they went to the same high school or college as you. You can edit this list, so feel free to add or remove people as necessary.

✦ **Work:** Similar to school lists, Facebook creates a list (or lists) based on your shared work history. Facebook tries to populate this list with others from your friend list who indicate they've also worked at a company you shared. If you manually add someone to a work list, Facebook notifies that person.

✦ **Your City:** This is another autopopulated and autoupdated list. Facebook places friends you're connected to in this list, and if anyone updates his information to include this city, he is added to this list automatically. Again, you can edit this list accordingly.

In addition to those smart lists, Facebook creates the Acquaintances and Close Friends lists. Technically, these aren't smart lists because Facebook doesn't automatically populate them or update them, but the lists are there for you to use. You can add people to and remove people from the lists as you like. You can see a catalog of your current Facebook lists in the left navigation column on your News Feed page (see Figure 3-6).

Figure 3-6:
Find your
lists in
the left
navigation
column.

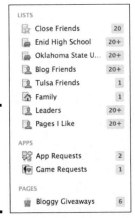

While you can't delete a list made by Facebook, you can add or remove people from those lists or hide the list.

Creating a new list

You don't have to use any of Facebook's premade lists, and you can definitely create your own. To create your own list, follow these steps:

1. **Click the Lists link in your left navigation column.**

2. **Click the Create List button at the top of the page.**

3. **Type the name of the new list in the dialog box that appears, and then click the Create button.**

4. **Click the Add Friends link to start populating your list.**

   Use the drop-down list on the dialog box to choose the type of information to use for population. You can choose Friends, Pages, or Subscriptions. You can even choose items from each of those options for inclusion in a single list.

5. **Click the Done button.**

   The list page appears again, this time populated with the updates from the friends (or Fan Page Timelines) you added to the list.

If you click the title of a list, you can type an update on that page that is visible only to the people included on that list.

Making a list a Favorite

The order of your lists in the left navigation column changes to show the one you most recently edited on top. If you find you have specific lists you want to check often, we suggest you add them to your Favorites (at the top of your left navigation column on the News Feed page; see Figure 3-7) so the lists are easily accessible.

Add a list to your Favorites by following these instructions:

1. **Move your mouse over the list you want to move to Favorites.**

   A pencil icon appears to the left of the list title.

2. **Click the pencil icon and choose Add to Favorites from the menu.**

   The list title moves from the Lists menu to the Favorites menu in the left navigation column.

Figure 3-7:
Your
Favorites
are shown
at the top
of the left
navigation
column.

You can change the order of the Favorites menu by moving your mouse over any item in the Favorites list, clicking the pencil icon that appears, and choosing Rearrange from the menu. At that point, you can click and drag any item to a new position in the list. When you're happy with the new order, click the Done link.

Managing how your lists work

Lists are most useful when they work in a way that fits your workflow. You may find that you need to rename a list; add or remove friends, Fan Page Timelines, or subscriptions from a list; customize what information is shared via a list; or delete a list that is no longer relevant. The editing options you have depend on the list you want to edit and may include renaming the list, adding or removing friends, choosing update types, or deleting the list. We explain each in the following sections.

Rename List option

Not all lists have the option to rename them (for example, you can't rename Close Friends). To rename a list, simply click the name of the list, click the Manage List button, and choose Rename List from the menu. A text box appears at the top of the page, as shown in Figure 3-8. Just type the new name there and click Save.

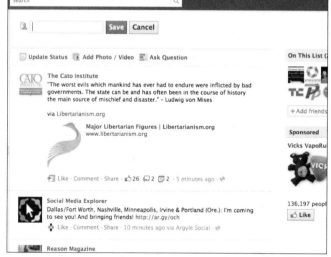

Figure 3-8:
Use the
text box at
the top of
the page to
rename your
list.

Add/Remove Friends option

The Add/Remove Friends option doesn't just apply to friends — you can also add or remove Fan Page Timelines or subscriptions to some lists. To add and remove friends from any list, regardless of whether you or Facebook created it, click the name of the list, and click the Manage List button. Choose Add/Remove Friends from the menu, and a dialog box appears, showing pictures of your friends. In the top-left corner, click the Friends drop-down list to see if Fan Pages and Subscriptions are available to edit for the list. You can also choose On This List to see people, Fan Pages, or subscriptions already included in a specific list. To add or remove a friend, Fan Page, or subscription, simply click the picture (a check mark appears by the picture to show it's selected), and then click Done.

When you accept a new friend or send a friend request, be sure to put that person in a list right then. This way, you don't forget, and the settings apply to your new friend immediately.

Choose Update Types option

Rather than see every update from the people on a given list, you can customize the information you see by following these steps:

1. **Click the name of the list you want to edit.**

   The News Feed switches to show the updates from people included in that list, and a Manage List button appears in the top-right corner.

2. **Click the Manage List button and choose the Choose Update Types option.**

   The menu now includes a list of the types of updates you see. The default is to show all types of updates. Updates you see in your News Feed or be alerted to are indicated by a check mark next to the update type.

3. **Click the type(s) of updates you don't want to see in your News Feed (for example, Games).**

4. **When you're done, click anywhere on the page to close the list, and your settings are saved.**

Delete List option

You can delete some lists if you find they aren't useful to you (again, not all lists have this option). Deletion can't be undone, but any content you shared with people on a list is still visible to those people even when the list is gone. To delete a list, click the name of the list you want to get rid of, click the Manage List button, and choose Delete List from the menu. A warning message appears to remind you that your actions are permanent and content is still visible to people on the list. Click Confirm to delete the list.

Discovering Interest Lists

Like regular lists, Interest lists allow you to subscribe to your favorite people, friends, and Fan Pages in one place. The difference between a regular list and Interest list is that when you set up your Interest list, others can subscribe to it — and you can subscribe to the Interest lists others create. It's another great way to control what you see in your News Feed.

At the time we're writing this book, Interest lists haven't been rolled out to all users. We're including it because by the time you have this book in your hands, you will likely have this feature.

It's becoming harder to have your Fan Page updates show up in people's News Feeds unless they regularly interact with your Fan Page Timeline. If your brand is on Facebook, Interest lists have the potential to increase your reach each time your Fan Page is included in a list. The reason is that the people subscribing to a list are particularly interested in those people and Fan Pages sharing relevant information — it's a very targeted audience that is more likely to interact with your content. In addition, Interest lists help those who have bought a campaign via the Reach Generator feature (see Book V, Chapter 5 for an explanation of Reach Generator) reach their goal of having 75 percent of fans see their posts.

To find your Interest list, navigate to your News Feed, and scroll down until you see the Interests category at the bottom of the left navigation column. If you don't see the Interests category, click the More link at the bottom of the left column. (If you still don't see Interests, it's possible that this feature hasn't been rolled out to all users yet. Keep checking; you'll have it soon.)

Below the Interests category title, you see the Interest lists you've created or subscribed to. Don't worry if you haven't created or subscribed to any lists; we explain how to do those things in the next section.

Creating or subscribing to an Interest list

If you'd like to keep tabs on groups of people and Fan Pages, you can create an Interest list to do that. As we explain earlier, Interest lists are handy because they aren't private to you (unless you set the list privacy settings to Only Me), and you can share your list(s) with others. This is an excellent way to promote topics, brands, or people you support. You can also subscribe to lists others create.

In the previous section, we explain how to find your Interest list in the left navigation panel. From there, you can create a new Interest list either by clicking the Add Interests link in the left navigation panel or by clicking the Add Interests button at the top of the main column. The main column shows a list of suggested Interest lists created by others that you may like. At this point, you can do three things:

✦ **Subscribe to a list.** To subscribe to a suggested list, click the Subscribe button next to any list you want to subscribe to.

✦ **Search for lists that may be of interest to you.** Type a topic or keyword into the Search text box, and Facebook autopopulates the list with relevant Interest lists you may want to subscribe to. Click the Subscribe button next to the lists you want to keep up with.

✦ **Create a new Interest list.** This involves a few extra steps, so we explain how to do that next.

To create a new list, follow these steps:

1. **Click the Create List button at the top of the main column.**

   The Create New List dialog box appears, as shown in Figure 3-9.

2. **(Optional) Click one of the category choices in the left sidebar.**

   If you choose Pages, Subscriptions, or Friends, you need to type a name into the Search text box at the top of the dialog box. Facebook autopopulates results based on what you type.

   If you choose one of the other categories (such as Art, Games, or Technology), Facebook finds and shows results related to that category (you may or may not already Like these Fan Page Timelines).

Figure 3-9:
The Create
New List
dialog
box offers
several
choices for
new Interest
lists.

3. **Click the picture of all items you want to include in your Interest list.**

You can also use the Search text box at the top of the dialog box to find friends and people you subscribe to or Fan Page Timelines you subscribe to, to add them to the list as well. Remember that you don't have to Like a Fan Page or subscribe to Timeline updates to add a Fan Page or person to an Interest list.

4. **Click Next when you're done (you can add to this list later).**

The settings page for your list appears.

5. **Type the name of your list in the List Name box.**

The list name can be whatever you like, but we suggest using common words that are descriptive of the list so others can find it easily.

6. **Select the radio button to determine your list's privacy settings.**

Your privacy choices are

- *Public:* Anyone on Facebook can find and subscribe to your list.

- *Friends:* Only your Facebook friends can find and subscribe to your list.

- *Only Me:* You are the only person who can see this list.

Subscribers can't add items to or delete items from your list.

7. **Click Done.**

Facebook immediately shows you the News Feed for your Interest list.

When you create an Interest list, it shows up in your regular News Feed. You also have the option of reading that Interest list's specific feed by clicking the name of your Interest list in the left navigation pane of your Facebook home page.

Managing your Interest list

Your Interests lists are meant to evolve. Maybe you'll decide to change your share settings so a wider audience can subscribe to your Interest list. Or you may find interesting Fan Pages or people to include as you meet others — on Facebook, another social media platform, or in real life. In the following sections, we explain how you can manage your Interest list.

Changing your Interest list share settings

While looking at the News Feed for the list you want to manage, at the top of the middle column, you see the title of your Interest list, who created the list (in this case, you), and how many people currently subscribe to your list. You also see an icon indicating the share settings for this list. You can click that icon and change the share settings for your list, as shown in Figure 3-10. Choose the settings that you want, and they take effect immediately.

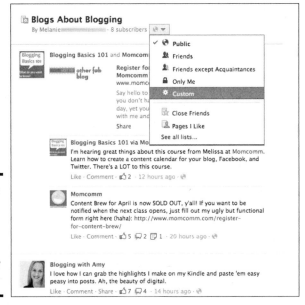

Figure 3-10:
Easily change the share settings of your list any time.

Managing other aspects of your Interest list

While looking at the news feed for the list you want to manage, you see the Manage List button at the top of the right column. Click this button to see the following options:

✦ **Rename List:** Choose this option if you want to rename your list. A text box appears at the top of the middle column, where you can type the new list name. Click the Save button to save and implement your changes.

✦ **Edit List:** Choose this option if you want to add or delete subscriptions, Fan Pages, or friend Timelines from your list. In the dialog box that appears, click the items you want to remove (you can add them back later, if you like). Use the drop-down list in the top left corner of the dialog box to filter your options by Friends, Pages, or Subscriptions, and then type a name in the text box in the top-right corner. Facebook auto-populates a list of items you can add to or delete from your Interest list. Click the Finish button to save your changes.

You can navigate directly to a Fan Page Timeline or personal Timeline to add it to your Interest list. For example, Melanie visited the Typ-A Parent Conference Facebook Page (`https://www.facebook.com/typeacon`) so she could add it to her Interest list for Blogging and Social Media Conferences (`https://www.facebook.com/lists/3502138472611`). Figure 3-11 shows how she used the gear icon and its menu to add the Fan Page Timeline to her Interest list.

Figure 3-11: Visit individual Fan Page Timelines or personal Timelines to add them to your Interest list.

✦ **Choose Update Types:** Just like with friends and subscriptions, you can choose which status updates appear in your Interest list news feed. Click Choose Update Types to see the list of options. By default, all options are chosen. To remove an option from the news feed, click it, and notice that the check mark disappears. That means that type of update (for instance, games updates from the friend, subscription, or Fan Page) won't show up in your Interest list News Feed. This is just one more way to exert even more control over the information you see in your News Feed so it's not cluttered with stuff you're not interested in.

✦ **Notification Settings:** This option enables you to control how you receive notifications about your Interest list. Use the drop-down list to choose which activity Facebook should notify you about. Click Save to save and implement your changes.

Any changes you make to your notification settings apply to all your Interest lists, not just the one you're currently editing.

✦ **Delete List:** You can delete an Interest list at any time. Choose Delete List, and the Delete *(Interest List Title)* dialog box appears. If you choose to delete a list, it's permanent. You can't reinstate the list later. However, you can create a new Interest list (with the same name, even) and add the same friends, subscriptions, or Fan Pages to it. Keep in mind, though, that anyone who subscribed to your list will have to resubscribe to your new list. Click Delete List if you want to continue to delete your list.

Sharing your Interest list with others

We mention earlier that one of the features that sets Interest lists apart from regular lists is that others can subscribe to your Interest lists. In order to gain subscribers, you need to share your list to get the ball rolling. To share a list with others, go to the main News Feed for that Interest list, and click the Share button at the top of the right column. The Share dialog box appears, and now you can share your list via your own Timeline, a friend's Timeline, in a Group, on your own Fan Page Timeline, or via private message. Use the drop-down list to choose the sharing option you want to use. Write a quick update inviting others to subscribe to your list (be sure to explain what your list contains and why people would want to subscribe) and then click the Share button.

You can't share Interest lists that are set to only show to you. To change the share settings for a list, see the "Changing your Interest list share settings" section, earlier in this chapter.

If you share your Interest list via a status update, several cool things happen:

✦ The status update shows a block of the people or Fan Pages included in your list. When a user or fan moves her mouse over that block of images, it expands as shown in Figure 3-12.

Figure 3-12:
Fans can
see a limited
list of the
Timelines
and Fan
Pages
in your
Interest list.

Now the user can click each link to go to that Fan Page Timeline or personal Timeline.

✦ The user can also click the See Full List link to see all the personal Timelines and Fan Page Timelines included in your Interest list. When the user clicks See Full List, a dialog box appears, similar to the one shown in Figure 3-13.

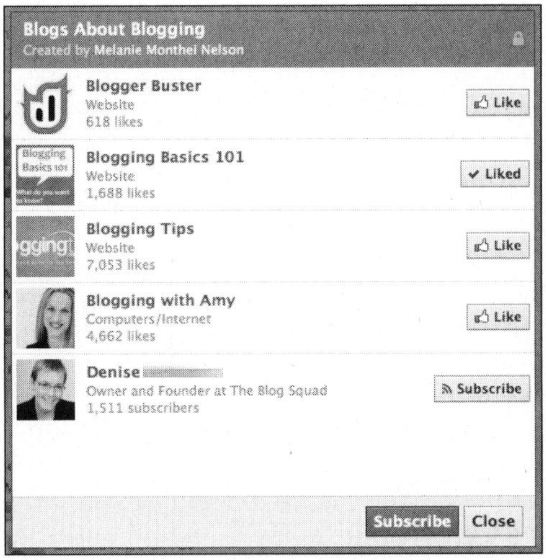

Figure 3-13:
A full list of
the personal
Timelines
and Fan
Page
Timelines
included
in your
Interest list.

The dialog box includes a link to each personal Timeline or Fan Page Timeline, as well as the option to Like individual Fan Pages or subscribe to Timeline updates. The user just has to click the Like or Subscribe button to complete those actions.

✦ The user can also click the Subscribe link either within the status update that links to the Interest list, or she can click the Subscribe link in the dialog box shown in Figure 3-13.

Chapter 4: Touring the Facebook Interface

In This Chapter

✔ **Understanding how each part of your News Feed works**

✔ **Managing your Ticker**

✔ **Curating your Timeline**

*F*acebook has many features including the News Feed, your personal Timeline, and Fan Page Timelines. Each offers a different way to view or access content. This chapter explains how the two most prominent pages — your News Feed and personal Timeline — work.

In this chapter, we share some screen shots of the News Feed and personal Timeline and explain the main elements of each. Both the News Feed and Timeline have a lot of functionality. There's a lot to cover, so let's get started!

Navigating Your Facebook News Feed Page

Your Facebook News Feed is your main Facebook page (we sometimes refer to it as your Facebook home page). You see it every time you log in, and it's where you find the most functionality for interacting on Facebook. Your Timeline is important too because it's where you archive your content, but your News Feed is where you'll spend most of your time.

We explain the News Feed page in terms of five main parts: top navigation, left navigation, your main News Feed, right navigation, and the Ticker and Chat panes (see Figure 4-1). Each of these parts has important functionality. The following sections explain how you can use them to get the most out of your Facebook experience.

Figure 4-1:
Your News
Feed page
has five
main parts.

Top navigation

The top navigation on your News Feed page consists of a blue toolbar. The elements on the toolbar are as follows:

✦ **Facebook link:** This link is the Facebook logo, and when you click it, you return to your main News Feed page.

✦ **Friend Request icon:** Any time you receive a friend request, you see this icon highlighted, with a number telling you how many requests you have. You can click the icon, whether it's highlighted or not, to see if you have any pending friend requests. From there, you can confirm the request or click Not Now to ignore the request. If you click Not Now, Facebook will ask you if you know the person outside Facebook. If you click Yes, nothing happens. If you click No, Facebook will not allow that person to send you any more friend requests. Remember, if you ignore the request, that person can still see your public updates.

✦ **Private Message icon:** When someone sends you a private message, this icon is highlighted, with a number telling you how many messages are new and waiting to be read. You can click this icon to see recent messages, send a new message, or see all your messages.

✦ **Notifications icon:** When someone interacts with your content, tags you in an update, responds to a comment thread you posted on, or posts to a Group you belong to, this icon is highlighted, with a number that shows you how many new updates your friends have added.

✦ **Search text box:** Use this text box to search for friends, Fan Page Timelines, or general information.

✦ **Link to Your Timeline:** This link appears with your profile picture and your name. When you click it, you go to your Timeline.

✦ **Home link:** This link brings you back to the News Feed page. It's the same as the Facebook link on the far-left side of the toolbar.

✦ **Account menu:** This link is marked only with a small down arrow. When you click the arrow, a menu appears, with the following options:

- Use Facebook as Page (see Book IV, Chapter 2)
- Account Settings (see Book I, Chapter 2)
- Privacy Settings (see Book I, Chapter 3)
- Log Out
- Help (see Book I, Chapter 5)

The top navigation toolbar is static and appears at the top of most interactive pages (for example, News Feed, Timeline, Groups, Messages, and so on). It's a handy way to quickly navigate to the main pages you use.

Left navigation

The left sidebar of your News Feed page houses links to your Timeline, Favorites, Groups, Friend Lists, Apps, Pages, and Interest lists. Because you use this navigation quite a bit, Facebook allows you to customize it somewhat to make it fit your habits. For instance, if you find that you visit a particular Facebook Group quite a bit, you can move that Group to your Favorites list so it's readily available at the top of your navigation list. In the next few sections, we explain each of the main navigation choices and provide instructions on moving an item to your Favorites list.

If you move your mouse over any of the main categories in the left navigation sidebar, you see the More option. When you click More, the main News Feed area shows you a list of your Groups, lists, Fan Pages, or apps. The list gives you the option to edit individual items and tells you how often you've used the item.

Timeline

At the top of the left navigation, you see your profile picture and your name. When you click either of these items, you go directly to your Timeline. Later in this chapter, we explain the features of your Timeline and how to use them to interact with your friends and colleagues.

Favorites

By default, the Favorites list contains links to your News Feed, Messages, and Events. You may or may not see a link labeled Find Friends (if you're new to Facebook, you'll probably see this option). The Favorites list is handy because you can keep all the Groups and lists you use the most in one place for easy access. (See Book II, Chapter 5 for information on using Facebook Groups and Book I, Chapter 3 for help creating lists.)

To move an item to your Favorites list, follow these steps:

1. **Move your cursor over the item (Group or list name) you want to move to the Favorites area.**

2. **Click the pencil icon.**

3. **Choose Add to Favorites from the menu.**

   The item appears in the Favorites list.

You can rearrange the order of your Favorites list by moving your cursor over one of the items in the Favorites list, clicking the pencil icon, and choosing Rearrange from the menu. Then you can click and drag items to change their position. The only item that cannot be moved is News Feeds; it stays static at the top of your Favorites list.

To remove an item from your Favorites list, move your cursor over the item you want to remove, click the pencil icon, and choose Remove from the menu. The item moves back to its original place in the navigation. For instance, if you remove a Group from your Favorites list, you can still find it under the Groups heading.

Groups

The Groups option won't appear in your left navigation unless you're actually part of one or more Facebook Groups. We explain how you can connect with others via Groups in Book II, Chapter 5. When you start participating in a Facebook Group, the title of that Group appears in the Groups section of the left navigation. You can click the title of a Group to find the latest updates to that Group.

Lists

In Book I, Chapter 3, we explain why lists are useful and how to create one (or several). Because the News Feed is ever changing, it's easy to miss updates from people you're interested in keeping up with. Facebook tries to guess what you're most interested in (by using an algorithm called EdgeRank — see Book V, Chapter 3), but it doesn't always get it right. Creating lists to organize your friends helps you quickly see recent updates by specific people. For example, we have lists for local friends, high school friends, blogging buddies, and family. When you click the title of each list, your News Feed switches from showing the Most Recent or Top Stories updates of everyone you're connected with to showing updates from the people you included in a particular list. We find we don't miss as many updates from important people when we use lists.

Apps and Pages

The Apps and Pages headers list the applications you have associated with your Facebook account and the Fan Page Timelines you administer, respectively. Both appear to list apps or Fan Pages based on how often you use an app or visit a Fan Page Timeline. We also noticed that the lists can be randomized. In other words, when you're looking at one page (for example, the News Feed), you see a list of items, but when you click to another page (such as a Group page), the order of that same list may change.

News Feed

You can update your status right from your News Feed. At the top of the page in the middle, you see options for Update Status, Add Photo/Video, and Ask Question. Just click the one you want to use, and share what's on your mind.

The main part of your News Feed page is — wait for it — your News Feed in the center of the page. This is where you see updates from your Facebook friends, Groups, people you subscribe to, and Fan Pages you've Liked.

Your News Feed is comprised of Top Stories and Most Recent Stories, and as Figure 4-2 shows, you can sort your News Feed between these two types of stories:

✦ **Top Stories** are from people or Fan Pages that Facebook deems most relevant to you based on your past interactions. Facebook uses an algorithm called EdgeRank to try to determine your affinity for each person and page you're associated with on Facebook — sometimes EdgeRank is right, sometimes it's wrong. (Read more about EdgeRank and other Facebook analytics in Book V, Chapter 3.)

✦ **Most Recent** shows a chronological list of the most recent updates from anyone you're associated with on Facebook and with whom you've interacted regularly. Both Top Stories and Most Recent stories can include updates from friends, people you subscribe to, Groups, apps, or Fan Page Timelines. Updates from people you haven't interacted with regularly are shown in the Ticker in the right sidebar. (We get to the Ticker later in this chapter.)

Figure 4-2:
Click the
Sort link
to switch
between
Highlighted
and Recent
Stories.

If you want to remove a story from your News Feed so it doesn't show, you can hover over the story until you see an arrow appear on the top right of the story. When you click the arrow, a menu appears, as shown in Figure 4-3. Choose Hide Story.

Figure 4-3:
It's easy to
hide a story
from your
News Feed.

The menu you see depends on whether you're looking at an update from a friend or a Fan Page Timeline. The following list explains all the menu options you may see:

✦ **Hide Story:** This option hides a story from your News Feed so you can't see it.

✦ **Report Story or Spam:** If you believe a story is spam or violates the Facebook terms of service, you can report it. When you click this option, Facebook removes the story from your News Feed and provides a link for you to report the item.

✦ **Change Your Subscriptions Preferences:** If an update is posted by a person rather than a Fan Page, you see the options regarding your subscription to that person's updates. You can change your subscription preferences for that person here instead of going to her Timeline.

✦ **Unsubscribe from *Name:*** If you choose this option, you unsubscribe from all of that person's content updates. In short, you're hiding him from your News Feed. You can always unhide him by going to his Timeline and resubscribing.

Unsubscribing from someone's updates is not the same as unfriending her. You're still Facebook friends with that person, but you won't see her updates unless you visit her Timeline. The exception is if she tags you in a status update, photo, or video. And good news! The person you unsubscribe from will not know that you've hidden her.

✦ **Unsubscribe from Status Updates from *Name:*** If you're not interested in seeing status updates from someone, you can stop receiving those by choosing this option.

✦ **Hide All by *Name of Application:*** You see this option only if the story was posted by a third-party application (such as HootSuite, FarmVille, or Instagram). When you choose this option, you can hide all updates that come from that application.

When you post your own status updates, or share photos, videos, or links, those show up in your friends' News Feeds (unless you've specifically applied a privacy setting to those updates; we explain how to do that in Book II, Chapter 2). As you can imagine, you should be careful about what you post because it's very likely many others will see it. (If you have questions about your Facebook privacy, see Book I, Chapter 3.)

Right navigation

Facebook tends to roll out changes here and there, and the right sidebar is where things sometimes jump around a bit. By the time you read this, the right navigation column may have changed yet again.

If your chat feature is off, at the top of the right navigation column, you see your Ticker (we explain it more in the next section). Below the Ticker, you have application alerts — these are usually about upcoming birthdays and Events (see Book II, Chapter 7 for more about Facebook Events). When you click the birthday person's name, the Today's Birthdays window pops up and provides a place for you to write a quick note to your friend, which is automatically posted to his Timeline. Similarly, if you click the name of an upcoming Event, the Event pop-up appears and gives an overview of the Event, complete with a link to the Event page and the option to RSVP to the Event.

Under application alerts, you can see Sponsored Stories. *Sponsored Stories* are a type of advertisement that rely on showing you which of your friends have interacted with a company or its Fan Page Timeline recently. We discuss Sponsored Stories more thoroughly in Book V, Chapter 5, along with other forms of Facebook advertising.

The right sidebar changes, depending on what type of Facebook page you're looking at. Following is a discussion of the basic options you're likely to see on specific types of pages:

✦ **Facebook Group Page:** The right navigation shows an overview of how many members are in the Group. Then you see a text box so you can add someone to the Group (just start typing his name, and you can choose him from the list Facebook shows; remember that you have to already be friends with someone in order to add him a Group). Then you see Sponsored Stories and links (ads).

✦ **Facebook List Feed:** The right navigation of any specific list shows the Manage List button. Click it to rename your list, edit the people on the list, choose which update types appear in the list, or archive the list. Next, you see the On This List section, which allows you to see a snapshot of the Facebook friends you've included on the list, as well as a See All link to show all the people in the list. Beneath that is a text box so you can add someone to the list (just start typing her name, and you can choose her from the list Facebook shows). The heading List Suggestions is next and provides a list of people Facebook suggests may fit with your list. You can click the Add button if you want to add a person to the list, or you can click the small X to tell Facebook the person suggested doesn't fit with the list and remove her from the suggestions list.

✦ **Facebook Messages:** The main Messages page doesn't have right-side navigation, but when you click to individual messages, you see sponsored ads on the right side.

Ticker and Chat panes

The Ticker and Chat panes appear at the far right of your Facebook page. The *Ticker* is a real-time update of what your friends are sharing. You also see updates from Fan Pages and Groups. The difference between your News Feed and the Ticker is that your News Feed focuses on showing you content from people and Fan Page Timelines you interact with most. The Ticker is a running stream of what everyone is doing, whether you regularly interact with them or not. *Chat* is exactly what it sounds like; it's texting in real time (or chatting) with someone via Facebook. Chats aren't broadcast via the News Feed, Ticker, or your Timeline; they are private. We explain chat in more detail in Book II, Chapter 8.

No matter what page you're looking at on Facebook — News Feed, Timeline, Messages, Groups, and so on — you'll see the Ticker and Chat panes. However, you can make the Ticker pane smaller by clicking and dragging the bar between the Ticker and Chat panes. Or you can close the Ticker and Chat column completely by clicking the Hide icon, as shown in Figure 4-4.

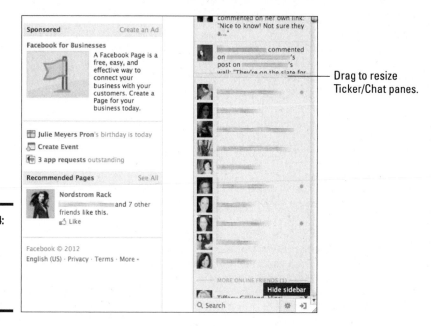

Drag to resize
Ticker/Chat panes.

Figure 4-4:
You can
hide the
chat and
Ticker
column.

As Facebook rolls out more activity applications, you'll see those updates in your Ticker. *Activity applications* are the new way Facebook wants you to interact with others. Facebook's take is that you're out there living life, and you want a more robust way to share what you're doing. Instead of just Liking a book, you can share that you've read the book. Or you can share that you hiked a trail, watched a movie, or played a game.

If you notice something come through your Ticker, and you want to see more about it, move your cursor over the update, and an expanded view appears. You see the status update and any comments to the status, and you can Like or comment on the status yourself.

When you notice that someone in your Ticker has commented on your Fan Page Timeline, you can respond to her right from the Ticker as your Fan Page! To do that, you need to ensure that you have your Fan Page's posting settings set to Always Comment and Post as Your Page. To double-check that setting, go to your Fan Page Timeline, and then click the following links: Edit Page⇨Your Settings⇨Posting Preferences. Then, when you want to respond to a comment on your Fan Page Timeline that you see in the Ticker, just hover over the comment, and a pop-up window appears with the option to comment, as shown in Figure 4-5.

Figure 4-5:
Comment
as your
Fan Page
directly from
your Ticker.

Navigating Your Personal Timeline

Your personal Timeline is a record of all the content you've shared through-out your time on Facebook. It's been referred to as a digital scrapbook, and that's fairly accurate. But if you're not the crafty type or not into scrapbook-ing, don't let that moniker deter you. Your Timeline is simply a way to orga-nize your Facebook interactions. You can highlight important events in your life (Facebook calls these *milestones)*, hide updates, or add events after the fact. For instance, maybe you took your first trip to Europe years before you joined Facebook. With Timeline, you can create a new update that shows up in the correct chronological spot in your Timeline. The update can include pictures, music you listened to while traveling, your own travel notes, a map of your travels, and more. When you've created the new event (or *story)*, you can feature it so others can have a complete picture of your experience — or you can relive the experience yourself.

Watch Facebook's video about how Timeline works at `https://www.facebook.com/about/timeline`.

Familiarizing yourself with Timeline's features

The Timeline has many features you can use to control how you share your content with others — even after you've already shared via the News Feed. First, though, you need to know how to find your Timeline. After you log in to Facebook, click anywhere you see your name (that is, either the left side-bar navigation or the top blue navigation toolbar). Your Timeline appears, similar to the one shown in Figure 4-6.

Figure 4-6:
An example
of a
Timeline on
Facebook.

As you can see from Figure 4-6, Timeline is all about the visual splash! The focus is on your cover photo, with your profile photo taking up just a little bit of real estate in the lower-left corner. Then you see a visual representation of your friends, photos you've uploaded or been tagged in, a map showing where you've recently checked in, and the Fan Pages you've Liked. In addition to the strong visual aspect, Facebook provides links to your biographical information and activity logs. Below these main items, you see your updates, all laid out in chronological order.

The following list discusses each of the items on your Timeline:

✦ **Cover photo:** The focus of your Timeline, your cover photo and can really have an impact when people visit your page. You can choose any of your previously uploaded pictures to use as your cover image, or you can upload a new image. It's handy to know that the cover image is 851 pixels wide by 315 pixels high so you can edit the photo before you upload it. You can use a picture that's smaller than 851 x 315, but Facebook stretches the photo to fit, so it may be distorted.

✦ **Profile photo:** The photo you choose as your profile photo becomes your Facebook *avatar* — it's the picture people see next to your status updates and stories. You can use a photo you've already uploaded to Facebook, or you can upload a new picture. Some people like to change profile pictures regularly, while others like to keep theirs the same. We suggest changing your profile photo only as necessary. Your friends will come to recognize your image, and because Facebook users tend to skim the News Feed, it's easier to find you because they recognize your picture.

✦ **Update Info:** Clicking this button takes you to your About page, where you can update your biographical information for work, education, relationships, quotes, where you live, contact information, and your short Basic Info and About Me blurbs.

✦ **Activity Log:** This button shows up only for you. Click this button to view and edit your previous status updates. You can see how a post was originally shared, how many Likes or comments it received, and even hide the story from your Timeline (by clicking the circle to the far right of the story). To change the share settings for an update, click the current share settings and choose a new setting from the menu (see Figure 4-7).

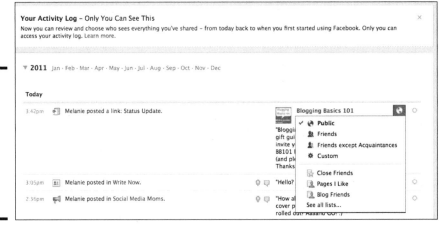

Figure 4-7:
Change
the share
settings
on a story
that's
already
been
published.

The default view for your Activity Logs is to show all your activity. Click the All button at the top of the page to see a menu of other options. For example, you can view only your activity related to Photos, Likes, or even Games. Or you can view the activity of others on your page.

Because Timeline makes it incredibly easy to find current and past status updates, it's a good idea to review your Activity Log and check the permissions on previous stories. You may want to hide some of those party pictures from your colleagues.

✦ **Settings:** Clicking the gear icon shows a drop-down list that enables you to view your Timeline as others see it (either the public at large or a specific Facebook friend). You can read more about that setting in Book I, Chapter 3. The other option available here is adding a Facebook badge to your site.

✦ **Biographical information:** Includes links to your current employer, education, current city of residence, and relationship status if you've shared that information. You can click the About link to expand the detail on these items or edit them.

✦ **Featured content categories:** The default featured content categories are Friends, Photos, Map, and Likes, but you can swap those out with other options. In Figure 4-6, you can see the number 6 and a down arrow after the Likes category. On your Timeline, the number may be different, but if you click that link, the featured categories list expands to show additional categories. Place your cursor over the category you want to feature, and click the pencil icon when it appears. From the menu, you can choose to swap positions with another category or delete the category from Favorites altogether. You cannot change the order of Friends or Photos; those two items will always be displayed as the first and second featured content categories.

Viewing your Timeline Content

Below the features described in the previous section is the meat of your Timeline: your past updates. To see past updates, you can scroll down your page and see stories in reverse chronological order, or you can jump to a specific month or year by clicking a date in the right navigation of your Timeline.

Each story (update) in your Timeline has a dot next to it. You may notice dots on the main Timeline (the line running down the center of your Timeline) that don't appear to have a story associated with them. If you move your cursor over those dots, the associated story appears. As we say throughout this book, Facebook likes to try to guess what's most important to you if you don't tell it outright. If you'd like to determine which stories are featured or highlighted on your Timeline (rather than hidden), we explain how in the next section.

TIP

If you move your cursor over each of the dots closest to the beginning of a year, you see an option to Show All Stories from *Year* (as shown in Figure 4-8). If you click that option, your Timeline expands to show everything you shared that year.

Featuring a story on your Timeline

As you review your Timeline, place your cursor over any story to see the star and pencil icons. Clicking the star icon allows you to feature a story on your Timeline. When a story is featured, Facebook makes it larger than surrounding updates. If you want to undo a highlight, you can place your cursor over the event and click the star again to minimize the event on your Timeline. Figure 4-9 shows how Melanie highlighted her first trip to New York City on her Timeline.

Figure 4-8:
You can expand your Timeline to show all stories from a given year.

Next to the star icon is the pencil icon. Clicking the pencil icon shows a menu that allows you to edit the status by changing the date, adding a location, hiding the update from the Timeline, or deleting the post completely. In addition, you can click the Share icon (usually a gear or a world icon, depending on how you originally shared the update) to change how a story is shared from this point forward. Together, these tools allow you to have complete control over how you share previous updates and content with others.

Hiding a story on your Timeline

While it's easy to focus on those stories you probably want to highlight on your Timeline, there might be a few updates you'd like to hide. No problem. To hide a story from your Timeline, you can either visit your Activity Log and edit your story there, or you can find it on your main Timeline and edit it there. Here's a little more information on each option.

Figure 4-9:
Highlighted
events are
bigger than
other events
on the
Timeline.

To edit your story via the Activity Log, find your story by clicking the correct month or year. When you find the story you want to edit, click the circle on the far right to bring up a menu, as shown in Figure 4-10. To hide your post, choose Hidden from Timeline.

Figure 4-10:
Use the
Activity Log
menu to
edit stories
on your
Timeline.

To edit a story via your main Timeline, find the story you want to edit, and move your cursor over it. When the pencil icon appears, click it to bring up a menu and then choose Hide from Timeline.

You can reinstate any story by returning to the Activity Log and choosing Allowed on Timeline.

Your Timeline can be an amazing tool to keep track of your major life moments and share those with others. Keep in mind, though, that you don't own your space on Facebook. While it's unlikely you'll lose your Timeline, there are no guarantees. We recommend that you keep backups of photos and important updates on your own computer (and create a backup of that as well). Facebook shouldn't be your only means of recording photos, video, or any other special content.

Adding a past event to your Timeline

Your Timeline is a chronological representation of the content you've shared with others. But really, your Timeline can be more than that. You can create a multimedia profile of your major life events to share with friends, family, and others. You can add photos, videos, and comments by year — even for the years before Facebook was around. You can start with the year you were born and go from there, or you can start at any point you like — you have that control.

As you scroll down your Timeline page and your cover photo disappears, a new toolbar appears in its place, as shown in Figure 4-11.

Figure 4-11:
The Timeline toolbar helps you manage your updates.

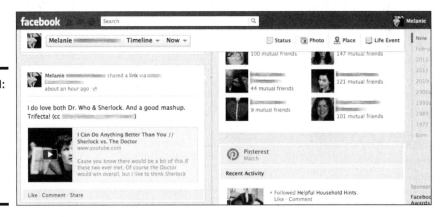

The toolbar lists the name of the person whose Timeline you're visiting, and has drop-down lists for Timeline and dates. Click Timeline to see a list of the pages associated with the Timeline (for example, choosing About will take you to the About page for this person). Or click Now to see a list of dates associated with the Timeline. When you navigate to a specific year, a new list appears: Highlights. Click Highlights to see a list of options for that year. The default is Highlights (showing the milestones from that year), but you can choose All Stories or a specific month to see other updates.

When you're ready to fill in past events on your Timeline, follow these steps:

1. **Use the list of years on the right side of your Timeline to choose where you want to add an event.**

   It's okay if the specific year isn't available; you can pick a year that's close — you can edit the year later. When you click the year, you jump to that spot on your Timeline.

2. **Move your cursor over the middle line and stop when it changes to a cross.**

   If the cursor doesn't change to a cross, you can use the toolbar shown in Figure 4-11 and click the Timeline button; then choose the type of event you want to add (for example, status, photo, place, or life event), and proceed to Step 5.

3. **Click the middle line.**

   A status update menu appears.

4. **Choose what type of status update you want to create here: a text update, Photo or Video, Place, or Life Event (such as marriage, birth of child, new job, and so on).**

5. **Complete the update as indicated and post the new update.**

You can add photos to your new event. The more pictures you include on your Timeline, the more visually interesting it is.

Chapter 5: Finding Help

A s you use Facebook, you'll invariably have questions about how to do something, where to find information, or whether an action is against the Facebook Terms of Service. In this chapter, we explain how to find the Facebook Help Center so you can find answers to your questions. We also show you where you can find information about online safety and privacy for both children and adults.

The Facebook help files cover many topics, and while most answers are pretty concise, some may not give you the complete answer you're looking for. Resources like this book and a few others we point you to later in this chapter will help you fill in the gaps.

Finding the Facebook Help Center

You can find the Facebook Help Center at `http://facebook.com/help.php`, or you can simply click the Account link on the blue toolbar at the top of the page (it looks like a down arrow). From the menu, choose Help.

The Facebook Help Center page (shown in Figure 5-1) provides links to overall help topics; a search text box so you can search for help on a specific topic; and the Facebook Help Feed, where you can find tips from Facebook about recent updates. You also find links to the Community Forum and Feedback. The following sections provide an overview of each help topic to help you find exactly what you're looking for.

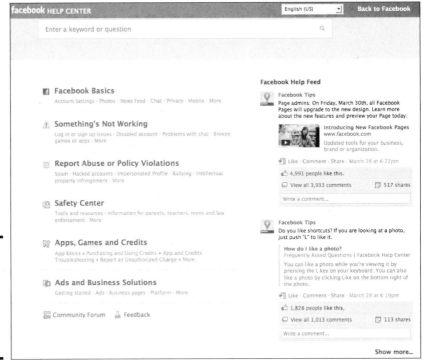

Figure 5-1:
The main
Facebook
Help Center
page offers
several
options.

Searching the Help Center

If you know what you need help with, it may be easiest to perform a search
on related topics. To do that, type a keyword or question in the text box.
As you type, Facebook autopopulates a list of related questions. You can
continue typing your question or term, or you can choose one from the list.
When you're done, click the Search button. Facebook returns related questions
and answers (even if they aren't exact matches). You can click a question to
expand it to show the full answer. If you want to share the question/answer with
others, you can click the permalink option under the question to see a single
page with the question/answer. Now you can copy/paste the URL (or permalink) for this article and share it on your blog, in an e-mail, on Twitter, or
anywhere else you may want to. Or you can click the Share link to share a
link to the question/answer on your personal Timeline, a friend's Timeline,
a Group, a Fan Page Timeline, or via a private message. Use the drop-down
list to choose which one to use. Type an explanation in the text box to give
some context, and then click the Share Help Content button to share the
question/answer.

Using Specific Help Topics

On the main Help Center page, Facebook provides a list of common help topics. Each of these topics is divided into several general categories that allow you to drill down to more specific topics that may fit your question or issue. When you click each main category, you're taken to a page that has more specific categories and related questions. You can click each question to expand it and see a detailed answer. In addition, each question/answer has its own permalink or the option to share the question/answer with others. Here is an overview of what you can expect in each category:

✦ **Facebook Basics:** If you're looking for answers to your general Facebook questions, this is where you want to start. You can find information about managing your account, popular Facebook features, using Facebook with mobile platforms (like your smartphone), and more.

✦ **Something's Not Working:** Visit the Something's Not Working section if you're having trouble logging in to your account or to find out how to change your personal settings (like passwords and privacy options). This section also provides a place to report broken features (for example, your photo upload feature isn't working).

✦ **Report Abuse or Policy Violations:** Facebook has fairly strict policies and terms of service to protect its users from inappropriate content, bullying, spamming, and other undesirable nuisances. If you see something that you feel violates the Facebook guidelines, you can report the user or status update here.

✦ **Safety Center:** The Facebook team takes your online safety and privacy very seriously, but they also believe you should control your own safety and privacy because you know best what you're personally comfortable with. To that end, Facebook provides links, videos, and information about several aspects of online safety. From the main Safety Center page, you can find links to Facebook's philosophy regarding online safety, tips on how to interact within the Facebook community (and report abuse or violations of the Facebook terms of service or community standards), and an explanation of how to use Facebook's tools. This last option, labeled Tools & Resources on the Safety Center page, is a particularly good section. It explains how you can protect your account and control who sees your information, and it covers the basics of unfriending or blocking someone. In addition, this section provides important links to more information about online child and family safety and online bullying.

At the bottom of the page, you see links to additional information for parents, teachers, teens, and law enforcement. Each of these links takes you to a page that provides articles that specifically address online safety and privacy issues. They're important articles to read, even if you feel you're a seasoned social media user — they're especially good if you have teens using Facebook. We encourage you to share these articles with your children and discuss how their behavior online can help or hurt them (or others) in the future.

Facebook has provisions to remove any content that violates its terms of service. If you believe a person or business is violating those terms, you can report them, and Facebook will take action if necessary. Any reports you make to Facebook are confidential. The person or business you report will not know it was you who alerted Facebook.

+ **Apps, Games, and Credits:** Any application not developed by Facebook is called a *third-party application.* Because most applications are third-party applications, Facebook does not troubleshoot or offer help for solving issues with specific applications. Instead, Facebook offers general information about using apps and understanding Facebook credits.

If you need help concerning a specific game or app, you'll have to rely on the information shared by the third party that developed that application.

+ **Ads and Business Solutions:** This section is geared less toward individual users and more toward businesses and brands, because those are the audiences who generally use Facebook ads and Featured Stories. Visit this section to find the Facebook Ad Guidelines, answer questions about scheduling and payment of ads, and much more.

+ **Community Forum:** If you can't find the answer you're looking for in the main Facebook help files, you may want to turn to the Community Forum, where you can interact with other Facebook users. Many times, crowdsourcing an issue leads to an answer. *Crowdsourcing* is when you assign a task to a crowd or community instead of an individual. In this instance, if you can't find what you're looking for within the help files, you can ask the Facebook forum community at large. Facebook's Community Forum provides a lot of functionality, so we'll cover that in depth in a minute.

+ **Feedback:** If you want to share your feedback or ideas with Facebook, this is where you start. The Suggestions and Feedback page has links to feedback forms for all of its features (and then some).

Using the Facebook Community Forum

When you click the Community Forum link on the main Help Center page, you're presented with the Community Help Topics page, as shown in Figure 5-2.

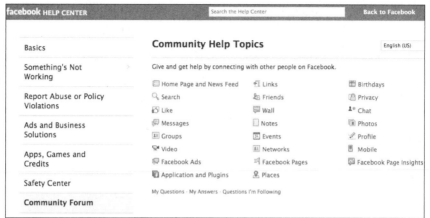

Figure 5-2:
The Community Help Topics page links to numerous community forums.

On this page, you have links to the main discussion topics, as well as the following links:

✦ **My Questions:** A list of the questions you've asked within the forums.

✦ **My Answers:** A list of the answers you've given to other questions. This is not a list of answers for a question you posted.

✦ **Questions I'm Following:** Each question in the forum has the option for you to follow it and be alerted when someone posts an answer. This is a list of the questions marked as something you want to follow.

When you click any of the topic icons or their respective links, you see a page similar to the one shown in Figure 5-3, with a list of general topic headings (the bulleted list at the top of the page; note that some pages have a list and others don't). You also see a list of questions from others in the Facebook community and a list of the most active members of the forum.

To ask a question in a forum, follow these steps:

1. **Navigate to the Facebook Help Center at** `https://www.facebook.com/help` **and click the Community Forum link.**

The Community Help Topics page appears.

2. **Click the topic that most closely matches your question.**

The forum page for that topic appears and shows a list of topics at the top.

3. **Click the general topic at the top of the page that is related to the question you want to ask.**

The forum page for that subtopic appears and is similar to the page shown in Figure 5-4.

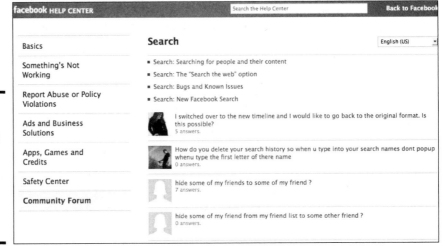

Figure 5-3:
A forum
page about
Groups
shows
topics,
questions,
and top
users.

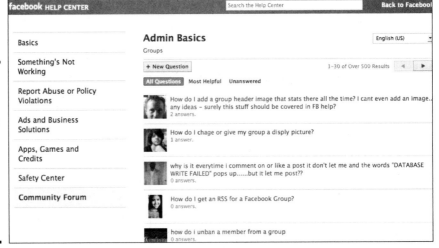

Figure 5-4:
Forum
subtopic
pages allow
you to ask
your own
question or
see what
others have
to say on
the subject.

4. **Click the + New Question button.**

   The Ask a Question page appears.

5. **Select the radio button next to the item that describes your issue and type your question in the text box.**

   Remember that anything you type here will be public and can be seen by anyone using Facebook. Your privacy settings do not apply here.

6. **Click the Ask This button.**

   A page appears with your question as it will appear in the forum.

7. **If you're happy with your question as it is, click the Post My Question button to post your question to the forum.**

   If you want to edit your question, click the Change My Question button.

Using the Facebook Help Feed

The Facebook Help Feed is populated by updates from the Facebook Tips Fan Page (https://www.facebook.com/facebooktips). This page isn't updated every day, but it seems to be updated at least a few times a month. If you don't want to check the Facebook Help Center for updates, you can Like the Facebook Tips Fan Page to see its updates in your News Feed.

Expecting a Response from Facebook

Facebook has over 800 million active users, but just over 2,000 employees (see http://facebook.com/press for more Facebook stats). As you can imagine, it's hard for Facebook to address individual inquiries. Unless your issue is legal in nature, Facebook doesn't usually respond to individual questions or issues. Instead, it's best to go through the proper channels and submit the Facebook form associated with the problem you want to solve. For instance, if you want to report a spam comment left on a status update you made, you can move your mouse over the comment, click the X in the right corner of the comment, and choose whether to delete the comment or report it as spam or abuse. If you need to report a Fan Page Timeline, you can click the gear icon under the cover photo and click the Report Page link.

Finding Links to Important Facebook Documents

Facebook has specific guideline documents and forms to address particular issues. The problem is that users may not know the documents exist or where to find them. Many times, these documents provide the most efficient way to answer your own questions or contact Facebook for help. Here are several web pages you may find helpful as you navigate Facebook:

✦ **Facebook Terms of Service:** https://www.facebook.com/terms.php

✦ **Facebook Pages Terms:** http://www.facebook.com/terms_pages.php

✦ **Promotions guidelines:** https://www.facebook.com/promotions_guidelines.php

✦ **Advertising guidelines:** https://www.facebook.com/ad_guidelines.php

✦ **Report an Infringing Username (this is useful when you own the trademark and need to enforce it):** `https://www.facebook.com/help/contact.php?show_form=username_infringement`

✦ **Reporting claims of copyright or intellectual property infringement:** `https://www.facebook.com/legal/copyright.php`

✦ **If your Fan Page Timeline is disabled:** `https://www.facebook.com/help/contact.php?show_form=page_disabled`

✦ **If your personal Timeline is disabled:** `https://www.facebook.com/help/contact.php?show_form=disabled`

✦ **Facebook Site Governance Page:** `https://www.facebook.com/fbsitegovernance`

Mari Smith has an excellent resource on her website listing 120 Facebook forms you may find useful. The list is current and updated regularly. You can find it at `www.marismith.com/how-to-contact-facebook-a-directory-of-120-forms`.

Finding Additional Facebook Resources

If you're interested in staying up-to-date on Facebook updates, we suggest checking out a few blogs that make it their business to share Facebook's newest features and how they may affect your personal Timeline or your fan page. Here are a few of our favorites:

✦ **All Facebook** (`www.allfacebook.com` and `https://www.facebook.com/allfacebook`) is an unofficial Facebook resource updated several times a day. Articles discuss everything from breaking Facebook news to weekly Top Pages at Facebook. You can also find tutorials and case studies.

✦ **Inside Facebook** (`www.insidefacebook.com` and `https://www.facebook.com/insidefacebook`) has been dedicated to Facebook since 2006 and is one of our go-to sources for Facebook updates, Facebook marketing, and ideas for using applications on Facebook in new ways. Inside Facebook is home to the *Facebook Marketing Bible,* an extensive how-to for getting the most out of your Facebook business efforts. While the book isn't free, this site regularly shares some of its content in abbreviated form for free.

✦ **The Facebook Blog** (`https://blog.facebook.com`) is the official Facebook blog. It's not updated regularly, but it will keep you abreast of major updates or changes to functionality across the platform.

✦ **EdgeRank Checker Blog** (`http://edgerankchecker.com/blog` and `https://www.facebook.com/edgerankchecker`) focuses on how Facebook's EdgeRank algorithm ranks content and determines how that content is seen within individual News Feeds. (Book V, Chapter 3 discusses Facebook analytics, including EdgeRank, in more depth.) Each time Facebook rolls out a new change to the interface, it affects the EdgeRank algorithm. If you're concerned about how your status updates (both for your personal Timeline and your Fan Page Timeline) are appearing, the EdgeRank Checker blog is a good place to start your research.

Book II

Connecting with Others

The 5th Wave   By Rich Tennant

"These are the parts of our life that aren't on Facebook."

Contents at a Glance

Chapter 1: Creating Your Social Media Persona

In This Chapter

✔ **Finding your voice on Facebook**

✔ **Displaying your personality and communicating effectively**

✔ **Developing your business and personal branding**

✔ **Planning messaging for Fan Page Timelines**

✔ **Becoming a resource for your friends**

✔ **Watching your words and behavior**

*F*acebook is a place where you can build a brand, you can connect with friends, you can be yourself, or you can be anyone you want (as long as you are yourself!). Facebook presents you an opportunity to share your thoughts and experiences with friends. The Update Status text box at the top of your screen asks "What's on your mind?" to help prompt you to share. (See Figure 1-1.)

Digging into Facebook is simple enough, but many people find themselves sitting in front of their screen wondering what to say. Sometimes "What's on your mind?" is the hardest question to answer.

This chapter helps you figure out what you should bring to Facebook. In this chapter, we cover how to best feature your personality through Facebook. We talk about this from the point of view of what we call *lifecasting,* as well as using Facebook to add value and enjoyment not only for yourself, but also for others.

Understanding the News Feed and Its Role on Facebook

When you log in to Facebook, the default view is your Home page, where you will see the Status Update text box and the News Feed. (See Figure 1-1.)

Figure 1-1:
Facebook asks "What's on your mind?" and shows your News Feed.

The News Feed gives you the top news (called Top Stories) at that moment based on Facebook's understanding of your interests and how you've interacted with other people and Fan Pages. You also have the option to select Most Recent, which shows all posts and activity from your friends starting with the most recently posted. By default, Facebook displays the Top Stories, as shown in Figure 1-1. In this view, the News Feed doesn't show everything your friends have shared. Facebook's News Feed is managed by an algorithm called EdgeRank that helps decipher what is most interesting and relevant to you based on your activity. To find out how EdgeRank works and what it means to you, take a look at Book V, Chapter 3.

Let us give you an example of how EdgeRank determines what shows up in your Tops Stories for your News Feed. If your mother posts Facebook updates every day about how much she loves her children, and you comment on each one, saying thank you, you will see all updates from her in your News Feed. If Bob the Builder (assuming you're friends with him) posts every day, but you never Like or comment on his posts, you will seldom see his updates in your News Feed's latest news. Facebook is designed to help you get the most out of it by highlighting the people you're most interested in and showing less of those things that you're not interested in.

With this knowledge, you can decide what makes sense to you on Facebook and what does not — and what to share (and what not to share). Knowing about Facebook's Top Stories and EdgeRank is important for the simple fact that you can begin to filter your News Feed as you like. On the flip side, you'll naturally develop an audience for your updates with those that are most interested in what you have to say. If your primary audience is your social friends, you may do better to talk about interesting experiences within your social life. If it's professional connections, you may find that they are more interested in what you're doing in your work or business. Perhaps it is all of the above. In most cases, there is a balance of social and professional interests.

The News Feed plays a big role in your Facebook success, and you're the star of the show! If you want to get the most out of Facebook, knowing your audience is critical, whether you're using Facebook for personal interests, professional interests, or a mix of both.

If you like to post irrelevant or annoying content, you should be aware of the power of the News Feed for your audience. Users have the option to unsubscribe from some or all updates from a certain user if they would prefer to not see them. Be careful not to be a nuisance on Facebook, or you may be subject to the unsubscribe option!

The beauty of Facebook is the power of permission. You connect with people that you give permission to. They see your updates only if they show an interest, and they can remove them if they wish. If you embrace this factor, you will get exactly what you want out of Facebook!

Finding Your Voice on Facebook

People are dynamic. We can be passionate, emotional, funny, or relaxed. If you're like the rest of the people in the world, you have parts of your character that you reserve for only a few. Consider that on Facebook.

To further illustrate this point, allow us to use an extreme but real example. One day, a lady has a bad day at work and vents by posting on Facebook that she hates her job. She forgot that she had added her boss as a friend on Facebook. He sees the update and adds a comment inviting her to not come in to work anymore. Remember that Facebook is very public, so while you can and should express your feelings, keep some reservation and think before you click that Post button.

That being said, Facebook is about being authentic. But determining your voice depends on a lot more than just being yourself. Before we go any further, consider your goals with Facebook. You might have one or more of the following goals:

✦ To share photos with family and friends

✦ To connect with friends to keep up to date on happenings

✦ To network and build professional relationships

✦ To find that special significant other

✦ To build a personal brand to establish who you are professionally

These different purposes each call for a different message. It's okay to have several of these or other reasons for using Facebook. Deciding on a goal will help you envision what you want to accomplish on Facebook and allow you to find your true voice.

Lifecasting

People are naturally inclined to share their life stories with others. That's why so many have joined Facebook! Since social networks have risen in popularity, sharing has come to a whole new level. Many people share their most notable life moments, and some people share moments that aren't notable at all. Sharing life moments on the Internet is the most common use of social networks. We call this *lifecasting.* The term *lifecasting* can refer to broadcasting your life (or portions of it) in any medium. On Facebook, it might be status updates about what you're doing, or photos and videos that highlight moments of your life.

Oftentimes, when people refer to lifecasting, they're thinking of people who post frequent updates stating what meaningless activity they're currently doing, because they manage to have access to a computer or mobile phone while doing so. Still others are just answering the question "What's on your mind?" Sharing life moments on Facebook is perfectly acceptable and is sometimes a great way of creating meaningful connections with friends and family. Figure 1-2 shows an example of lifecasting.

Figure 1-2:
Sharing a homemade recipe.

Notice the post about homemade fudge. This is a great example of lifecasting. This user is probably very proud of his fudge and wants to share his creation with others! What easier way to do that than to simply snap a photo on his smartphone and post it right on Facebook?

Avoid putting sensitive information on Facebook. (If the user's fudge really looks good, he might have tons of people wanting to get their hands on his confectionary creation!) In all seriousness, most times, sharing with your friends is perfectly safe. Showcasing food is not likely to put you at risk, but some things can. Suppose you're hanging out in the driveway, and you snap a shot of your friends in front of the open garage. This gives people the opportunity to see all the valuables within view of the camera and may show your house numbers as well. If you have your Timeline set to be visible to the public, anyone can see that photo. Again, most times you're safe, but if you're concerned, you might want to consider what you feel comfortable posting on Facebook. There's a little information about the potential dangers of photos taken from smartphones at `http://technorati.com/technology/gadgets/article/why-iphone-photos-are-dangerous/`. Consider your Facebook privacy settings as well. For the lowdown on privacy, see Book I, Chapter 3.

People can see only what you allow them to see. You can not only control the level of privacy of different portions of your Timeline, but also the privacy of specific posts. If you want to post something that is appropriate only for certain people, you have the ability to do that when posting a status.

Embracing differences

Facebook is a great private network or a great open network. Decide what works best for your goals, and go for it.

For example, Daniel likes to use Facebook to connect with new people and grow new relationships. One of his Facebook goals is to build his personal brand. His Facebook privacy settings are completely open, and he welcomes new connections! In fact, go ahead and add Daniel as a Facebook friend! By contrast, Melanie uses Facebook to connect mostly with family and close friends. She allows people to subscribe to her public updates, but she limits her personal connections on Facebook to people she's actually met and talks to regularly, and her privacy settings are more strict.

Neither one of these approaches to using Facebook is wrong, because everybody has a different goal. You shouldn't feel bad if you want to be more open or more private; don't take it personally if someone else chooses to be more private.

Knowing what people read

If you want to use Facebook as an effective tool for getting the word out about an event, promoting a blog, or simply increasing the level of connection you have with people, it is important to understand what people read and respond to. We recently had a conversation with some friends about how people share on Facebook. Chris stated that when people post on Facebook, they want people to comment or like their posts. Carrie begged to differ! She said she often posts with no desire or expectation for a response. She made her point the next day with a status update to that effect (see Figure 1-3).

Figure 1-3:
Some
people are
looking for
comments;
others
aren't.

She may have been satirical with her point, but here's something we can learn — people read and respond to things that are most interesting to them. Here are some of the types of updates that have a tendency to get a lot of views and clicks because they catch people's interest:

✦ Simple and concise updates

✦ Updates they're tagged in

✦ Updates that are funny

✦ Interesting pictures or videos

✦ Controversial statements

Most people respond very well to photo and video posts, with a runner-up being simple and concise updates. Remember that Facebook users skim their News Feed and are interested in reading headlines, and then deciding what conversations they want to dive into.

How can you use the knowledge of what your friends are likely to click, comment, or read? Suppose you're trying to promote a yard sale. Instead of posting a text update, you could post a picture of the yard-sale sign. In a comment below, you can list some of the items you're selling. Because people see photos more easily in their News Feed, and they are more likely to engage with photos, you'll likely have greater success getting the info out because you understand what people respond to.

Status updates are like headlines — they should be short and simple. If you want to share more than a few sentences, use Notes to get into more detail. Those who want the rest of the story will read your Notes, and those who aren't interested will be spared a long story in their News Feed.

Using humor and controversy

Using humor is a great way to engage people. Being lighthearted is very inviting. Who couldn't use a laugh every now and then? One of Daniel's favorite things to post is something ironic or funny. Facebook is just an opportunity to share that thought and invite others to share their witty retorts.

Controversy is a great way to start a proverbial fire! People are passionate about ethics, religion, politics, and many other topics. Be careful when you post your own opinions on these topics. It's pretty easy for someone to get upset about what you posted or to get offended by other commenters. While debate can be fun, it can also be dangerous. If you're okay with starting a spirited debate, go for it! However, if you take people's differences of opinions personally, maybe you should stick to the humorous side of things.

Speaking to your audience

Who are you trying to reach? In this chapter, we assume that you have a goal of some sort on Facebook, such as building a brand for your business or strengthening your personal connections with friends. Either way, your goal should help you determine how to connect with your audience and be relevant when you speak to them.

How do you know what is relevant to your audience? People have a tendency to attract who they speak to. What we mean is that if you talk about sports, you're going to have better connections with other people who are also interested in sports. If you're an avid business networker, your Facebook friends list will show a slant toward other people who are avid networkers.

Think about your goal(s) regularly to reassess what you would like to gain from Facebook. Doing this will help you be clear about what you should share on Facebook.

Building a Brand

Facebook is a great place to build a brand. One of Daniel's goals with Facebook is to build a personal brand (in fact, you can add him right now at `www.facebook.com/danielherndon`; please say hello!). Building a personal brand and building a brand for your business are a little bit different, so we cover them both.

Building your personal brand

Your personal brand is simply an expression of who you are. In many cases, this is the real you, but in a professional context. For example, Daniel has created his professional persona on his personal Timeline. His personal brand reflects the value that he provides for his clientele. His personal brand reflects that he's an active networker. On the other hand, Melanie develops her personal brand via her Fan Page Timelines and tends to keep her personal Timeline limited to friends she's met in person and family. However, Melanie does have the Subscription feature enabled and allows (and encourages!) subscribers. That way, she can publish something publicly and keep other things more private.

Following are some ways that you can express and establish your personal brand via your personal Timeline:

✦ With your profile picture

✦ With the type of posts that you respond to

✦ With the kind of information you share

Building your brand might just be about sharing your personality. Daniel likes to make people laugh and likes to connect with new people, so this helps shape what he shares on Facebook. His passions include people, marketing, and humor. While he shares general personal topics, most likely, the topic of conversation is humor, connecting with people, and occasionally marketing.

To strengthen the professional side of his brand, Daniel had a professional photo taken for a featurette in *Indianapolis Business Journal*. He's also considerate of the fact that he values his connections, regardless of differences in opinions, so he's respectful of people's thoughts even if he weighs in on a debate.

Building a brand for your business

The biggest thing to consider when building a brand for your business is that you're representing a group of people (your company) rather than a single person. The personality of your brand on Facebook can be just as lively, but with some different considerations:

✦ Create a Facebook Fan Page Timeline rather than a personal Timeline for your business. This is a must. The Facebook terms of service do not allow businesses to create personal Timelines; if you do, you could lose your page and your community. We think you'll prefer creating a Fan Page Timeline anyway because there are so many more features for those Timelines (for example, custom applications). Book IV explains more about Fan Page Timelines.

✦ Communicate clearly what your company does.

✦ Create or install customized applications (for example, a newsletter sign-up or RSS feed for your blog).

✦ Strengthen connections by talking to your customers and responding when they engage.

The ways to build your brand are as vast as the number of business types. Remember that businesses are made up of people. While you're typically speaking to a broader audience with a business Fan Page Timeline than with a personal Timeline, it's still important to be authentic. If you want to increase customer connections through Facebook, talking about sales isn't going to create the brand perception you want. Merely broadcasting special offers may achieve a goal, but oftentimes, it's less inviting and doesn't attract interaction from your customers on Facebook. A better approach might be to ask questions of customers and start conversations. Establish yourself as the go-to source in your niche by solving a problem, entertaining your audience, or educating your audience. By giving your customers a reason to come back and inviting them to engage with you, you're strengthening connections.

Planning Content for a Fan Page Timeline

Oftentimes, companies want to plan their content for their Fan Page Timeline rather than simply posting at will. We say that's a good thing! Here are some of the things that you might include in Facebook on your Fan Page Timeline:

+ Notes or links to blogs

+ Promoting coming events

+ Special offers

+ Engaging questions for fans

The easiest way to plan your updates is to schedule them the moment you determine what your messaging is. Focus on getting to know your audience, what they respond to, and what time of day they are most active on your Fan Page Timeline — your Facebook Insights (see Book V, Chapter 3). Use that information to determine your posting strategy.

What's important is to offer valuable content. Provide information that draws your customers to interact. If they don't connect with you or interact in any way, your updates will stop showing up in their News Feed. We cover several ideas and best practices for creating a strong Fan Page Timeline (see Book IV), but we also suggest you check out *Facebook Marketing All-in-One For Dummies,* by Amy Porterfield, Phyllis Khare, and Andrea Vahl (John Wiley & Sons, Inc.).

Being a Resource

A friend of ours once spoke of his addiction to news and described Facebook as "hyperlocal news." That's a great description of how Facebook is a resource to some people. Make sure that you're a resource to your readers.

One great way to be a resource is to share other content that you find interesting online, especially if you believe that your friends and fans will find it interesting as well. All you have to do is simply copy the link into the Status Update text box after typing any thoughts that you might want to add.

Consider proper spelling and grammar

The social media world is often approached with a more casual and genuine attitude. While that's perfectly acceptable, it's all too common for people to let the informal nature go too far and write posts with poor spelling, a bare nod at grammar, little or no punctuation, and text-message abbreviations. While it's perfectly acceptable to be genuine, remember that everything that you write is a reflection of you (or your company). So grammar, spelling, and punctuation are important!

Facebook detects any pictures on the web page you're sharing and offers you the opportunity to select a different picture (known as a thumbnail) if there are several on the page.

For example, on her Fan Page Timelines, Melanie shares news and important information that's relevant to her community as well as her niche (social media). When you share useful information with your audience, it helps build your brand and adds real value to your interactions. If you're using Facebook for your company, consider how you can provide valuable resources for your customers.

If you still don't know what to say, don't sweat it! Be yourself, but know who you're talking to. The more value you add to others, the more you will get out of Facebook. It's not only about you; it's also about those you connect and share with.

Avoiding Inflammatory or Spammy Behavior

Sure, you don't mean to be a spammer, but if you (accidentally) do the same things that spammers do, how will people know the difference? This especially applies to those using Facebook for business networking or running a Fan Page Timeline, because some of your fans who are connected to your business may not know you personally.

Here are some simple tips to avoid being mistaken for a Facebook spammer:

✦ **Don't write updates with ALL CAPS.** This is usually done either by someone who lacks the skill or discipline to capitalize properly or someone who's trying to get attention from people who are not interested in his updates. Online, when you type in all caps, it's the same as yelling at someone. You definitely don't want to yell at your customers and friends.

✦ **Don't mass-add friends.** When you add friends without any sort of context of why you should be connected, many will be deterred and will reject your friend request.

If you want to add someone you're not well acquainted with and think he may not remember you, send him a private Facebook message, and tell him why you would like to be connected.

✦ **Do use your own photo as your profile picture.** Remember, this is *Face*book. People appreciate seeing the real you (if it's your personal Timeline) or even your logo (if it's your Fan Page Timeline).

✦ **Don't send private messages with questionable links.** If you do share links in a private message, be sure to explain to the recipient what the link is and where it will take them. Sometimes, people won't click a link because it looks too much like phishing. (Phishing sites are designed to make people's private information vulnerable to hackers.)

Respecting others' privacy

One of Facebook's biggest success factors has been the ability for people to choose their level of privacy. Some choose to limit their Timeline's visibility to only friends; some even choose to have varying levels of privacy for friends as well. Understanding your friends' (and even nonfriends') desire to protect their own privacy, however they choose to do so, is important.

Another important thing to consider (as you would in everyday life) is understanding what was shared openly with you but not with others. Take the following tips into consideration when it comes to the privacy of others:

✔ Don't post information on someone's Timeline unless you're sure it's welcome knowledge for all his friends on Facebook.

✔ Don't post on the Timeline of someone you don't know well.

✔ Do be sure you disclose how you know each other if you send a private message to someone who may not be sure who you are.

✔ Do be careful to recognize that your comments on a friend's post are public. For example, if a friend posts about having a bad day, she may not be willing to share details in comments.

✔ Do be careful to recognize that when you tag someone in a post, all your friends can see your post, regardless of the tagged friend's privacy settings. Make sure you don't post something that he would not like to be public!

Chapter 2: Posting and Sharing

In This Chapter

✓ Creating status updates

✓ Tagging people and Fan Pages in updates

✓ Deleting comments or updates

✓ Interacting with others on Facebook

✓ Understanding the Subscribe feature

The crux of Facebook is sharing real-time information with family, friends, and colleagues. Facebook offers several ways for you to share content with others and to respond to content from others. This chapter explains how you can create and interact with stories (updates), photos, and video using your personal Facebook account. We also show you how you can use the Subscribe feature to share updates with people you aren't friends with (and why you may want to) and how you can use it to keep up with people you aren't friends with.

If you're looking for info on interacting on your Fan Page Timeline, flip over to Book IV, Chapter 3.

Creating a Status Update

A status update, also called a *story,* is a short explanation of something you want to share with your Facebook friends. A status update can include just about anything: text, pictures, video, links to a website, and so on. Status updates are the main way you share information with others. (You can also use private messages, chat, and comments, but this section is focused on basic status updates.)

To create a status update, you need to type in the Status Update text box. You find that box in one of two places: your News Feed or your personal Timeline. On your News Feed, there is a link at the top labeled Update Status; when you click that link, a text box appears. You can type your status update, tag people, include your location, and customize who can see your update. The Status Update text box in your Timeline offers a little more customization. In addition to tagging, location, and customized sharing, you can add a year or signify that this update is a Life Event. Figure 2-1 shows the Timeline Status Update text box.

Figure 2-1:
The
Timeline
Status
Update text
box lets
you share
content with
friends.

As Figure 2-1 shows, you can post a story as any of the following:

✦ **Status:** This option allows you to post a regular text status update. If you want, you can include a link to a blog or website in the update, and a preview of the web page will show with the status update. As we explain in Table 2-1, you also have the option here to tag others, add a year, assign a geographic place, and set the share settings.

✦ **Photo:** If you want to add photos or video, click the Photo link. We explain in detail how to share photos and video in Book II, Chapters 3 and 4, respectively.

✦ **Place:** You can choose to relate your update to a specific address or general location when you click the Place icon. You can achieve the same thing by creating a regular status update and changing your Place option (see Table 2-1).

✦ **Life Event:** When you click the Life Event option, you're given a menu with the following options:

• Work & Education

• Family & Relationships

• Home & Living

• Health & Wellness

• Travel & Experiences

Because life events are usually more important than an average text status update, each of these options has its own submenu that leads to a form to fill out with additional information. You can include pictures, dates, location, and a complete story with each Life Event update. The Life Events option is particularly useful as you update and complete your Timeline. Book I, Chapter 4 explains how the Timeline works in general and why you may want to add events to your Timeline.

Figure 2-1 also shows a group of icons beneath the text box where you type your status updates. Table 2-1 explains those icons in more detail.

Table 2-1		Status Update Icons
Icon	*Name*	*What It Does*
	Tag People	Click this icon and start typing the names of people you want to tag in your update.
	Add Year	Click this icon to add a year to your status update. If the year is different from the current year, the status update will appear in the correct chronological place on your Timeline rather than being posted as a current update.
	Place	Click this icon and start typing your location. You can type the name of a business (say, a restaurant), a city, state, or even a specific address — it really depends on how much information you want to share.
Public ▼	Share Settings	Click this icon to customize how you share any update. You can share or restrict access to any person or list via this option. You can change the Share settings even after you've published a story.

Adjusting how you share content

If you want to change the privacy of a piece of content, you can do that easily — both before and after an item is published. When you initially publish something (for example, a text update or link), you can click the Share icon (it looks like a gear, the Earth, or two people, depending on your current share settings). From the menu, choose to share your update with Everyone (Public), a specific list, specific people, or otherwise customize how you share the item. If you want to change the Share settings for an item you previously published, just click the Share icon and change the Share setting. Yes, it's that easy!

Remember that everything you share ends up in your friends' News Feeds. If you post too much or post uninteresting things, your friends may choose to hide you from their stream or unfriend you completely. On the other hand, you may find you don't like seeing certain updates from friends, and you may choose to hide them as well. To hide a certain type of update, you can visit the friends' Timeline and choose which updates you see you in your News Feed. For example, if your friend Kathy is sharing too many pun-related updates or game requests, you can follow these steps to hide those types of updates:

1. **Go to the Timeline of the person whose updates you want to control in your News Feed.**

    At the top of the page, you see three buttons: Friends, Message, and a gear icon.

    Alternatively, you can move your cursor over a person's name in your News Feed and a pop-up appears, showing the Friends button. Move your cursor over the Friends button, choose Settings, and then proceed to Step 3.

2. **Click the Friends button and choose Settings from the menu.**

    A menu appears, with check marks next to the updates you currently see in your News Feed from this person.

3. **Click the item(s) you no longer want to see in your News Feed.**

    For example, if you don't want to see FarmVille or other gaming updates, you can click Games to remove the check mark. When this friend shares updates for any games, you won't see them in your News Feed.

 Alternatively, you can change your general subscription options right from your News Feed. When you see an update from that person, mouse over the story, and then click the arrow on the right side. When the menu appears, choose whether you want to subscribe to all updates, most updates, or only important updates from this person. If you want to hide someone completely, you can choose the unsubscribe option. They'll still be able to see your updates, but you won't see theirs (and no, Facebook doesn't tell them you unsubscribed).

Taking a poll

The top of your News Feed page offers options for updating your status so you don't always have to go to your Timeline if you want to share something. The options are a bit different on the News Feed, but you can do essentially the same kinds of updates. One difference is the option to take a poll. The Ask Question link at the top of the News Feed page allows you to ask a question and provide multiple-choice answers. This option is basically a way to create a poll for your Facebook connections. To create a poll, follow these instructions:

1. **Navigate to your News Feed page and click the Ask Question link at the top of the page.**

2. **Type your question in the text box provided.**

3. **Click the Add Poll Options link.**

    More text boxes appear below the question box, as shown in Figure 2-2.

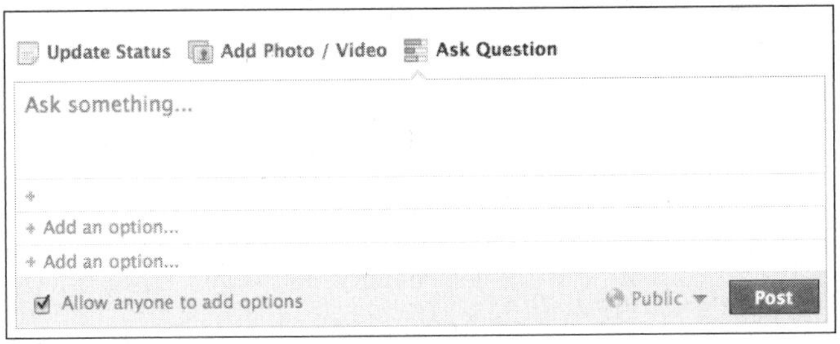

Figure 2-2:
Adding
a poll as
a status
update is
easy.

> Update Status   Add Photo / Video   Ask Question
>
> Ask something...
>
> + Add an option...
> + Add an option...
>
> ☑ Allow anyone to add options   Public ▼   Post

4. **Type an answer or choice in as many of the Add an Option text boxes as you wish.**

   You can have as many choices as you like. Each time you click in the last Add an Option text box, a new one appears. You don't have to use each text box.

5. **Deselect the check box next to Allow Anyone to Add Options if you want people to choose only your predefined answers or choices.**

   If you don't mind if people add their own answers, you can leave that check box selected. Melanie once left the Allow Anyone to Add Options check box selected, and every time she posted a question, someone added an answer relating to Justin Bieber. Be prepared to have a sense of humor.

6. **(Optional) Set your Share settings.**

7. **Click Post to share the poll with your Facebook connections.**

Tagging friends and Fan Pages

Tagging is when you write a status update and provide a link to someone's personal Timeline or a Fan Page Timeline. When you tag a person or Fan Page, that person is alerted that you've shared something about her. Figure 2-3 shows a status update where Melanie tagged her friend Debbie and the Fan Page for her business. When people see the update, they can click Debbie's name to visit her personal Timeline or click her business name to visit the Fan Page Timeline. Facebook will alert Debbie that Melanie tagged her and her Fan Page in a post.

If you tag a friend in a status update, that doesn't mean everyone has access to her information. What people see when they click to her Timeline will depend on her current privacy settings (see Book I, Chapter 3 for advice on setting up your Facebook account and privacy settings).

Figure 2-3:
An example
of how
tags look
in a status
update.

Tagging a person or Fan Page in an update is easy. Type @ and start typing
the name of the person or Fan Page you want to tag. For example, if you want
to tag the Blogging Basics 101 Fan Page Timeline in an update, start typing @
Blog, and Facebook creates and shows a list of related people and Fan Pages
for you to choose among, as shown in Figure 2-4.

Figure 2-4:
Use the list
Facebook
creates to
choose who
to tag.

'ew tips about tagging:

n tag up to ten people or Fan Pages in a single status update.

sing your Timeline, you can tag people when writing a status
r when commenting on a status update.

ag Fan Page Timelines even if you haven't Liked them.

can't tag individuals in a status update.

an tag other Fan Pages even if the Fan Page hasn't been
3ook IV, Chapter 3, to find out more about how Fan Pages
with other Fan Pages and individual fans.)

tag individuals in comments if that individual left a previ-
n the thread. For instance, the upcoming Figure 2-5 shows
ommented on a post at the Blogging Basics 101 Fan Page
ie isn't Facebook friends with this person, so she can't
s update and tag that commenter. However, because

the person commented on a status update, she can now respond to him or her in the comments section of that same thread and tag that person. The benefit of this is that Facebook lets the person know Melanie tagged him or her, and he or she can come read her response.

 It's best to tag people only if you know they won't mind. It's especially important to ask people if you can tag them when you're using Facebook's check-in feature (see Book II, Chapter 5 and Book IV, Chapter 4 for an explanation of Facebook Places, check ins, and Deals).

 If you'd like to control whether people can tag you, adjust your privacy settings. Click the down arrow next to the Home link, click Privacy Settings, click Edit Settings next to How Tags Work, and click Timeline Review. (Check out Book I, Chapter 3 for a discussion of your Facebook privacy.)

Removing Updates or Comments

There will be times when you rethink something you shared, and you want to remove it. In fact, as you update your Timeline, you may want to remove some of your past updates as your circle of friends grows or your life changes. Or maybe you commented on someone's status update, and you wish you'd been a little more eloquent.

You can delete comments (yours as well as those from others on your updates), but before you do, think about your reasons for doing so. Social media is about open sharing and accessibility. It's about discourse and sharing all sides of a story or issue. Ideally, that discourse will be respectful, but sometimes it gets out of hand. No one likes to have his or her voice removed (or, in this case, comment), but sometimes it's best in order to keep the peace. On the other hand, if you remove a comment (either yours or someone else's), be prepared for the possibility of being called out for censoring the conversation. There are two sides to this. One is that your Timeline is your space, and you can decide what is or isn't appropriate for that space. It's important to explain your stance to your circle of friends so they understand your point of view. The other side is that if you post content to Facebook, you're essentially inviting people to interact with you and share their opinions on that content. If you choose to remove comments you disagree with, others may not feel welcome to comment on your updates.

If you administrate a Fan Page Timeline, removing comments becomes an even bigger issue. Some businesses will remove inflammatory or unflattering comments, but that can be a mistake. Your customers expect your Fan Page Timeline to be a place where they can interact with you — both positively and negatively. If you whitewash your Facebook Timeline, allowing good comments and deleting anything questionable, your fans will rebel. (We explain the etiquette and overall management of Fan Page Timelines in further detail in Book IV.)

Say you really do need to remove a status update or comment. If that's the case, follow these instructions:

1. **Find the status update or comment on your Timeline (or go to your Timeline and click the Activity Log button).**

2. **Move your mouse over the update or comment to reveal the pencil icon (for status updates) or the X (for comments).**

3. **Continue as follows:**

   • *To remove a status update:* Click the pencil icon and choose Hide from Timeline or Delete Post from the menu.

   • *To remove a comment:* Click the X.

When you delete a post or comment, it's permanently deleted. You can't get it back. If you don't want to permanently delete a post, you can always change the Share settings or hide it from your Timeline instead.

Interacting with Other People's Updates

When you share content on Facebook, you're probably doing it so others will interact with it. Let's face it, if everyone just broadcast updates, pictures, and video without receiving feedback, it would be pretty boring — and not terribly fulfilling. When we share something, our intent is to have friends comment or Like the content. That interaction is validation that others agree or disagree with us. Or it's just an acknowledgement that someone else noticed we're around and sharing stuff. Either way, we get a sense of satisfaction from those interactions.

Depending on how interesting you found an update, you can interact in the following ways:

✦ **Like:** Clicking the Like button is the easiest way to interact with content on Facebook. When you click Like, you're basically acknowledging that you agree with the status update or like the content of it (whether it's text, a link, a picture, or video). Clicking Like in a comment is also a way to let commenters know you've seen their input if you can't respond right away.

✦ **Comment:** Responding with a typed message takes a bit longer, but trust us when we say that everyone loves a comment. It's especially nice when those comments lead to a civil discourse on interesting subjects — or build on each other for humorous observations.

✦ **Share:** This is the ultimate in validation because you like something enough to share it with your own circle. The person or Fan Page that originally shared an item can see how many times it's been shared.

You can do most of your content interaction via your News Feed or the feed for a specific list (see Book I, Chapter 3 for information on lists); you don't have to click to someone's personal Timeline or Fan Page Timeline to interact with their updates. As you see something in your News Feed, you can Like, comment, or share at will.

To share an item, follow these instructions:

1. **Click the Share link below the content.**

   The Share This window appears.

2. **Use the drop-down list to choose where to share the content.**

   You can share it on your own Timeline, on a friend's Timeline, in a Facebook Group you belong to, on a Fan Page Timeline you administer, or via a private message.

3. **Set the Share settings for your update.**

4. **Write a status update introducing the content.**

5. **Click the Share button.**

When you share something, it appears on your Timeline and in your friends' News Feeds (depending on who you shared the update with, of course), and others can see where you found the shared content, as shown in Figure 2-5.

Book II
Chapter 2

Posting and Sharing

Figure 2-5:
Melanie
shared a
link found
via her
friend Amy
Tucker.

Understanding How Subscriptions Work

The Subscribe feature allows people to subscribe to your public updates without being your Facebook friend. Likewise, you can subscribe to others' public updates. However, you can subscribe to someone's public updates only if they've enabled the Subscribe feature.

You have to be 18 to turn on the Subscribe feature. It's a handy feature to enable if you're a celebrity or public figure who may have a quite a following but like to keep your Facebook friends somewhat private, or at least confined to those people you've met in person. Or maybe you like to be available to network but still want to keep some things private. If you have the Subscribe feature enabled for your account, any time you post content and set the Share settings to Public, your subscribers will see your updates. Those subscribers will not see any updates that have customized share settings (like Friends Only). At the time we wrote this book, the Subscribe feature was available only for personal Timelines, not Fan Page Timelines.

Turning on the subscribe feature for your account

Before you decide to turn on the Subscribe feature for your account, you may want to do a quick review to make sure that your account is ready for public consumption. Click the View As option in your settings (click the gear icon under your cover photo) to see how the public will view your Timeline. You can change the Share settings for any content you don't want publicly available.

When you turn on the Subscribe feature, Facebook shares your Timeline on the People to Subscribe To suggestion list for others, and your bio appears under your name. Now is a good time to double-check what you have as your current work status and change it accordingly. To edit your information, go to your Timeline, click Update Info, and click the Edit button next to the information you want to update.

To turn on the Subscribe feature on your account, follow these instructions:

1. **Click the Settings link on the blue Facebook toolbar (it looks like a triangle) and choose Account Settings from the menu.**

   The General Account Settings page appears.

2. **Click the Subscribers link in the left navigation column.**

   The Subscribe Settings page appears.

   Alternatively, point your browser to `https://www.facebook.com/about/subscribe` and click the green Allow Subscribers button.

3. **Select the Allow Subscribers check box.**

   A new menu of editable options appears.

   Additionally, if you have your privacy settings set so that only friends or friends of friends can search and find you, you'll see the highlighted Subscriber Search alert. This alert reminds you that if you want to reach all your potential subscribers, you should change your settings.

4. **Select the Subscriber Search check box if you'd like to change your settings.**

If you want to keep your settings the same, don't select the check box. Subscriptions will be turned on, but you still won't be visible in public search.

5. **Click the Edit link beside the Subscriber Comments and Subscriber Notification options and use the drop-down lists to refine who can leave comments and what kinds of notifications you'll receive.**

When you turn on the Subscribe feature, visitors to your Timeline will see the Subscribe button. Anyone who clicks the Subscribe button, whether they are actually connected to you on Facebook or not, will see your Public updates. Subscribers will not, however, see your personal data (like your birthday).

Subscribing to other people's updates

You can subscribe to anyone's update as long as they have the Subscription feature turned on for their account. To subscribe, just go to someone's Timeline and click the Subscribe button, and you'll start receiving their public updates immediately. You can customize which updates you receive by clicking the Subscribe button again to bring up a menu like the one shown in Figure 2-6. (You may have to choose Subscribe⇨Settings to get the What Types of Updates list.)

Book II
Chapter 2

Posting and Sharing

> ○ **Subscribed**   Message   ✱
>
> How many updates?
> ✓ **All Updates**
>   Most Updates
>   Only Important
>
> What types of updates?
> ✓ Life Events
> ✓ Status Updates
> ✓ Photos
> ✓ Games
>   Comments and Likes
> ✓ Music and Videos
>   Other Activity
>
>   Unsubscribe

Figure 2-6: Use the Subscribed menu to fine-tune what you see from others.

You can choose to receive All Updates, Most Updates, or only Important Updates. You can further customize your interaction by clicking the items you don't want to receive updates about (Games, Music and Videos, and so on). If there's a check mark beside a topic, you'll receive an update about it. You can edit these settings later by clicking the Subscriptions category in your Favorites. (The four images under the cover photo in your

Timeline; this list usually starts with Friends, Photos, and so on. If you don't see Subscriptions, click the down arrow to see more options.) On the Subscription page, click the Subscribed button next to the person whose updates you want to control and choose Settings. Click to deselect any topics you don't want updates for.

When you subscribe to someone's updates, you can respond to those updates publicly if they allow it (they may allow only friends to comment). If you post something publicly and have someone reply who isn't a friend (or even a friend of a friend), check to see if you have your Subscribe feature turned on, and determine if you want to have that option available or not.

Your Facebook friends are subscribed to you automatically. Even if you turn off the Subscribe feature, they'll receive your updates. The exception is if you restrict them from your updates. (See the "Adjusting how you share content" section, earlier in this chapter, for an explanation of how to restrict updates, and flip to the section on lists in Book I, Chapter 3 for additional information.)

Chapter 3: Sharing Your Photos on Facebook

In This Chapter

✔ Taking pictures within Facebook to share with friends

✔ Uploading pictures to Facebook from your computer

✔ Making albums to hold your photos

✔ Knowing when and how to tag friends in your photos

✔ Using applications to share photos on Facebook

*I*t doesn't take long to realize that photos and videos catch your attention in your News Feed more than simple text updates do. Also, pictures stand out and have a better chance of encouraging interaction (such as a Like, comment, or share). Interaction is what determines how often you show up in someone else's News Feed. Simply put, the more an individual interacts with your content, the more Facebook thinks that person wants to see your updates, and the more your updates appear in his or her News Feed. (For more discussion on how Facebook determines what shows up in the News Feed, see Book V, Chapter 3.)

In this chapter, we explain how to upload images to your personal Timeline and your Fan Page Timeline, how to create and edit photo albums, and how to tag people in the images you upload. We also introduce you to some third-party applications you can use on your smartphone to upload images to your Facebook Timeline.

Taking Pictures with Facebook's Photo Application

Photos are usually eye-catchers, but the size of photos in the News Feed really stands out to Facebook readers in a list of text updates. Usually, you upload photos from your camera, computer, or smartphone to Facebook, but sometimes you may want to take a picture with your webcam and upload it to your News Feed because it's fast and easy. For example, Melanie is in a Facebook group where the members like to greet one another by posting photos of themselves drinking coffee or tea each morning. It would be tedious to try to take a picture (or have someone in her family take a picture) of her drinking tea every morning, download it to her computer, and finally upload it to Facebook. The situation calls for a more efficient and impromptu option, such as using Facebook's photo application and a webcam.

You need to have a webcam installed in order to use Facebook's photo application to take a picture and post it directly to your News Feed. Facebook uses Adobe Flash to connect to your computer's webcam. If you haven't already given permission for Facebook to use Flash and connect to your computer's webcam, you may see an alert like the one in Figure 3-1 when you try to take your picture.

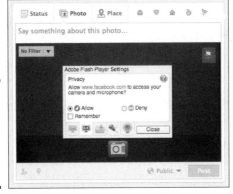

Figure 3-1:
Allow
Facebook to
access your
computer's
webcam.

Within the alert pop-up, select the Allow radio button, and if you want Facebook to remember that you've given it permission, select the Remember check box. Click the Close button.

To take a picture with the Facebook application (or *app)* via your personal Timeline or Fan Page Timeline, follow these instructions:

1. **Use your browser to navigate to your personal Timeline or Fan Page Timeline, and then click the Add Photo link above the Status Update text box.**

   Three choices appear. You can upload a photo from your computer, use your webcam to take a photo, or create a photo album.

2. **Click the Use Webcam option.**

   Facebook displays a screen showing the view through your webcam. Adjust your webcam as needed.

   The default for your webcam on Facebook is video. Click the small photo icon in the top right of your webcam picture to switch from video to photo.

3. **(Optional) Choose a filter from the drop-down list in the top-left corner of the display if you'd like to apply a special effect to your photo.**

4. **Click the Camera button to take a picture.**

   Facebook counts down from three to one before taking your picture. You can retake your picture as many times as you like. When you're happy with the result, continue to Step 5.

5. **Click the Say Something about This Photo text box and type a status update about your photo.**

6. **If you're working within your Timeline, use the toolbar below your picture to tag people, assign a location to the picture, and/or customize who you want to share the picture with.**

   Note that if you're working within your Fan Page Timeline, you can customize only who you want to share the photo with (targeted by language and location); you can't tag people or assign a location.

7. **Click the Post button to publish your picture and status update in your News Feed.**

Uploading Images from Your Computer

Facebook displays your uploaded photos as shown in Figure 3-2, with a large photo (if you just upload a single image) or a large photo and two smaller photos (if you upload several images at a time).

The instructions for uploading images to your personal Timeline or a Fan Page Timeline are essentially the same, with minor differences in the way the menu is labeled and the ability to tag people when uploading the image. You can upload images to your Timeline or directly to a new photo album. Any photos you post to your Timeline are placed in a photo album called Timeline Photos. Whether you post your photos to your Timeline or a specific photo album, they appear in your News Feed unless you customize your sharing options.

Figure 3-2: Facebook displays your photos in the News Feed.

If you want to upload photos to your Fan Page Timeline, you need to navigate directly to your Fan Page Timeline and start from there, but if you want to upload an image and have it associated with your Timeline, you have a few options. You can

✦ Click the Add Photo/Video link at the top of your News Feed page.

✦ Navigate to your Timeline and click the Photo link above your Status Update text box.

✦ Navigate to your Timeline and click the Photos link to the right of your personal information under your cover photo.

To upload your image via a regular status update (either on your personal Timeline or a Fan Page Timeline), follow these instructions:

🔲 Photo

1. **Click the Photo link above the Status Update text box, as shown in the margin.**

Three choices appear. You can upload a photo from your computer, use your webcam to take a photo, or create a photo album.

2. **Click the Upload Photo/Video link.**

3. **Type a status update related to your photo.**

4. **Click the Browse button and choose the file you want to upload to Facebook.**

5. **Tag people, link a Place, and/or customize who will see your image using the icons in the gray strip below your Status Update text box.**

Note that if you're working within your Fan Page Timeline, you can customize only who you want to share the photo with and assign a date; you can't tag people or assign a location.

6. **Click the Post button to publish your picture and status update in your News Feed.**

Your image is immediately shown in your News Feed and placed in the Timeline Photos album. Note that who sees your image is dependent on your customizations in Step 5. Anyone you tag in the image will be able to see the image.

You may want to use photo editing software to manipulate your image before you upload it to Facebook. Some photo editing software allows you to save your image for the web. What that setting does is pull out extraneous digital information and allow your image to load faster on a web page. Unfortunately, saving your images for the web may also cause them to appear grainy when you upload them to Facebook. Photos look their best on Facebook when you save them as .jpg files; other images, such as line art or cartoons, look best when saved as .png files.

Creating and Editing Albums

Melanie's Great-Grandma Anna used to keep a scrapbook of all the photos she took around her farm. She had formal photos as well as impromptu and illusion photos where she had tried her hand at playing with depth of field to make it look like Grandpa Wayne was holding a pumpkin bigger than he was. All the photos went into an album — and those albums are in a box in a closet. Likewise, Melanie has ten or so albums filled with her kids' baby pictures in her closet. Sometimes those albums get pulled out of the closet, but not often. Let's face it, printed photos and albums are passé: Just about everyone is taking photos with their digital cameras or smartphones, storing those photos on their computers, and sharing them with friends via sites like Facebook and Flickr (www.flickr.com) or personal blogs.

Digital albums are handy because you can access your photos any time and share them with friends and family (or the public at large), and they don't take up valuable closet space. Facebook makes it fairly easy to create your own digital photo albums and share your memories (or the latest in your string of shenanigans) with whoever you like. What hasn't changed is the need for organization; storing photos in specific albums on Facebook makes them easier to find later. In this section, we explain how Facebook sorts your photos into albums, and how you can create new albums and control the privacy of those albums.

Any time you upload a photo, Facebook places that photo into an album. Which album your photo ends up in depends on how you uploaded and used the image:

✦ When you upload an image directly to your Timeline via a status update, Facebook puts the photo into the Timeline Photos album.

✦ When you want a picture to be part of a specific album, you can upload the photo directly to that album or, if the album doesn't already exist, create a new album.

✦ When you share a picture from your phone or other mobile device, Facebook puts the photo into the Mobile Uploads album. See Book II, Chapter 6 for more information on how you can make regular updates with your mobile device.

To create a new album, you just need to upload photos to Facebook. You can create as many Facebook albums as you want, and you can upload 200 images into an album before Facebook considers it full and automatically creates a new album for you (you can edit the new album's name and privacy). The exception is your Mobile Uploads album — it holds only 100 images before it's full.

To create a new album, you can start from one of two places:

✦ Click the Photo link above your Status Update text box and choose Create Photo Album. This option works for both personal Timelines and Fan Page Timelines.

✦ Click the Photo link under your cover photo, as shown in Figure 3-3, and then click the +Add Photos button in the top-right corner of the page. This option is available only for your personal Timeline.

Figure 3-3:
The Photos link on your personal Timeline allows you to upload pictures to a new album.

Melanie ▒▒▒▒▒▒

🏢 Works at Blogging Basics 101
🎓 Studied M.A. Technical Writing at Oklahoma State...
🏠 Lives in Tulsa, Oklahoma
💜 Married to ▒▒▒▒▒▒

About   Friends 524   Photos 114   Ma

Regardless of your starting point, the Photo Album window appears, as shown in Figure 3-4, and shows the following:

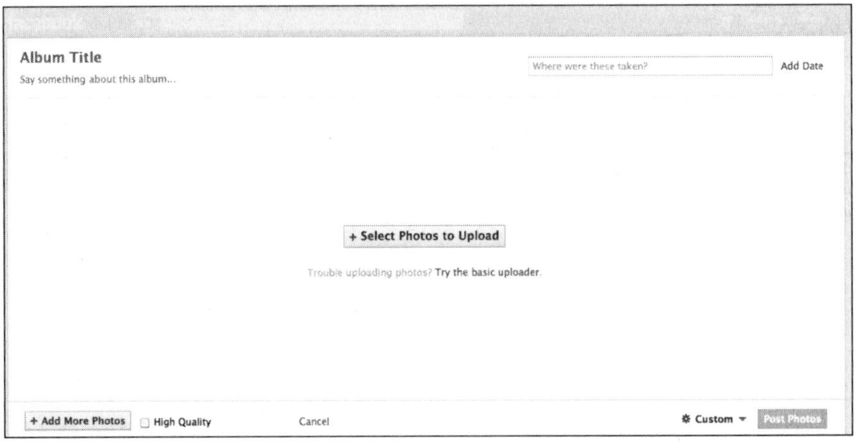

Album Title
Say something about this album...   Where were these taken?   Add Date

+ Select Photos to Upload

Trouble uploading photos? Try the basic uploader.

+ Add More Photos   ☐ High Quality   Cancel   ⚙ Custom ▾   Post Photos

Figure 3-4:
The Photo Albums window allows you to name the album for your photos.

✦ **+Select Photos to Upload:** Click this button to choose individual photos to upload to this album. When the photo starts uploading, you see the status of your upload (the upload status bar disappears when your image is fully loaded).

✦ **Album Title:** Click Album Title, and you can type the name of the album where you want to place your image. Even if you type the name of an existing album, your photos are placed in a new album with the same name rather than in the existing album. To place photos in a specific album, see the instructions in the later section "Uploading new photos into an existing album."

✦ **Say Something about This Album:** Click here and type a description of the album and its contents.

✦ **Location and Add Date:** You can type the name of the location where the image was taken. If you like, you can click the Add Date link and include the year, month, and day the picture was taken. Fan Page Timelines do not offer the option to include a date.

✦ **+Add More Photos:** This button allows you to upload more images to your album.

✦ **Quality:** Click to select High Quality if you want to upload the best version of an image. If you do not select High Quality, there's a chance the standard version of your image may be grainy. A high-resolution version of the image may take longer to upload, but it may be clearer. Note that Facebook can't upload a higher resolution of your image than you currently have. In other words, if you have a poor image to begin with, it will likely still look poor when you upload it to Facebook.

✦ **Sharing options:** You can customize who can (and can't) see your album and the images inside. Note that this option isn't available for Fan Page Timelines.

Book II
Chapter 3

Sharing Your Photos on Facebook

With the Photo Album window showing, continue with these instructions to upload photos:

1. **Click the +Select Photos to Upload button and choose the image file(s) you want to share on Facebook.**

   When your image is loaded, it appears similar to Figure 3-5, and you can customize information associated with it (see Step 2).

2. **Type the information you want to include in the album (name of album, description, location, and date).**

   You can also customize the information associated with the photo, as shown in Figure 3-5. You can include a comment, tag people, set the date and time the photo was taken, and even provide additional location information.

3. **Use the sharing options in the drop-down list to set the album's privacy.**

4. **Click the +Add More Photos button if you want to upload more photos to this album.**

Album Title

Say something about this album...

Say something about this photo...

+ Add More Photos   ☐ High Quality   Cancel

Figure 3-5:
After your
new image
uploads, you
can tag it,
comment on
it, or assign
a location.

5. **Click the Post Photos button.**

   The Album page appears. From there, you can view the photos in your album or edit your album.

As you create albums, you may find that you want to edit them. To edit an album, go to your personal Timeline or your Fan Page Timeline and click the Photos link under your cover photo. The Photos page appears and shows your albums at the top. Click the title of the album you want to edit (if you don't see it, click the See All link) to open it. Click the Edit Album link.

The Edit Album page offers editing several options:

✦ **Album Name:** You can change the name of the album by deleting the old name and typing a new one. This option is available for both personal Timeline and Fan Page Timeline albums.

✦ **Where:** Change the location associated with your album or refine it even more. For example, if you assigned a state location to an album (say, New York), you could change it to reflect the city (New York City), a part of the city (Manhattan), or even a specific location (Dylan's Candy Bar). This option is available for both personal Timeline and Fan Page Timeline albums.

✦ **Date:** Assign a year and month to your album. You can add a specific date by clicking the +Add Day link. This option is available only for personal Timeline albums.

✦ **Description:** You can add or change the description of your album here. This option is available for both personal Timeline and Fan Page Timeline albums.

✦ **Privacy:** Use the drop-down list to customize your privacy settings for this album. Remember that anyone tagged in a photo that resides in the album can see the photo. This option is available only for personal Timeline albums.

✦ **Edit Photos:** This tab enables you to type a description for individual pictures, assign a location to a picture, and tag people in the picture. You can also choose which picture is the album cover by selecting the This Is the Album Cover radio button under the picture you want. Or, if you uploaded the wrong picture, you can select the Delete check box, and Facebook deletes that photo when you save your changes. Finally, you can move a picture to another album, if you want. Just use the Move To drop-down list to choose the album where you want the picture to appear. This option is available for both personal Timeline and Fan Page Timeline albums.

✦ **Edit Info:** This tab enables you to change the album name, assign a location (where you were when the photo was taken), add a description of the entire album, and set the album's privacy. This option is available for both personal Timeline and Fan Page Timeline albums.

✦ **Delete:** If you no longer want your album to appear on Facebook, you can delete it. Click the Delete button, and Facebook removes the album completely from your personal Timeline or Fan Page Timeline.

Uploading new photos into an existing album

Photo albums are rarely static things, and you probably want to add to them over the course of time. No problem! After you create an album, it's easy to add more pictures to it. Just follow these steps:

1. **Navigate to your personal Timeline or Fan Page Timeline and click the Photos link under your cover photo.**

The Albums page appears and shows your existing albums at the top of the page.

2. **Click the album you want to add pictures to.**

You're taken to a page for that album that shows all the photos included in that album.

3. **Click the Add Photos button in the top-right corner.**

The Upload Photos pop-up window appears.

4. **Click the +Select Photos to Add button, choose the photo(s) you want to upload to your album, and click Open.**

The Upload Photos dialog box reappears and shows the status of your upload. While you're waiting for your photos to upload, you can select the quality of the photo and assign location information to this batch of photos, if you like.

5. **Click the Post Photos button.**

The album page reappears and shows all the pictures in that album, including the one(s) you just uploaded. If your picture(s) have a recognizable face, the Who's in These Photos page appears. Type the names of the people in the pictures and click Save or click the Skip Tagging Friends link. If your photo doesn't have recognizable faces, the Edit Album page displays.

Each album allows you to have 200 photos (except the Mobile Upload album, which allows only 100). When you reach that limit, the Add Photos button disappears, and you'll need to create a new album for your new photos. Additionally, you won't see the Add Photos button in the following albums:

✦ **Timeline Photos:** Photos appear in this album only when you post them directly to your Timeline via a status update.

✦ **Mobile Uploads:** Photos appear in this album only when you upload them from your mobile device.

✦ **Cover Photos:** This album holds only photos you've used as cover photos. (See Book I, Chapter 2 for instructions on how to set your cover photo.)

✦ **Profile Pictures:** This album holds only photos you've used as your personal profile picture. (See Book I, Chapter 2 for instructions on how to set your profile picture.)

✦ **Some third-party app albums:** If you're using a mobile app like Instagram, you won't be able to manually add pictures to those albums.

Moving photos from one album to another

To move a photo from one album to another, navigate to your personal Timeline or Fan Page Timeline. Click the Photos link under your cover photo to go to your Albums page. From there, just follow these steps to move your photos from one album to another:

1. **Click the album where the picture currently resides.**

A page appears showing all the pictures in that album.

2. **Click the Edit Album link.**

The Edit Album pop-up window appears. (The only albums that don't offer this option are Profile Pictures and Cover Photos.)

3. **Click the Edit Photos link in the lower-left corner.**

   A new page appears, similar to the one shown in Figure 3-6.

Figure 3-6:
Use the
Move To
drop-down
list to move
photos from
one album
to another.

4. **Click the Move To drop-down list under the picture you want to move, and then select the album you want to move the picture to.**

5. **Click the Save Changes button.**

   The Album page for the original album appears, but the picture you moved is gone. To see the picture, click the Albums link. On the Albums page that comes up, click the album you chose to move the picture to, and you will see it there.

Editing privacy settings for albums

Privacy is a big issue, especially when it comes to pictures and video. (See Book I, Chapter 3 for further discussion of online privacy and how you can protect yourself and others.) You can not only customize the overall privacy settings for your Facebook account, but also customize privacy for individual photo albums in your personal Timeline (Fan Page albums are automatically Public). To do that, first navigate to your Timeline and then follow these steps:

1. **Click the Photos link on your main dashboard.**

   The Albums page appears.

2. **Click the sharing icon to show a drop-down list (as shown in Figure 3-7) and choose who can see your albums.**

You can choose a general category or list, such as Public or Friends. For finer control, choose Custom. If you choose Custom, the Custom Privacy dialog box appears.

3. **(Optional) Select an option from the Make Visible To drop-down list, type the name of the people or lists you want to hide the album from in the Hide This From text box, and click Save Changes.**

Figure 3-7: The Privacy drop-down list enables you to determine who can or can't see your pictures.

There are a few important things to be aware of when you're sharing pictures on Facebook:

✦ Only the album owner can change the privacy settings. That means you're in charge of your albums, regardless of who you share them with. It also means that if someone shares an album with your picture in it, they control who sees it, not you.

✦ While you can't change the privacy settings for the Mobile Uploads album, you can change the privacy settings for each picture within that album.

To change the privacy for the individual pictures in the Mobile Uploads albums, click the album, and then click the picture you want to work with. The photo viewer appears, with that picture, as shown in Figure 3-8. From the Share drop-down list, select a privacy setting for this picture. Save your changes, and you're done.

✦ If you share an album or picture with others, they can download those pictures to their computers. If you don't want people to save or share a particular photo (say, if you doing something questionable or embarrassing), you probably shouldn't upload the photo to Facebook (or anywhere online, for that matter).

Figure 3-8:
Use the Share with pull-down menu to control who sees your pictures.

Editing Pictures

Facebook doesn't currently offer the options of full-fledged photo editing software. If you want control over removing red-eye, enhancing the color, or cropping an image, you need to do that with photo editing software on your computer, such as Adobe Photoshop, Photoshop Elements, or GIMP (free at http://gimp.org). However, you can do basic edits such as tagging people in a photo, adding a location tag or date to your photo, and rotating your photo.

To find the picture you want to edit, navigate to your personal Timeline or Fan Page Timeline, and click the Photos link to view your album, photo, and video page. The albums you've created are at the top of the page. You can click any of these to work with a specific photo you uploaded, or if you scroll down a bit more, you'll see photos and video that you've been tagged in but were uploaded by others. You can click any of these pictures to edit them. Find the picture you want to edit, and click it; the image appears in the photo viewer, as shown in Figure 3-9.

The Facebook photo viewer page has options to

✦ **Tag Photo/Tag This Photo:** Facebook allows you to tag people in photos, videos, and status updates. *Tagging* is like labeling your photo with the names of people who appear in the picture. When you tag someone, the photo shows up in their News Feed, and they are alerted that you've uploaded a picture of them. To tag someone in your picture, click the Tag Photo button or the Tag This Photo link, and then click the person's face. A box appears around the place where you clicked, and a menu appears. Start typing the name of the person you want to tag. You can repeat the process for each person in your picture, if you like.

Figure 3-9:
The photo viewer shows pictures full size and allows you to make several edits.

If you posted this picture to a Fan Page Timeline, you can't tag individual fans unless you're connected with them via your Timeline (in other words, you need to be Facebook friends with them).

It's considered bad form to tag people or Fan Page Timelines that aren't actually in your photo. Although Facebook is a social platform, not everyone has the same ideas about how to share on Facebook. You may be fine with others tagging you in photos; others may find it to be an invasion of their personal privacy. Melanie has one friend who scanned in high school senior pictures of people and invited them to tag themselves (few did). We're glad the friend who uploaded the photos didn't tag them herself, but we might go one step further and suggest that if it's not a picture of you, ask permission before posting it. Not everyone likes to share everything.

Finally, there's the issue of spamming. When you tag someone who isn't relevant to your picture (for example, a Facebook friend who isn't pictured or a Fan Page Timeline that doesn't relate to your image), you're spamming them — and no one likes to be spammed.

✦ **Edit:** This link allows you to change the description of the photo, tag people who were with you, and set the location of where you took the photo. Just click within the text box; start typing a description, someone's name, or the location; and then click the Save button.

✦ **Like/Unlike or Comment:** If you want to Like or Unlike your photo, click this button or the link under the photo description. On the left side of the photo viewer, you see a list of comments people have made about the picture. You can respond to comments, delete comments, and Like or Unlike the picture or individual comments.

✦ **Follow/Unfollow Post:** When you post a picture or comment on a picture, Facebook automatically assumes you want to know when others comment or Like the photo as well. These updates appear in your Notifications (the icon of the world at the top of your Facebook page next to the Search text box). If you don't want a notification when people interact with your photo, click Unfollow Post. If you change your mind, return to the picture and click Follow Post.

✦ **Share:** When you upload a photo, it appears in your News Feed. However, you may want to share a picture again later or share the picture with a wider audience. Click the Share link, and use the Share On drop-down list on your own Timeline to choose where you'd like to share the photo. You have the option of sharing this photo on your own Timeline (meaning your personal Timeline), on a friend's Timeline, in a group, on your Fan Page Timeline (if you administer more than one Fan Page Timeline, you see a list of all the Fan Pages you're affiliated with), or via private message. When you've chosen where to share the photo, type a short introduction of the image to give your audience context, and click the Share Photo button.

When someone else shares a picture of you and tags you in it, you can click it to edit it, but you'll find that you have limited options because the photo doesn't belong to you — it belongs to whoever shared it.

Figure 3-10 shows what a shared photo looks like when you click it.

**Book II
Chapter 3**

Sharing Your Photos on Facebook

Figure 3-10:
You can't fully edit pictures uploaded by someone else.

The top of the right column shows who shared the photo, when they shared it, and who they shared it with. You can see who they shared it with by clicking the icon (usually a gear, heads, or the Earth, depending on the share settings). Beneath that is the On Your Timeline notification. It's grayed out if the image is shown in your Timeline. You can click the Remove link to remove the picture from your Timeline.

Be aware that removing a photo from your Timeline or page doesn't remove the photo from Facebook. The picture is still visible via the person who posted it originally.

When you click the Remove link, a dialog box appears, alerting you that the photo is no longer on your Timeline. You also have the option to Report/Remove Tag or Send *[Original Poster]* a message. If you think someone has tagged you unnecessarily in a photo just to get your attention (that is, you're not really in the picture), you can click this link to mark the image as spam and report it to Facebook. When you click this link, a dialog box appears, as shown in Figure 3-11. Select the radio button next to the issue(s) you want to report, click the Continue button, and follow the directions. If you accidentally click this link, just click Cancel.

Figure 3-11: Report and remove offensive or spammy photos.

The next item you see is the caption the original poster gave the photo, followed by the names of everyone tagged in the photo. Below this, you have the option to Like, Comment, Unfollow the post, or Share the image with your own friends.

At the top of the right column next to the X, you see a gear. Click it to reveal a drop-down list with these options:

✦ **Add or Edit Location:** You have the option of associating a location with your photo. Click this option and type the city or country you want associated with your picture in the Where Was This Photo Taken text box. Click Save to save your changes.

✦ **Change Rotation:** If you originally shared the photo, you see the option to rotate your photos left or right.

✦ **Download:** If you want to save the photo to your computer, click the Download link. A dialog box appears, asking if you'd like to save the file. Click OK, and the file is saved on your computer. You may want to rename the file after you download it because Facebook uses long strings of random numbers as filenames.

✦ **Make Profile Picture:** If you want to make a specific image the profile picture for your Timeline, click this link. A crop box appears on your image so you can crop it to show exactly what you want in your profile picture — just drag the corners until the image is cropped the way you want. Click the Done Cropping link under the picture, and the picture is now your profile image. Your Timeline shows your new profile picture.

✦ **Delete This Photo:** If you are the person who originally shared a photo, you can delete the photo by clicking the Delete This Photo link. After you click the link, a dialog box appears, asking if you're sure you want to delete your photo. Click the Confirm button to delete your picture from Facebook.

✦ **Report This Photo:** As explained earlier in this section, if you want to report a photo as being spammy or inappropriate, you can do so here. You see this option if you aren't the original person who shared this photo.

**Book II
Chapter 3**

Sharing Your Photos on Facebook

Using Smartphone Apps to Share Photos on Facebook

Of course, you aren't always sitting at your computer when you want to upload photos to Facebook. Sometimes you're out and about, and you want to share what you're doing or document an event you're attending. Luckily, there are several applications you can install on your smartphone that allow you to take a picture and share it directly to Facebook. A few you may want to consider are

✦ **Instagram (**`http://instagr.am/`**; free):** This app allows you to take a picture and choose among several filters to apply before you share the photo. Instagram is one of the most popular photo apps for sharing pictures on Facebook.

✦ **GLMPS (**`http://glmps.com/`**; free):** This innovative camera app is currently available only for the iPhone. What makes it stand out from the other apps is that it takes a few seconds of video before it snaps the picture, giving you a better idea of the moment you captured in the picture.

✦ **Camera+ (**`http://cam1.us/`**; 99 cents):** This app provides a lot of bang for just a buck. You can set the exposure and focus separately, choose among four shooting modes (including stabilizer and timer), and use the onscreen grid to ensure your photos aren't crooked. When you're done with the shot, share to Facebook, Twitter, or Flickr.

And, of course, you can download the Facebook app for your smartphone. The Facebook app allows you to take photos, write updates associated with your photos, tag people, and post everything right from your smartphone. (For more information about using mobile Facebook, check out Book II, Chapter 6.)

Chapter 4: Sharing Vi[deo]
on Facebook

In This Chapter

✔ **Using video to encourage sharing**

✔ **Shooting video with Facebook's app**

✔ **Uploading video to Facebook**

✔ **Using apps to share your other video channels on Facebook**

✔ **Making the most of your video efforts**

*P*eople on Facebook love video links! After all, the primary goal of Facebook is to connect with people and to share. Video is interesting and easily shared. Also, when you deal with people online primarily through text, sharing a bit of yourself through video allows you to connect with your friends or fans in a much more personal way.

Facebook makes it easy for fans and friends to view video: They just click the video and watch it in their News Feed. They don't have to view a slideshow (as with images), and they don't leave Facebook (as with clicking a link). Video allows you to interact with your fans and friends on their terms, without asking them to leave their Facebook News Feed. When you make Facebook interaction easy for your friends and fans, Facebook rewards you by showing your updates in your friends' and fans' News Feeds more often. (Facebook uses EdgeRank software to weight your interactions within Facebook; for more about EdgeRank, turn to Book V, Chapter 3.) Video is win-win!

This chapter explains how you can integrate video with your personal Timeline as well as your Fan Page Timeline. We show you how to shoot video right from your Facebook page, upload video from your computer, and integrate videos from your other channels (such as YouTube or Vimeo). We also give you some tips on what kinds of video to share and how to produce great videos.

Creating Video for Your Fan Page Timeline to Promote Sharing

The goal of creating video and sharing it on Facebook is to have others also view and share your video content. You probably want all your content shared, but you really want video shared because it counts for so much in EdgeRank.

Consider that the average number of friends a Facebook fan has is 130. (Of course, because 130 is an average; some have more friends, some have fewer.) When a fan or friend shares your video, that video has the potential to be seen by all the fans or friends of that person. When you consider the reach of just one person, you can imagine how a video could go viral fairly quickly if it's shared by several people.

Not many people are using video on Facebook to its full potential. Right now is a great time to be the pioneer and draw people into your Fan Page Timeline. Be the first in your niche to embrace it! You can shoot video anywhere and upload on the fly if you have your laptop or smartphone with you. It's never been easier to be a roving reporter or share your latest event with those who couldn't make it.

What kind of video should you share? That depends on your audience. Book IV, Chapter 3 explains the importance of knowing your audience and giving them what they need (that need may be solving a problem, educating, or entertaining). Sharing video that gives your audience what they need (or just makes them laugh) is the best way to encourage sharing. Here are a few ideas for video to create and share:

✦ **Showcase the best.** Every week, you can showcase a specific product or service to your audience. Sometimes a video does a better job of showing off a product's features than a photo can.

✦ **Conduct an interview.** Whether you're interviewing customers with testimonials or simply interviewing an expert in your niche, a video is much more interesting than a written transcript.

✦ **Create a tutorial.** Instructional videos are priceless. Many times written instructions are hard to follow, but a short video showing exactly how to do something is news you can use.

✦ **Be funny.** Most videos shared by friends and fans have one thing in common: They make us laugh. Sharing tutorials or interviews may appeal to part of your audience, but if you want to reach past your audience to their friends, you need to make them laugh. Not every video can be humorous, and that's okay. Just don't be afraid to try something new or step out of your comfort zone.

Shooting Video with Facebook's App

Sometimes you may feel the need to connect with your friends and fans in a different way from standard text updates or shared links. If you have something to say fairly quickly, you can create a short video update right from your personal Timeline or Fan Page Timeline. Facebook video recordings can be a little rough, but they serve the purpose of being a fast way to share information with your friends or fans. If you're interested in shooting a video right from Facebook but aren't sure what to discuss, here are a few ideas:

+ **Ask a short question to start a discussion.** We've seen a few social media Fan Page Timelines do this — fans love it and respond with many comments! Start by asking a general question, briefly give your take on it, and open it up to your fans. Melanie once shot a video asking whether people like salty cookies or sweet cookies and received over 30 responses! We think you'll find that people are intrigued by the video question.

+ **Give a concise answer to a frequently asked question.** If you're receiving the same question over and over, you may want to address it quickly on your Fan Page Timeline with a video response. Or, on your personal Timeline, you can provide updates to family members (because your most frequently asked question is probably what you're up to personally).

+ **Promote an event or share highlights from past events.** Offline events are a great way to make a personal connection with your fans. You can create a video invitation to your upcoming conference, book signing, workshop, open house — whatever you're planning. If you have access to video editing software, you can create a video that includes highlights from previous events, and then upload it to your Fan Page Timeline to show fans how much fun they'll have at your event. After your event, use your video editing software to create and share another highlight reel showcasing your fans who attended (or some of your headlining talent).

+ **Show off your haul.** Over the past few years, bloggers and vloggers (video bloggers) have started sharing their *haul* (deals they find while shopping). Rather than typing out where you found the deals, what you bought, and how you saved, you can create a video and show off your deal-snagging prowess (and your excitement).

Book II
Chapter 4

Sharing Videos on Facebook

You need to have a webcam installed in order to record a video from your computer directly to your Facebook page.

Facebook uses Adobe Flash to connect to your computer's webcam and microphone. If you haven't already given permission for Facebook to use Flash and connect to your computer's webcam and mic, you may see an alert like the one shown in Figure 4-1 when you try to record your video.

Figure 4-1:
Allow
Facebook to
access your
computer's
webcam
and
microphone.

Within the alert dialog box, select the Allow radio button, and if you want Facebook to remember that you've given it permission, select the Remember check box. Then click the Close button.

To create a video with the Facebook video application (or *app)* on your personal Timeline or Fan Page Timeline, follow these instructions:

1. **Use your browser to navigate to your personal Timeline or Fan Page Timeline.**

2. **Click the Photo link above the Status Update text box.**

Alternatively, if you're viewing your News Feed as your personal Timeline (or as your Fan Page Timeline — see Book IV, Chapter 2 for more about that), click the Add Photo / Video link.

Three choices appear, as shown in Figure 4-2: Upload Photo / Video, Use Webcam, and Create Photo Album.

Figure 4-2:
On your
Timeline,
you have
three
choices.

3. **Click Use Webcam.**

Facebook displays a screen showing what your webcam sees. Adjust your webcam as needed.

4. **Click the Record button (red square with a white dot) to begin recording your video.**

5. **Click the Stop button (white square) when you're finished.**

   You see a still picture of the video. You have the choice to Play or Reset. Play allows you to preview your video before you share it on your Timeline; Reset allows you to re-record your video. When you're ready to share your video, proceed to Step 6.

6. **Click the text box that contains Say Something about This Video, as shown in Figure 4-3, and type a status update about your video.**

   For example, give your friends or fans a quick synopsis of the video so they know what to expect.

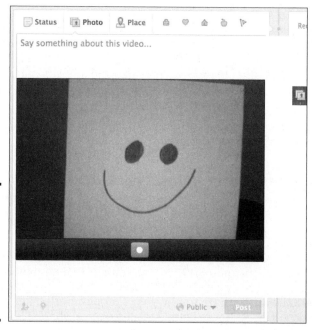

Figure 4-3: Type a status update telling fans and friends what they can expect.

7. **(Optional) Use the toolbar below the video to tag people, assign a location to the video, and/or customize who you want to share the video with.**

   You can tag a Fan Page Timeline without Liking it, but you must be Facebook friends to tag another individual.

8. **Click the Post button to have the video and your status update appear in the News Feed.**

   You can edit the title and description of the video, but it's already live on your Timeline and in your News Feed without those customizations.

Sometimes when you share your video, it will appear in your News Feed; then it may seem to disappear. Check back in a few minutes, and the video should be there. Facebook needs a few minutes to render the video.

Uploading Video to Facebook

More often than not, you want to share video that you didn't take with Facebook's video app. On Facebook, you can share video from just about any source: a video file from your computer, a video from another social media channel (such as YouTube), or even your smartphone.

Two benefits of loading a video directly into Facebook, especially for a Fan Page Timeline, rather than sharing a link to video that resides on another platform (such as YouTube) are that

+ When you upload a video directly to your Fan Page Timeline, Facebook places a link in the top-left corner of the video that encourages people to Like your Fan Page Timeline. This link appears only when the user hovers the mouse cursor over the video and appears only to people who haven't already Liked your page.

+ You can tag others in your video if you're uploading via your Timeline. When someone is tagged, it shows up in her News Feed and has the potential to be shared among multiple users.

Sharing video from your computer

Before you share video from your computer, check to ensure that the video is less than 1,024MB and under 20 minutes long, and that you own the video (in other words, you or your friends made the video).

Whether you're posting video to your personal Timeline or your Fan Page Timeline, you can customize the sharing settings to determine who sees your video in their News Feed. Next to the Post button, you see a down arrow. Click the arrow to customize your sharing settings. Remember that Fan Page Timelines are more limited on customized sharing because they are meant to be public platforms.

Be aware that although you can limit which fans see your video in their News Feed, anyone (fan or not) can visit your Fan Page Timeline and click the Video link in the left sidebar navigation to see all the videos you've uploaded to your Fan Page Timeline (but may have excluded them from seeing in their News Feed).

If your video is within the parameters previously listed, follow these instructions to upload a video file to your personal Timeline or your Fan Page Timeline from your computer:

1. **Navigate to your News Feed or Timeline and click the Photo (or Add Photo / Video) link above the Status Update text box.**

Facebook gives you three choices: Upload Photo / Video, Use Webcam, and Create Photo Album.

2. **Click Upload Photo / Video.**

A menu appears, as shown in Figure 4-4.

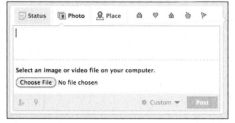

Figure 4-4: Choose your video.

3. **Type a short status update introducing your video.**

4. **Click the Browse button to find the video file you want to share.**

5. **(Optional) Use the toolbar to tag people in your video, assign a location to the video, and/or set your sharing preferences.**

6. **Click the Post button to publish the video to your Timeline.**

A new window opens, telling you your video is being uploaded. When the video upload is complete, you have the option to edit your video or close the page (see Figure 4-5).

Whether you choose to edit your video settings or not, your video is already posted to your Timeline and is visible to your friends.

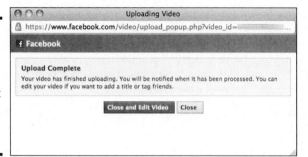

Figure 4-5: After your video is uploaded, you can edit the video or close the page.

Sharing video from your phone

You can share video from your smartphone in a few ways. We cover using the Facebook smartphone app here, but you can also check out Book II, Chapter 6 for an explanation and instructions on using Facebook's mobile upload service.

The Facebook smartphone app doesn't allow you to take and share video to your Facebook Fan Page Timeline. You can share video only via your Timeline.

An easy way to share video directly from your smartphone is to download the Facebook app from the application store associated with your brand of phone (such as the App Store for iPhones or the Android Market for Android phones).

When you have the Facebook app installed on your smartphone, follow these steps to take video with your phone and share it immediately on Facebook:

1. **Open the Facebook application on your smartphone.**

2. **Navigate to your Timeline.**

3. **Tap the Photo button.**

A menu appears with three options:

- *Take Photo or Video* enables you to take a new photo or video. Remember that your smartphone must have video capability in order to use this feature.

- *Upload Photo* enables you to choose among photos or videos you've already taken that are stored on your phone.

- *Cancel* returns to your Timeline without sharing a photo or video.

4. **Tap the Take a Photo or Video button.**

Your phone's camera opens.

5. **Take a video as you normally would with your phone.**

The mobile Facebook app gives you the same options as the Facebook website. You can play back your video before you post it, retake the video, or post it immediately.

6. **When you're done recording your video, tap the Use button.**

A new page appears with text boxes for Title and Description.

7. **Tap inside the Title text box and type a title for your video.**

This is the title of your video and appears next to your video in your News Feed.

8. **Tap the Description text box and type a description of your video.**

   This description appears as your status update above the video in your News Feed.

9. **Tap the Upload button in the top-right corner of the screen.**

   Your video shortly appears in your News Feed.

Sharing video from another social media channel

You won't always want to create new video or share video from your computer. Instead, you may find videos to share via websites like YouTube or Vimeo (two of the most popular video-sharing sites). This section explains how to share videos from those sites to your personal Timeline or your Fan Page Timeline.

Sharing video from YouTube

When you find a video on YouTube that you'd like to share — maybe it's one from your own YouTube channel or one you just found — you can share the video by following these steps:

1. **Click the Share button below the video.**

   An expanded menu appears, as shown in Figure 4-6.

Figure 4-6: The expanded Share menu on YouTube.

2. **Click the Facebook icon.**

   A new tab opens in your browser showing the Share This Link page, as shown in Figure 4-7.

3. **Type a status update in the text box to give the video context.**

   You can choose where you share this video by using the drop-down list above the status text box. You can share the video to your Timeline, a specific friend's Timeline, a Group, on your Fan Page Timeline, or even via a private message.

4. **Click the Share Link button in the lower-right corner.**

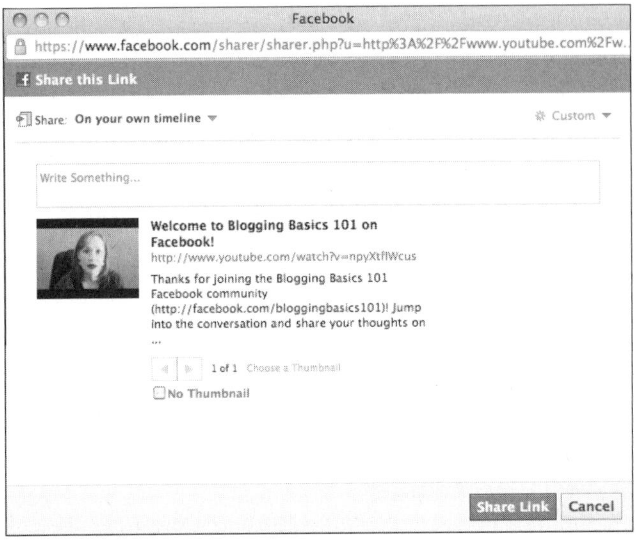

Figure 4-7: The Share This Link page lets you easily share content.

Sharing video from Vimeo

When you find a video on Vimeo that you want to share on Facebook, just follow these instructions:

1. **Click the Share button.**

   Figure 4-8 shows that the Share button is located on the right side of the video itself.

   The Share This Video dialog box appears.

Figure 4-8: The Vimeo Share button.

2. **Click the Facebook icon at the bottom of the dialog box, as shown in Figure 4-9.**

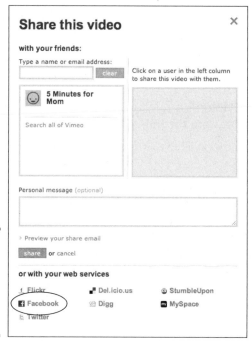

Figure 4-9:
The Facebook icon at the bottom of the window.

A new tab opens in your browser, showing the Share This Link page.

3. **Type a status update in the text box to give the video context.**

You can choose where you share this video by using the drop-down list above the status text box. You can share the video to your Timeline, a specific friend's Timeline, a group, on your Fan Page Timeline, or even via a private message.

4. **Click the Share Link button in the lower-right corner.**

Customizing Your Video

After you've shared a video and it's out in the wild, you can let it run its course, or you can customize a few aspects (such as tagging people in the video or editing the title of the video). Before you can customize those aspects, though, you need to find the video you want to work with. The following sections explain how to find a video you've uploaded to your personal Timeline or Fan Page Timeline and how to customize the video.

Finding a video on your Timeline

To find a video you recently shared on your personal Timeline or Fan Page Timeline, you can look on your Timeline to see if it's still visible. If it is, click the title of the video (which is probably something generic like the date and time you recorded the video). If you don't see the video listed on your Timeline, you can follow these instructions to find it:

1. **Go to your Timeline and click the Photos link under your cover image.**

Your Photos page appears.

2. **On the Photos page, click the Video link, as shown in Figure 4-10.**

A page appears, showing all the videos you've created or uploaded or have been tagged in.

Figure 4-10: Click the Video link to see a list of your videos that you can edit.

3. **Click the video you want to edit.**

A page appears that shows your video and the editing features. See the "Editing your video" section, later in this chapter, for instructions on customizing specific aspects of your video.

Editing your video

Facebook doesn't currently offer the options of full-fledged video editing software. If you want control over frame-by-frame content or want to enhance a video with music or text, you need to do that with video-editing software on your computer, such as Final Cut Pro, Adobe Premiere, or iMovie.

When you click a video to edit it, regardless of whether you uploaded the video to your Timeline or Fan Page Timeline, you see a page that looks similar to the page shown in Figure 4-11.

Figure 4-11:
The Video page looks the same for videos shared on your Timeline or your Fan Page Timeline.

The Facebook Video page allows you to

✦ **Like or Comment:** On the right side of the page, you see a list of comments people have made about the video. You can respond to comments, delete comments, and Like or Unlike the video or comments.

✦ **Share:** Click the Share link and use the Share on Your Own Timeline drop-down list to choose where you'd like to share the video. You have the option of sharing this video on your own Timeline (meaning your personal Timeline), on a friend's Timeline, in a Group, on your Fan Page Timeline (if you administer more than one Fan Page, you'll see a list of all the pages you're affiliated with), or via private message. After you choose where to share the video, type a short introduction of the video to give your audience context, and then click the Share Video button.

✦ **Tag This Video:** Click the Tag This Video link, and a menu appears under the video. Click the Who Were with You text box and type the name of the person or people you want to tag in the video. You also have the option of associating a location with your video (perhaps where the video was shot). Click the Where Was This Video Taken text box and type the city or country you want associated with your video.

It's spammy to tag people or pages that aren't actually in your video or photo. If you posted this video to a Fan Page Timeline, you can't tag individual fans unless you're connected with them via your Timeline (in other words, you need to be Facebook friends with them).

✦ **Edit:** Click the Edit link to do the main customization of your video. The Edit Video page, shown in Figure 4-12, has the following options:

- *In This Video:* You can tag people in your video. Start typing the name of the person you want to tag and then choose them from the menu. You must already be connected to a person via your Timeline in order to tag them. You can tag other Fan Pages whether you have Liked them or not.

- *Title:* Give your video a name. The default title is the date and time you recorded the video.

- *Description:* Type an overview of what fans can expect to see when they watch your video. Go ahead and use keywords within your paragraph if you can, especially if this video appears on your Fan Page Timeline. Keywords will help others search for and find your video.

- *Privacy:* If you're posting the video to your Timeline, you can determine who can see the video, using the Privacy drop-down list. If you're posting the video on your Fan Page Timeline, anyone can view the video. Your Fan Page Timeline is not tied to your Timeline privacy settings, and the video will be public.

- *Choose a Thumbnail:* Scroll through the optional thumbnail pictures (if available), and stop on the one you like.

- *Save, Delete, or Cancel:* If you click Save, your updates (title, description, tags, and so on) are saved. If you click Delete, your video is permanently deleted — no take-backs. If you click Cancel, your updates are not saved, and your video is still published to your Timeline.

✦ **Embed This Video:** If you'd like to embed your video in your blog or website, click the Embed This Video link. A dialog box appears, with the necessary embed code. Copy this code and paste it into your blog post or website as you normally would with a third-party video (for example, YouTube or Vimeo).

Using Facebook Applications to Share Existing Video on Your Fan Page Timeline

One of the attractive features of Fan Page Timelines is that they have an option not available to personal Timelines: You can install Facebook applications. A Facebook application (or *app)* provides additional functionality for a Fan Page Timeline. If your business already has a video channel established outside Facebook (for example, on YouTube), you can use a Facebook app to import your video library to your Facebook Fan Page Timeline. Flip to Book VI, Chapter 3 for instructions on how to install a third-party Facebook app on your Fan Page Timeline.

Book II
Chapter 4

Sharing Videos on Facebook

Facebook video applications are abundant. Here are three you may like to try:

✦ **Involver YouTube Channel app** (available at `https://apps.facebook.com/involver_appjgeph/`): This is app is free and allows your fans to comment on and subscribe to your videos. You can upgrade to the Professional version of this app to control colors and add a banner to your video tab.

✦ **Shortstack's video applet** (available at `www.shortstack.com`): Shortstack offers free Facebook applications for up to 2,000 fans. If you have more than 2,000 fans, you can view its pricing structure at `www.shortstack.com/pricing`. The Shortstack app allows you to automatically update your Facebook page with your YouTube or Vimeo playlists.

✦ **North Social** (available at `http://northsocial.com/apps/`): North Social isn't free. You pay a monthly fee to have access to all of their apps. The monthly fees range from $19.99 to $149.99 and are based on the number of fans you have and/or features you need (see `http://northsocial.com/pricing/` for a full explanation of North Social pricing). The North Social video channel app offers a customizable banner, optional Like-gating, featured video, and user comments that post to the user's News Feed with a link to your video.

Producing Great Video Clips

Shooting good video takes practice. It would be great if we all had access to hair and makeup artists and professional videographers at our whim. (Melanie would love to have an actress playing her so she didn't even have to be in front of the camera.) Even without those people at your disposal, you can still ensure that the video you create is the best it can be. Here are a few tried-and-true tips:

+ **Have a script.** Depending on what you want to accomplish, it's almost always better to put some thought into what you'd like to say *before* you try to say it. You can write a complete script or just an outline.

+ **Keep practicing.** As with everything, practice makes perfect. If you're not comfortable in front of the camera, don't give up. Film a few practice runs, and watch them. Make notes about what you want to change, and practice again. It may be uncomfortable in the beginning, but you'll get used to it — and your video will improve.

+ **Slow your speech.** A common mistake people make when recording video is speaking at their normal rate. Slow things down a little. If you're nervous, you'll probably speak even faster than normal, so keep that in mind and consciously slow your speech. Remember, it's okay to pause. That's a normal part of speech.

+ **Consider your background.** It's possible you've stopped seeing that pile of laundry in the corner that you're going to put away tomorrow, but we promise that your friends and fans will notice. Find a background that won't distract from you and your message.

+ **Check your lighting.** It's a real bummer when you nail the script, but you can't see yourself because you forgot to do a test run to ensure that your lighting was bright enough.

+ **Film someplace quiet.** Sometimes you become so used to background noise (kids, pets, the TV, even the heat or air conditioner running), you don't hear it anymore. Unfortunately, your camera picks it up. Background noise is very distracting, and in some cases, it can be louder than your own message.

+ **Use a tripod.** Even if you're a brain surgeon with super-steady hands, don't try to hold the camera while you're filming yourself. When you speak, you move; you gesticulate to enforce your point. Your video will suffer. Using a tripod ensures that your video will be smooth.

Chapter 5: Connecting with Groups, Places, and Fan Pages

*B*esides enabling you to connect with your friends one on one, Facebook allows you to create connections based on similar interests and activities and get access to special features. In this chapter, we talk about interacting with Facebook Groups, Places, and Fan Pages. We explain the value of each of these features to you as a consumer. Here are some examples of ways you may find value:

✦ Connecting online with groups you're involved with offline

✦ Finding out what friends are doing right now

✦ Taking advantage of Fan Page Timeline discounts and announcements

But this is only the beginning. Groups, Places, and Fan Page Timelines offer many options for interaction and expanding your network. In this chapter, we explain how you can use these features.

Discovering Groups

Facebook describes Groups as places to share with the most important groups in your life. Groups allow you to create a place (private or public) for your group where you can post pictures, upload videos, post messages, share documents, chat, or schedule events within the Group. Pretty much all the features that you experience within Facebook as a whole can be focused specifically to friends within a Group.

Groups can be completely private or totally open to the public. Groups even be secret, where you can see that the Group exists only if you are a member. We discuss these options a little later in the chapter.

Participating in Groups

Participating in Groups is a big reason why people join Facebook. Groups allow you to build a meeting place specific to people with similar interests so they can connect, share documents, chat, and post updates within Facebook. Facebook Groups are useful because they allow you to

✦ Organize and communicate with a group of co-workers

✦ Share important, yet private, information within a Closed Group

✦ Plan an event or other collaborative project

✦ Build a community for those with similar interests

Facebook Groups are valuable for creating an additional connection with people you are linked within an organization such as a church, school, or job. They are also a great way to meet people with common interests, such as baseball card collectors. A Group provides a place where you can meet these people and develop connections before you extend the invitation for a one-on-one friend relationship.

If you want to see which groups you belong to already, look on the left side of your home screen (click the Facebook logo at the top of the screen to go to your home screen), as shown in Figure 5-1. In the left navigation column you see the Favorites, Groups, Pages, Lists, and Apps categories (among others). (For more about this part of your home page, see Book I, Chapter 4.)

Figure 5-1:
Click the
Create
Groups link.

GROUPS
- Frankie Does LA
- Marketing Folks
- Create Group...
MORE ▾

The Groups section displays some of the Groups you have been made a part of, and typically those in which you're most active. By default, when someone invites you into a Group, you're automatically included in that Group. We tell you how to leave a group later in this chapter.

Creating a Group

Of course, you may want to create your own Facebook Group. That's pretty easy. When you create a Group, you are automatically assigned as the administrator of that Group. The Group admin can edit the Group's description and settings, add other administrators, and remove or ban members. To create your own Group, follow these steps:

1. **At the bottom of the Groups list, click Create Group.**

A dialog box pops up, asking for a Group name, what friends you would like to add to the Group, and the privacy settings of that Group. See Figure 5-2.

Figure 5-2:
Creating
a Group
and adding
members.

2. **Give the Group a name by typing in the Group Name text box.**

The best way to name a Group is to give it a descriptive name. That way, the intended topic of the Group is clear, and it's easier for interested parties to find it (if it's not a Secret Group).

3. **Add members to the Group by typing names in the Members text box.**

4. **Select the privacy settings of the Group:**

- *Open:* Anyone can see the Group, who's in it, and what members post.

- *Closed:* Anyone can see the Group and who's in it, but only members can see posts.

- *Secret:* Only members see the Group, who's in it, and what is posted.

5. **Click the Create button.**

As you can see in Figure 5-3, the Group page is very similar to your home screen, except what you see is all contained within the Group. If the Group is set to private, only you and other Group members will be able to see the posts.

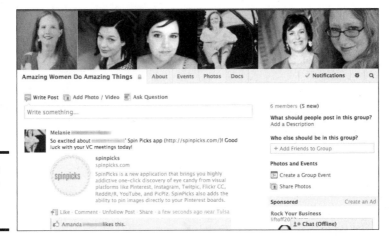

Figure 5-3:
The Group
home
screen.

Updates to a Group appear in members' News Feed. However, those updates aren't showing up in nonmembers' News Feeds. It depends on the privacy settings of the Group (Open, Closed, or Private).

After creating your Group, you can invite friends to the Group (you must be connected with someone in order to invite them to your Group) and begin posting. Your friends will receive a notification that they have been invited into the Group.

You can also grant administrative privileges to other Group members. To do that, click the Members link under the Group cover image. A list of members appears. Click the Make Admin link for the Group member you want to add as an admin. A dialog box appears, letting you know that if you make that person an admin, they can edit Group settings, add members, and make others admins as well. If you agree, click the Make Admin button. It's important to note that if you make someone an admin, they can take away your admin status (we hope they wouldn't, but it could happen). To take away admin status, just click the Remove Admin link for that person.

Personalizing the image for your Group

Groups are always more personal with a little customization. When you create a Group, the Group page shows a row of members' profile pictures (see Figure 5-4). These photos rotate each time the Group page is refreshed (if there are enough members).

If you're an administrator of a Group, you can also upload and display a customized graphic like the one in Figure 5-5 (just be sure it's 400 pixels wide).

Figure 5-4:
Group
member
profile
pictures are
the default
Group
header.

Figure 5-5:
Groups
can have
customized
graphic
headers.

Here are a few ideas of what you can use for your custom graphic:

✦ A logo (if you own the rights to it)

✦ A picture of the people in the Group

✦ A picture of a common meeting place

✦ Any image that is descriptive of the Group

The image will be seen on the home screen of your Group. If you're the admin for a Group, you can upload a picture by following these steps:

1. **Navigate to the Group page.**

2. **Hover your cursor over the main image at the top of the page.**

By default, the main image is a grayed-out display of Group members' profile pictures. When you hover your cursor over the image, it changes to a full-color version and displays a small icon, as shown in Figure 5-6.

Figure 5-6:
The icon to
change your
Group's
cover
image.

Click to upload a photo

3. **Click the icon.**

   The Upload a Photo option appears.

4. **Click the Upload a Photo option.**

5. **Choose an image file from your computer.**

   The photo appears as the Group's new cover image.

6. **(Optional) Click and hold to drag the image; reposition it if necessary.**

7. **Click Save Changes.**

You can change the Group cover image again any time you like. Or you can revert to the member profile pictures. To change your Group cover image, move your cursor over the Group image, and click the Change Group Photo button that appears. A menu appears, with three options:

✦ **Upload a Photo:** You can upload a new photo from your computer for your Group cover image.

✦ **Reposition Photo:** You can move the existing cover image around.

✦ **Remove Photo:** You can remove the current cover image, and the Group member profile pictures will reappear as the cover image.

Establishing the settings for your Group

The default settings for your Group were set when you created it, with the option to make your Group Open, Closed, or Secret. If you're the administrator for a group, you can modify a few additional settings within the Edit Group settings area. Find the Edit Group settings by clicking the gear icon at the top of the right column of the Group page and choosing Edit Group from the menu. The settings you can change include the following:

✦ **Group Name:** To rename the Group, simply click inside this text box, highlight the current name, and then type over the name to change it.

✦ **Group icon:** The Group icon, by default, is a generic Group image. By clicking the Group Name drop-down list (shown in Figure 5-7), you are presented with around 50 options for icons. Select one that is relevant to your Group's purpose. This icon appears in the left navigation of the Group member's Facebook home page next to the Group's name, and also on the Group's main page at the bottom of the Group's cover image. It does not appear in the News Feed when members update the Group.

✦ **Privacy:** Below the name section on the Edit screen are the Group visibility options: Open, Closed, and Secret. Select the privacy level you want.

✦ **Membership approval:** Select whether any member can add or approve members or whether an admin has to approve new members.

Figure 5-7:
Icons help
describe
a Group's
purpose.

Book II
Chapter 5

Connecting with
Groups, Places, and
Fan Pages

✦ **Email Address:** You have the option of setting up an email address for
the entire Group. Any message sent to this e-mail address will go out
to each member of the Group. Click the Set Up Group Email button,
and type a prefix for the e-mail address. The domain is `@groups.`
`facebook.com`. (See Figure 5-8.) Click Create Email to finish.

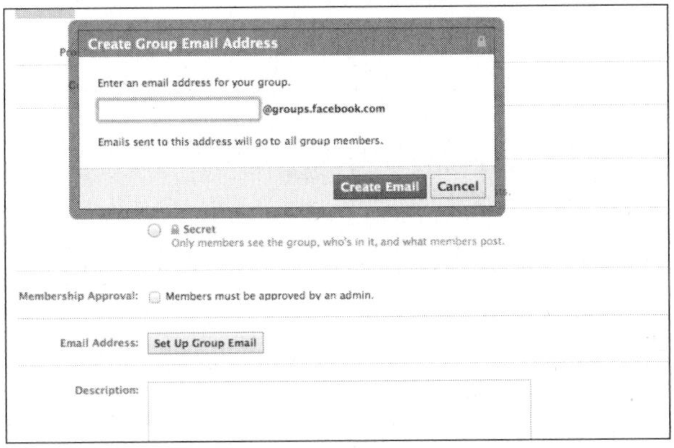

Figure 5-8:
Creating
an e-mail
address for
your Group.

✦ **Description:** Type a description of your Group in the Description text
box. Be aware that if your settings are not set to Secret, nonmembers
can see the description.

✦ **Posting Permissions:** Select who can post to the group — only members
or only administrators. Although there may be some instances where
you'd want to limit posting, we think it's best to allow members to post
to the Group. After all, you created it to share your thoughts and interests, right? Communities thrive on give and take.

Be sure to click the Save button to save your changes, or they'll be lost when
you navigate away from the Edit Group settings page.

Inviting members

Inviting members to your Group is quite simple. The only requirement is that you be connected to them as a friend on Facebook. You can invite friends into a Group one of three ways:

✦ Add people to the Group when you create it

✦ Add people to the Group at any time after it has been created

✦ Accept requests to join your Group

Adding members when you create a Group

When you create the Group, the first step after naming the Group is to select friends to be a part of the Group. You do this by entering names in the dialog box (refer to Figure 5-2).

Start by typing the names of people you want to add, and Facebook automatically displays relevant names (as well as shows their profile picture) as you type the name. For example, if you type **chri**, you will see people from your friends list whose names start with *Chri,* such as Christy, Christopher, Christina, and so on. When you find the correct person, simply move your mouse over that particular result, and click it.

Adding members to a Group any time

You can always add new members to your Group. In the right column of your Group page, you see a text box labeled Who Else Should Be in This Group? Click inside the box and start typing a name (remember, you need to be Facebook friends with someone to add them). Facebook will autopopulate a list of possible people to add. Simply choose the person from the list, and they are added to the Group.

Accepting a request to join your Group

When someone discovers your Group and wants to join, she might issue a request to join. People can find your Group if it is an Open or Closed Group, but not if it's a Secret Group.

When someone wants to join your Group, he clicks the Ask to Join Group button, as shown in Figure 5-9.

When someone clicks the Ask to Join Group button, you as a Group member (or as an administrator) will see a notification that someone has requested to join your Group. (See Figure 5-10.)

Figure 5-9:
Ask to Join
Group.

Figure 5-10:
Group
request
notifications.

On the Group screen, you also see the request on the right side of your
screen, with a check-mark icon and an X icon, as shown in Figure 5-11. Click
the check-mark icon to add this person to your Group, or click the X icon to
reject his request.

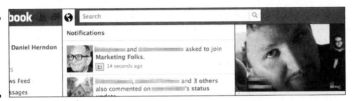

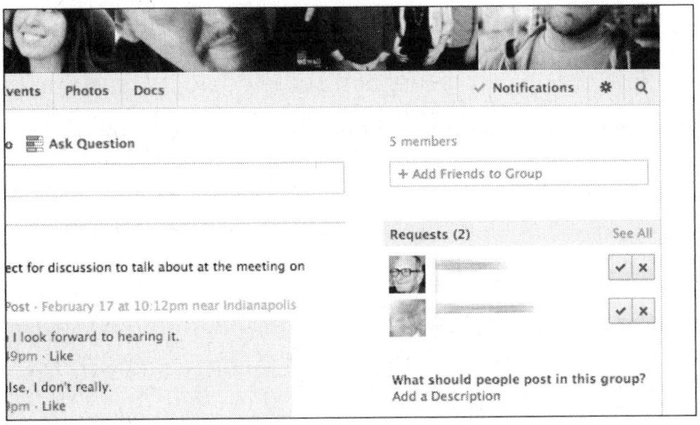

Figure 5-11:
Group
request on
the Group
screen.

Posting to a Group

The posting permissions on the Edit Group settings page determine who can post to a Group. The admin of a Group can choose to allow all Group members to post or only admins to post. As we say earlier, we think it's best if all members of a Group are allowed to interact — it just makes for a more interesting community.

To post an update to a Group, follow these steps:

1. **Click the Group title (on the left side of the page, under your profile picture).**

   The most common Groups you interact with will show up here. If the Group you're looking for does not appear, you can select More, which appears above the Group list as you hover your mouse pointer over it.

   If you don't find the Group here, you can just as easily go to the Search text box at the top of your browser screen and type in the name of the Group. As you type, relevant results show up below the Search text box. Click the Group you are looking for to go to the Group page.

2. **At the top of the Group screen is the Update text box; click where it says Write Something and type your update.**

   The Update Status text box looks identical to the one on your Timeline.

3. **(Optional) Click Photo, Video, or Question to add a photo, video, or poll to your update, respectively.**

4. **Click Post to post your update.**

More details on posting updates, such as adding a link, video, or picture, can be found in Book II, Chapter 2.

Sharing documents in a Group

Members of a Group can create and share documents within the Group. Documents can be edited by any member of the Group at any time. Group members may find this to be a valuable tool for a number of reasons. Here are some examples of when you may want to use the documents feature in Groups:

+ You're collaborating on a list of items to bring to an event.

+ You're working together to write a plan for your business or organization.

+ You're collecting pictures with a narrative of a recent trip members of the Group took together.

Face it, you can use this feature for any reason to create and share a document. To create a Group document, click the Doc link in the lower-right corner of the Group cover image, and the document editor appears. You can give your document a title and start typing in the large text box. Documents have basic formatting options, including bold and italic text, numbered lists, and bulleted lists. You also have the option to add pictures to the document. When you're done typing and formatting your document, click the Create Doc button to save your changes and publish the document to the Group.

When a document is created, Group members will see a preview of the document as they would any update in the Group's News Feed. The Doc link under the Group cover image will have a number next to it that shows how many documents the Group has. When a member clicks the Doc link, a page appears, with each of the documents created. The member can then click a title to view the full document. To edit the document, a member just needs to click the Edit Doc link. Members can comment below documents as well. Only Group admins can delete a document; to do that, just click the Delete link.

Leaving a Group

After a while, you might lose interest in a Group and want to remove yourself. To do so, all you have to do is click the gear icon under the Group cover image and choose Leave Group from the menu.

A warning dialog box appears, asking if you're sure you want to leave the Group. If you're certain, click Leave Group. If you've changed your mind and want to stay, click Cancel.

If you're the sole administrator for the group, we highly recommend appointing someone else as the admin for the Group before you leave. However, if you don't, the Group will continue, and another member can make themselves the admin.

When you click Leave Group, you are also given the option to report the Group if it is malicious or inappropriate (see Figure 5-12). You'll see a link to the bottom left of the dialog box that says Report Group. Some reasons you might report a Group are

✦ The Group is harassing you or a friend.

✦ The Group sends out spam or is a scam.

✦ The Group promotes hate speech, violence, or harmful behavior.

✦ The Group is sexually explicit.

Figure 5-12:
Reporting a
Group.

Report a Group only if there is a legitimate reason to do so. When you report the Group, Facebook will review the info and determine whether to disable the Group.

Checking In to Places

When you are out and about, Facebook Places allows you to check in to a physical location with your mobile phone (for instance, a restaurant). Your check in becomes a status update in the News Feed, with location information telling your friends where you are. Places is a social utility to connect with friends who work, live, or study around you. Because people use Facebook to connect with others, Places is a way to connect with others in real life while also connecting on Facebook.

To use Places, you need to enable Location Services on your smartphone so that Facebook can search for Places near you based on your GPS location. Places allows you to see other people who have checked in to that Places location, as well as tag friends who are with you at that time. Being tagged in Places by a friend is much like being mentioned in a status update.

Using Places to Connect

Facebook Places are locations listed within Facebook where people can post an update that they are there, or comment and find out who else has checked in to that Place. In some cases, a business may have merged their Places listing with their Fan Page Timeline, which makes the Place and the Page one and the same. In this case, when you check in at that business, your update will link to the Fan Page Timeline.

Have you ever gone to a concert or sporting event, only to find out later that your friends were there as well? With Facebook Places, you can connect in real time with friends who choose to check in to Places. This allows you that real-time connection to friends who happen to be nearby. Another example is when you discover a great new restaurant or other location, you can share with friends that you're at the restaurant.

Recently, Daniel went to a hockey game and checked in via Facebook Places. As he checked in, he discovered a friend had checked in as well! While there were thousands of people at the game, Places allowed Daniel to discover friends who were there.

You can use Places on iPhone or Android devices, as well as using the browser of any web-enabled mobile device. The examples in the following sections use the mobile version of Facebook. The iPhone and Android apps may look a little bit different, but most of the functionality is the same.

Using Location Services

To use Facebook Places, you can access the function from your smartphone (using GPS or Location Services), or you can access it from your computer (such as a laptop while you're at a Place). To access Places with a mobile device, you need a smartphone to access the full mobile browser capabilities. You must allow Location Services so that Facebook.com can access your phone's location and find Places near you. If it's the first time you've used Places, you see a button on your screen asking you to allow Facebook permission to access Location Services. You should have to do this only once.

**Book II
Chapter 5**

**Connecting with
Groups, Places, and
Fan Pages**

Finding your Place

When you're at a location where you would like to check in, pull out your mobile phone and open Facebook. (You can open Facebook through your phone's browser or use the Facebook app.) Tap the Status button at the top of the screen. A box appears, where you can enter your status.

If you are using one of Facebook's official apps (on iPhone or Android devices), what you see on the device may look a little different from Figure 5-13.

Figure 5-13:
Checking
in to a
Place via
Facebook
mobile.

To check in to a Place on your smartphone, follow these steps:

1. **Tap the Places icon at the bottom of the Status Update text box.**

   The Places icon looks like an upside-down teardrop or a pin (presumably poked into a map to identify a Place, right?).

   Alternatively, you can tap Check In on the opening screen of your mobile app. The result is about the same.

2. **A list of nearby Places appears; select the appropriate Place.**

   If you don't see the Place in the list, search for it by name. If the Place isn't already in your Places list, you see the option to add it.

3. **Enter your status.**

   After you select the Place and add a status update, that Place becomes a link within your status update.

4. **(Optional) Tag Friends who are with you by tapping the Friends icon below the Update Status text box; type your friends' names in the Who Are You With area.**

   The Friends icon appears as a person with a plus sign. When you tag friends, Facebook links to their Timelines in your update and indicates that they are with you where you checked in. If they're already using Places, it will be as if they checked in without having to do anything. Tagging a friend will appear in your check-in details, as well as on your friends' Timelines.

   If you accidentally tag the wrong person, before you click Check In, you can remove the friend by tapping the X that appears next to his name.

Finding your friends on Places

You can find out who else is on Places in two ways:

✦ Checking into a Place and seeing who is already there and has checked in.

✦ Looking at recent check ins from your friends after clicking Places from your home screen.

You can only see people that are your friends on Facebook on Places. This protects users by allowing a location only to be seen by those that friends (who, presumably, you trust).

Interacting with Fan Page Timelines

Fan Page Timelines are sometimes called Business Pages or just simply Pages. If you see these terms, you know that the page is for a business (or possibly a celebrity), and not an individual.

Fan Page Timelines are ever-evolving parts of Facebook. They are designed for businesses, brands, products, celebrities, and other professional entities to create a Timeline that is fitting to the way that businesses and their "fans" interact with them. They provide several features that are different from the personal Timeline, allowing businesses to market themselves and fans to get the most out of their experience.

Fan Page Timelines operate on an *opt-in platform,* meaning that you can follow a Fan Page by Liking it. To do this, you simply click the Like button at the top of the Fan Page Timeline, as shown in Figure 5-14. The Fan Page owner is not required to do anything in response. Liking a Fan Page is just a way for you to subscribe to the updates that that Fan Page Timeline offers. After you click Like, you see that Fan Page's updates in your News Feed.

EdgeRank is a feature of Facebook that learns what Fan Pages and people you are most interested in. If you never interact with or click a particular Fan Page, you're less likely to see its updates in your News Feed. Those Fan Pages that you show interest in (by commenting on updates or Liking posts) are more likely to appear in your News Feed.

Because people interact differently with companies and brands than they do with their individual friends, Facebook has formulated the features of a Fan Page Timeline to accommodate that distinction. For instance, Fan Page Timelines can have unlimited fans (or Likes), have apps installed, and provide metrics about how fans are interacting with the Page. Personal Timelines can't do those things. See Book IV for a complete explanation of how Fan Page Timelines work.

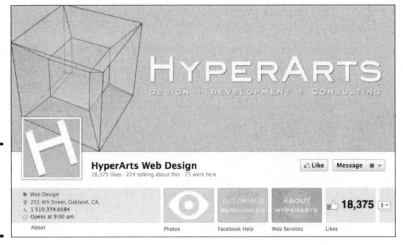

Figure 5-14:
Click the
Like button
to see
updates.

Posting comments, reviews, and photos on Fan Page Timelines

Fan Page Timelines invite you to Like them by clicking the Like button at the top of the Timeline. Doing so subscribes you to that Fan Page's updates so that you see them in your News Feed.

Instead of just listening to what a company is saying, you can interact. You can share your thoughts with a business you like as well as others that like it, too. Facebook Page Timelines allow you to post comments, links or reviews, and (if the Fan Page admin has enabled these features) check in and access deals through the Fan Page Timeline.

When you share something on a Fan Page Timeline, your privacy settings still apply. For example, if you have your privacy set to friends only, and you post a picture to a Fan Page Timeline or tag a Fan Page Timleine, the Fan Page's admin will see the notification, but the rest of the fans won't (unless those fans are your friends on Facebook).

Posting on a Facebook Fan Page Timeline

To post an update to a Fan Page Timeline, follow these steps:

1. **Go to the Fan Page Timeline.**

   To find the Fan Page Timeline, you can type the name of the Fan Page in the Search text box at the top of your home screen. Alternatively, click an update from the Fan Page in your News Feed.

   When you arrive at the Fan Page Timeline, you see a Status Update text box at the top that says Write Something. This looks similar to the Status Update text box on your personal Timeline.

2. **Click where it says Write Something and type your update.**

3. **(Optional) Click Photo, Video, Link, or Question to add a photo, video, link, or poll to your update, respectively.**

   Any post you create during Step 3 or 4 will show up on the Fan Page Timeline, just like a post on a friend's Timeline. You can see an example of how Kelly Trent posted to a Fan Page Timeline in Figure 5-15.

4. **Click the Share button.**

   All those who visit the Fan Page Timeline can see the update. In addition, it will appear on your Timeline in your Recent Activity feed. However, the update will not appear in the News Feed of other fans. The only way other fans will see your update is if they return to the Fan Page Timeline and see it there or if they are friends with you.

Figure 5-15:
Posting on
a Fan Page
Timeline.

You can find more detail on posting updates such as a link, video, or picture in Book II, Chapter 2.

Sharing a recommendation on a Fan Page Timeline

Recommendations are a feature for local businesses, and they allow you to tell others what you think about a business on its Fan Page Timeline. Because Fan Page owners have the option to turn the recommendation feature on or off, you will see it only if they have it enabled. If the recommendation feature is enabled, you'll see it on the right side of the Fan Page Timeline under Recent Posts by Others. To write a recommendation, click inside the text box, and type your review just as if you were posting a comment.

Sharing photos on a Fan Page Timeline

Have you ever wanted to share a great experience at a restaurant? Have you ever bought a car from a dealer and wanted to share it with your friends and feature the dealer? Sharing pictures through Fan Page Timelines is a great way to do this. Simply select the Upload Photo option on the top of the Fan Page Timeline, and follow the directions (or flip over to Book II, Chapter 3).

Tagging a Fan Page Timeline

Another way that you can share with the Fan Page is by tagging the Fan Page in your status update. You can do this only if you have Liked the Fan Page. When you type your status update, typing the @ symbol at the beginning of the name, as shown in Figure 5-16, will bring up a search for relevant Fan Pages or friends to tag. Tagging the Fan Page Timeline alerts the page admin and shares your picture with its viewers. Remember, though, that other fans will see your tag only if they visit the Fan Page Timeline or are already friends with you and see your post in their News Feed.

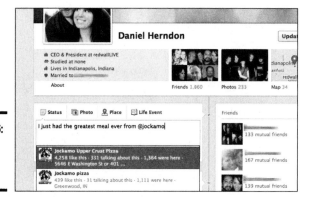

Figure 5-16:
Tagging a
Fan Page
you like.

Chapter 6: Going Mobile with Facebook

In This Chapter

✔ Using the Facebook smartphone app

✔ Dialing into the Facebook mobile website

✔ Using Facebook on simple mobile phones

The ability to go mobile is certainly a big reason why Facebook has experienced such success. Picture this: You're at a ball game, you catch a fly ball (we've seen it on TV so we know it happens), and you want to share that excitement with your friends. What do you do? You share it on Facebook, but not just a status update, a picture of that ball so that you have visual proof of your story. The reason why Facebook can enhance your life is because you don't have to be tied to a desk to get online. You can take Facebook with you to capture parts of your life and share it with family and friends. No longer do you have to carry a photo album with that sticky clear cover over each page holding the photos down. Just share your story on Facebook, along with a video or photo to tell that story a little better.

Facebook also has implemented Location Services into the mobile experience. That's where Facebook uses GPS and other services to note where you are in an update, if you allow it to. With Location Services on, you can check in to venues and tag that Place on your update. (See Book II, Chapter 5 for details on Facebook Places.) In this chapter, we talk about what Facebook is like when you go mobile.

Location Services allow apps on your phone to use cellular, Wi-Fi, and Global Positioning System (GPS) to identify your approximate location. This is all of course limited to whether these settings on your smartphone are turned on and connected to their respective networks. The information is always collected anonymously, and your personal information is not used or identified. Using Location Services with Facebook allows Facebook to associate a location with your update. Furthermore, you can search for Events or Places in your area using Location Services within Facebook.

Going Mobile

We heard a quote that goes something like the solution to impatience is to do something in the mean time. If that is so, then Facebook has been the solution to boredom and impatience for many. Many of the Facebook features you're familiar with on your full-screen computer browser can be accessed through the mobile site or a mobile app on your smartphone. The site is reformatted to fit the phone's screen, along with the fact that you use touchscreen features in most cases. Facebook is a little bit different in your mobile browser or smartphone app, but it's still familiar.

Not only can you update statuses, share photos, and more, but you can also take advantage of the Locations Services that many smartphones have these days. So while you give up some features from the standard Facebook site, you gain other features. Furthermore, most phones have cameras, so you can very easily share a little piece of every experience you have by snapping a shot and sending it directly to Facebook.

Going mobile really is a great way to enjoy Facebook. As Facebook continues to improve its mobile site and apps, it enables you to access more and more of the features that previously were limited to only the desktop version of the site. As shown in Figure 6-1, Facebook mobile allows you to access search, your Timeline, the News Feed (just as you would see it on your desktop), not to mention chat services, all your Groups, and you can even jump over to your Fan Pages.

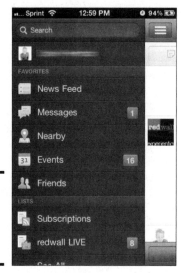

Figure 6-1:
Accessing
the various
parts of
Facebook.

Using the Facebook Smartphone App

The Facebook smartphone app is one of the most popular apps for smartphones. Because there are many different smartphones, the Facebook app on your particular phone may look different from the screenshots you see in this chapter, and it may have some different features as well. (We use the Facebook app on the iPhone to capture the images in this chapter.)

Features of the smartphone app

Here's a little about the major features of the smartphone app.

✦ **The News Feed:** When you first open your Facebook app, the default screen is the News Feed, shown in Figure 6-2. The News Feed shows the full status updates of your friends similarly to the desktop view. Use the Sort button at the top of the screen to sort your Feed by Top Stories or Most Recent. As you browse your mobile News Feed, you see previews of pictures, along with the option to Like or comment on an update. You also see a note of how many comments or Likes the post has received. Both of these are links to comments on the post.

Figure 6-2:
The News Feed on the smartphone app.

✦ **Liking or commenting on a post:** If you want to interact with a post you have several options:

- Tap the Like link to immediately Like the post.

- Tap the Comment link to leave a comment. When you click the Comment link, the Comment screen appears, as shown in Figure 6-3. Type your comment and tap the Post button.

• Tap the Thumbs-up icon or the speech bubble icon at the bottom of the post to see the whole thread of comments related to a post. You also have the option to type a comment and join the conversation. See Figure 6-4.

Figure 6-3:
A Facebook Comment text box on iPhone.

Figure 6-4:
The comments thread on iPhone.

✦ **Filtering your News Feed:** Some of the latest improvements of Facebook for smartphones are that you now have the ability to filter your News Feed based on certain preferences. By tapping the newsfeed filter at the top left of your screen (it looks like three lines stacked on top of each other), you can choose to see updates from your lists, Groups, subscriptions, or even a single person. Figure 6-5 shows an example of a filter menu. When you see your filter menu, choose what you want to see in your News Feed, then click the Filter icon again to return to the News Feed.

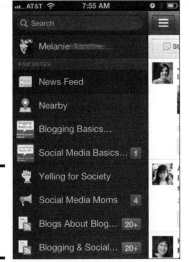

Figure 6-5:
Filtering
your News
Feed with
lists.

✦ **Notifications.** All your notifications appear at the top of your screen, similar to what you see on the top left of your screen on Facebook's desktop version. A red badge appears on the icon to inform you if you have Notifications. These icons are:

• *Friend Request:* The silhouette of the heads of two individuals indicates you have a friend request pending. Tap the icon to respond to this friend request.

• *Messages:* The chat boxes indicate you have a message in your inbox. Tapping this takes you to your inbox.

• *General Notifications:* The globe tells you that you have general notifications. This includes someone Liking or commenting on your post, inviting you to an Event, and more. Tap the General Notifications icon to see a list view of your most recent notifications.

✦ **Creating updates:** You can create a mobile status update from the News Feed screen or your personal Timeline. If you're looking at your main News Feed, near the top of your screen are the Status, Photo, and Check In buttons. To write a simple text update, tap the Status button and begin typing in the text box that appears. You can tag others with you, share where you are, take a picture, and even customize your sharing options for this update. If you want to share a photo or video, tap the Photo button. Tap the Take Photo or Video to begin shooting, or tap the Choose From Library button to select a photo or video you've already captured. Tap the Check In button to select a Place near you. If you need to add a new Place, start typing the name of the Place in the Search text box. If the Place doesn't appear as you type, you can add it by tapping the Add "*Place Name*" option, as shown in Figure 6-6.

Figure 6-6:
Adding a
Place.

Updating your status on the Facebook app

To post a status update using the Facebook app, follow these steps:

1. **Tap Status.**

The Update Status screen appears, as shown in Figure 6-7.

2. **Begin typing whatever you would like to share.**

3. **(Optional) To tag a friend in your status update, tap the Friend icon.**

The Friend icon looks like a silhouette with a plus sign on it. A screen appears with a list of friends in alphabetical order. Use the Search text box at the top to narrow down to who you're looking for.

Figure 6-7:
The Update
Status
screen.

4. **(Optional) Tap the Pinpoint icon to indicate where you are.**

   This is the same thing as checking into a place.

5. **(Optional) Add a photo or video by tapping the Photo icon (it looks like a camera).**

6. **(Optional) Select the audience for whom you would like to share your update by tapping the Audience icon (the globe icon).**

   A list appears, which allows you to select whether to make your update Public, to share only with Friends, or to be more selective. The icon changes after you update this setting.

7. **Tap the Post button to share your update.**

You can only post as yourself when using the mobile Facebook app; you can't post as your Fan Page Timeline (see Book IV, Chapter 2 for a full explanation of how to use Facebook as yourself or as your Fan Page Timeline). That means if you post an update to your Fan Page Timeline from your mobile device, you're posting as you, not your Fan Page. The result is that your fans won't see your updates unless they are friends with your personal Timeline on Facebook.

Understanding the limitations of the Facebook app

The limitations of mobile apps grow smaller and smaller as the capabilities of mobile devices increase. The main limitation is a smartphone's smaller screen size, which changes the way you use the functions of Facebook. For the most part, touchscreen devices are the direction mobile is going, which also changes the way you interact with the application.

Depending on the type of smartphone you have, you have further limitations with fewer features. Because iOS (the iPhone, iPod touch, and iPad operating system) and the Android operating system are the most popular smartphone and tablet OSes, less development attention is payed to less popular mobile OSes.

Accessing Facebook Mobile for Touchscreen Smartphones and Tablets

Facebook's mobile website is called Facebook Touch Mobile. The look and functionality of the Facebook mobile website (not the smartphone app) differs very little from one mobile device to the next. This is because much of the user interface is built into the website itself instead of the device's operating system. With the mobile site, Facebook detects what browser you're using and loads the compatible version of the mobile site.

To access Facebook Touch Mobile, all you have to do is open your (touchscreen) mobile device's browser and type in the address `touch.facebook.com`. Your browser is automatically detected and the mobile site loads. Figure 6-8 shows the Facebook Touch Mobile site on an iPhone. This site looks similar on Android devices as well.

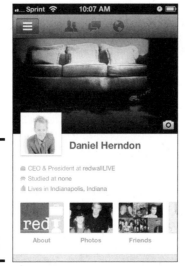

Figure 6-8:
A Timeline on Facebook Mobile (shown on an iPhone).

One of the major limitations of the mobile site is that some browsers (iPhone's Safari is one of them) don't support uploading pictures. For this reason, you have to use the mobile app to upload photos or videos. As well, when you comment on other people's photos using the Facebook Touch Mobile site, the appearance is slightly different than on the Facebook app.

Tablets in almost all cases operate on an equivalent operating system as smartphones. For example, Android is a common operating system for smartphones and tablets. Similarly, the Apple iPhone, iPod touch, and iPad devices all use the same iOS operating system. All the functions are almost exactly the same on tablets as they are on smartphones. The main difference is that the larger screen size of a tablet allows for a bit larger layout.

Using Facebook Mobile on a Cellphone

If you want to go mobile, but you don't have a smartphone, you can still post Facebook updates using text message on a regular cellphone. With Facebook's text based services, you can do the following:

✦ Update your status

✦ Add a friend by name or phone number

✦ Subscribe to someone's status for mobile updates

✦ Unsubscribe from someone's status updates

✦ Upload photos

All these features are done by texting the appropriate code to Facebook's short code 32665 (which spells FBOOK on your alphanumeric phone keypad).

Unless you have unlimited texts with your cellphone plan, keep in mind that text messaging rates apply to texts you send to Facebook. Don't blame us if you get a huge cellphone bill next month because you texted a few hundred status updates, photos, and such.

Setting up your Facebook account to accept text messages

To be able to use Facebook via SMS (that is, text messages), you first have to set up your mobile phone with your Facebook account. To do so, follow these steps.

1. **Log in to Facebook and go to your home screen.**

2. **Choose Home⇨Account Settings.**

The General Account Settings page appears.

3. **Click the Mobile link (found on the left) to edit the mobile settings.**

The Mobile Settings page appears, where you can add your mobile phone to your Facebook account.

4. **Click Add a Phone to Your Account and select your carrier.**

5. **When prompted, text the letter F to 32665 from your phone.**

   The Activate Facebook Texts dialog box appears, shown in Figure 6-9, asking for the confirmation code. You should receive a text message with that code within a few minutes.

6. **Enter the confirmation code and click Next.**

   You have completed the process of enabling Facebook SMS messages for your phone.

Figure 6-9:
Enter the confirmation code.

Updating your status via text

After you confirm your cellphone with Facebook, you can use Facebook SMS features to keep up with your friends and keep them up to date, no matter what kind of mobile phone you have. Here's how:

✦ **To update your status,** simply text the status to 32665 from your mobile phone.

✦ **To add a friend,** text the name of your friend (for example, John Smith) or your friend's phone number to 32665.

✦ **To subscribe to a friends updates** so that they come directly to your phone as text messages, text **Subscribe** and your friend's name **to** 32665 (for example, text **Subscribe Jane Smith**). Text **Unsubscribe** along with the friends name to cancel the friend's updates.

✦ **To stop SMS updates,** text **Stop** to 32665.

After you have added your mobile phone number to your account, your number appears on the info page of your Timeline. This also allows friends to send you text messages via Facebook messages. (Discover more about messages in Book II, Chapter 8). If you don't want your Facebook friends to have access to your mobile number via Facebook, all you have to do is disable the setting. As you can see in Figure 6-10, two check boxes allow friends to send you text messages and to share your number with friends. Deselect these check boxes to keep your mobile number private.

Figure 6-10:
Allow (or restrict) your friends from sending you texts via Facebook.

Changing your mobile number

If you need to change the mobile number associated with your account, choose Home↪Account Settings, click Mobile, and click the Remove link next to your mobile number on the Mobile Settings page. After doing this, you need to go through the set up process to add a new phone number, as described in the earlier section, "Setting up your Facebook account to accept text messages."

Using send to Facebook, uploading pictures, and more

If you want to send pictures to Facebook from a simple cellphone, you can do so by sending an MMS message (also known as picture mail). To do this, text **photos** to 32665, and you will receive an message back telling you the e-mail address to send pictures to. If your mobile plan and phone support picture mail, then you can send a message to an e-mail address the same way you would send to a phone number. When you MMS a picture to the Facebook e-mail address, Facebook automatically updates your status with the photo that you include in your message.

Chapter 7: Keeping Up with Events

In This Chapter

✔ **Finding Events on Facebook**

✔ **Creating your own Events**

✔ **Privacy settings for Events**

✔ **Using Facebook to promote Events**

Facebook is a great tool for connecting with your friends and finding out what they're doing. Facebook Events allow you to easily plan ahead. With Events, you can plan your occasion, invite friends, promote it, and see who has RSVPed or is planning to attend.

Planning and keeping track of events in life can be challenging. Facebook makes it simple to set up small Events such as a dinner party for six or a large-scale concert you are trying to promote beyond your own network. Facebook makes it easy to see what Events you're attending and who else is going. You can even coordinate Events with some of the most popular online calendars such as Google Calendar or Mac's iCal.

What makes Facebook Events so great is their integration into other Facebook activities. Users can share with friends and comment on Events they are invited to. Public Events even appear in your News Feed, so you have the opportunity to let your friends know what's going on. Your friends then have a link to find out more, share information, include pictures, and join the Event. If you want to get the word out about your Event, friends that RSVP to the Event can invite their friends on Facebook, too!

In this chapter, we show you how to use Facebook to manage all the Events you are attending, RSVP to Events, and interact with friends within the Event screen. We also show you how you can use Facebook Events to create your own Events and promote them to friends and beyond. (At the time that Daniel wrote this chapter, he was preparing to celebrate his eleventh year of marriage. We use that Event as an example for planning your own Events.)

Introducing Events

Events are an easy way to interact with others. To plan an Event in Facebook, you need to understand how people discover Events in Facebook. When an Event is created and you invite people, they see it in two areas:

✦ In their Notifications (see Figure 7-1)

✦ In the App Requests section right below the Ticker

Notifications for Event invitations are mixed in with other notifications, so if you don't pay close attention to notifications, you might miss one. Keep in mind that it is no different for your friends.

Events describe the time, place, and details about the gathering, and also list the attendees. The great thing about the virtual world is that the Event place can be anywhere. For example, if you are planning a worldwide "hug a puppy" day, a Facebook Event is the ideal way to do so. People that respond to the Event invitation are shown as attending. They can post links, pictures, and videos, as well as share the Event and invite others. When people join an Event, they're notified any time someone posts something within the group. A Facebook Event can be a way to bring people together, even if they're not actually physically close together.

Figure 7-1:
Event
notifications.

Understanding Events Basics

There's a lot more to the Facebook Events feature than just sending out invitations. Events enable you to do the following:

✦ Create an Event

✦ Define the details and location

✦ Invite your friends to attend

✦ Share the Event as a status update

✦ Share pictures, links, and videos within the Event screen

✦ Make the Event private or public

✦ See what Events are going on now and in the future

✦ RSVP for Events and see who else is attending

✦ Synchronize Facebook Events with your online calendar (such as iCal or Google Calendar)

You can find the Events section in the left navigation of your News Feed page under the Favorites category. Click Events and you'll see the current Events you're invited to and have the option to create your own Event (just click the +Create Event button at the top of the page. If you want to view other Events, click the button with the magnifying glass and a new menu appears that allows you to view suggested events, past events, birthdays, and more. Click on any Event to go directly to the official Event page where you can find out specific information.

Getting the lay of the land

As shown in Figure 7-2, a Facebook Event has a very concise layout that allows you to see all the basic details of the Event, and interact with those invited to the Event.

The Event page shows the following details:

✦ **Picture:** When creating an Event, you can upload a picture to help describe it.

✦ **Time, Location, Created By:** This is standard information about the Event. When you create your Event be sure to include basic information like when the Event starts and where it's located. When you create an Event, the page includes a link so people can click directly to your Facebook Timeline (or to a Fan Page Timeline).

✦ **More Info:** Part of an effectively planned Event is explaining what the Event is, why you're hosting, and any other relevant information attendees may find useful.

**Book II
Chapter 7**

**Keeping Up
with Events**

Figure 7-2:
The Event
page.

✦ **The Event Wall:** This is a great way for the invitees to share with each other. You (and attendees) can post links, videos, photos, and any text post that you want, which is shared with all the invitees.

✦ **Edit Event, Message Guests:** Visible only to the Event creator, the Edit Event and Message Guests buttons enable you to make changes to the Event, or send a message to everyone that has RSVPed.

✦ **+Join, Maybe, Decline:** If you're not the creator of an Event, you'll see these buttons at the top right of an Events page. Click Join if you will be attending the Event; click Maybe if you're not sure; and click Decline if you will not attend the Event. When you click Join or Maybe, you'll have the option to invite more friends. If you click Decline, you're given the option to write a post on the Wall with your regrets (remember this shows up publicly on the Event Wall). You don't have to do this; you can click Skip if you'd rather not leave a note. If you change your mind about your RSVP, you can click the Going button at the top of the page and change your RSVP status.

Kinds of Events

You can plan, promote and host an unlimited variety of gatherings within Facebook Events. Events fall into two categories:

✦ **Public Events:** If your Event is at a public venue and anyone is welcome to attend, Public Events are perfect. With Public Events, anyone can find the Event and add themselves to the guest list. Concerts, rallys, festivals, and town meetings are all ideal to be set as Public Events. You can tell if an Event is public simply by looking at the Event screen. The title of the Event at the top of the screen will say that it is a Public Event. You also have the option to invite friends, share the Event via your Timeline, and RSVP to the Event. Any user can search for and find Public Events using the Facebook Search function found at the top of the screen.

✦ **Private Events:** Private Events are for private parties where the attendance is by invitation only. Private Events can be seen only by those that are on the invitation list. Private Events also don't appear in search results. Some great uses of the Private Events function are private birthday parties, business meetings, and weddings. If you're planning to surprise someone and are organizing the plan on Facebook, we recommend a Private Event. The administrator (creator) of a Private Event can allow users to invite others in the Event Settings screen, or limit it to the Event administrator only.

Later in this chapter, we explain how to create these sorts of Events and establish the Event permissions as public or private. On an Event Description page, you can clearly tell whether it is a Public or Private Event. Refer to Figure 7-2 for an example of a Public Event. Figure 7-3 shows the same Event as a Private Event.

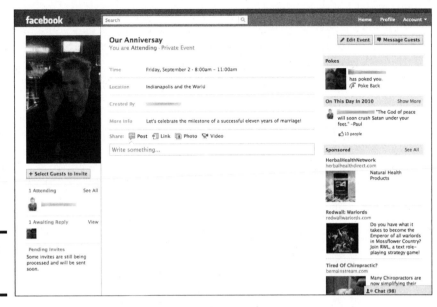

Figure 7-3:
A Private
Event.

Finding and Interacting with Events

If you're looking for something to do this weekend, Facebook Events might be the place to go. Maybe you're looking for concerts in the area, or perhaps something fun to take the kids to. Perhaps you just want to see what other friends are doing to plan their day or weekend. You can use the Event search function for all these reasons.

Some people may make their Event public, but not necessarily because it is truly a public occasion. Perhaps they made the Event settings public to be sure that the people that they have forgotten to put on the guest list can still find the Event.

Searching Events

To find an Event you've been invited to, start on your main News Feed page. If you have recently been invited to any Events, you see these in the app requests section on the right side of your home page. (See Figure 7-4.) If you have several Events, this section shows how many Event invitations you have. Click here to show the Event invitations. You can "Join" (RSVP) from here or click the title of an Event to go to the Event Description area.

Below your profile picture on your home page is an Events link. This link takes you to the page where you can view all Events that are on your Event list. This includes invitations, as well as Events that you have RSVPed to.

Figure 7-4:
Events
you're
invited to
appear on
the right
side.

When you click the Events link below your profile photo, an additional option appears that says Friends' Events. This allows you to see all the upcoming Public Events that have been created by your friends. The Events you see here are organized into three groups:

✦ Today

✦ This Week

✦ This Month

These Events include Events that your friends are going to, even if you are not friends with the Event creator. Click the title of any of these Events to find out details and RSVP to the Event.

The Facebook Search tool is at the top of your home screen. The Search tool allows you to explore a variety of content on Facebook and the web. To find Public Events, you can use Facebook Search as follows:

1. **Type keyword(s) describing an Event into the Search text box.**

For example, suppose you're searching for concerts in Indianapolis. Type **concerts in Indianapolis** into the Search text box.

2. **Instead of pressing Enter, click the magnifying glass on the right side of the Search text box.**

(If you press Enter, you select the first result displayed below the Search text box.) Clicking the magnifying glass brings you to the Facebook search advanced screen.

3. **On the left side of the screen, click the Events link as shown in Figure 7-5.**

   This searches specifically for Events based on the keywords of your search. The results that appear include the keywords in the title.

The Events that you find here are all Public Events. Click any one of these Events to see details or RSVP to the Event. You may not find it necessary to RSVP if it is an open Event such as a concert or festival, but finding out who will be at the Event is part of the fun. It's a great way to know who to look for and connect with other friends.

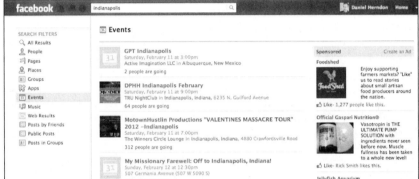

Figure 7-5: Finding others' Events.

Book II
Chapter 7

Keeping Up
with Events

RSVP to an Event

When you are invited to an Event, you receive a Notification indicating that your friend has invited you. That Event invitation also appears in your Events listing when you click the Events link underneath your profile picture. There are three simple ways that you can respond to an Event.

To respond to an Event invitation on your Events page, follow these steps:

1. **On your home screen, click the Events link below your profile picture to go to the Events page.**

   On the Events page, you see any Events that you have been invited to. To the right of each Event are links for Join and Decline.

2. **Click Join to confirm you're attending or click Decline to confirm you're not.**

   When you Decline the invitation you also have the option to ignore future invitations from this sender.

You can also respond to Events via the App Notifications section on the right side of your home page. If you've been invited to an Event, it's listed here. If you have been invited to several Events, the Events are consolidated. Figure 7-6 illustrates this.

Figure 7-6:
The Event preview on the right.

To RSVP to an Event in the Event preview, click the Events link to see a preview of the Events you're invited to. Click the Join link if you plan to attend. If you want to see more information about the Event or RSVP as a maybe or decline altogether, click the title of the Event to visit that Event's page where you'll have more options.

If you've been invited to several Events, they may not all show up in the preview pane; you'll have to click over to the Events page using the link in the left navigation bar.

If you move your mouse over the Event title in this section without clicking, you see a menu that shows you some details about the Event, as well as the options to RSVP.

You can click directly to any Event Description page if you want to get the whole scoop before making your decision to attend. Just follow these steps:

1. **Click the Event title to go directly to the Event.**

   You can also click the Events link below your profile picture.

2. **Click Join, Maybe, or Decline to RSVP (look at the top right of the Event Details page).**

Checking out who is attending the Event

Face it, the cool factor is important for most people. Who wants to go to a party if no one awesome is going to be there? To better plan your appearances, you can see who has already stated they're attending an Event. Figure 7-7 shows the left bar of the Event page, where you can see who submitted their RSVP to the Event.

As long as the guest list has been made public, you can see who responded as Attending, Maybe, and Not attending. If the administrator has chosen to not show the guest list on the Event page, you can't see who is attending.

Figure 7-7:
Those
that have
RSVPed to
an Event.

Interacting on the Event Wall

The Event Wall allows you to connect with others on the guest list before
and even after the Event. You can write on the Event Wall whether you are
attending the Event or not. Figure 7-8 shows some interaction that Daniel's
wife Carrie and he had when they were gearing up for their anniversary. He
even posted after the Event. Pretty cute, huh?

Figure 7-8:
Interacting
on an Event
Wall.

Synchronizing Events with Your Online Calendar

If you're like us, you've grown to depend on the mobile calendar on your smartphone, or through iCal or Google Calendars that you access via your computer. If you're going to take your Facebook Events seriously, synchronizing your calendar is a must. You can synchronize Events with your calendars three ways:

✦ Sync a single Event by e-mail

✦ Sync a single Event by downloading the calendar file

✦ Sync all your Facebook Events by subscribing to the calendar feed

You may find it valuable to synchronize all Events if you're close with all the people you connect with on Facebook, or if you like to see what's going on at a glance from your online calendar. Some people like to have all their friends' birthdays in their calendar, and this is a great way to do that. You'll never miss a birthday again.

If you prefer to be more selective with what goes on your calendar, you may feel that a single appointment here and there is all you will need to transfer over. You can do this easily, too.

Synchronizing all your Events

To synchronize all your Events on Facebook with your other calendars, follow these steps:

1. **Click the Events link underneath your profile picture to go to the Events page.**

2. **Click the Export link.**

Look for the Export link in small text at the bottom of your Events screen. (See Figure 7-9.)

As shown in Figure 7-10, a dialog box appears that explains your next step. You can export any Event, or export all Events.

3. **Copy the link (or click it).**

If you're using iCal or Microsoft Outlook, clicking the link opens that calendar tool and asks you to confirm that you're subscribing to the calendar. If you are using an online calendar, such as Google Calendar, you need to copy the link and enter it in your calendar.

Figure 7-9:
Export
Events
to other
calendars.

Figure 7-10:
The Export
Calendar
link.

Synchronizing a single Event

To synchronize a single Event to your calendar, navigate to the Event page and follow these steps:

1. **Click the Export link found at the bottom of the left navigation column on the Event page.**

The Export Event dialog box appears.

2. **Choose whether to download the Event in a calendar appointment file or have the Event e-mailed to you.**

You can select from any of the e-mail addresses you have associated with your Facebook account.

3. **If you chose to download the Event, double-click it to open your default calendar program and add the entry. If you had it e-mailed to you, you receive a calendar invite by e-mail; click Add to Calendar in the e-mail message.**

Creating Your Own Events

Creating Events requires some basic information about the Event and a few friends to invite. In just a couple of minutes, you can tell all your friends what's going on, when, and where. To create an Event and fill in the details, follow these steps:

1. **Navigate to the Events page, and then click the + Create an Event button.**

   The Create New Event dialog box appears, as shown in Figure 7-11.

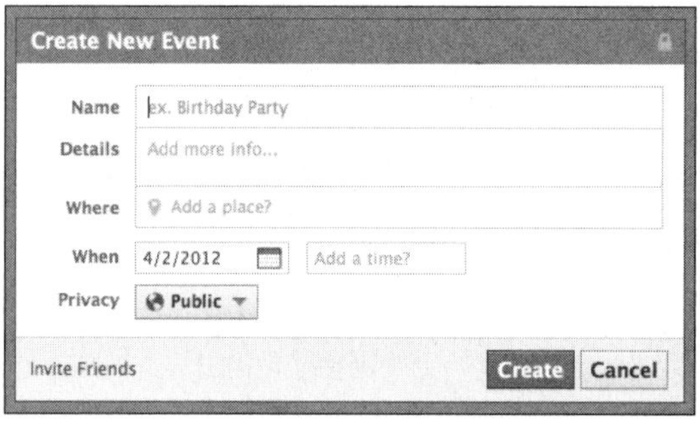

Figure 7-11: Create your Event and fill in all the details.

2. **Type a name for the Event in the Name text box.**

3. **Type the details of the Event in the Details text box.**

   Tell your guests what to wear (casual or black tie, for example), what to expect, or what to bring (a dish if you're hosting a potluck, for example). You can type anything you want in the Details text box.

4. **Type the meeting place in the Where text box.**

   Typing in this text box starts a search for places with that name. You can type the name of a place (like Meadowbrook Country Club) or you can type the actual address of the venue.

5. **Click the calendar icon in the When box to choose the date of your Event.**

6. **Type the time of your Event in the Add a Time text box.**

This is intended to be the actual time of the Event. (If you have friends that always show up late, you could make the time about 30 minutes early.)

7. **Click the Public button to choose whether your Event is viewable to the Public, Friends, or Invitees only.**

   Here's a little more information about your privacy choices:

   - Public: Anyone can find and view your Event.
   - Friends: Only invitees and their friends can view and join the Event.
   - Invite Only: Only people you invite can view and join the Event.

8. **Click the Invite Friends link at the bottom of the box, and in the Invite Friends dialog box, select the check boxes next to the friends you're inviting.**

   Facebook sends the selected friends a Notification that you have invited them to the Event.

9. **Click the Create button.**

   You see the Create Event page again.

Privacy settings for the Event

The privacy settings are essentially two forms, Public or Private. Public Events are open for everyone to see and anyone can RSVP to the Event. Public Events also show up in search results. People who visit the Public Event's page can post on the Event Wall, including uploading pictures, links, and videos.

If you wish to keep the Event private, make sure you choose Invite Only (see the previous section). Invite Only Events can only be seen by people that have been added to the guest list. If you want to cast your net a little wider you can choose Friends as your Event privacy setting. With Friends Events, invited guests can invite other people you may not be connected to. This means that the Event will not be seen by those that are not on the guest list, but anyone on the guest list can add others to the guest list.

The Show Guest List on the Event Page check box applies to both Public and Private Events. You might deselect this option when you don't want it to be public information ahead of time who is and isn't invited. Or you might deselect this option for an Event where you don't want people to decide whether to go based on the guest list.

For any Event that you want to promote and get others to promote, be sure to make it a Public Event so that it can be found and shared by others. Doing this may open up the opportunity for people to share the Event and help you to promote it.

Adding a picture to your Event

The Event picture is not required but it sure helps, especially if you want to get people excited. You can present the Event better with a great picture that tells a little about the Event. Figure 7-12 is a great example of a descriptive picture. YMI is a nonprofit mentoring organization that is having a Putt-A-Palooza Event to raise funds for its organization. The picture shows its name on golf balls (and stacked up in a cool fashion!). People are often visual, so a good picture helps describe the Event.

Figure 7-12: A descriptive picture always helps.

To upload a picture for your Event, navigate to your Event page and follow these steps:

1. **Click the gray box at the top of the left navigation column.**

The Add Event Photo dialog box appears.

(Optional) You can also click the gear icon at the top right of the page and choose Add Event Photo from the menu.

This works the same when you have already created the Event and you are in edit mode.

2. **Click Browse.**

The Choose File to Upload dialog box opens.

3. **Select a picture from your computer and click Open.**

After you complete your selection, the picture for your Event is set.

Inviting friends

When you invite friends, you can send them a basic invitation or you can send them a personal message explaining what the Event is and why you want them to come. You can invite friends when creating the Event or after the Event is created. Guests can also invite friends if you allow them to do so.

To invite friends to an Event, follow these steps:

1. **When you're creating an Event, click the Invite Friends link.**

   Note: If you're inviting guests to an Event after it has been created, whether you're the Event creator or just on the guest list, click the Invite Friends button at the top right of the Event's page.

   The Invite Friends dialog box appears, as shown in Figure 7-13.

**Book II
Chapter 7**

Keeping Up
with Events

Figure 7-13:
Select the
check box
next to
people you
would like
to meet.

2. **Select the check box that appears next to each profile picture for each friend you want to invite.**

   (Optional) Type a name in the Search By Name text box at the top to search for friends, and select the check box next to the friend you want to invite.

   As you type, the list of friends narrows to match the name you're typing.

3. **Click the Send button.**

   Your invitations are now sent!

Promoting Events on Facebook

The features described in this chapter are designed to make it easier to promote Events. With as many Event invitations that people send out, it can be easy to miss or gloss over Events that don't catch their attention. Here are some simple best practices that can help you make a Facebook Event more successful:

✦ Make sure your Event is Public, so it is easy for people to see the Event, or find it in search.

✦ Give the Event a name that makes it clear why someone would want to come to the Event. For example, if it is a concert, be sure to include the name of the artist(s). It also helps to include the city name so that people searching for local Events can find it.

✦ Share the Event in your status update with a link to the Event page. That gives people an additional place to find out about the Event if they didn't see an invitation. You can do this by copying the link from your browser when you're on the Event page. Better yet, just click Share at the top of the Event page!

✦ Send out messages to guests with updates about the upcoming Event. Getting people more involved before the Event makes a big difference. Just be sure you're not sending too many updates. People don't like to feel overwhelmed with updates.

✦ Post pictures and videos on the Event Wall. These notifications will go to everyone that is on the guest list. Pictures get a lot of clicks because they're eye catching and engaging. Pictures help people think about your Event.

✦ Send a personal message to a few people that you know can help you to promote the Event and ask them if they can help you share your Event.

✦ Only invite people who you know would be interested in your Event. For instance, if you're holding a local event, just invite your local friends (unless you know an out-of-towner will be visiting). Many people stop checking their Event invitations simply because so many are irrelevant to them.

Chapter 8: Having Private Conversations

In This Chapter

✔ Starting messages, chats, and video calls

✔ Chatting with multiple friends

✔ Using Facebook e-mail addresses

✔ Limiting chat availability

Communicating with your friends goes far beyond the Timeline, where everyone can see your conversation. Private conversations on Facebook come in several different forms. With Facebook's messaging features, you can connect with friends by text chat (or instant messaging), by video calls, through private e-mail–like messages, and from your message Inbox. You can even create chat conversations with groups of friends.

In this chapter, we cover all the aspects of private messaging on Facebook. We describe how to initiate messages or chats with your friends, as well as how to initiate video calls or group chats. We also cover how to take your conversations on the road with Facebook mobile chat and messaging. Lastly, we make sure you're equipped for messaging via e-mail or mobile phone outside of Facebook. You can use Facebook e-mail for sending and receiving messages from any e-mail account.

Introducing Facebook Messaging Options

The many options for communicating on Facebook give you a lot to think about. Fear not, for all of Facebook's messaging features are integrated seamlessly together. We're going to give you an overview of the types of message options, then we'll explain how each works and how you can use them in later sections. When it comes to private conversations, Facebook has the following messaging functions:

✦ **Messages:** Messages are like e-mail within Facebook. Much like your typical e-mail, you have an Inbox, and places where other messages are stored such as Sent Messages or Archived Messages. This is all contained within the Facebook messaging platform and you receive notifications of new messages along with your other Facebook notifications in your Facebook toolbar (the blue strip across the top of all Facebook pages). Figure 8-1 shows the messages screen (the Inbox) and a red number at the top with all the notifications indicating that one of the messages is new.

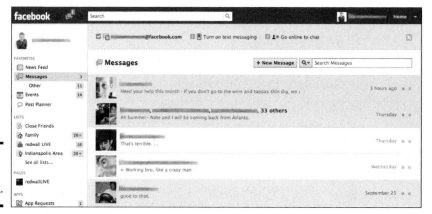

Figure 8-1: Messages in Facebook.

✦ **Chats:** Chats are the same as instant messages — real-time text conversations between friends. Chats appear on the bottom of your screen within the browser with the friend's name at the top of the message. You can have several active chats at a time. If you chat with several friends, you would simply have a chat box open for each conversation, as shown in Figure 8-2.

Figure 8-2: Chat boxes in Facebook.

✦ **Video calls:** Video calls are just like phone calls between two people, except that you have the added benefit of being able to see the person you're talking to on your screen. Video calls use your computer's web camera and microphone. A video call conversation with people far away makes them seem close.

✦ **Pokes:** Pokes are, perhaps, the least significant part of this chapter. No one really knows what a poke is. Essentially, Facebook has a feature (the Poke) which allows you to send a completely meaningless notice to any friend. Because pokes are between two people, we include them with private conversations. To Poke someone, you navigate to their personal Timeline and click the gear icon under the cover photo. Choose Poke from the menu that appears.

✦ **Group chat:** Chatting with multiple people in the same conversation is the only defining factor of group chats. It works just like regular chat, except you can get all your friends in the same "room" at the same time; we explain how a little later in the chapter.

✦ **Facebook e-mail addresses:** When you set up your Timeline, Facebook allows you to set up a Facebook e-mail address, which ends in `@facebook.com`. This address enables people to send messages directly to your Facebook account from any e-mail provider, as shown in Figure 8-3.

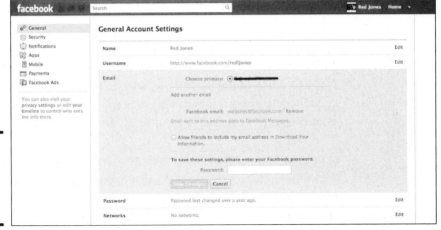

Figure 8-3:
An
@facebook.
com e-mail
address.

You can send messages on Facebook several ways. The following sections discuss your options.

Sending Messages

Facebook message is one of the most popular ways to interact privately with friends, Fan Pages Timelines, and others you may not be connected with yet. Messages are closely integrated with Facebook chat — those two features often overlap. This section explains how to use Facebook messaging to contact others (we'll explain chat right after).

Messaging Friends

Messages between you and your friend are organized in one continuous stream. Chat and message histories are threaded together. Essentially, all your private communication with a friend is combined in one place, regardless of the format of the conversation. If you turn on text updates, messages exchanged with friends via text are stored in the message thread as well.

You can send a friend a message from a few different places in Facebook. The two primary places to send a message are from the friend's Timeline (click the Message button under his cover photo) or from your messages screen. To get to your Messages screen, you can click the Message icon in the blue toolbar at the top of all Facebook pages (it looks like two speech bubbles), or you can navigate to your main News Feed page. There, below your profile picture, is a Messages link (you may have to scroll down a bit if you have a lot of items listed in your Favorites category). Clicking the Messages link opens your Messages page and shows your Facebook Inbox.

To send a message to a friend, navigate to your Facebook Inbox and follow these steps:

1. **Click the New Message button at the top of the Messages page.**

   A new message box opens where you can compose your message.

2. **Type the name of the person you wish to message in the To text box.**

   As you begin typing, relevant names of friends appear. As you type, the results narrow. You can press Enter to select the option on top or click one below.

3. **Type your message in the Message section.**

   Below the message text are icons of a paperclip, a cell phone, and a camera:

   • *Click the paperclip to attach a file to your message.* You can attach just about anything you can attach to a traditional e-mail message.

   • *Select the Send to Mobile check box next to the cell phone icon to send the message to the recipient's mobile phone.* (Note that the friend must have that option enabled to receive your message or she'll just see it in their Facebook Inbox as usual.) See Figure 8-4.

Figure 8-4:
Sending to mobile.

If you're sending a message that is too long for a single text message (more than 160 characters), consider deselecting this option as a courtesy to your friend.

- *Click the camera icon to take a picture or video of yourself and include it in the message you're sending.* If you have a message that is too long to type, or you just want to make it more personal, this is a great feature to include in your messages.

When you type or paste a link in your message, Facebook automatically generates a preview. Facebook pulls images from the link site into the preview. If there are multiple images to choose from on the site, you have the option to select which image appears. Directly below the image is a left and right arrow that scrolls through your options. Select one that shows the recipient what to expect (and not a generic icon that happens to appear from that site).

5. **Click Send and your message is off!**

   Your friend receives a notification of the message almost instantly.

When you receive messages from friends, at the bottom of the message is the Quick Reply Mode check box, shown in Figure 8-5. If you select this check box, Facebook automatically sends the message when you press Enter. If you want to create a line break to start a new paragraph within the message, you can do so by pressing Shift+Enter. If you deselect the Quick Reply Mode check box, pressing Enter creates new paragraphs as normal; you click the Reply button to send your message.

**Book II
Chapter 8**

**Having Private
Conversations**

Figure 8-5:
Quick Reply
Mode check
box.

Messaging non-friends

Sending messages to someone that is not a friend (someone who is not on your Facebook Friends list) works similarly to sending messages to friends. Because she isn't on your Friends list, when you type her name in from the New Message screen, her name will not show up. To send her a message, you will have to start by visiting her Timeline.

To get to someone's Timeline, type her name in the Search text box at the top of your home page. Relevant results appear as you type. Click the name of the person to whom you want to send the message to go to her Timeline. When you are on her Timeline, click the Message button at the top of the Timeline. The New Message dialog box appears; type your message as normal.

Users have the option to disallow messages from people that are not their friends (or at least friends of friends) within their privacy settings. If a user chooses that level of privacy, you won't be able to send them a message. If their privacy settings are more open, then you may send a message without first being their friend.

When someone receives messages from a person they don't know, they may be naturally suspicious. To avoid that, make sure you provide context in the content of your message. You're more likely to receive a response if you explain how you know each other (mutual friends, for example) and why you're contacting him. In other words, include things such as, "We met at the Indianapolis Volleyball Competition." Explaining who you are right from the get go reminds the person of who you are, which will make him more receptive.

Links from strangers are suspicious. If you must share a link, it's best if the link includes a preview of the destination site. Keep in mind that people are less likely to click a link shared with them by a stranger because of the threats of spam and phishing sites.

Chatting with Friends

When you and a friend are logged into Facebook at the same time, you can exchange messages instantly and enjoy a real time conversation. Real-time messaging also comes in the form of video calls within the chat screen — Facebook integrates with Skype to provide this feature (we'll discuss that in a bit).

The Facebook Chat features are designed to work seamlessly with the Facebook Messaging features. When you send a chat message to one of your friends, and she goes offline before receiving it, the chat message is automatically sent to her message Inbox.

Initiating a chat message

When you are logged in to Facebook, there is a small box to the right that says Chat. (If you don't see it, navigate to your News Feed page and look at the bottom of your left navigation bar. There may be a notification that says you're currently offline and will provide a link to go online to chat.) When you click the Chat box on the right side of your screen, a list of friends will appear to the right with green dots by their names. These are your friends that are online (or were recently online). If you previously had your chat sidebar open, it may display this way by default when you log in again. Click any one of the names, and a chat box appears at the bottom of your browser screen. Type your message in the text box to chat.

To the right of someone's name on your chat list is a dot indicating availability. A green dot indicates that she's online and available for chat. When someone remains idle for a period of time or logs off, he doesn't have a dot next to his name, indicating that he isn't available for chat.

Chatting with more than one friend

How about getting all your friends together, no matter what part of the world they are in? You can easily invite several people into a chat conversation. To do so, follow these steps:

1. **After initiating a chat, click the little gear on the top of your chat box and select Add Friends to Chat.**

You can see the gear icon in Figure 8-6.

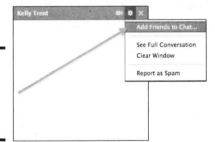

Figure 8-6: Chatting with more than one friend.

2. **Begin typing the names of the people you want to add to the chat and select their names, as shown in Figure 8-7.**

This invites the additional friends into your chat conversation.

Figure 8-7: Selecting friends to add to a chat.

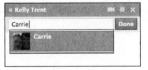

Going offline or limiting your availability

You have the option to turn chat off while you are logged on to Facebook. Certainly, sometimes you would rather not be bothered. Simply click the gear at the bottom of your Chat list and choose the Go Offline option.

You can also turn on or off sounds. Click the gear icon and select or deselect Chat Sounds. When a check mark appears next to Chat Sounds, you hear a little blip sound when someone sends you a chat.

If you want to limit your chat availability to people in certain groups, you can do so. Limiting your availability can be nearly as specific as the Privacy Settings for your Timeline and status updates. With Facebook's group settings (which we talk about in Book II, Chapter 5), you can make yourself available only to specific lists or available to anyone except a specific list. Figure 8-8 shows how you can hide yourself from a friend. Click the friend's name, then click the gear icon in the dialog box that appears. Choose Go Offline to *[Name]* and that person won't see you as available to chat.

Figure 8-8: Limiting your chat availability.

Figure 8-9 shows how you can use your Advanced Chat settings to limit who sees you on Chat. To use the Advanced Chat settings, click the gear icon at the bottom of your chat column and choose Advanced Settings from the menu. The dialog box in Figure 8-9 appears. From here, just choose the settings you want to implement and click Save.

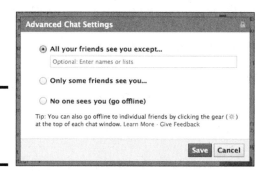

Figure 8-9: Advanced chat settings.

Making a Video Call

Talking with your friends face to face no longer requires that you be in the same room. Facebook has integrated Skype video calling features that make it possible for you to video chat with any of your friends, so long as you both have a web camera connected to your computers. When you initiate a video call for the first time, you need to complete a quick one-time setup. After you complete the setup, you see a Call button on friends' Timelines if they have also set up video chat.

To set up video chat, you must first initiate a call with a friend:

**Book II
Chapter 8**

1. **Click the gear (the Options button) on the top-right side of the friends' Timeline who you want to call (right below their cover image), and click Call in the menu that appears.**

   You're asked to set up video calling, as shown in Figure 8-10.

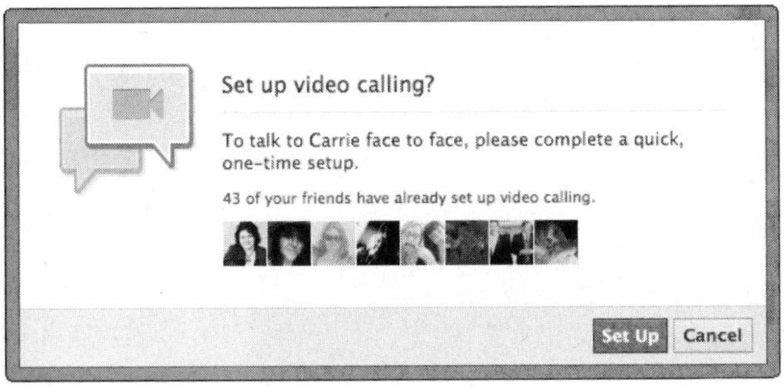

Figure 8-10: Setting up video calling.

Set up video calling?

To talk to Carrie face to face, please complete a quick, one-time setup.

43 of your friends have already set up video calling.

Set Up   Cancel

2. **Click the Setup button.**

   Your browser may ask you to save a file. This will look a little different in each browser.

3. **Click Save.**

4. **After the file has downloaded, open and run the downloaded file.**

   This is the plugin that Facebook needs you to have on your computer for video calling to work.

   After the file is installed, Facebook will initiate the call with your friend. Next time you initiate a call from your computer, you will not have to install the plugin.

   In the top-right portion of the screen, you see a small picture of what your computer's web camera is showing. The big picture is where you see your friend. (See Figure 8-11.)

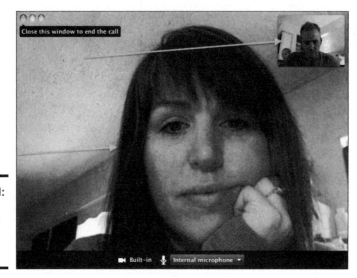

Figure 8-11:
You and
your friend
on a video
call.

5. **To end the call, click the Close (X) button or the red button.**

   The call ends immediately, as shown in Figure 8-12.

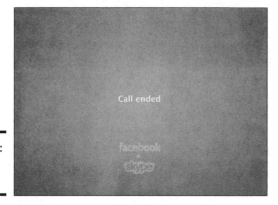

Figure 8-12:
Ending a
video call.

Creating a Facebook E-Mail Address

Facebook e-mail addresses provide an e-mail platform that is similar to traditional e-mail services (like Gmail or Yahoo). Facebook e-mail addresses provide a seamless integration with your Facebook messaging, which essentially expands your communications reach.

Having e-mail within Facebook allows you to communicate with the last couple of people that may not have a Facebook account. Some Facebook power users may rely heavily on Facebook for their communication, and with Facebook e-mail addresses, this does not limit you to communicating with Facebook users only. An added benefit of a Facebook e-mail address is the inherent security features that Facebook provides. Any limitations are ultimately to eliminate the threats of dangerous content being attached to messages.

The biggest limitation to Facebook e-mail is that a message that you send to an e-mail from Facebook is limited in terms of content by Facebook's features. You can only attach what Facebook allows you to attach, and there is no Subject line. It's a minor limitation, so go ahead and dive in!

Setting up your Facebook e-mail account

To set up your Facebook e-mail account, follow these steps:

1. **Click the little arrow link at the top right of your screen on the blue bar and choose Account Settings.**

    The Account Settings page for your Facebook account appears.

2. **Click the Edit link on the right side of the Email row.**

    The row expands to show more e-mail options.

3. **Click the Activate Facebook Email link.**

    A menu appears, telling you what your Facebook e-mail address is.

4. **Click the Activate Email button on the menu.**

5. **Click Next to complete setting up your Facebook e-mail.**

Sending a message from Facebook to e-mail

You can send a message to any e-mail address from Facebook after you have your Facebook e-mail activated. To send a message with your Facebook e-mail, follow these steps:

1. **Click the Messages link under your cover photo.**

2. **Click New Message.**

3. **In the To field, type the e-mail address of the person you want to send a message to.**

4. **Compose your message in the Message text area.**

5. **Click Send!**

If the person you e-mailed replies to your message, you receive the reply in your Facebook Inbox, just as you do with any other message.

 All the different ways that you can communicate with your friends are always organized into a unified stream of messages in Facebook. This means that when conversations start with a chat or a video call, then continue to a private message and even into e-mail and text environments, they are automatically combined in a single conversation in your Facebook Inbox.

Using Mobile Chat and Messaging

To chat or message via your mobile phone, you must enable mobile services. After you do so, you can chat directly with your friends on your mobile phone. Facebook associates your mobile phone number with your Facebook Timeline and directs the messages send to you on Facebook to your phone. You send Facebook messages to the short number 32665 (which spells FBOOK on your traditional phone number pad).

To enable mobile services, follow the steps in the section about setting up your Facebook account to receive text messages in Book II, Chapter 6.

After you enable your Facebook account to accept text messages, you can go to the Mobile Settings page to change specific settings. (Click the arrow beside Home and choose Account Settings, and then click the Mobile link on the left side of the page.) You can choose which types of messages are delivered to you (all or only those where Send to Phone is selected). You can also turn text messaging on or off, or specify a daily limit.

Sending a message from Facebook to a phone

When you are sending a message to a friend that has mobile texts enabled, you can select the Send to Mobile check box at the bottom of the message. When you send this message, it arrives on your friend's phone (if she has mobile services enabled, of course). Remember that normal text message charges may apply. Consider whether your friends are being charged for receiving your texts!

Sending a message from your phone to a Facebook friend

If you have received a message from a friend, all you have to do is reply to the message to respond directly to that friend. To send an original message directly from your phone, follow these steps:

1. **Start an SMS text message to 32665 from your mobile phone.**

2. **Type** msg **and your friend's name to indicate to Facebook that this is a message to that friend.**

   For example, if you want to send a message to John Smith, type **msg John Smith** at the beginning of the text message.

   If you don't start the text message with **msg John Smith**, your message will show up as a status update to your Timeline. The number that you are sending to is the same; it's the code at the beginning that tells Facebook what to do with the message.

3. **Type the content of the message and send it.**

   The message goes to the relevant person on your friends list.

Book II
Chapter 8

Having Private
Conversations

Chapter 9: Playing Games with Friends

In This Chapter

✔ **Finding games on Facebook**

✔ **Changing game settings and permissions**

✔ **Collecting Facebook credits**

✔ **Viewing Ticker within games**

✔ **Playing Facebook mobile games**

Remember when you were a kid and you had a game system? (Maybe you're even old enough to remember those cartridge-based game machines, or when you had to go to an arcade to play video games.) If you wanted to enjoy playing games with your friends, they had to come over. (You were the cool kid if you had a game machine.) Now you can play games with friends on Facebook, and you don't even need to have friends come over or blow the dust out of your game cartridges.

Facebook, by design, is dedicated to connecting people for whatever purpose they choose. Some people make business connections, some make social connections to keep up with friends and family. With Facebook's integration with apps and games, you can also enjoy the fun of a game or two with your friends, even if they are located on the other side of the world. Facebook games also allow you to have the latest games without having to leave your home to buy or rent the game.

Games on Facebook

Games, in most cases, are created by third-party application developers. The game apps can be plugged into your Facebook experience. Games often use Facebook's core features through Facebook Connect to make playing more social. (See Book III, Chapter 2 to find out more about Facebook Connect.) Some of the features native to Facebook that make playing games more fun and more social are the following:

✦ Inviting your friends to join you in games

✦ Tracking progress with your Timeline to earn points or badges

✦ Sharing your badges on your Facebook Timeline

✦ Seeing which of your friends are also currently playing a game

✦ Finding new games that your friends are playing

Facebook uses the term *apps* (short for *applications*) to describe any tool and functionality that enhances features or adds more features to your Facebook experience. Essentially, apps are any third-party software, regardless of what they're designed for. Games are just apps whose purpose is game play. For this reason, a lot of the help topics apply to all apps, which includes games.

The games people play on Facebook are not made by Facebook, and are not part of Facebook.com. Because Facebook allows third party integration of games and other apps, anyone with web software development skill can follow the appropriate procedures to build games. Some Facebook games are made by larger software development firms that specialize in Facebook games, while some are made by individuals. There are presumably thousands of developers who make Facebook games and other Facebook apps.

In the old arcade days, you dropped a quarter or token into the machine to play the game. Facebook games work similarly, but in most cases, it's free to play the game in the beginning, and you pay small amounts of money to level up or buy virtual items within the game. Usually, players buy credits and use them to continue through the game. Credit increments can range as much or as little as a game developer decides — game credits prices range from $5 to $100 and can be spent over time. We cover buying credits in Book I, Chapter 2.

Some games are sponsored by brands looking to expand visibility of their products to game players. For example, *The Sims Social* struck a deal to "run on Dunkin'," so Dunkin' Donuts brand consumable items appear within the game. (See Figure 9-1.) While it is paid for by advertising, it creatively embeds the product into the game itself.

It's also very common for advertising to appear on display off to the side of the game you're playing. Advertisers attempt to pair products that appeal to the same people that a particular game would appeal to. Some advertisements prompt for users to Like the company's Facebook Page or perhaps even make a purchase right on the spot.

Figure 9-1:
Branded
items
appear in
games.

Finding Your Favorite Games on Facebook

Games are hosted in a specific place on Facebook (www.facebook.com/games). The Apps and Games page is also called the Games Dashboard. The top of the screen displays some of your latest game notifications, which include invitations to games, or a notice that your friend has made a move and it is your turn. (You need to be logged in to Facebook to see the game invitations from friends on the dashboard.) The bottom part of the Games Dashboard displays information about other games, as shown in Figure 9-2. The links here include

✦ **Recommended Games:** Shows games that Facebook recommends because your friends have played or interacted with recently.

✦ **Friends Using:** Games that your friends are playing currently.

✦ **Recommended Apps:** This list shows apps that are popular, especially among your friends, just like the Recommended Games link.

✦ **Newest:** Some of the latest games made available on Facebook.

The Games Dashboard also displays featured games as a feed to the right of the screen. These are games that are popular or have been featured by Facebook.

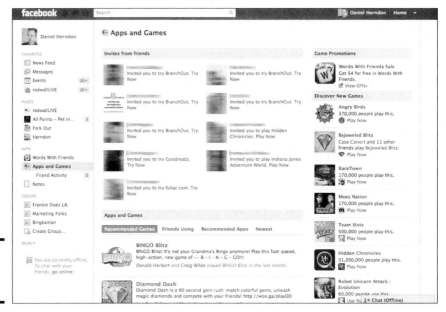

Figure 9-2:
The Games
Dashboard.

Finding out what games your friends are playing

If you want to find out what other games your friends are playing so you can join in on the fun, you can find out in the following ways:

✦ **Look on the game Ticker.** Games played within Facebook (not on a mobile device) always have a Ticker, similar to the Ticker that you see on your home screen. The game's Ticker shows news of the latest activity from your friends within that game.

✦ **Look on the Games Dashboard.** When you go to www.facebook.com/ games, you see which games your friends are playing. Scroll down, and click the Recommended Games, Newest, and Friends Using links. Clicking these links shows a list of games and other apps with links indicating which friends are playing these games (or using these apps), as shown in Figure 9-3.

✦ **Invites and News Feed updates.** If you're invited to a game by a friend, you can rest assured that she has been playing that game. Many of the games have an Invite option within them. This is what makes Facebook games social!

Figure 9-3:
Find games
being
played by
friends.

Allowing games to access your Timeline

Whether you are discovering games on your own, or you received an invitation from a friend, games request access to your Timeline in advance. (See Figure 9-4.)

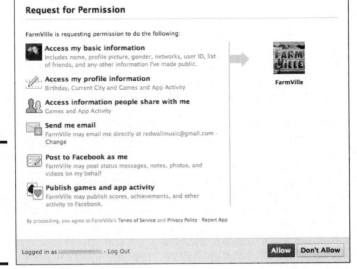

Figure 9-4:
Allowing
games
permission
to access
your
Timeline.

The permissions that games need vary, but in most cases it includes the following:

✦ **Basic Information:** This includes general information contained within your Timeline, such as your name, profile picture, gender, networks you're a part of, user ID, and your list of friends. There are many reasons why this information may be needed by the game. Some examples are accessing your friends' list to suggest people to invite, and using your name or gender to properly address you with questions or notices within the game. Other uses might be for marketing purposes, meaning they use basic info about you to display ads that are more relevant to you.

✦ **Send Email:** The e-mail address associated with your Facebook account might be shared so that the game can send you notifications related to the game, or other e-mail content. The e-mail content will always be related to the game in some way, but it might include suggestions of other games made by the same developer or notifications that it's your turn if you've been engaged in a game with a friend.

✦ **Access Timeline Information:** This includes items about you that are in your Timeline that you have made public, such as your birthday. In the case of your birthday, the game might have special features, such as a birthday bonus.

✦ **Publish Games and App Activity:** The activity includes your scores within a game or other accomplishments. These might be published on your Timeline. Your activity is populated automatically when you use Facebook. Games and any other apps have to be granted permission to do this.

✦ **Publish to Facebook as Me:** This permission means that an app can post an update on your Timeline as if you posted it. It will post something related to the game, which may include status messages, notes, photos, or videos. Usually, you have to click a Confirm button before the game can publish information on your Timeline.

It's up to you to allow games to access your Timeline, however in most cases, the game will only request permissions for the functions required for you to use the game. Some permissions are optional, which means that you can still allow it, but have to confirm before the game takes the specified action, such as posting on your Timeline or sending invitations to your friends. These actions are permitted in advance, but don't happen without your knowledge. They are parts of the game activity.

To permit access to a game, click the game and you're prompted automatically. Click Allow if you wish to allow the game access to your Timeline as it describes. If you choose to decline by clicking Don't Allow, you usually see a screen that further explains each of the permissions and how the game uses that information. If you decline to allow access, you decline to use the app in most cases.

Inviting your friends to a game

After you enter a game, and you clicked Allow on the Request for Permission screen, the next step is to play. Because games are more fun with friends, many games prompt you to invite your friends and share the game with them. Some games are designed to play with others, such as Words With Friends, a game similar to Scrabble. Words With Friends is played between two players, and each player takes a turn at his or her own pace. If you'd like to begin playing Words With Friends, you need to first invite someone to play. When you enter the game, the game prompts you to invite or challenge a friend, as shown in Figure 9-5.

This is the same principle with most games. Many games give you the option to send an invite out to a group of friends by selecting from your entire friends list as shown in Figure 9-6. This is usually an option that is prompted. In the case in Figure 9-6, the game DoubleDown Casino gives you more chips for game play when you invite your friends.

Figure 9-5:
Inviting
a friend
to play
Words With
Friends.

Figure 9-6:
Inviting all
friends to
play Double
Down
Casino.

Accepting invitations from friends

When you go to the Games Dashboard, you see your pending game invitations from friends. These invitations allow you to accept or decline the invitation. To accept, all you have to do is click the Accept button on the right side of the invitation, and the game opens. (Remember that the app will ask you for access permissions at this point.)

Blocking unwanted games

It's always an option to decline invitations to games, but you can take it a step further and block invitations from that game. When you receive an invitation from a game you want to block, click the Ignore All link within the text of the game invite. (It's usually in gray and appears to the right of the game title.) By clicking Ignore All, you will no longer receive invitations from any of these games. You can always go directly to that game to gain access if you change your mind later.

Credits within Games: Facebook's Virtual Currency

Games aren't produced for free. Game developers make money for their services through advertising and sponsorship, as well as from players paying to play the game. To accommodate this, Facebook created a currency to provide credits for in-game purchases. Credits allow you to have your own personal arcade anywhere where you have your computer and Internet access.

Facebook is known for focusing on their user's privacy, and credits are no exception. Credits allow you a secure way to spend money on the entertainment that games offer with the peace of mind that your financial information is safe with Facebook. Facebook then acts as the middle man to tender funds to the third-party game provider.

Credits are automatically associated with your Timeline, and spent when you give an app permission to do so. Most games allow you to replenish your credits within the game, using Facebook's purchasing methods.

To establish credits, follow these steps:

1. **Choose Home⇨Account Settings.**

2. **Click Payments.**

   The Payments options appears on the left side of the page. The Payments Settings page appears, as shown in Figure 9-7.

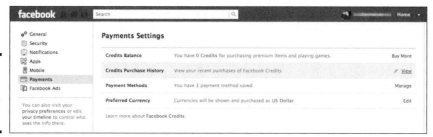

Book II
Chapter 9

Figure 9-7:
Click
Payments to
buy credits.

Playing Games
with Friends

3. **Click the Buy More link to purchase credits.**

4. **Select your form of payment and click Continue.**

   Facebook allows you to pay with a standard credit card, your mobile
   phone provider, a gift card, or your PayPal account, as shown in
   Figure 9-8.

Figure 9-8:
Payment
options to
purchase
credits.

5. **Select how many credits you want to purchase, and click Continue.**

6. **Fill out the form with your payment information and click Complete
   Purchase.**

After you've completed your purchase, you see a dialog box confirming that
you've purchased credits. You can begin using your credits immediately.
You cannot transfer credits you've purchased to another Facebook user.

Ticker for Games and Apps

The Ticker within games appears to the top right of your screen on the Games dashboard, as shown in Figure 9-9. This is a stream showing friends' game scores, achievements, and activity in games. This Ticker allows you more opportunities to see what other games friends are playing and what they're achieving within them. With the Ticker, you can comment on each of the stories from your friends, or click through and start playing the game right away.

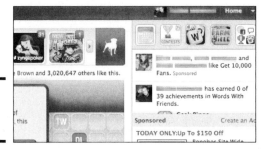

Figure 9-9:
The Ticker
for games.

You can control what your friends see in the Ticker from your games. Maybe you want friends to see updates from a game you enjoy being competitive with, but with another game you play, you want to wind down and relax and ignore any competition.

To control these settings, follow these steps:

1. **Choose Home⇨Account Settings.**

2. **Click Apps on the left side of the page.**

   The Apps Settings page appears, showing all the apps you have granted permission, as shown in Figure 9-10.

3. **Click the Edit link to the right of the app you want to change.**

   The app's settings and permissions appear. At the bottom, you see the App Activity Privacy section.

4. **Click the button to the right (it says Public by default) to change the game's privacy setting to Public, Private, or a more specific setting such as sharing activity only with one of your lists.**

   This is shown in Figure 9-11.

5. **Click Close.**

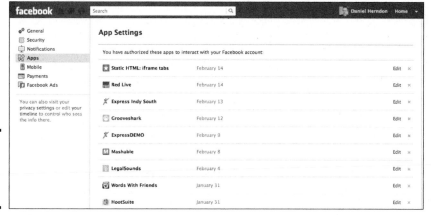

Figure 9-10:
Settings for
your apps
and games.

Figure 9-11:
Setting
privacy for
specific
apps.

Games on Facebook Mobile

Some Facebook games are available on your iPhone or iPad. As well, most
mobile browsers allow you to view the full desktop version of Facebook, so
you can play Facebook games that way. (It often isn't as enjoyable as playing
it on the computer, though.)

You can find games on the Facebook mobile site (m.facebook.com) by
typing the name of the app into the Search text box. You're directed to the
app, where you're asked to grant permission to access your Timeline just
like you are on your desktop computer. After you grant permission, you can
begin playing the game. You typically don't need to grant permission again if
you have already granted permissions from your desktop computer.

If you're using an iPhone or iPad, you can search for the app within the
Search text box of the Facebook iPhone/iPad app. (If you don't already have
the Facebook app, you can download the app from the Apple App Store.)

After you type the name of the game you want to play into the Search text box within the Facebook app, you're directed to the App Store if you have not already downloaded the game, and it will prompt you to download the game to your device. For example, type **Bejeweled** into the Search text box to find Bejeweled Blitz, download the Bejeweled Blitz app from the App Store, and start making those hypercubes and blowing up gems. After you've downloaded the game, you can go to it directly from Facebook to play.

When you play games on the Facebook app or through the Facebook mobile site, your activity will be posted in the Ticker the same way that it would if you were playing on your desktop computer.

Chapter 10: Professional Networking

In This Chapter

✔ Using Facebook for networking

✔ Growing your network

✔ Building stronger engagement

✔ Using Fan Page Timelines for networking

*E*xpanding your reach in business isn't easy — it takes tons of meetings and a lot of effort to keep in touch with your contacts. The key is to be remembered by the people that you build a network with, so that when they need your services, or they know someone who does, they will deliver the business to you. While you can do only so many face-to-face meetings in a day, you can use Facebook to expand your visibility to your network, and make sure that you're always on their mind when it comes to your services.

Facebook is not a replacement for face-to-face meetings, but it is a way for those meetings to reach further. In this chapter, we talk about how you can use Facebook as a tool that extends the reach of your networking and enhances business relationships. We even talk about some innovative ideas that can take your networking efforts from staying in touch to power user.

Understanding What You Need to Know before Networking

Everybody is a little different in the way that they use Facebook. It's important to keep in mind that some people are very private and others are very open. If people prefer not to add professional contacts to their friends list, don't take it personally.

The reverse is that you should definitely be conscious of what you say online. For obvious reasons, if you're using Facebook as a networking platform, airing dirty laundry is not a good ingredient to add into the mix. The good news is that you can filter who sees which updates if you must be inappropriate (or otherwise have private content to share).

Most of all, keep in mind what people see on your Timeline, and be conscious of the message you're sending. This includes your profile photo or all of your photos for that matter, your Info page and its contents, your status updates, and even your friends' responses.

Customizing your profile photo for networking

So you're trying to put your best foot forward, and a great thing to consider is the appearance of your Timeline. The best place to start is your profile picture, which is perhaps the most important part of your Timeline. Your profile photo is a way of identifying you and makes a suggestion of who you are. You want to determine where you want to be between a professional appearance and a friendly personality. Figure 10-1 shows Daniel's profile picture. He wanted to present who he really was, yet with a professional appearance.

Figure 10-1:
A professional yet casual profile photo.

This is your Facebook Timeline, so you can do whatever you want. There is no right or wrong way to use Facebook (within reasonable boundaries). We're merely presenting you with what many have found to be successful.

Getting to know the space

After the profile picture, there is still a little bit more work to do for a complete Timeline. Some of the areas that you want to be sure to be aware of are

+ **The cover photo:** The cover photo is an image that covers the top of your Timeline. Users are encouraged to choose an image that represents you or something you think looks nice.

+ **The About Me section:** Tell a little bit about yourself. Be genuine, and be sure to share a bit about what you do for a living and why you love what you do.

✦ **Work and Education:** Make sure your Work and Education information are filled out. This is one of the first places people look when learning about new connections.

✦ **Contact Info:** Here people can find out how to connect with you outside of social media.

Anything beyond these areas is optional.

Using Facebook for Professional Networking

Two things are very important when you're using Facebook to network: being professional; and being genuine and personal. These may sound like contradictory ideas in some ways, but they aren't. In fact, they should complement each other. Facebook is all about making personal connections. People appreciate that you're a real person with real things going on in your life. We think the best professionals to connect with are those that are regular people as well. When you let those two areas of your life — personal and professional — blend, you can make some very good connections. Facebook allows you to do that.

Most businesses are relationship-based. People are more likely to buy products and services from people that they know, like, and trust, so one of your goals may be to connect with other professionals in your niche via Facebook. When you make connections on Facebook, you can share life experiences and have conversations; you can begin to get to know others and build trusting relationships. The concern some may have is how to connect with business contacts on Facebook without seeming overzealous. That is certainly a valid concern, and we have some ideas about how you can approach your professional networking on Facebook.

Most networking starts with some sort of meeting. If you're looking to grow your network, you're going to have to have a cup of coffee with someone every now and then. Talking with someone face-to-face almost always helps strengthen a relationship. After you've met with someone that you'd like to connect with on Facebook, send them a personal message saying something like "Hey, Tom, great getting together for coffee! Thought I would go ahead and connect on Facebook," and then send them a friend request. Of course, not everyone likes to mix professional and personal lives, so don't be offended if Tom replies, "I enjoyed coffee too, but I like to keep my Facebook for family and friends. Why don't you connect with me on my Fan Page Timeline?" Remember that Facebook is a personal space and everyone uses it differently. Tom may need to get to know you better in person before he feels comfortable connecting with you on Facebook.

An important part of networking is connecting people to others who can help them. As it's appropriate, you may want to promote your professional contacts to your Facebook friends by posting an update suggesting others do business with them. Melanie has a friend who sells comfy hoodies with a logo that says "Runner Chick." Melanie also has several friends who run regularly. When a race was coming up, it made sense for Melanie to write a status update that suggested her running friends check out (and maybe buy) the hoodies as a reward for running the half marathon. Melanie was sure to tag all parties (friends and business owner alike) and the Fan Page Timeline of the company selling the hoodies in her update. She also provided a link to the website's store. She managed several networking strategies in that one update: a call to action (check out the hoodies), a way to complete the action (a link to the online store), and networking (she introduced her friend's business to four new customers). Figure 10-2 shows a status update Daniel wrote to promote himself to one of his new contacts.

Figure 10-2:
Promoting people by tagging them on Facebook.

When you do connect with professional contacts on Facebook, be sure to continue the relationship by commenting on their Facebook updates. Connecting casually through some simple conversation keeps you at the top of mind. Your conversations don't have to be at all about business. Just build the relationship! Daniel suggests asking your contact if she would like to connect in person or on video chat just to catch up on what's new. Or you may simply ask how you can be of service — helping your new friend make additional connections is a great way to build that relationship.

Having personal and professional conversations

It's okay to engage in a conversation about every day life, as well as the more sensitive topics, as long as you have mutual respect and decency. Opportunities to connect with friends of friends can open up in these sorts of conversations. When two people join in on a conversation within the post of a mutual friend, you've been virtually introduced, and this might be a great time to send a friend request if you think you might be good connections for one another.

The important thing to remember is that your professional contacts are regular people like you are, and they have lives, families, friends, and experiences to share. It's okay to talk business, and it's okay to talk personal, but just don't put too much energy into a strict outline. Be yourself and have a little fun.

Building connections with professional contacts

If you'd like to expand your Timeline network to include professional peers, you can use your e-mail account's Contact list to invite people to Friend you on Facebook. You may like this option because it offers you the chance to connect with those people in a more casual environment. Importing your e-mail Contact list is perhaps one of the easiest ways to quickly grow your network. All you have to do is upload the properly formatted list of your friends' names and e-mail addresses, and they will automatically be sent an invitation to connect with you on Facebook.

Follow these steps to import your e-mail Contact list and send friend requests:

1. **Click the Friends icon at the top of the screen, and click the Find Friends link, as shown in Figure 10-3.**

Figure 10-3:
Click Find
Friends.

The Friends page appears and shows the following:

- Any outstanding Friend requests
- The option to manage your Friend Lists
- The option to import contacts from Skype and various e-mail clients
- A list of people you may know, but are not connected with yet

2. **Scroll to find the Add Personal Contacts as Friends section and click the source from which you would like to upload.**

You see several options, as shown in Figure 10-4.

Book II
Chapter 10

Professional
Networking

Figure 10-4:
Choose
where you
would like to
find friends.

When you choose an option, you see further options on how to access contacts from that source and upload them to Facebook. Follow the instructions on your screen to download or access a list of contacts to add as friends.

3. **(This step may vary, depending on your e-mail.) Click the Choose File button, select the file you just created, and then click Upload contacts, as shown in Figure 10-5.**

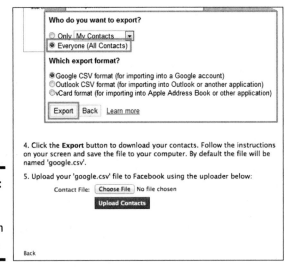

Figure 10-5:
Upload the
file to send
an invitation
to connect.

You're alerted to how many people will be invited to join you on Facebook.

Facebook recognizes e-mail addresses that are associated with an account on Facebook. Those e-mail addresses that are not recognized will show up in a second list. You have the opportunity to invite these friends to join Facebook and connect with you.

4. **Click Confirm to send the invitations.**

Some people set up Facebook with one e-mail address, and do all their regular e-mail communications through another e-mail address. If someone's e-mail shows up on the list of people not found on Facebook, it doesn't mean that she isn't actually on Facebook. Try searching for that person by name or by another e-mail address. (See Book I, Chapter 2 for more about finding friends.)

Growing Your Network

It's easier than you think to grow your network on Facebook if you're actively connecting with people. Keep in mind that if you're randomly adding people, but aren't connecting with them well, then you aren't likely to benefit from that network (and neither are they). The same is true if you're collecting Likes, but not nurturing your Fan Page Timeline community. It's important to make meaningful connections. The following sections describe some ways to grow your network organically.

Providing exclusive content to fans

One way to get more connected with your network via your Fan Page Timeline is to provide exclusive content for your fans. We've seen several businesses offer coupons, free e-books or chapters, and other value-add items to their new fans. The catch is that the value-add item is Like-gated. In other words, the business uses a third-party application (like North Social, ShortStack, or Wildfire) to create two distinct pages: The first encourages the new user to Like the Page in order to download the value-add item. When the user clicks Like, a new page appears with a link to the downloadable item.

Establishing yourself as an authority

When you're growing a network, the kind of information you share has an effect on whether others want to connect with you (either via your personal Timeline or your Fan Page Timeline). People that share puddles of annoying updates often lose the connections with people who are interested in the latest news, business ideas, or clean humor. Think about whom you're trying to reach so that you can share the right kind of information to grow that audience.

If you provide great content, then it's easy to create an incentive for people to connect with you on Facebook. This keeps you top of mind for them when they're considering the kinds of services that you offer. For example, a business consultant may provide expert advice to businesses to grow and succeed. On a daily basis, he shares content that contains highly useful advice. The great advice he offers people is an incentive to be his friend or fan on Facebook.

Rocking the boat

Daniel notes that you don't always have to play it safe. If you know your audience well enough, you may be able to introduce some moderated controversy into your status updates (either on your personal Timeline or your Fan Page Timeline — it really depends on your goals and your audience for each). For example, Daniel's friend Nathan knew that if he built his social media audience, he could attract new business for his company. One of his core goals was to engage with his fans and friends on Facebook through controversial conversation about politics. While you may think that this could be a turnoff, he looked at it in a different way. His predominantly professional audience often considers politics an important topic of conversation. Mutual respect is shared with those who engage in such conversation, even if they're on opposing sides. If you decide to try this method, Melanie suggests that you clearly define the rules with your audience. For instance, any comments with derogatory remarks or name-calling will be deleted. Establishing the guidelines for debate is especially important for your Fan Page Timeline as those tend to come under closer scrutiny. Fans don't like to be censored, and if you delete their comments without clear reason, the backlash can be intense.

Building Stronger Engagement

Engagement is the key to nurturing any network. The more you can encourage people to talk back to you, share your content, or tell their friends about you, the stronger your Facebook community is — and the more people want to connect with you. Facebook uses an algorithm called EdgeRank that, in very simple terms, keeps track of the personal Timelines and Fan Page Timelines you interact with most. You can read more about EdgeRank in Book V, Chapter 3, but we wanted to mention it here because it has an effect on how you create and share content with your audiences.

Here are a few tips to use to build engagement with your fans and friends:

✦ **Post something fun every now and then.** EdgeRank promotes stories from people that you show more interest in. This means that if you Like and comment on someone's stories regularly, then you see more from that user in your News Feed. If you think you have to be stiff just because you're posting to your Fan Page Timeline, we want to encourage you to loosen up! If you lighten up the mood and share stuff that is fun, people will engage a bit more, and that will help your Fan Page Timeline updates show up in your fans' News Feeds more often.

✦ **Don't share long status updates.** The News Feed is fast paced. Keeping your updates short ensures that you can capture the attention of your readers. Longer updates are commonly overlooked when people are scanning the News Feed for the latest interesting news. For this reason, a short update is going to catch more attention than a long one will. If you need to share more information, we suggest providing a link to a blog post.

✦ **Share pictures, video, and links.** Statistically, updates with pictures capture the most engagement because Facebook is very visual. Couple that with the quickly moving News Feed and it's easy to see how a photo or video catches the eye more quickly than a text update. When you share a link, Facebook automatically pulls a picture from the page so viewers can see a preview of the link. This helps to increase the chance that people will take notice and click through to see more. This is good advice whether you're posting via your personal Timeline or your Fan Page Timeline.

✦ **Comment on your friends' posts.** Building community means you have to be part of that community. Unless you're a celebrity (if you are, congratulations and thanks for reading this book) you won't always attract activity to your Fan Page Timeline without taking the time to connect with others. If you want to gather more comments on your Fan Page Timeline, be sure you're taking the time to comment on other Fan Page Timelines (either as yourself or as your Fan Page — we explain how to do that in Book IV, Chapter 2). If you're networking more with your personal Timeline, commenting on a friend's status update may prompt her to take a look at what stories you're sharing. The truth is, if you want better engagement, then go ahead and engage with people!

Networking via Your Fan Page Timeline

If you want to network in a different way, you may also promote a Fan Page (see Book IV for information on Fan Page Timelines). Fan Pages allow you to promote your business while keeping your personal Timeline separate. However, you don't have to stick to business only! You can definitely let your personality shine through on your Fan Page Timeline (and your customers will appreciate the effort). In this section we discuss how you can introduce your Fan Page Timeline to new and existing contacts.

Sharing a Fan Page with a friend

It's simple to share your Fan Page with your current Facebook friends. All you have to do is go to your Fan Page Timeline dashboard and click the

Build Audience button. From there, choose Invite Friends from the menu and a dialog box opens, as shown in Figure 10-6. In the Suggest *Page Name* to Friends dialog box, you see a list of all your friends; select the check box next to each friend you would like to ask to Like your Fan Page Timeline and click Submit.

The default list shows people who have had recent interactions with your page, but you can click the Recent Interactions pull-down list and choose friends based on where they live, whether they're in other Facebook Groups with you, or which lists you have. Or you can search all your friends and invite specific people.

Figure 10-6: Select the friends you would like to invite.

Another way to share your Fan Page Timeline is to use the Share Page feature. The Share Page option is available either from your Admin Panel (Build Audience ➪ Share Page) or from your Fan Page Timeline (click the gear icon under your cover photo and choose Share from the list). When you do, the Share This Page dialog box appears (see Figure 10-7) and allows you to share the Fan Page Timeline on your Timeline, on a friend's Timeline, in a Group, on your page (we know it doesn't really make sense), or via a private message. Choose where you want to share your Fan Page Timeline, type a note in the text box, and then click Share Page.

**Book II
Chapter 10**

Professional
Networking

Figure 10-7:
Share a Fan
Page.

Inviting e-mail contacts to Like your Fan Page

Maybe you've gotten to the point where you would like to expand your connections a little further than they are. Facebook allows you to invite your e-mail contacts. Here's how to do this:

1. **Go to your Fan Page Timeline Admin Panel.**

   If you don't see your Admin Panel displayed at the top of your Fan Page, click the Admin Panel button to the right of your cover image.

2. **Click Build Audience⇨Invite Email Contacts.**

   The Invite Email Contacts dialog box appears as shown in Figure 10-8.

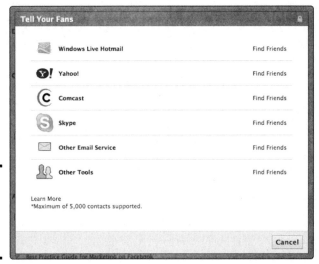

Figure 10-8:
Invite
people
via e-mail
upload.

3. **Click the Find Friends link beside the e-mail provider you want to use, and log in to the e-mail account.**

   After you confirm, an invitation to Like your Fan Page Timeline will be sent to your contacts.

Chapter 11: Managing Connections Gone Awry

In This Chapter

✔ **Unfriending or hiding a friend's updates**

✔ **Leaving Groups and Unliking Fan Pages**

✔ **Blocking unwanted apps**

✔ **Removing content from your timeline**

✔ **Fixing your compromised account**

While you're building connections and reaching out to new people, you may find that more people start reaching out to you. This is because your name starts to show up in more places as you share mutual friends with others or interact with friends by commenting on a friend's post. Maybe you'll find that some of your new-found friends like to invite you into their Groups, invite you to random strangers' birthday bashes, or ask you to play games with them as they post tons of updates about their latest win in AquaVille or some other game. That's an exaggeration of a situation, but sometimes you find yourself with connections on Facebook that just turn bad.

If you have found you need to purge your social connections, there is hope. In this chapter we help you to navigate through Facebook to remove connections and keep your social sphere in order. We also illustrate how to remove content from your own Timeline if you find that you've shared some things that you may want to keep out of the wrong hands.

The last thing we cover is Facebook viruses. No one ever asks for a virus, but in most cases, they can be avoided — and we explain how. If you have found your Facebook account infected with a virus, we tell you how to cure it and fix your account.

Unfriending or Hiding

When you first sign up for Facebook, it's so easy to get excited about adding every friend you've ever had since preschool. This becomes an issue when you find that some of these long-lost friends are a little overzealous with their sharing, inviting, and gaming. As you accumulate friends, you may find that you need to purge your friends list. Here are a few reasons why you may want to do this:

✦ A friend frequently shares offensive or defamatory updates.

✦ A friend inappropriately comments on your posts.

✦ You want to maintain a higher level of privacy.

✦ You want to purge connections for a more easily managed friends list.

✦ You're entering the witness protection program.

All kidding aside, sometimes you just find you have to make some changes to your Facebook friend list. In some cases, you may want to unfriend someone completely; in other cases, you may just want to hide someone's updates, but keep them as a friend. No problem. The next few sections explain how to do that.

Hiding updates from a friend

If you don't want to see the updates of a particular person, whether because they are offensive or simply boring, hiding the friend's updates is an alternative to unfriending her. Sometimes, you may not want to completely remove someone as a connection on Facebook just because you don't want to see her updates in your News Feed.

Hiding a friend's updates is an easy task. You can hide updates from any friend right from your News Feed. The people that show up in your News Feed are those that you are subscribed to. Initially, this is determined by EdgeRank (which you can find out more about in Book V, Chapter 3). You can manually remove updates that you don't want to see. To hide updates from someone, follow these steps:

1. **Find an update from the person you wish to unsubscribe from within your News Feed.**

2. **Move your mouse pointer to the right side of the update and click the button to see a drop-down list, as shown in Figure 11-1.**

The options that appear are related to what updates you see from this friend in your News Feed.

3. **To never see updates from this friend in your News Feed, click Unsubscribe from *[Name]*.**

You still have this person as a connection (or friend), but you will no longer see his updates in your News Feed.

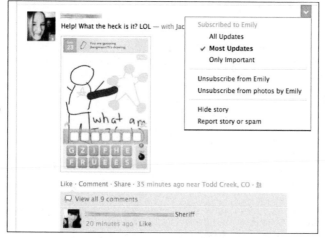

Figure 11-1:
Subscribe or unsubscribe from a friend's updates.

Hiding a friend's updates doesn't prevent him from seeing your updates, nor does it disallow the friend from commenting on your posts. It only removes his updates from your News Feed. If you would like to comment on a post of his, you can go directly to his Timeline by typing his name in the Search text box at the top of your home page.

Removing someone as a friend

When you unfriend someone on Facebook, you prevent her from commenting on your posts (unless they are shared publicly) or seeing any pictures or updates that you have not made public. And, because you're no longer friends, you can't see her private content either.

Former friends will not receive any notice that you have unfriended them. They will only be able to see that you aren't connected by going to your Timeline and seeing the +1 Add Friend button or looking through their friends list.

Remove someone from your friends list by following these steps:

1. **Go to the friend's Timeline by clicking his name in your News Feed or typing his name in the Search text box.**

2. **Click the Friends button at the top of his Timeline.**

A drop-down list appears as soon as you move your mouse over it, as shown in Figure 11-2. The options you see here also include adding the friend to one of your Groups or smart lists.

3. Click Unfriend.

Currently, Facebook doesn't allow you to unfriend users in mass. If you have multiple people you would like to unfriend, you have to visit each person's Timeline and unfriend them one by one.

Blocking Someone

If things have really gone bad, and you want to ensure that a certain person does not have the ability to send friend requests, messages, or see your information, you can block that person. This is especially helpful if you have found someone who is spammy or malicious.

To block someone, follow these steps:

1. **Go to her Timeline by clicking her name in your News Feed or typing her name in the Search text box.**

2. **Click the gear icon under the cover photo and choose Report/Block from the drop-down list, as shown in Figure 11-3.**

The Report and/or Block This Person dialog box appears (see Figure 11-4) with additional options to complete the process. You can choose to unsubscribe, unfriend, or block the person.

Figure 11-4:
Additional
options
to block
or report
someone.

3. **To block her, select the Block** *[Name]* **radio button.**

4. **(Optional) Select the appropriate radio button if you want to report
this friend if you believe her content is spam or inappropriate.**

5. **Click Continue.**

After you click Continue, you have blocked the individual and can no
longer communicate with her on Facebook (and she can't communicate
with you). You see a dialog box that confirms this. The dialog box also
gives you a link to the Family Safety Center, which offers information on
how to handle harassment.

Only report someone when absolutely necessary. What you believe to be
inappropriate may not violate the Facebook terms. If you are offended by
something that someone has posted, send him a message about it directly
or unfriend him. If you're certain that his content violates Facebook terms,
select the appropriate radio button in the Report and/or Block This Person
dialog box. After this you've done your part, and you can move on.

When it comes to blocking people, that is between you and the person you
blocked. Blocking doesn't remove her from Facebook or report her to the
Facebook compliance team. Blocking only prevents you and the individual
from being able to communicate on Facebook. If you find that you made a mistake, you can edit your block list in your privacy settings (see Book I, Chapter
3 for more information about finding and choosing your privacy settings).

Leaving Groups

If you're the creator and/or administrator of a Group, you can add anyone
you're Facebook friends with to the Group. When you do, that person will
then be included in all updates within that Group. What this means is that
when someone thinks you should be in a Group, they can go ahead and

add you in (even if you didn't want to be a member of the Group). For this reason, you may discover that you have become a part of a Group that you would rather remove yourself from.

Follow these steps to remove yourself from a Group:

1. **To view what Groups you are a member of, click the More link by the Groups section on the left side of your home screen, as shown in Figure 11-5.**

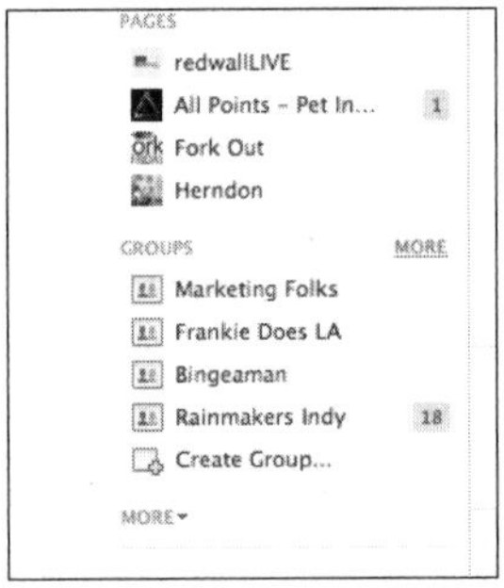

PAGES

▪ redwallLIVE

▪ All Points – Pet In...   1

▪ Fork Out

▪ Herndon

GROUPS   MORE

▪ Marketing Folks

▪ Frankie Does LA

▪ Bingeaman

▪ Rainmakers Indy   18

▪ Create Group...

MORE ▾

Figure 11-5:
Click More
to view all
Groups you
are in.

This displays all the Groups that you are a member of.

2. **Click the pencil icon to the left of the Group name.**

You have the options to add the Group to your favorites, edit your notification settings, or leave the Group.

3. **Click Leave the Group, and you will no longer be on the Group membership lists or receive any updates from the Group.**

Unliking Fan Page Timelines

Fan Page Timelines are opt-in, which means you have to Like the Page Timeline in order to see the Page Timeline updates in your News Feed. Sometimes a Page Timeline turns out to be something you're no longer interested in. It could be that the Page is posting too much, or not enough, or maybe the content just isn't interesting to you. In those cases, you may want to Unlike the Fan Page Timeline — and that's an easy task.

To Unlike a Fan Page, you have to go to the Fan Page Timeline and click on the down arrow (next to the gear icon under the cover photo) to see a drop-down list. Click Unlike (see Figure 11-6) and you are finished. You will no longer see the Fan Page Timeline's updates in your News Feed.

Figure 11-6:
Unliking a
Fan Page.

Unliking multiple Fan Pages at a time is not possible with Facebook's current design.

Blocking Apps

Apps are any games or applications that are designed to add functionality to Facebook. There are thousands of third-party apps that include a wide variety of functions. In order to use an app, you have to permit it to access your Timeline (either your personal Timeline or your Fan Page Timeline), and often times, especially with games, the app will prompt you to invite others to participate as well. Your friends may (without even realizing it) be inviting you to the same game repeatedly, whether you have previously declined an app's invitation or not. To stop receiving invitations or announcements from apps, you can block the app.

When you receive an invitation from an app that you'd like to block, click Decline to the right of the app and then click the Block All Invites from *App Name* link. You can also go to the app's Fan Page Timeline and click the Block App link on the left side of the page.

If at any time you want to unblock an app or just review which apps you've blocked, you can do that. To manage your blocked apps, follow these steps:

1. **Click the down arrow on the top blue bar and choose Privacy Settings from the list.**

   The Privacy Settings page appears, as shown in Figure 11-7.

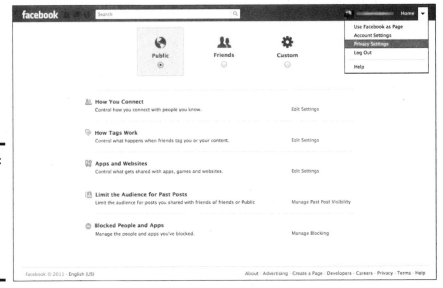

Figure 11-7:
Click
Manage
Blocking to
view and
manage
blocked
apps.

2. **In the Blocked People and Apps row, click the Manage Blocking link.**

    The Manage Blocking page appears. At the bottom of the page you can
    view which apps you've blocked, and you can choose to unblock them.
    To unblock an app, just click the Unblock link next to its title.

Removing Content from Your Timeline

If someone has spammed you or posted inappropriate content on your
Timeline, you will most certainly want to remove those posts. To do this,
just move your cursor over the post and click the pencil icon that appears at
the top right, as shown in Figure 11-8. A menu appears; click Remove Post to
remove the post from your Timeline. If you were tagged in the post, choosing Remove Post removes that tag (and removes the content from your personal Timeline). If the content is something that you have posted, but want
to remove, you have the option to delete the entire post.

Figure 11-8:
Removing
content
from your
Timeline.

Avoiding Facebook Viruses

A *virus* is malicious code that can wreak havoc on your (and your friends') Facebook account. You can only get a virus by clicking a link and downloading something (usually an `.exe` file) or clicking a link and allowing an infected application to access your Facebook account. When your Facebook account is infected with a virus, the virus will access your account and post infected updates to your friends' Timelines and make it difficult for you to use Facebook. As you can imagine, it's best to avoid them.

Spotting a virus

The reason Facebook viruses spread so quickly is that they are hard to discern from regular status updates, and they appear to be shared by people you trust. Many times, the virus link piques your interest and you almost can't help yourself because you can't believe someone would share that information online. That morbid curiosity is exactly what the hackers are counting on.

One of the most popular viruses contains a link that claims to tell you who has been looking at your Facebook Timeline. Although you may be interested to see who's been looking at your Timeline, Facebook doesn't share that information with anyone. There is no app that allows you to see who has looked at your Timeline, so you know it's a fake link.

Another popular trick is to use a link that allows you to watch a video of something "you won't believe!" or even a supposed video of you doing something funny or humiliating. If it's a legitimate video, it will play when you click on it. If you're asked to download anything or allow an app to have access to your account, it's probably not a legitimate link and you should cancel immediately.

The way Facebook apps work is that they ask you to allow them to access your personal Timeline information. (See Book VI for a full explanation of Facebook apps and how they work.) It's a tricky business knowing which Facebook applications to allow and which to click away from. A lot of it is simply experience and knowing what companies are legitimate. For instance, after you enter a giveaway or contest on a Fan Page Timeline, the application for the promotion may ask if you'd like to share the link with your friends. To share the link, you have to allow the application to have access to your Timeline. Or if you want to buy something from the Payvment Shopping Mall on Facebook (`https://apps.facebook.com/payvment`), the Payvment app asks permission to access your account. Those are both instances where you must allow the application access to your account in order to complete your task, and the app is from a legitimate company. If you click a video, photo, or sales link and are asked to allow an app to complete a transaction, you may want to research the company further or click away from that page.

One way to avoid getting a dreaded virus is to pay attention to what's showing up in your News Feed. Many times, a virus will become so prolific that all
your friends seem to be sharing the same link. In order to avoid Facebook
viruses, consider the following questions:

✦ **Does the link have a questionable image?** Sometimes you can surmise
that it's a virus just by the picture attached to the update. If it's inappropriate or graphic in any way, it's probably a virus. Facebook is pretty
strict about pornography and shuts down pages that are considered
adult, so if you see a racy image with a status update, it's likely a virus
link.

✦ **Is this the type of link my friend usually shares?** If not, don't click. If
you're tempted to click, first hover your mouse over the link and look in
the lower-left corner of your browser. You see the URL attached to that
link. If it's not a URL you're familiar with, don't click the link. Many virus
links use `.info` in the URL.

✦ **Is this link related to a hot topic or current event?** You can expect a
new rash of viruses when important current events occur. For example,
when Osama bin Laden was killed, links surfaced on Facebook suggesting you could watch the raid or see Osama's dead body. People who
clicked that link quickly discovered the link was fake and their accounts
were infected.

✦ **Do I know the person who claims to have tagged me in a photo or
video?** Beware of any message, link, or video claiming someone has
tagged or commented on a photo of you. Look to see if you know the
person who supposedly tagged you. If you don't know her, don't click
the link. If you do click the link and you see a blank page, change your
password immediately. If you're asked to allow an app, do not click the
Allow button — just click away from the page.

✦ **Am I on a legitimate Facebook page?** Occasionally, you may mistype
the main Facebook URL and end up on a fake Facebook login page. If you
type in your login information and click Submit, that page takes your
information and accesses your Facebook account (technically this isn't
a virus; it's called *phishing*). Always double-check that you're browser is
pointed to `https://www.facebook.com/index.php` before you type
your login information.

If you ever end up on a page that says your Facebook session has timed
out, do not type in your login information. Facebook sessions don't time
out. Instead, point your browser to `https://www.facebook.com/
index.php` and log in as necessary.

Fixing your account

The first thing you must do when you discover you have a Facebook virus is change your Facebook password. To do that, follow these instructions:

1. **Log in to your Facebook account.**
2. **Click the down arrow on the blue bar and choose Account Settings.**

   The Account Settings page appears.
3. **Click the Edit link on the Password row.**

   Three text boxes appear, labeled Current, New, and Re-type New.
4. **Type your current password into the Current text box.**
5. **Type a new password in the New text box.**
6. **Type the new password again in the Re-type New text box.**
7. **Click the Save Changes button.**

Now that you've changed your password, write a status update alerting your friends that you clicked a bad link and had a Facebook virus. Tell your friends not to click any links that appear to be from you (then refrain from posting any links for a while so people don't worry about which links are good or bad).

If you know specific people received a viral link from you, head over to their Facebook Timelines and delete the message if you can. Also let your friend know not to click the link.

Finally, check to be sure the application carrying the virus isn't lurking on your account. (It's probably not, but it's best to be sure and now is a good time to clean out the apps you're not using any more anyway.) To check the apps connected to your account, follow these steps:

1. **Log in to your Facebook account.**
2. **Click the down arrow on the blue bar and choose Privacy Settings.**

   The Privacy Settings page appears.
3. **Click the Edit Settings link in the Apps and Websites row.**

   The Apps, Games, and Websites page appears.
4. **Click the Edit Settings button next to Apps You Use.**

   The Application Settings page appears and lists all the apps you allowed to have access to your Facebook account.

5. **Click the Edit link next to any apps you don't remember installing or that you don't use regularly.**

   The app information expands to give a full overview of the app.

6. **Click the Remove App link.**

   A dialog box appears, reminding you that if you remove the app, it can no longer access your account.

7. **Click the Remove button.**

   The Application Removed dialog box appears to let you know the application was successfully removed.

8. **Click the Okay button.**

If you don't see an app that looks like it's related to the virus, that's okay. It may not be there. Changing your password is what really matters; checking for the app and removing it is just insurance.

Book III

Connecting Facebook and Other Social Media

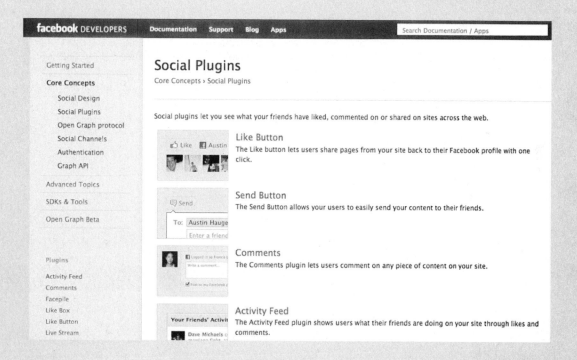

Contents at a Glance

Chapter 1: What Is Social M

In This Chapter

✔ **Defining social media**

✔ **Delving into what makes up social media**

✔ **Understanding how Facebook compares and competes**

✔ **Garnering what social media means to you and to marketers**

*1*n this chapter, we explain more about what social media is and how you can use it. We also introduce you to some other social media platforms like Twitter and LinkedIn and tell you how they're different from Facebook and why you may want to check them out. Throughout the chapter, we'll primarily focus on what social media means to marketers, but much of what we share can also be applied to your daily personal life as well. Even though you may not be selling a product, you're still building your online reputation.

Defining Social Media

Social media is connecting with people using digital tools — like Facebook. Facebook has taken the fundamental elements of how people connect, and made it possible to do much more with those connections. You can meet new friends in parts of the country (or world) you've never visited, network with business peers and share ideas, create interactive marketing campaigns that bring more sales, and bring a new level customer service to your clients. Or, if you prefer to use social media just to keep up with friends and family, you can do that too. Sharing photos, videos, and day-to-day updates about your life has never been easier. The personal aspect of social media brings endless options.

As the number of users of online social communities grow, businesses have found opportunities to join the conversation, too. *Social media evangelists* (people who make it their mission to promote and teach social media) insist that if you're in business, you must use social media because that is where your customers are connecting. Those customers are seeking new interactions, rating products, and making buying decisions based on the feedback of their peers.

In the past, media had been mostly broadcast and reserved for people who had the money to spend on it. Advertising is a good example. When a company wants to promote a product or service, they may buy television or radio ad space and broadcast their message to you. You don't have the option of interacting with that ad; you just absorb the information or ignore it. The communication in those instances is one-way. In the mid-1990s, Marc Andreesen developed a friendly face for the world wide web (the web browser), and the internet as we know it started becoming main stream. Companies started building websites (static at first, then more fluid) to broadcast their messages. Customers started using the internet to find information, comparison shop, and yes, kill time.

Over the past 20 years, the Internet has evolved. Companies can no longer get by with just an online brochure and customers know that well-written and well-placed reviews can help or hurt a company. Customers know they have a certain amount of say in the conversation that they haven't had before. The growth of social media — the open conversations between friends or companies via digital platforms — has changed the way we live and do business.

Media is no longer top-down; it starts with the individual, not the company. Consider our earlier example of television and radio advertising. In those situations, you have the option of turning off the device or changing the channel. Social media platforms (like Facebook) allow the user to have more control over who she interacts with. She decides who she wants to hear from and what she wants to hear from them — she can finely fileter the messages she sees. More importantly, she also has the option to weigh in and voice her opinion, and her actions may influence her friends to do the same.

Connecting — either with friends via their personal Timeline or with businesses via their Fan Page Timeline — is the centerpiece of social media. Facebook didn't invent the friending feature of social networking sites, but it sure has made a good use of it with the ability to adjust the levels of connection you have with people and businesses. You can share or consume more information with certain groups and less with others. (If you want to take your social media connections up a notch, flip to Book II, Chapter 10 where we discuss advice for social networking.)

The ability to filter content in a way that makes sense to you is important when you're choosing who to interact with. Most social media platforms have a list feature that allows you to group your connections and friends into categories that make sense so you can filter their shared information in your social media feeds. You can learn more about Facebook lists in Book I, Chapter 3.

People accumulate friends via social media for a number of reasons. It might be for professional networking or simply to keep in touch with family. If you are trying to build your network, start by friending people that you know personally, and then create new relationships through the mutual connections of those friends by engaging in conversations.

Blogging and microblogging

The term *blog* (a combination of web and log) was coined in the 90s to describe the phenomonon of online journals. It all started in the late 70s with Usenet, a digital bulletin board where anyone could post a message for all to see. People would be alerted of the latest updates (called posts or articles) through an alert system called a news feed. The first blogs required that the user know some basic HTML to insert the content. Later, content management software was created that made creating and maintaining a blog easy enough those who weren't interested in learning HTML or other coding.

Blogs allow people to have their own websites where they can post entries, writing about whatever they want, and visitors can respond to posts by leaving comments. Some blogging platforms allow for communities where users can post stories or questions to other users in the community. While some bloggers use their blogs as a form of an online diary, many bloggers write articles, reviews, host giveaways, and much more. Blogging can even be a source of income from ads and sponsorships.

Similar to blogging, *microblogging* is an update on your personal page on the web, except (yep, you guessed it) with very short posts. A microblog post is typically a sentence or two at the most. Posting status updates on Facebook is a form of microblogging. Other common microblogging hosts are Twitter and Tumblr.

Making the Internet Friendly

Book III
Chapter 1

What Is Social
Media?

Years ago, Daniel was looking for something on the Internet and didn't know how to find it. Someone at work advised him to go to a website called Ask Jeeves, where you could type a question and Jeeves would return an answer. But every time Daniel asked a question, Jeeves would just return a list of websites that may or may not have been what he was looking for. Daniel didn't find this very useful.

Social media sites like Facebook have changed the terrain of the web in a big way. Now you can ask all your friends the questions you would previously ask that imaginary butler. The ability to ask online (or *crowdsource*) and share your experiences (providing social proof) makes a major impact on your decisions. For example, if you're searching for a contractor to put a new roof on your house, you might give preference to the company that a friend recommends.

The Internet is not just about reading information, it's about connecting with your friends and building relationships as well. People make purchasing decisions, plan activities, and build friendships all with the use of the Internet. The Internet in its infancy was used more for its utilitarian purposes, but human nature has put an emphasis on what matters most to us — relationships.

ng to Know Other Social Media Platforms

Although you bought this book to find out all about Facebook, we want to introduce you to some other social media platforms as well. Facebook is just one of many options for connecting with others online. And, while Facebook is the largest social network, each of the others has important features and uses.

Introducing Twitter

Twitter is a microblogging site that enables you to post short updates of 140 characters. Twitter feeds real time *tweets* (posts) from all the people that you follow, and also feeds all of your real time tweets to those that follow you. Twitter is opt-in based, meaning you don't send a friend request, you simply subscribe to the feed of an individual you want to follow. Others can choose to subscribe to your tweets the same way.

Many like the simplicity of Twitter. Because posts are limited to 140 characters (shown in Figure 1-1), Twitter provides a concise sharing and communicating experience.

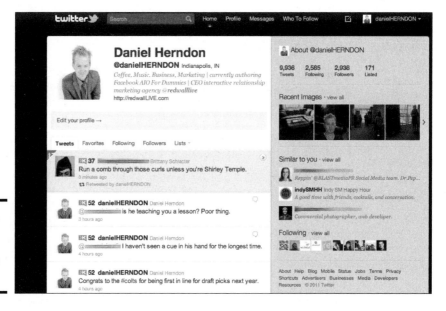

Figure 1-1: Sharing in 140 characters or less.

Twitter is a simple platform and the original interface (at `http://twitter.com`) offers few features. You can post statuses, and share links to photos, videos, articles. Like Facebook, Twitter allows you to create lists of people based on any criteria and therefore filter what you see in your Twitter stream so you can focus on what you want and ignore what you don't. Unlike Facebook, though, on Twitter there are no Fan Pages, Group pages, Events, and so forth.

Twitter relies on third-party apps (such as Hootsuite or TweetDeck) to provide additional features, and those freatures are delivered outside of Twitter. That means you have to visit the third-party's website or install an application on your computer or phone. This isn't a big deal and most people find using these applications enhances and streamlines their Twitter experience.

Introducing LinkedIn

LinkedIn is designed for professional networking (see Figure 1-2), and it's a bit more closed than Facebook when it comes to making connections. By design, LinkedIn tries to limit your connections to those people that you know or have done business with. When you add a person as a connection, LinkedIn asks for some verification of how you're connected to her in real life. That way (if everyone follows the rules) being connected on LinkedIn means you're really connected to that person in reality. The reason LinkedIn prefers you to really know your connections is that it's a site where recommendations and introductions are key. If you're connecting to everyone willy-nilly, you can't really vouch for their professional integrity. On LinkedIn, when you see that someone is connected to someone else, that connection is a kind of social proof. If Melanie is connected to someone Daniel wants to meet, he can ask her for an introduction. Likewise, if Melanie is looking for someone to hire and finds someone connected to Daniel, she could ask him for more information about that person's abilities and how she handles changing deadlines. In both cases, we rely on the other's connections to be based on actual interaction and experience.

Your LinkedIn profile is your online resume and highlights your skills, experience, and reccomendations. When you have provided a service to someone, or worked with someone, you might ask for him to write a letter of recommendation for you on LinkedIn. LinkedIn allows you to put these recommendations right on your profile, alongside the experience that you list.

Although LinkedIn doesn't provide the same kind of socializing you find on Facebook, it's still a great way to connect with your professional peers. LinkedIn offers Groups based on interests, career niches, and many general topics. These Groups are similar to online professional organizations and are places where you can bounce ideas off others or ask (and answer) questions. In fact, these groups are an excellent way to network with other professionals and establish yourself as the go-to person for answers in your niche.

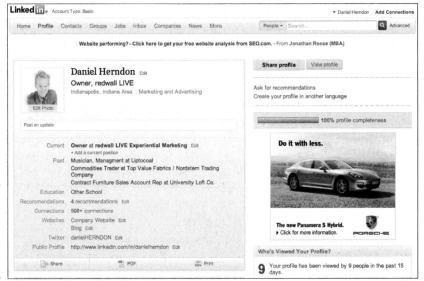

Figure 1-2:
Professional
networking
online on
LinkedIn.

Like Facebook, you can post updates on LinkedIn as shown in Figure 1-3. Users can Like and comment on someone's post, as well as share it with friends.

Figure 1-3:
Sharing and
commenting
on LinkedIn.

Introducing Google+

If you have a Gmail address, you can sign up for Google+ in a matter of seconds. Google+ (pronounced Google Plus) is Google's answer to social networking. Many say Google+ is designed as a Facebook competitor. (Figure 1-4 shows how Google+ looks similar to Facebook.) Google clearly studied the market to see what what's working and what's not, and built its social network accordingly.

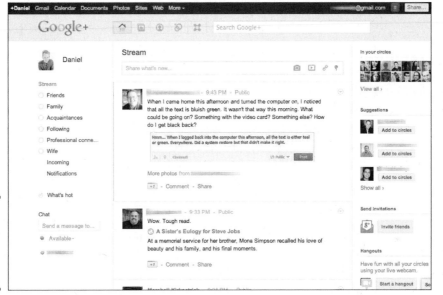

Figure 1-4: Google+ uses status updates and comments.

Google has created a suite of online tools (like its search engine, Gmail, Picasa — which is a photo sharing and editing tool, and many others) and Google+ is integrated with all of them via the black toolbar across the top of the screen (you can see it in Figure 1-4). This is handy because you can have all of your Google tools at your fingertips.

Google+ also makes it easy to add friends, especially for Gmail users. When you create your account, Google+ uses the names in your Gmail address book to suggest people that you might want to connect with. If you want to add someone later, just type their name in the search bar at the top of the page and Google+ returns a list of possible matches. Click their name and you can quickly add them to your Circles (which we explain next).

Like Facebook and Twitter, Google+ allows you flexibile privacy and custom sharing that is built into what it calls Circles. *Circles* are the same as the list feature on Facebook: They're a way of organizing your users into categories so you can filter the information you share and interact with. Circles let you limit who sees what updates, and if you wish, you can only look at updates from specific Circles.

Much like Facebook, Google+ allows you to share photos, videos, links, and more within a News Feed-like environment. While you can view both pictures and videos within the News Feed, Google+ presents them in a much bigger, more visually catchy way.

Understanding What Social Media Means to Marketers

Marketing always follows people. People watch TV, so companies spend big money to be in front of those viewers through commercials. The same is true for billboards on busy streets, the pages of popular magazines, and almost any other media source you can imagine. Social networks provide a unique form of visibility for brands. On social networks, people don't just passively watch, they interact. This opens up the opportunity for businesses to reach consumers through both interaction and standard advertising.

Interaction is a unique yet very important way for a company to connect with its customers. Facebook allows this interaction through Fan Page Timelines, where a brand or business can create a conversation instead of a canned ad. This conversation-based mentality has proven to be linked to higher brand loyalty for consumers. So, if your brand lends to customer loyalty, Facebook is a great place to cultivate that loyalty. When it comes to your company, you should determine for yourself if your company should be on Facebook. For many brands and companies, it isn't an option, but a critical piece of doing business.

Facebook and advertising

Advertising on Facebook is one of the best ways to target a very specific demographic of people. Every day, marketers try to discover where their customers are and what message to send to them through advertisement. Facebook has the potential to remove some of this mystery. Facebook advertising can be based on the fine details that someone shares on his Timeline, including age, location, likes and interests, and other demographic info. Facebook ads are also based on a pay-per-click model, which means that any small or large business can run a Facebook ad and still work within their marketing budget. To find out more about Facebook advertising, see Book V, Chapter 5.

Chapter 2: Connecting Facebook with Everything Else

In This Chapter

✔ **Understanding the basics of Facebook Platform**

✔ **Connecting your Twitter account to Facebook**

✔ **Using Facebook badges**

✔ **Integrating Facebook into all your marketing efforts**

*F*acebook is a lot more than a place for status updates. It offers fantastic ways for people to connect with friends and for businesses to connect with customers while they enjoy all the features of Facebook across the web. This chapter introduces the ways that you can connect your Facebook Timeline (both personal and Fan Page) in the areas of your choosing. We explain how to integrate Facebook with Twitter, add social sharing tools to your website and blog, and add a social networking element to your offline marketing activities.

Understanding the Basics of Facebook Platform

Developers are provided with a set of tools globally called *Facebook Platform*. Facebook Platform refers to the API (Application Programming Interface) that developers use to connect a website or app to Facebook. Any time you use Facebook to log into a site or you click the Like button on a website, the website owner has used Facebook Platform to provide these features within the website. Facebook Platform is used in many ways, and in the context of websites, it is often called Facebook for Websites. Facebook for Websites allows you to enjoy all the social features of Facebook while also maintaining the safety features that prevent your data from being accessed maliciously. Facebook offers several options to website and app developers to make your experience on the web more social.

Facebook for Websites enables you to sign in to other sites or online services using your Facebook e-mail login and password and automatically take your Facebook profile information to your favorite sites. Because of Facebook's tremendous popularity, it's very common to find sites and applications that have utilized Facebook for Websites. This offers you a lot of benefits to simplify your online activity. For example, if you use Pinterest, you can log in using Facebook. This means that you don't have to create another user profile to create a Pinterest account.

Many of the sites using Facebook for Websites require you to give them permission to access certain information on your Timeline, as shown in Figure 2-1. Facebook describes this function as an application (or app) and requires you to give the app specific permission to access your Timeline. The information that the app accesses is normally just what it needs for the function and purpose of the app. For example, if you're using the social check-in site foursquare, you might receive badges posted on your Timeline as a trophy or award when completing certain check ins. For this reason, foursquare needs to access your Timeline feed. Some websites or applications are designed to enhance Facebook Fan Pages. If you're managing a Fan Page Timeline and attach an app to it, the app's access will be to Fan Page Timelines you administer (you can determine which ones; when you install an app, it doesn't have to apply to all your Fan Page Timelines). When the app requests access, the request shows the specific things that the app needs to access. For instance, in Figure 2-1, Daniel is installing the Twitter app on his personal Timeline. The app needs to access Daniel's basic information and post to Facebook as him. Why does the app need to to post as Facebook as him? Well, Daniel is installing the Twitter app so that when he posts to Twitter, the same update is broadcast in both Twitter and Facebook. This way, Daniel doesn't have to go to Twitter and write a status update then visit Facebook to make the same update. By allowing Twitter to post on his personal Timeline, Daniel can post a status update to Twitter and Twitter will post it on Facebook for him.

Figure 2-1:
Apps
request
permission
to access
your
Timeline.

Facebook's OAuth service allows applications to follow a standardized way of ensuring privacy and security while letting apps you choose connect with Facebook and engage with the features and functions of the platform. *OAuth* is the permission tool that verifies that your information is safe and only accessible as authorized. For you as a user, authorizing other applications is quite simple. Most applications have an easy process by which you give them permnission to access Facebook, as shown in Figure 2-1.

The OAuth process allows you to have peace of mind when using certain services or applications. Some sites completely eliminate their own form of sign in and exclusively use Facebook Platform. For example, popular sites like Pinterest.com, Etsy.com, and Shortstack.com allow you to sign up or log in with your Facebook account rather than an e-mail and password. It's a great way to manage your online connections without having to frequently create new accounts.

Finding Common Uses for Facebook Platform

Facebook Platform allows developers and site owners to use various Facebook features outside of Facebook. The following list describes ways you might use Facebook Platform:

✦ **Transfer your login information:** Facebook for Websites eliminates the need for you to create a new user account on a site. Instead, you sign into Facebook, and Facebook signs you into the site. Figure 2-2 shows the Connect with Facebook button on the Klout site, which enables you to log into the Klout site using your Facebook account.

Facebook Platform is handy for people who would like to use the features and benefits of Facebook within other websites or applications. When you log into another site using Facebook, you gain access to tools for sharing, commenting, and connecting in the same way as in Facebook. It's secure because you log in to Facebook as normal and then connect to the site with the click of a button.

Shopping is a great example of this. Bing Shopping offers you the option to login with Facebook. Any time that you use online stores, you typically create a user account before you can make your first purchase. Logging in with Facebook adds certain benefits such as gift suggestions for your friends that have birthdays coming up.

**Book III
Chapter 2**

**Connecting
Facebook with
Everything Else**

Figure 2-2:
Click
Connect
with
Facebook to
log in.

✦ **Facebook games and apps:** Apps within Facebook are tools with specific functionality that allow you to do, add, or access certain functions such as communicate with your friends lists. Games such as Angry Birds are a kind of app. (See Figure 2-3.)

Figure 2-3:
Playing
games in
Facebook.

✦ **Facebook comments on other sites:** You can leave comments on blogs or other sites that use the Facebook Comment feature just as in Facebook. When a blog or article includes Facebook comments, the comments section shows your Facebook profile picture, as shown in Figure 2-4. It looks very much like the comments see on a Facebook post. Comments posted on a website are visible within the website, regardless of the user's privacy settings. The comment is posted to your Timeline, which will still be private to those who normally are permitted to see your timeline.

Figure 2-4: Comments on other sites.

✦ **Social bookmarking:** Sites such as Pinterest, a social media site for pinning photos that you find on the Internet and want to reference later (for say, home decorating ideas), also enables you to use Facebook to log in. Log into Pinterest using your Facebook account by clicking the Sign In with Facebook button, shown in Figure 2-5, and you can easily find out which of your Facebook friends are also using Pinterest. This saves you the work of searching for friends you want follow on Pinterest manually.

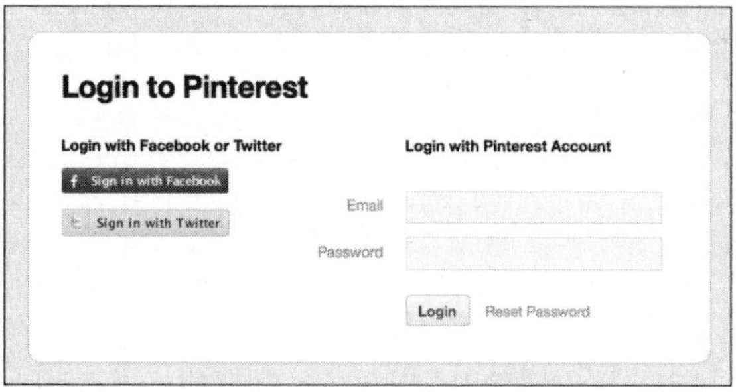

Figure 2-5: Use Facebook to log into social bookmarking sites.

✦ **Like, Share, or Recommend buttons:** These buttons can be embedded into any site by the site owner, as shown in Figure 2-6. The buttons allow you to share interesting content from sites with your friends with the click of a button. When you click the Like, Share, or Recommend buttons, a story appears in your friends' News Feeds with a link back to the site. In some cases you can write a short note about the link to give it context.

Figure 2-6:
A Like button on a website.

✦ **Posting tweets to Facebook with the Facebook app for Twitter:** As you create tweets within Twitter, the Facebook Twitter app allows you to post your tweets directly into your Facebook stream automatically. (See Figure 2-7.) This is helpful if you would like to seamlessly syndicate each tweet as a Facebook status as well. Similarly, many social media sites such as foursquare and Gowalla (two check-in sites) offer you the ability to automatically include your activity into your Facebook activity.

Figure 2-7:
Use the Twitter app to send tweets to Facebook.

There is some debate about integrating Twitter and Facebook. Remember that you don't always have the same audience in both places so the information you share on each platform may not be relevant in both places. Or, if you do have the same audience, you want to be sure you're not inundating them with the same information at the same time in several places.

✦ **Sharing your blog posts on Facebook:** Bloggers may find it useful to share blog posts on Facebook as a way of alerting their readers that they have added a new post. Some third-party tools allow a blogger to syndicate the entire blog post as a Note on Facebook, or post a status update previewing the post along with a link directing readers right to the blog post.

Connecting Your Blog to Facebook

If you want to drive traffic to your blog site using Facebook, you can use a third-party app to connect your blog to Facebook. Using an app such as HootSuite or Tweetdeck allows you to post a status update with a link to the blog post on your site. This method differs based on the specific app that you use. For example, Ping.fm and Seesmic Ping are tools that offer you the ability to post the entire blog as a Note, or you can post status updates and syndicate them to multiple sites at the same time (like Facebook, Twitter, and LinkedIn). HootSuite is typically used for posting status updates to several accounts from one screen. HootSuite also enables you to control when the updates are posted by scheduling them in advance. (See Book III, Chapter 3 for more about scheduling updates with HootSuite.)

To connect your blog and Facebook in Hootsuite, follow these steps:

1. **Log into Hootsuite at** `http://hootsuite.com`.

2. **Click Settings (the gear icon on the left panel) and select Social Networks.**

3. **Click Add Social Network, and select the specific type of network you would like to add (Facebook, Blog, and so on).**

4. **Enter your username and password, and click Submit.**

Hootsuite is one of the most popular social management sites, and is easy to manage. Because the specific steps to connect your blog to Facebook vary by which app you choose, we can't detail them all. Note, however, that any tool will ask you to authorize permission for the app to post on your Timeline feed.

Connecting Your Twitter Account to Facebook

Some Twitter users connect with people in a different way than they do on Facebook, while others prefer to syndicate their Twitter updates to the status updates on their Facebook personal Timeline (this doesn't work with your Fan Page Timeline).

Connecting your personal Timeline to Twitter is easy. Of course, you need to have active Twitter and Facebook accounts. To connect your Twitter and Facebook accounts, follow these steps:

1. **Go to your personal Timeline home page, and type Twitter in the Search text box at the top of the screen.**

   The first result in the list is most likely the original application. The app you're looking for is simply named Twitter and displays the Twitter name and bird logo.

2. **Click the application link to proceed to the Twitter app canvas page (shown in Figure 2-8) where you can install the application.**

   The app canvas page appears with a button asking you to go to your Twitter Settings to start.

3. **Click the yellow button to go to your Twitter settings.**

   The Twitter log in screen appears.

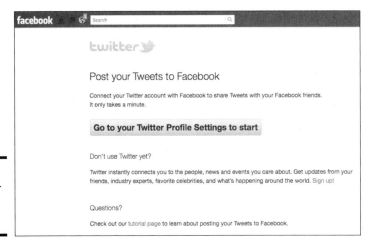

Figure 2-8:
The Twitter
Fan Page
Timeline.

4. **Type your Twitter username or e-mail and your password in the correct text boxes and click Sign In.**

   Your Twitter Profile page appears. At the bottom it notes that you've connected your Twitter account to Facebook.

5. **Click Save Changes.**

   Now all of your updates on Twitter will also post as a Facebook status update. Keep in mind that @replies and direct messages will not post to your Facebook status.

The nature of Twitter allows people to update frequently. Facebook is a very different environment. You may want to keep your status updates at a lower frequency. If you are a busy tweeter, consider whether or not it makes sense for you to syndicate your Twitter feed to Facebook.

Using Facebook Social Plugins

When you're browsing the web, you often see several features that make the web more social using Facebook Platform. It's like all the elements you use within Facebook extend to the rest of the web. The biggest benefit is a single sign in for many website. Facebook plugins are found at `http://developers.facebook.com/docs/plugins/`, as shown in Figure 2-9.

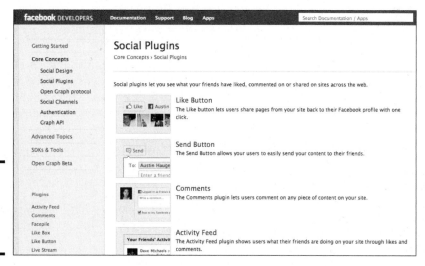

Figure 2-9:
Add Like
and Send
buttons to
your blog.

In most cases, the social plugins don't require you to do anything to use them if you're signed into Facebook. Your browser can keep you signed in (you need to select the Keep Me Logged In check box when you first log in to Facebook). If you're signed in to Facebook, you are automatically authenticated for use of social plugins on other sites. These plugins include the following.

✦ **Add to Timeline:** Allows application-specific functions to be added as an update to a user's Timline.

✦ **Like or Share buttons:** Allow you share links to articles or pages from sites directly to your Facebook Timeline.

✦ **Send button:** Allows you to send content directly to your friends.

✦ **Comments:** Lets you comment on any content on a site.

✦ **Activity Feed:** Shows you what your friends are doing on a site.

✦ **Recomendations:** Suggest to your friends what pages you like, much like clicking the Like button.

✦ **Like box:** Like a Fan Page and view its stream directly from the website it's located on.

✦ **Login button:** Allows you to log into a site using your Facebook account.

✦ **Registration:** Easily sign up for a website using your Facebook account.

✦ **Facepile:** Shows the pictures of people who have Liked a Fan Page or registered for a site.

✦ **Live Stream:** Allows people to connect in real time with comments as they interact during an event.

Using social plugins such as the Share, Like, and Recommend buttons makes your site more social. Facebook's social plugins are great for giving your visitors a way to recommend your site to their friends. Here are some places where you might want to use social plugins:

✦ **Using buttons for individual posts/articles.** By providing fresh, interesting content, blogging drives new traffic to your site. Asking your readers to click Share is an easy way to increase that traffic to your blog entry. Using the Share button as social proof also tells the reader ahead of time how interesting the article may be because Social Share buttons show how many people have already shared the article. If others see that your link has been shared a lot, they may click through (and share) as well because so many others have done so.

✦ **Using buttons for individual products in an online store.** If you sell products on your site, getting referrals from other customers is the best way to get new business. That's the beauty of the Like and Share buttons. Those that share your product are instantly sharing your product with all their friends. The best sales pitch for your product is a recommendation from a happy customer.

Increasing traffic by giving your loyal readers and visitors an easy way to share with their friends is important. People are more likely to do what is easy, so Facebook's social plugins can help increase your website's popularity! The Facebook social tools allow you to share within Facebook in two primary ways:

✦ **As a Like or Recommend:** These show up in your activity feed. A Like or Recommend may appear in News Feeds if your friends have the broadest view settings. It will also appear on your personal Timeline, as shown in Figure 2-10.

Figure 2-10: Likes show up on your Timeline.

✦ **As a status update:** Readers click a button like the one shown in Figure 2-11, which prompts them to share an article as a status update or add it to their Timelines.

Figure 2-11: Sharing as a status update.

There is debate on whether it is better to put the Share button on the bottom of the blog or the top of the blog. Some say the buttons at the top allow readers to instantly see the social proof if the story has been read, others say that people don't want to scroll to the top to share an article or blog post after they're done reading. In most cases, Daniel thinks the top is the optimal place to put the Share button. Melanie, on the other hand, likes to put one at the top of the article (for example, how many people have already Liked the article), then put the rest at the bottom of the article. These can include share buttons for Facebook, Twitter, Google+, etc. By putting the social proof at the top (how many people Like the article) you encourage others to read it. By also putting share buttons at the bottom, the reader can quickly share the article to multiple social media platforms without scrolling back to the top. You can see how Melanie does it her site: `http://bloggingbasics101.com`. She uses a WordPress plugin called DiggDigg to display the social sharing icons. The bottom line? Put the Share button wherever you feel is best, but make sure you consider the two schools of thought when setting up your site.

Using Facebook Badges for Social Proof

Badges are add-ons that you can place on your site to show a little bit of information from Facebook such as text from your Fan Page Timeline or your favorite Facebook photos. (See Figure 2-12.) It's one way that you can use your personal site to attract more friends, followers, or interaction on Facebook. One of the things that badges can do for your site is show how many people have Liked your Fan Page as proof to visitors that they should as well.

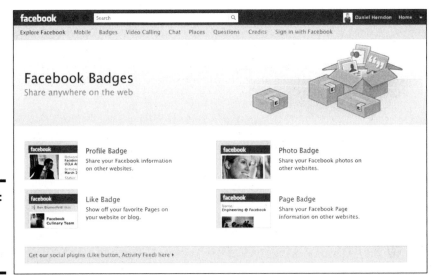

Figure 2-12:
Add Facebook badges to your site.

You can add the following types of Facebook badges to your site:

✦ **Profile badges** link directly to your Timeline and show information about you. (See Figure 2-13.)

✦ **Like badges** shows off Fan Pages that you Like.

✦ **Photo badges** showcases your favorite pictures on Facebook on other sites.

✦ **Page badges** promote your Fan Page on other sites. It shows your picture and how many like your Fan Page, as shown in Figure 2-14.

Figure 2-13: Profile badges include your Timeline info on your site.

Figure 2-14: Page badges shows off your Fan Page.

Integrating Facebook with Marketing Efforts for Your Business

To get the most out of Facebook, you have to take it a step further and integrate Facebook into all your other marketing efforts. Connecting a Fan Page Timeline to your blog or website, and other social networks such as Twitter, is one way to broaden your reach when using Facebook as a marketing tool.

Facebook provides brands and networkers a way to extend the relationship with their customers further than limited in-person interaction. Often, when customers have another way to communicate with you, however simple it may be, it increases the value of that relationship. The following section discuss a few ways to foster that relationship and invite your customers, friends, and those you network with to connect with you on Facebook as well.

Business cards

In the business world, you hand your business card out to nearly everyone you talk to. Business cards are obviously designed to provide someone the details of how they can contact you at a later time. Include your Facebook username on your business card so that when people are connecting with you for business, you're also offering them the opportunity to connect with you socially as well.

Some fear that the mix between business and personal is not a wise idea. Daniel disagrees. If you enjoy and belive in what you do, then you should be more than happy to offer that to your friends. Also, when you reach out to someone in a friendly manner (by friending them on Facebook), it adds a friendship factor to the relationship that in many cases increases the chances that people will buy from you. On the other hand, Melanie prefers to invite people to connect with her on her Fan Page Timelines if they are interested in doing business with her. Although she has subscriptions enabled on her personal Timeline, she only friends people she knows well. She likes to keep a personal space for her and her family and friends.

Website or blog

If you own a business or blog, put a link to your Fan Page Timeline on your website. Sometimes, all you have to do to give people the opportunity to connect is to let them know that you would like to be connected on Facebook.

Sign or QR code in store or print materials

If you own a retail business, people can't click a button to connect with you on Facebook in your store to Like your Fan Page on Facebook. On the other hand, many people carry smartphones, so you can use QR codes to direct customers to your Fan Page Timeline. *QR codes* are a bar code–like box that, when using a bar code scanner (available on smartphones — we like the i-nigma app for iPhone), can direct the device directly to your site of choice. In Figure 2-15, you can see a QR code that directs a smartphone right to Daniel's Fan Page Timeline. Feel free to give it a try and add Daniel.

This method is a great way to make it simple for people to find your Fan Page Timeline when they're not likely to write down the URL and visit it later. Be sure and create a sign that explains what people will find when they scan the code!

Figure 2-15:
QR codes
direct
people to
Facebook.

Wherever you had your phone number in the year 2000

Facebook is one of today's most common ways of communicating. It was only a few years ago that the best way to reach people was by phone. Remember when you used to write down your phone number on a gum wrapper when you wanted to give someone a way to reach you? Well, put your Facebook username there! This goes the same for business. If you provide yard work, wouldn't it be great if everyone that saw your truck with your logo on it also saw the URL of your Facebook Fan Page Timeline?

Chapter 3: Flying on Auto Pilot

In This Chapter

✔ **Automating your Facebook marketing**

✔ **Setting up notifications for Fan Page Timelines**

✔ **Scheduling posts to Facebook with third-party tools**

✔ **Making contests and tabs work for you**

With all the third-party tools designed to manage your social media activity, the Facebook developer API (Application Programming Interface) has opened the door to great efficiency and automation. Automation is most interesting to those who manage social media for the purpose of marketing. Marketing can be a big job, and it's important not to miss a beat. This means that you have to be on Facebook all the time to make sure that you reach as many customers as possible. Because there is no way for that to happen, you need to turn to some Facebook productivity tools to make sure that you have the furthest reach without having to maintain a non-stop connection.

Facebook's API allows third-party sites and web services to help you make your Facebook activity more manageable. In this chapter, we explain some of the ways that you can make it easier to keep your Fan Page Timelines and personal Timeline active without having to sacrifice all your time.

Automating Facebook to Achieve Marketing Goals

Since you can't be online all the time to post updates, respond to comments, add friends, or suggest likes, you may decide to automate some Facebook tasks. Before you start automating, consider the purpose of automating your Facebook marketing. Think about your goals. If you're a marketer, you probably want to accomplish some or all of the following goals:

✦ Increase Fan Page Likes

✦ Deliver quality content to fans and friends

✦ Drive traffic from Facebook to your blog or website

✦ Monitor the public use of keywords using search

✦ Maintain enagegment with customers and fans

These goals aren't accomplished through a "set it and forget it" mentality. Flying on auto pilot works only with these important points in mind: You must have great content, consistent content, and you must have activity that engages your consumers and fans. In other words, you have to connect with your supporters so they will continue to connect with you. Here are some ways to automate with such goals in mind:

✦ Syncronize and/or schedule content to decrease the number of times you have to log on to post recurring or predetermined updates.

✦ Set up alerts so that you know when you need to respond to a comment (or not).

✦ Be sure that each one of your blogs gets posted on Facebook to drive traffic to your other sites as well.

Facebook values manual posting over using third-party tools. If you rely on those tools to update your Facebook status with your new blog post link, those posts may not be easily seen by your fans. Facebook groups the updates that use the same tool and yours may not be on top. If that's the case, your fans will have to click the See More Like This link — and it's less likely they'll do that if they're skimming their News Feed. In addition, many third-party tools that automatically share your blog's newest post will post those links when they are published. If you publish your blog articles at 6am because that's the best time for your blog, that means your Timeline is also publishing the link at 6am. That may not be the peak time to reach your Facebook audience and they'll miss the link. Whenever possible, we encourage you to manually post links to your new blog posts with a teaser or a bit of context to entice your fans to click through.

Scheduling Updates in Advance with TweetDeck or HootSuite

Scheduling updates in advance using a third-party tool such as HootSuite or TweetDeck is a great way to consolidate your marketing activities to be more efficient. Some reasons why you might want to do this are

✦ You have an event you're promoting and need to share updates throughout the week.

✦ You have a blog or contest you want to share now, but also later when other viewers may be online.

✦ You want to increase your efficiency for general status posts by creating several at one time, but scheduling them to post intermittently.

✦ You want to share several things but don't want to flood your readers all at once.

TweetDeck and HootSuite are useful tools for users at any level. You will find one of these tools useful if you're sharing information on multiple social networks or if you want to be more productive by sharing specific marketing messages planned throughout the week, month, and so on. Both TweetDeck and HootSuite allow you to manage both your personal Timeline and your Fan Page Timeline, as well as Twitter accounts and other social networks. See Figures 3-1 and 3-2 for examples of the screen view of both HootSuite and TweetDeck, respectively.

We find these tools most useful for creating updates of any kind that you want to share on multiple social networks. Both are free, and you can access them online through a browser. TweetDeck is also available in a desktop app. The functionality that is most relevant to automating Facebook is available in the desktop version, so we reference that version throughout this chapter.

HootSuite and TweetDeck for the most part have the same features. The difference between the two lies predominantly in the user interface and user experience, meaning the look, feel and functionality of the product. Refer to Figures 3-1 and 3-2 for a look of the two. Both allow multiple accounts, both allow scheduling, and both can be accessed through the web. You'll have to determine your prefered application based on your own opinion. They both work great.

**Book III
Chapter 3**

Flying on Auto Pilot

Figure 3-1:
HootSuite
for
managing
Facebook.

Figure 3-2:
TweetDeck for managing Facebook.

Both applications also work with Fan Page Timelines as well as personal Timelines. If you have one or several Fan Page Timelines, this is one reason why you might choose to use an efficiency tool such as HootSuite of TweetDeck. Here are some of the functions of Facebook you can manage from either of these tools:

✦ **Posting status updates:** The core function of any Facebook user is posting an update. You can do this just about the same in either HootSuite or TweetDeck.

✦ **Scheduling updates to post in the future:** HootSuite offers post scheduling, including a batch upload via a `.csv` (comma separated values) spreadsheet for bulk uploading of updates. TweetDeck offers scheduling if you're using the Chrome browser and download the Chrome-based browser app for TweetDeck.

✦ **Commenting on your own and other people's posts:** Hootsuite and Tweetdeck both display content in vertical streams. Your newsfeed column is one of the standard column options, and you can create others. When you see a friends upate in the News Feed column, then you can comment on it righter there within either Hootsuite. In Tweetdeck, you cannot comment on the posts within the application.

✦ **Seeing your notifications:** TweetDeck offers notifications (such as people commenting on your posts) only in its browser-based app (as opposed to the desktop app), which is available only for Google Chrome.

(However, TweetDeck is beta testing other browsers as of this writing.) HootSuite does not feed your notifications (as of this writing).

✦ **Creating keyword searches:** Creating a keyword searches based on your brand name or topics related to your industry is perhaps one of the most interesting ways to learn about your market, or find out when someone is asking about the services you provide. HootSuite can perform keyword searches, as shown in Figure 3-3. TweetDeck doesn't currently offer keyword searches for Facebook.

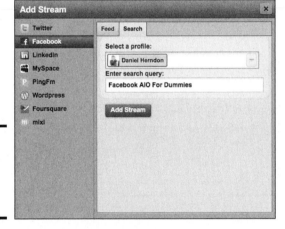

Figure 3-3:
Creating a
keyword
search in
HootSuite.

Scheduling updates can come across as lacking authenticity or seem canned at times. The biggest downside to scheduling your posts is the loss of real-time relevancy. We don't recommend relying on scheduled updates as your main way of interacting with your social accounts. Instead, post manually as often as possible to keep the content fresh and relevant. In fact, Facebook prefers that you update your Timelines (both personal and business) manually. The Facebook algorithm called EdgeRank ranks automated posts and their interaction below manual posts. In other words, if you're not posting manually, your EdgeRank may suffer and your updates may not be showing up in your fans' News Feed as often as you'd like. You can read more about EdgeRank in Book V, Chapter 3.

If you're updating a Fan Page Timeline and a personal Timeline at the same time, consider who is the audience of each of these the two networks. If many of your Facebook friends are also fans of your Fan Page, then they are likely to see the same post back to back. We highly reccomend separating these by at least a few minutes. It might also be wise to differentiate the content so that it comes across as fresh.

Setting Up Notifications for Individual Fan Page Timelines

When you're flying on auto pilot, you need to make sure that you still personally respond to comments on your Fan Page Timelines. Setting up notifications for your Fan Page Timelines is a great way to be alerted when you have something you need to respond to. Here's how:

1. **Visit the Fan Page Timelines you would like to receive notifications from by typing the name of the Fan Page Timelines into the Search text box at the top of the screen or going directly to the URL (for example,** www.facebook.com/redwalllive**).**

The admin panel of your Fan Page Timeline should be showing. If it isn't, click the Admin Panel button at the top of your Fan Page Timeline.

2. **On the Admin Panel, click Manage and select Edit Page from the drop-down list that appears, as shown in Figure 3-4.**

3. **Click the Your Settings link at the top left of the page, as shown in Figure 3-5.**

Figure 3-4:
Click Edit
Page to edit
the page
settings.

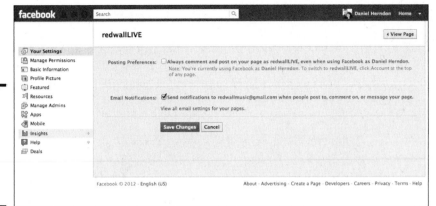

Figure 3-5:
Click Your
Settings to
see your
Fan Page
Timeline
settings.

4. **Select the Send Notifications to *[E-mail Address]* When People Post or Comment on Your Page check box.**

   You may want to confirm that the e-mail notification settings are turned on for that particular Fan Page through your Timeline.

5. **Click the View All E-mail Settings for Your Page link just below the check box.**

   You see a list of options, including those shown in Figure 3-6.

6. **Click the Change E-mail Settings for Individual Pages link.**

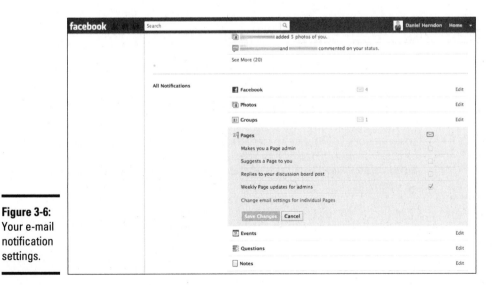

Figure 3-6:
Your e-mail
notification
settings.

You see the Fan Page Timelines you administer in the Page E-mail Settings dialog box, as shown in Figure 3-7.

7. **Select the Fan Page Timeline(s) you want notifications for, and then click Save.**

    You will now receive notifications when people intereact with your Fan Page Timeline.

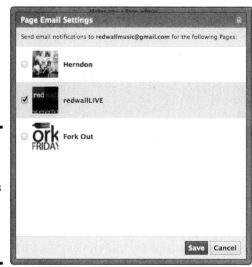

Figure 3-7: Turning on e-mail notifications for individual Fan Page Timelines.

Publishing Your Blog to Facebook with Ping.fm

One of the easiest ways to push your blogs directly to Facebook while posting on other sites is to integrate your Facebook Timeline with Ping.fm. The website address is `http://ping.fm`, so many people call it Ping.fm, but it is also known simply as Ping. This tool is very useful for productivity on Facebook and many other sites it supports (of which there are many). The sole purpose of Ping.fm is to distribute content to more than one social or blog site from one interface. When you post an update to Ping.fm, that content is distributed to all the social networks you've connected to your Ping.fm account.

Posting to social media sites simultaneously

If you wish to share a link to your blog with a teaser on Facebook as well as several other sites (such as Twitter and LinkedIn), Ping is great for that. Here are some of the reasons you might use Ping.fm with Facebook:

✔ You want to share an update with your professional network on LinkedIn and your

personal netorks on Facebook and Twitter at the same time.

✔ You want to post to your blog site and copy it to Facebook Notes.

✔ You want to post status updates to Facebook and other social networks simultaneously by e-mail or SMS (text messaging).

Setting up Facebook with Ping is quite simple, after you set up your Ping account (you went to Ping.fm already, right?). All you have to do is add Facebook as one of your networks. Here's how:

1. **Log into your Ping.fm account and look below the left column with all your social networks.**

2. **Click Add More Networks.**

3. **Click the Add Network link next to Facebook and/or Facebook Pages (depending on what you want to connect), and enter your username and password as required.**

   The Facebook OAuth screen appears.

4. **Authorize Facebook by clicking Allow.**

After you have Ping connected, it's up to you when and how you use it. You have to log in to Ping.fm to use it, but the good news is, if you don't want every update going to other social networks or blog sites, you have that option.

Connecting Your WordPress Blog to Facebook

Often times, the biggest source of traffic to a blog or website is social media sharing. You can post your blog on an Application Page through an RSS feed (see Book III, Chapter 2), but this doesn't drive traffic to your blog site. If you're trying to drive traffic, perhaps to monetize your blog, you may want to use a third-party tool that automatically shares your blog posts to Facebook.

If you have a WordPress website (a common blogging platform), you can choose from any number of plugins to connect your blog to Facebook.

 Creating a Facebook Developer Application is required by some plugins or services because Facebook uses the Facebook developer platform to connect to other sites. You can create the application by going to `https://developers.facebook.com/apps`, where you click the Create New App button at the top of the screen. This application is the foundation used for all kinds of ways of connecting to Facebook features on other sites.

Here is a brief description of a few popular plugins:

✦ **Simple Facebook Connect:** A framework and series of subsystems designed to make it easier for you to add any kind of Facebook functionality that you would like with much less code writing. It's extensive enough that we recommend this for the more expert user who's looking for a lot of Facebook features (including but not limited to sharing blogs on your Fan Page Timeline).

To use this plugin, first you have to install the plugin onto your WordpPress site and activate it, and then you need to create a Facebook Application Page so you can enable individual features that it provides as you choose. Simple Facebook Connect provides the following:

• Users can comment using Facebook credentials

• Automatically publish new posts to Facebook

• Integrate comments made on Facebook back into your own site.

• Implements Open Graph tags entirely automatically.

✦ **Wordbooker:** Enables you to cross post your blog posts to your Fan Page Timeline (it also supports posting to personal Timelines as well). It's easy to install and easy to authorize.

After you've downloaded and installed the plugin on your blog, all you have to do is go to the plugin settings page, where you're prompted to authorize Facebook to connect to the plugin. Then you're ready to go. Check the Wordbooker settings page for other customizations. Wordbooker allows you to select which Fan Page Timeline (and even groups) you would like to publish to with each post if you're the administrator of more than one.

✦ **Facebook Page Publish:** Publishes your blog posts directly to your personal Timeline, Fan Page Timeline, or application. You have to create a Facebook application for this plugin as well, which acts as a platform to connect your website, Fan Page Timeline, and the plugin itself.

With Facebook Page Publish, you can specify certain categories from your WordPress blog to post to Facebook. After installing the plugin, you need to create the application, and then authorize the plugin to access your Timeline through the application you created.

You can always take the shorter route and simply use Share buttons on your blog. There are several including Share This, Digg Digg, and others. These are placed on the blog itself so the reader (or you) can share the blog easily to Facebook by clicking a button. This only sends the post to the Facebook Timeline that you're logged into, and not to Fan Page Timelines, but it is much simpler to set up if you're not app savvy.

If you're ready to dive in, follow these steps to set up an application to connect your WordPress blog to Facebook:

1. **To create an app, point your browser to** `https://developers.facebook.com/apps` **and click the Create New App button.**

2. **Type in the app name of your choice.**

   The app name can be anything you want it to be, as long as the name isn't already taken.

3. **Click Create App in the center part of your screen. Make sure you select Agree.**

   You may be asked to verify you're a real person by deciphering the CAPTCHA code. (CAPTCHA is simply words and other characters that appear on your screen to manually verify you're a real person.)

4. **Type the CAPTCHA in the text box, and then click Submit.**

   You land on the app's About or Basic page. There are several fields that don't apply to this particular purpose. Just make sure your contact e-mail is accurate and you have a proper description.

5. **On the top left, click Web Site and complete this section.**

   The site URL is your blog site URL, and the site domain is the simple address without the `http://` prefix (such as `example.com`).

6. **After you've completed these steps, save your changes.**

   You can see the completed app page after you save changes. You can also find it by pointing your browser to `https://developers.facebook.com/apps`.

   Typically when you are connecting sites using a Facebook Application, you will need the App ID, App secret, and sometimes the API Key. You find this on the app home page.

Avoiding Automation Blunders

The two primary functions of any automation are to syndicate content that you're posting on other sites or social networks, and scheduling posts in advance.

It's important to keep tabs on that content, because when you post automatically rather than manually, it's easy to forget that you have content posting from third-party apps. The result can be that you mistakenly post the same content manually or fail to respond to comments, and so on.

When scheduling updates in advance, be conscious of the date and time that your update is going out. It's important to revisit your scheduled content and adjust as necessary. For example, if you have an automatic post going out that says something like "Looking forward to a great day," but it happens to be the day that there is a major disaster, you'll look extremely insensitive.

If you're syndicating updates from other sources such as a blog or Twitter, make sure you're aware of the balance of content coming from that source in addition to any updates you may post directly to Facebook. Otherwise, you could risk updating too much, and lose interest from your readers.

Book IV

Building a Fan Page Timeline

The 5th Wave · By Rich Tennant

"Jim and I do a lot of business together on Facebook. By the way, Jim, did you get the sales spreadsheet and little blue pony I sent you?"

Contents at a Glance

Chapter 1: Creating a Fan Page Timeline for Your Business

In This Chapter

✔ Setting up your Facebook Fan Page Timeline

✔ Customizing your Fan Page Timeline

✔ Optimizing your Fan Page Timeline for search engines

✔ Creating a customized Facebook URL

"*B*ut I already have a website, do I really need a Facebook Fan Page?" you ask. In most cases, yes, you do. Facebook has proven to be an outstanding marketing tool. By integrating Facebook into your overall strategy, you expand your reach by millions. Consider these numbers:

✦ Facebook is the number two site on the Internet (only Google has more visitors).

✦ Over 800 million people have active Facebook accounts.

✦ Over 400 million people log in to Facebook every day.

✦ The average user has 130 friends and is connected to 80 community pages, groups, and events.

Those are *your* customers. Your customers are on Facebook *looking* for ways to interact with you. Why not meet them where they are? Facebook Fan Page Timelines are an easy way to connect with your fans (and introduce yourself to new fans!).

This chapter explains how a Fan Page Timeline works and how you can create one in just a few minutes. After you create your Fan Page Timeline, you want to customize it, or *brand* it. Facebook offers a few customization options, but we show you some Facebook applications that really help you take your Fan Page to the next level and help you engage with your readers.

Deciding to Create a Facebook Fan Page Timeline

Before we show you how to create a Facebook Fan Page Timeline, let us explain the options you may see on Facebook. Facebook has three types of pages, but businesses can only use Fan Page Timelines to create and interact with a community. The three types of pages on Facebook are

✦ **Personal Timeline:** These are personal Facebook pages that relate to your private life. This type of page is usually referred to simply as one's *Timeline.* (Note that the Timeline is relatively recent as of this writing; previously, you had *personal profiles.*) (See Book I for a full discussion of personal Timelines.) You can't use a personal Timeline page to promote a business; personal Timelines are strictly for personal use.

✦ **Fan Page Timelines:** Facebook created Fan Pages to give businesses, products/services, celebrities, artists, and causes their own space on Facebook. Fan Pages are sometimes called *Business Pages* or just *Pages,* but we stick to the terms Fan Pages or Fan Page Timelines.

✦ **Generic community pages:** These are Facebook-generated pages that are not owned by anyone in particular (except Facebook), so you can't control the information shared. These pages are generally populated by Wikipedia information and related status updates from Fan Pages and personal Timelines. Very few Facebook users refer to generic community pages with any consistency.

Generic community pages should not be confused with creating a Fan Page Timeline for a community or cause. If you choose to make your own Fan Page Timeline dedicated to a community or cause, you have complete control over how that Fan Page Timeline looks, which applications are installed, and how information is shared.

One thing you'll notice is that Fan Page Timelines look similar to personal Timelines. Look ahead to Figures 1-4 and 1-5 to see what a few completed, customized Fan Page Timelines look like.

Fan Pages weren't part of the initial Facebook options. The result is that some businesses created personal Timelines rather than Fan Page Timelines for their businesses. Now that Fan Page Timelines are mainstream and fully integrated into the Facebook experience, using a personal Timeline for your business is against Facebook policy. This separation is actually a good thing. Facebook is aware that personal Timelines and Fan Page Timelines have different needs and they've addressed those by giving Fan Page Timelines more marketing functionality than personal Timelines. If you're contemplating marketing your business, service, or product on Facebook, you probably want as much exposure as possible for your product or business. Table 1-1 shows that a personal Timeline simply doesn't offer the marketing flexibility that a Fan Page Timeline does.

Table 1-1	Differences Between Personal Timelines and Fan Page Timelines	
Personal Timeline	*Fan Page Timeline*	
Limited to 5,000 friends	No limit on fans or Likes	
Not allowed to install applications	Allowed to install multiple applications to streamline your social media efforts	
Only searchable within Facebook	Fully searchable inside and outside of Facebook	

Creating separate entities for yourself and your business (in other words, keeping your personal Timeline and your Fan Page Timeline separate) allows you to connect with your friends personally while keeping your business contacts separate. Although there may be some overlap, your everyday friends will appreciate that they aren't being subjected to your business discussions, promotions, and information (because that will be done via your Fan Page and they can opt in to that Fan Page). Likewise, your business associates or fans aren't subjected to your personal status updates or to cute photos of your puppy and kids.

Make Facebook a component of your strategy, not your only strategy

Facebook has a lot of features and opportunities for branding and customization. In fact, you can customize your Fan Page Timeline so completely that you may be tempted to ditch your blog or website to focus your energy on your Facebook presence. We strongly advise against that.

All your social media efforts should work together. Think of your website as your hub. From there, you may have spokes (links) out to your Facebook Fan Page, Twitter account, YouTube channel, and LinkedIn communities. Each of those spokes is owned by a third party; only your website is fully owned by your company.

You don't own your space in Facebookland — Facebook owns it and can evict you if it sees fit. Eviction (that is, deletion of your Fan Page

Timeline) doesn't happen often, but if your Fan Page violates Facebook terms of service or any of the numerous guidelines, Facebook can and will remove your Fan Page Timeline. The awful thing is, you don't have a say. Facebook doesn't contact you to warn you; it doesn't e-mail or call to discuss your options. Your Fan Page (and all you've built — community, content, trust, *everything*) is erased. You'll have to rebuild from scratch — Facebook will not reinstate a Fan Page Timeline it deleted.

It's never a good idea to put all your eggs in one basket for the simple reason that your audience doesn't gather in a single venue. Many people may look for you on Facebook, but others will seek out your website or blog or follow you on Twitter.

Creating Your Fan Page Timeline

The length of this chapter may suggest that setting up a Fan Page Timeline is complicated. Nothing could be further from the truth! With a few clicks, you'll be up and running. To get started, follow these instructions:

1. **Use your browser to navigate to** `http://facebook.com/pages/create.php`.

You see six boxes representing different categories, as shown in Figure 1-1.

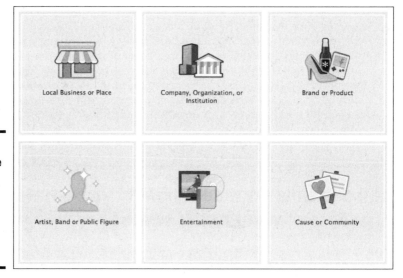

Figure 1-1:
Choose one of these six broad categories for your Fan Page Timeline.

Many of the main categories offer similar options for your business. For instance, if you are creating a Fan Page for a book store, you could choose Local Business or Place⇨Book Store or Entertainment⇨Book Store. The result is the same.

Here is an overview of each category to help you choose which one best fits your needs:

• *Local Business or Place:* Best choice if you have a single bricks and mortar store. This type of Fan Page focuses on the location instead of product. You can share business hours, parking information, and so on.

- *Company, Organization, or Institution:* Best choice if your business has multiple stores. You still have the option to include addresses. Note that the Fan Page Timeline you create will be a representation of your brand, not each store. Facebook isn't offering that functionality to the masses yet. You can make individual Fan Page Timelines for each store, but it may be confusing for your customers and you can only use your business name once as your username (discussed later in this chapter). One of Melanie's clients has two stores in the same town. Rather than make two Fan Page Timelines, they use one and cross-promote the stores on the single page without any problem.

- *Brand or Product:* Best choice if you don't have a bricks and mortar storefront and/or want to focus on your product. You can share your website address, products, company overview, and so on. If you're a blogger creating a Fan Page, this category is an excellent choice.

- *Artist, Band, or Public Figure:* Best choice if one of those descriptors fits you. You must be the official authorized representative (not just the biggest fan) of the artist, band, or public figure in order to create a Fan Page.

- *Entertainment:* Best choice if your business is movies, theater, books, sports, music, and so on.

- *Cause or Community:* Best choice if you're creating a Fan Page for a cause (Kids With Food Allergies) or a community (such as Points of Light).

2. **Click the box that best represents your business, product, or service.**

   A drop-down list to narrow down the category and a text box for your Fan Page Timeline name appear.

3. **Use the drop-down list to choose the sub-category for your Fan Page Timeline.**

4. **Type the title you want your Fan Page Timeline to have in the Name text box.**

   The name is the title of your Fan Page and is searchable both inside and outside of Facebook.

   Depending on the type of Fan Page you chose, the Name text box may be labeled as follows:

   - Business or Place

   - Company Name

   - Brand or Product

   - Name

   - Cause or Community

You can change your Fan Page Timeline title until you have 100 fans. When your 100th fan Likes your Fan Page, your title becomes permanent. Facebook figures that as you grow, it's important to keep your brand intact and not confuse your readers with changing information.

5. **If you're creating a Fan Page for a Local Business or Place, type your street address, city/state, zip code, and phone number in the relevant text boxes.**

6. **Select the I Agree to Facebook Pages Terms check box.**

7. **Click the Get Started button.**

   The Set Up page (part one of two) for your Fan Page Timeline appears and suggests you upload a profile image.

8. **(Optional) Upload an image to serve as your profile picture from your computer or import one from your website and click Next.**

   If you don't set your profile image at this point, you can add it later (we tell you how later in this chapter).

   If you do upload a picture, this image appears any time you post as your Fan Page Timeline. We provide advice on choosing your profile image later in this chapter.

   The Set Up page (part two of two) for your Fan Page Timeline appears and asks you to provide some basic information about your page.

9. **Type a description of your Fan Page in the first text box, and then add your blog or website URL, your Twitter handle, or other pertinent links in the second text box.**

10. **Click Save Info.**

    Your Fan Page Timeline appears, similar to the one shown in Figure 1-2. Facebook walks you through the important parts of your Fan Page Timeline and how you can customize it.

Figure 1-2: A brand new Fan Page Timeline in need of customization.

Creating a business account

If you don't have a Facebook account, you can use what's called a *business account*. These accounts have limited functionality and only allow you to administer Fan Page Timelines or ads.

Warning: If you already have a personal Timeline, you may not set up a business account. Facebook's terms of service clearly state that each user may only have one account. Business accounts are only for those people who don't want a personal Timeline, but need to administer a Fan Page Timeline or ad campaign. Facebook will delete all of your accounts if they discover you have more than one.

Setting up a business account is a fairly simple affair. Just follow these steps:

1. **Create a Fan Page Timeline (refer to the instructions earlier in this chapter).**

   The Create Facebook Account page appears.

Alternatively, you can begin by creating a Facebook ad (refer to Book V, Chapter 5 for instructions on setting up an ad).

2. **Select the I Do Not Have a Facebook Account radio button, and then complete the rest of the form.**

3. **Select the check box that confirms you have read and agree to the Facebook terms of service.**

4. **Click the Sign Up Now! button.**

   You will receive a confirmation e-mail at the address you entered on the form.

5. **Follow the instructions in the confirmation e-mail to complete your business account set up.**

You can read more about Facebook business accounts at `http://on.fb.me/ BusinessAccount`.

Customizing Your Fan Page Settings

Part of what's appealing about creating a Facebook Fan Page is the way you can customize it to reinforce your brand. Figure 1-2 shows the suggestions Facebook has for helping you get started. There are few things you'll want to do to customize your Fan Page Timeline before you share it with the masses:

✦ Create and load a profile image.

✦ Create and load a cover photo.

✦ Like your Fan Page.

✦ Invite your friends and e-mail contacts to Like your Fan Page.

✦ Review your dashboard settings.

✦ Install a few applications to encourage interaction on your Fan Page Timeline.

In the following sections, we explain how to complete each of those items and give you some tried and true advice that will help you put your best foot forward.

Choosing a profile image

Your profile image is what people will come to associate with your presence on Facebook. We (and Facebook) suggest using your logo or a company symbol. The image you choose should be recognizable and consistent with the other business branding you do outside of Facebook. By branding yourself consistently across platforms (Facebook, Twitter, your website, and so on), you make it easy for fans and potential fans to recognize your brand and engage with you.

We suggest using an image that is 180 x 180 pixels for your profile image. Facebook will scale it down to 32 x 32 pixels in the News Feed. You can use a larger image, but it may not look as good. Experiment with what you have to see what you like best. As you consider what image to use for your profile picture, remember that you don't have a lot of real estate. Choose something that is easily recognizable (and readable if necessary) when shown in the smaller size.

Figure 1-3 shows some examples of profile images; notice how impactful they are with very little information. The most important thing is for you to choose an image that reinforces the brand you're trying to create and share. You can see how the profile images in Figure 1-3 look when paired with their cover photos here:

✦ For Dummies: `https://www.facebook.com/ForDummies`

✦ Hyperarts: `https://www.facebook.com/HYPERARTS`

✦ Hubspot: `https://www.facebook.com/hubspot`

✦ Blogging Basics 101: `https://www.facebook.com/BloggingBasics101`

Figure 1-3: Smaller profile images that still make an impact.

Before you upload your profile image, check to be sure it matches this criteria:

✦ **Your image should be at least 180 pixels wide.** The largest dimensions a profile image will display at are 180 pixels wide by 180 pixels high. (If your image is larger than 180 x 180 pixels, Facebook will resize it to fit within the display.) It's important that your image is 180 pixels wide (or wider). If it's less than 180 pixels wide, Facebook won't allow you to upload it. If by chance you can upload it, the image Facebook will stretch your image to make it fit the space and you may end up with a distorted picture that looks blurry.

✦ **Your image should not be larger than 4MB.** Remember that smaller files load faster than large ones.

✦ **You must own the rights to the image you use.** If you use an image that you don't own, you risk losing your Fan Page Timeline.

✦ **Your image should be saved as a PNG (.png) file.** These files tend to upload better to Facebook and they have the added bonus of being small files! You can also use .jpg files.

✦ **If you import your image from your website, know the exact URL for the image you want to use.** You can enter the main URL for your site (for example, http://www.domain.com) and Facebook will pull an image from the site. However, this image may not be the one you want to use. To ensure Facebook pulls the correct image, use the image's URL.

To find the URL for an image from your site, right-click the image. Depending on your browser, you have these options:

- *Firefox:* Choose View Image from the menu. A new page appears showing the image. Notice the new URL in your browser's address bar. That's the URL you'll need if you want to import your image to Facebook from your website.

- *Google Chrome:* Choose Copy Image URL from the menu.

- *Internet Explorer:* Click the Properties option to find the image URL.

Uploading an image

If you didn't upload a profile image when you created your page, you can do that any time. When you visit your new Fan Page Timeline, there are several options for installing your profile image. You can choose from photos you've already uploaded to albums (which you probably haven't done yet if your Fan Page Timeline is brand new), take a photo with your webcam, or upload an image from your computer.

To upload an image from your computer, follow these instructions:

1. **Click the Upload an Image link.**

The Upload a Profile Picture dialog box appears.

2. **Click the Browse button.**

3. **Choose the file you want to upload to Facebook.**

4. **Click Open.**

Your image immediately appears as your profile image.

If you'd rather install your profile image via your Fan Page Timeline dashboard, skip ahead to the "Profile Picture tab" section, later in this chapter.

Don't change your profile image frequently. As we note throughout this book, Facebook moves quickly and users scan information instead of reading it thoroughly. Your fans come to associate your profile picture with your updates. When you change the picture, fans may miss your updates because the picture isn't familiar.

Choosing a cover photo

Online, looks are everything. A great design can make or break your success. The more professional your web pages appear, the more authority you're perceived to wield. Your Facebook Fan Page Timeline is no exception. Because your cover photo is likely a visitor's first interaction with your Fan Page Timeline, it can set the tone and expectation of your Fan Page Timeline, as well as reinforce your brand. Figures 1-4 and 1-5 show the cover photos for two of our favorite Fan Pages, Hyperarts and Hubspot, respectively. Notice how the cover image and profile pictures work together. When you first visit the Fan Page Timelines, you have a sense of how things fit together, but when you see the profile image by itself in your News Feed, there is no doubt which page it belongs to.

Figure 1-4: The Hyperarts Fan Page Timeline cover photo and profile picture.

As we mention throughout this book, Facebook likes to focus on the visual impact of content. In that vein, Facebook encourages you to use your cover photo in an aesthetically pleasing way without strong-selling your audience. Although your cover photo is an excellent place to reinforce your brand, Facebook has rules about what you can and can't include in your cover photo. Your cover photo can't have:

- ✦ Calls to action (such as Get it now! or Visit our website!)

- ✦ References to Facebook actions (such as an arrow pointing to the Like button or asking people to share your page with their friends or comment on your posts)

- ✦ Pricing, discounts, or special codes

- ✦ Contact information (including, but not limited to, your or your company's e-mail address, phone number, website address, and physical address — if it's information that would fit under your About section, it doesn't belong in your cover photo)

Be safe: Don't include any of these items in your cover photo unless you're willing to risk Facebook deleting your Fan Page Timeline.

Facebook encourages Fan Page Timeline admins to change out the cover photo as often as you like to keep things interesting for your fans. The actual dimensions for a cover photo are 851 pixels wide and 315 pixels high. You can upload a picture with a minimum width of 399 pixels, but your image will be stretched to fill the 850-pixel space and will likely be distorted.

Figure 1-5:
The Hubspot
Fan Page
Timeline
cover photo
and profile
picture.

Finding and using your dashboard

To find your dashboard, navigate to your Fan Page Timeline. Your Admin panel may or may not be visible to you above your cover photo. If it isn't, click the Admin Panel button in the top-right corner of your Fan Page Timeline to reveal it (see Figure 1-6 for an example of an Admin panel; we explain the admin panel more completely in Book IV, Chapter 2).

Click the Manage button to reveal a drop-down list of options. Choose Edit Page to see your full Fan Page Timeline dashboard. Your dashboard consists of 11 tabs that enable you to manage or customize a specific aspect of your Fan Page Timeline (you may have 12 tabs if you're using Facebook Deals, which we discuss in Book IV, Chapter 4). We explain each tab in the following sections.

**Book IV
Chapter 1**

Creating a Fan Page
Timeline for Your
Business

Figure 1-6:
A Fan Page
Admin
panel.

Your Settings tab

From the Your Settings tab, you can set your posting preferences and your e-mail notifications. When you post on your Fan Page Timeline, you have the option of either posting as your Fan Page (for example, Melanie usually posts as Social Media Basics 101) or yourself (your personal Timeline). Select the Always Comment and Post on Your Page As check box, and all status updates, comments, or other interactions you post on the Fan Page Timeline will appear to come from the Fan Page itself. For example, Melanie posts to the Social Media Basics 101 Fan Page as the Fan Page so all updates appear to be from Social Media Basics 101, not Melanie Nelson. If you don't select the Always Comment and Post on Your Page As check box, then every time you interact with your Fan Page, your comments, status updates, and so on appear to be from your personal Timeline, not the Fan Page Timeline.

One reason you may choose to interact as your Fan Page is that not all your fans know you personally. Some people suggest that because social media is so personal, it's a good idea to interact as yourself. That's a valid point. The bottom line is that you have to figure out what works best for you and your fans, and stick with that. Many businesses strike a compromise by allowing multiple employees to update the Fan Page, setting each post to appear as the brand, but each employee signs the post he or she makes. The result is that fans know the update, comments, and responses are from the brand, but begin to recognize individual employees as well.

Another reason, possibly more important than the previous one, is that if you comment as yourself, your Fan Page may not be as visible in the News Feed — especially if you have your privacy settings as anything other than Public. If your personal Timeline privacy is set to Friends or even Friends of Friends, anyone who isn't connected to you or one of your friends can't see your updates. If you have your personal Timeline set to Public, it's possible that more people will see your update, but that update will look like it's coming from you, not your Fan Page Timeline. We recommend posting to your Fan Page Timeline as your Fan Page, not your personal Timeline, if you want to reach as many of your fans as possible.

If you'd like to receive e-mail notification when someone posts or comments on your Fan Page, select the Send Notifications to *Your E-mail Address* check box. It's handy to have these e-mails sent to you. They ensure that you don't miss comments or updates from fans, and allow you to respond to fans quickly. Keep in mind, though, that sometimes Facebook hiccups and we miss some updates. Check your Fan Page Timeline regularly to ensure you're seeing all your interactions.

Sometimes the e-mail feature doesn't work. When Facebook is making major changes, sometimes certain features are glitchy. If you want a backup plan, sign up with Postling (`https://postling.com`). This service has several features, but the one we've really taken advantage of is the Recaps. Every 24 hours, Postling sends a digest of all the responses you receive on Facebook and Twitter. Postling is a paid tool, but it's only $1 for the first month, then it's $3 per month. Not bad for a back up plan.

Manage Permissions tab

The Manage Permissions tab is your default dashboard tab. Any time you click Manage and then the Edit Page button on your Fan Page Timeline, you go to the Manage Permissions tab on your dashboard. From here, you can do things such as manage restrictions for your Fan Page, determine fans' posting and tagging abilities, control whether fans can send private messages to your Fan Page Timeline, moderate blocklists and profanity, or delete your Fan Page Timeline permanently. Figure 1-7 shows the various options you have on this tab.

Each option on the Manage Permissions tab has a specific action. The following list explains each:

✦ **Page Visibility:** If your Fan Page Timeline isn't quite ready for public consumption, you can select the Unpublish Page (Only Admins Can See This Page) check box to keep it private and visible only to admins. When you're ready to interact with fans and grow your community, you can deselect the check box and your Fan Page is published publicly. The default for new Fan Pages is to publish automatically, so if you want to keep your Fan Page under wraps until you have it just right, be sure to visit this option first.

✦ **Country Restrictions:** If you want to restrict which countries can see and interact on your Fan Page Timeline, type the name of the country in the text box provided. Next, choose whether you want to hide your content from users in these countries or exclude all countries but that one. For instance, if you want to only show your Fan Page Timeline to users in the United States, type **United States** into the text box, and select the Only Show This Page to Viewers in These Countries radio button. However, if you want your Fan Page to be visible to all countries *except* the United States, type **United States** in the text box, but select the Hide This Page from Viewers in These Countries radio button.

✦ **Age Restrictions:** Some products and content are not appropriate for underage users. The drop-down list allows you to choose the age restrictions for your Fan Page Timeline. If you choose Anyone 13+, you're choosing to publish your Fan Page Timeline to everyone using Facebook (except those you may have restricted based on country). If you choose to restrict your Fan Page Timeline to users who are 17+, 18+, 19+, or 21+, then you are only publishing your Fan Page Timeline to Facebook members who are that age or older. If you are creating an alcohol-related Fan Page, you must choose the Alcohol-Related option from the drop-down list. Facebook notes that the Alcohol-Related option sets the restriction for your Fan Page Timeline based on the user's location. For instance, in the USA, your Fan Page Timeline would be restricted to users 21 and over; in Canada, your Fan Page Timeline would be restricted to users 19 and over.

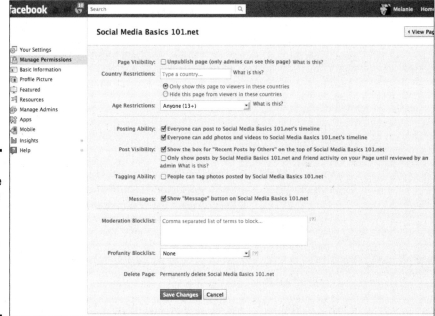

Figure 1-7: The Manage Permissions tab allows you to restrict access to your Fan Page Timeline.

✦ **Posting Ability:** Select (or deselect) the options that fit your needs. We suggest allowing everyone to post to your Timeline and allowing everyone to add photos and video to your Timeline. You may have to remove some comments occasionally, but you're building community. People love to see themselves in print and/or have your attention directed to them. They want to interact with you. Make it easy for them to do so. If you find you're dealing with too much spam, you can change these settings for a while and explain your actions to your fans. They'll appreciate that you're keeping the space professional.

✦ **Post Visibility:** Select (or deselect) the options that fit your needs. If you want your fan's posts, questions, and tags to show up on your Timeline, select the Show check box for Recent Posts by Others. Select the check box next to Only Show Posts by *Fan Page* and Friend Activity on Your Page until Reviewed by an Admin if you don't want posts by fans (and non-fans) to be public until you've approved them via the Activity Log.

✦ **Tagging Ability:** Select this option to allow people to tag themselves in photos you share. We like to allow our fans full access to our Timelines, and that includes tagging themselves. We meet a lot of fans at various conferences and we like to take pictures with them and share those photos on our Timeline. We want to make it easy for those fans to interact with us and tag themselves.

✦ **Messages:** In an effort to make customer service even easier for brands and Facebook users, Facebook allows people (both fans and non-fans) to send a private message to a Fan Page. Select this option to turn the feature on; deselect to turn the feature off. When the feature is on, the Message button appears under your cover photo. When you receive a message, you see a notice in the Messages section of your Admin panel above your cover photo as seen in Figure 1-6 (we discuss the Admin panel in more detail in Book IV, Chapter 2). When you click on the new message, you can type a reply message. Remember that your reply will always appear to be from your Fan Page Timeline, not your personal Timeline, regardless of how you set your Posting Preferences (discussed earlier in this chapter).

✦ **Moderation Blocklist:** If there are specific words you don't want showing up on your Fan Page Timeline, you can type them in the Moderation Blocklist text box. Use a comma to separate words and phrases. Be aware that any comment or post that uses the words listed here will be automatically marked as spam and removed from your Timeline.

✦ **Profanity Blocklist:** You can use this drop-down list to set the profanity filter to None (no filters; it's possible you or your audience will use or see profanity), Medium (mild profanity is not filtered), or Strong (almost no profanity allowed).

✦ **Delete Page:** If you'd like to delete your Fan Page Timeline, click the Delete *PageName* link (refer to Figure 1-7). If you choose to delete your Fan Page Timeline, you have 14 days to restore it. After that, your Fan Page Timeline is permanently deleted. Alternatively, you can choose to simply unpublish it (make it only visible to admins) indefinitely.

Book IV
Chapter 1

Creating a Fan Page
Timeline for Your
Business

Basic Information tab

The material you share on the Basic Information tab appears publicly on the About link of your Fan Page Timeline. As you look at the Basic Information tab, you see that it has many options for sharing information about your company. The options you see are dependent on the category you chose when you created your Fan Page Timeline. Considering there are six main page categories and each of those categories has around 30 sub-categories, it doesn't make sense to try to explain every option possible. However, most Fan Pages have similar options, so we explain the most common and important options in the following list:

✦ **Category:** You can use the two drop-down lists here to change your Fan Page's sub-category and group, respectively. Choosing the correct sub-category and group will help people find your Fan Page Timeline.

✦ **Community Page:** Facebook's generic Community Pages cover just about every topic imaginable, and you can now connect your Fan Page Timeline to those Community Pages. However, we don't see a big value in connecting your Fan Page Timeline to a generic Community Page — your Fan Page Timeline is likely more specific than a generic Community Page, and by providing a link to the generic Community Page, you're giving your readers another way to leave your Fan Page Timeline.

If you decide to connect your Fan Page Timeline to a generic Community Page, you can type a topic related to your Fan Page in the Community Page text box. As you type, you see the Community Page options available in a menu. Select the Community Page you want associated with your Fan Page Timeline. When you click the Save button at the bottom of the page, Facebook puts a link to the Community Page beneath the title of your Fan Page Timeline (visible on the main Fan Page, not your dashboard). Figure 1-8 shows a page with the link.

Figure 1-8:
You can include a link to a related Community Page on your Fan Page Timeline.

Great Golf Getaways

Community Page about Golf

Message

✦ **Username:** When you've accrued 25 fans, you can change your Facebook Fan Page URL from a long, hard-to-remember address to a shorter, easier-to-remember address. We discuss usernames (also called *vanity URLs*) later in this chapter. We want to point out that you don't always need 25 fans before you can claim your username. Sometimes you can claim it immediately after you've created your page; others times you need 25 fans. We wish we had a better answer for you about why that is, but sometimes Facebook doesn't lend itself to easy answers.

You don't have to set your custom URL via the Fan Page dashboard. You may see the option in your Admin Panel (above the cover photo on your Fan Page Timeline) in the Page Tips box, as shown in Figure 1-6.

✦ **About:** The information you provide here shows up on your Fan Page's About Page (you find the link just above your Timeline updates). The About box is a good place to share your website address or a link to your Twitter handle (provide the URL to your Twitter page — `http://twitter.com/`*username* — so your fans can click and connect rather than trying to find you themselves).

Any time you include a web address, be sure to type `http://` as part of it so the link is clickable. Without the `http://` prefix, Facebook doesn't know you're sharing a link, so it won't be clickable. For example, type `http://bloggingbasics101.com` instead of `bloggingbasics 101.com`.

✦ **Company Overview:** Write a paragraph about your company. You could include how you started or your business philosophy. Alternatively, you could include your contact information (e-mail, phone number, Twitter handle, or website address). It's really up to you what you include here.

✦ **Description:** This is another option to include more information about your company, products, or niche. The description doesn't need to be as long as your company overview. In fact, you may not need both a Description and a Company Overview. It's fine to have one or both.

✦ **Products:** You can list your products or services in this text box.

Your Fan Page and its contents are searchable outside of Facebook. We suggest using keywords associated with your company, product, or niche as appropriate in the About, Description, Company Overview, and Products sections. You don't want to *stuff* (overuse certain keywords or include irrelevant keywords) your descriptions with keywords — that's considered bad form. Instead, see how you can use keywords seamlessly with your existing marketing content that you may be reusing here.

✦ **Address, City/Town, Postal Code:** If you have a brick-and-mortar location that customers and fans can physically visit, type in the necessary information. Doing so allows your customers to check into your venue and allows you to set up Facebook Check-In Deals (see Book IV, Chapter 4 for more information).

✦ **E-mail:** Type your e-mail address here. Be aware that this information will be publicly available when fans click the About link. Instead of sharing your personal e-mail address, it's a good idea to create a general e-mail address (info@yourcompany.com or facebook@your company.com).

✦ **Website:** Type the URL of your website in this text box. Remember to type the entire address, including http://.

The information you share on the Basic Information tab in your dashboard shows up on the About Page for your Fan Page Timeline. This information is publicly available — both inside and outside of Facebook.

Profile Picture tab

The Profile Picture tab allows you to manage your profile picture. From here you can Edit your current thumbnail (the image that appears next to your Timeline updates and comments).

To edit your thumbnail, follow these instructions:

1. **Click the Edit Thumbnail link.**

   The Edit Thumbnail window appears. When you move your cursor over the image, notice that the cursor arrow becomes a hand or a cross with arrows at each point.

2. **Click and hold the crop box to drag it to the portion of the image you want to appear as the thumbnail.**

   Alternatively, you can select the Scale to Fit check box. This option shrinks your image to fit within the thumbnail parameters. Be aware that many times shrinking your image makes it unreadable, so this may not be the best option for you.

3. **Click Save.**

You can remove your current profile picture by clicking the Remove Your Picture link under your current profile image. A dialog box appears, asking you to confirm that you want to remove your current image. Click OK if you're sure; click Cancel if you want to keep your image. Your profile image returns to the default gray background with a white question mark. The image you removed is still in your Profile Pictures photo album.

You can change your profile picture by uploading a file from your computer. Just click the Choose File button and select the file you want to upload.

Alternatively, you can take a new photo via your computer's camera and use it. To do that, follow these steps:

1. Click the Take a Picture button.

The Take a Profile Picture window appears and shows an image of what your computer camera sees.

If you see an Adobe Flash Player Settings window, select the Allow radio button. Select the Remember check box if you want Facebook to remember that you've granted permission for it to access your camera and microphone. Click the Close button.

2. Click the camera icon to take a picture.

3. If you're happy with the picture, click the Save button.

If you'd like to re-take your photo, click the camera icon. If you change your mind and don't want to take a photo, click the Cancel button.

Whether you're choosing an image file from your computer or taking a new photo, as soon as you upload the image or save the new photo, that picture immediately becomes the profile image for your Fan Page Timeline.

Featured tab

The Featured tab allows you to showcase specific Fan Pages you have Liked as your Fan Page (see the section in Book IV, Chapter 2 about using Facebook as your Fan Page or Timeline for an explanation of how to Like a Fan Page as your Fan Page — it's not as confusing as it sounds!) and to feature admins of your Fan Page Timeline if you desire.

In general, you can Like as many Fan Pages as you want, and five of those Fan Pages appear randomly on the right side of your Fan Page Timeline, as shown in Figure 1-9.

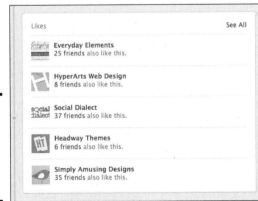

Figure 1-9:
Other Fan
Pages your
Fan Page
Timeline
Likes.

If you'd rather showcase specific Fan Pages instead of a random sampling of all the Fan Pages you Like, you can do that by following these steps:

1. **Click the Edit Featured Likes button.**

   The Edit Featured Likes button window appears with a list of all the Fan Pages you have Liked as your Fan Page.

   If you haven't previously selected other Fan Pages to feature, then you may see the "Add Featured Likes" button. Click that to get to the "Edit Featured Likes" button.

2. **Select the check boxes next to the five Fan Pages you want to showcase.**

3. **Click Save.**

   The Fan Pages you selected now show up in random order each time your Fan Page Timeline is visited or refreshed in the visitor's browser.

The order of the Fan Pages displayed is not static and you can't control that. The Fan Pages will only appear in random rotation.

You may want to share who your admins are with your fans, especially if you're mostly interacting as your brand (your Fan Page) instead of your personal Timeline. By featuring your admins on your About page, any fans visiting your Fan Page Timeline can put a personal face to status updates and comments.

When you feature an admin Timeline, the name is listed on the Fan Page's About page and linked to her Timeline. Visitors (whether they are fans or not) can click that link to view the Timeline and send a friend request to that Timeline. It's important to consider your privacy settings and how you'll respond to friend requests. You are under no obligation to accept requests. If you'd like to keep your Timeline private, you can respond by thanking the fan for the request and explaining that you reserve your personal Timeline for family and friends you've met in real life; if they'd like to connect with you, they can do so on your Fan Page.

Resources tab

The Resources tab lists Facebook resources where you can find answers to many of your questions. You can find links regarding everything from best practices for creating an engaging Fan Page to how to link your Fan Page Timeline with your Twitter account to the general Facebook Help files — and everything in between. (Or you can just keep reading this book. We cover everything you need to know, but it's nice to know Facebook has you covered with links on your dashboard.)

Manage Admins tab

When you want to add someone to your admin list (or delete someone), Manage Admins is the tab you need. To add someone as an admin for your Fan Page, you must first be connected to him on Facebook (in other words, you need to be Facebook friends). When you are friends, you can start typing his name into the provided text box. A list of your friends appears, and you can either finish typing or choose a name from the list. Click Save Changes and you're done! Facebook sends an e-mail to the person you added as an admin to alert him to his new role. We strongly suggest adding at least one other admin to your Fan Page as a security measure. That way, if you are locked out for some reason, you have someone you trust who can reinstate you as an admin.

To remove an admin, simply click the Remove link next to the name of the person you wish to eliminate as admin for your Fan Page Timeline. When you click Save Changes, that person will no longer have administrative privileges for your Fan Page Timeline. If you accidentally click the Remove link, but don't actually want to remove that admin, click Cancel. A dialog box appears, asking if you want to leave this page with unsaved changes. Click Leave this Page. You end up on your Fan Page Timeline, instead of your dashboard, but your admin panel will be intact.

Any admin can delete another admin. Be very careful when choosing who to award admin privileges to.

Apps tab

The Apps tab lists all the applications (or *apps*) you have installed on your Facebook Fan Page. Facebook apps provide additional functionality for a Fan Page. By default, all Fan Page Timelines have the following apps installed and ready to use:

✦ **Photos:** Allows you to upload and share images with your friends and fans. Book II, Chapter 4 provides instructions on how to share and hide photos, as well as sort them into albums.

✦ **Links:** Provides a list of all the links you and your fans have shared on your Fan Page for the last week or so.

✦ **Events:** Allows you to create a special page to promote an event you're hosting. Book II, Chapter 7 explains how to find and create events, as well as explains the etiquette behind Event invitations.

✦ **Notes:** Provides a way for you to write longer posts for your audience. Notes allow limited formatting, and you can include photos with them. It's been rumored that Facebook is phasing out this feature.

✦ **Video:** Enables you to create video messages right from your Fan Page and keep them stored on your Video tab. Find out more about using video with Facebook in Book II, Chapter 4.

Under each app listed on the Apps tab, you see links. Depending on the app, you may see a link for the following options:

✦ **Go to Application:** Click this link to go directly to a page that allows you to choose the settings for your app. These settings vary greatly, depending on the app.

✦ **Edit Settings:** This sparse tab usually has just one or two options and tells you if the app is added as a tab on your Fan Page Timeline or not. If you want to remove an app from your Fan Page Timeline, click the Remove link, and that tab is removed from your main Fan Page navigation, but remains in your list of apps on the dashboard. You aren't deleting the app from your Fan Page Timeline completely, so you can reinstate it later if you desire.

To delete an app from your Fan Page Timeline completely, click the X to the far right of the app. A dialog box appears, asking if you're sure you want to remove this application. Click Remove if you're sure; click Cancel if you want to keep the app. When you remove an app in this manner, it's no longer associated with your Fan Page Timeline. It no longer appears in your Fan Page navigation, nor does it appear in your list of apps. If you want to use it again, you need to reinstall it. (See Book VI, Chapter 3 for instructions on how to install an application on your Fan Page Timeline.)

If the app is not currently active, the Edit Settings window shows Available (Add). Click the Add link to include the app in your Fan Page navigation and make the app live.

Some apps may have another tab besides the Add/Remove option labeled Additional Permission. Click this tab to set any additional permissions for this app. Those permissions generally include what the app has permission to access, but these options vary depending on the app.

✦ **Link to This Tab:** Every app you install becomes a tab on your Fan Page Timeline left navigation list. Each tab has its own URL or *permalink*. This is handy, for instance, if you want to link directly to a Note you shared or want to remind fans about a promotion you're running on your Fan Page Timeline and provide a link directly to the entry form. You can write a status update directing your fans to the link for that tab instead of sending them to your general Timeline and hoping they find what you're referring to. When you click the Link to this Tab link, a dialog box appears with the permalink for that tab.

Don't worry if you don't see a Link to this Tab link under an app. You can still find its permalink. Navigate back to your Fan Page Timeline, look at the App list, and click the app you want to link to. When the new page comes up, copy the URL and paste it wherever you need to place your link (a status update, e-newsletter, your blog, and so on).

Mobile tab

You don't have to have your computer handy to post updates to your Fan Page. You can send status updates via e-mail, mobile web, your smartphone's Facebook application, or text. If you want to sign up for these free options, click the green Sign Up for SMS button in the lower-right corner and follow the instructions in the dialog boxes. Alternatively, you can flip to Book II, Chapter 6 for further instructions and explanations of your mobile Facebook options.

Insights tab

Insights is Facebook's analytics information. From here, you can see how your fans interact with your content, Likes and Unlikes, basic demographic information for your fans, tab views, referrers, and more. We explain Insights thoroughly in Book V, Chapter 3. For now, you can just be aware that your dashboard has a link to your Insights and you can also find a View Insights link on your Fan Page Timeline in the Admin panel above your cover photo.

Help tab

When you click the Help tab in your dashboard, you are directed to the Facebook Help Center page related to Fan Pages. This page provides a list of general topics related to Fan Pages and links so you can ask your own questions, report a bug, or make a suggestion. The left side of this page has links to the main Facebook help topics.

Deals tab

You only see the Deals tab if you've enabled the Deals feature. Deals allow you to reward your loyal fans when they check in to your brick-and-mortar place of business. (See Book IV, Chapter 4 for more about this tab.)

Installing useful apps on your Fan Page Timeline

The ability to install applications is one of our favorite things about Facebook Fan Page Timelines. Applications (often referred to simply as *apps*) offer a level of functionality that you can't get on your personal Timeline. We explain apps further in Book IV, Chapter 5 and building and using apps in Book VI. Here, we introduce you to our favorite general applications for new Facebook Fan Page Timelines:

✦ **A contact form:** Although Facebook offers your audience the option to message you directly, you may want to design your own contact form that collects specific information (for example, their e-mail address, name, or whether they are a returning customer). You can create a contact form via ShortStack (`http://shortstack.com`), Involver (`http://involver.com`), or Appbistro (`http://appbistro.com`).

✦ **E-mail newsletter sign up form:** If you're trying every which way to grow your e-list, here's one more. If people are visiting your Fan Page, they may also see your newsletter sign up and join. Or, because every tab has its own permalink, you can link directly to your newsletter sign up with a strong call to action in your status update. People hate to leave FB, so if you're linking to your sign up that's housed on your Fan Page, that's good. If you're using MailChimp (`http://mailchimp.com`) or Constant Contact (`http://www.constantcontact.com`), they have apps you can install. If you use a different service, contact the help desk and ask if the service has a Facebook application you can install.

Ensuring Your Fan Page Timeline Is Optimized for Search Engines

While personal Timelines are only searchable within Facebook, Fan Pages are searchable both inside and outside of Facebook. Yes, Google and Bing can see your Fan Page Timelines and they are indexing them. What that means is another opportunity to have your business information appear in search results. The key is knowing how to optimize your Fan Page Timeline. The most important place to optimize is your About page, which is populated by the Basic Information tab on your dashboard. (We discuss this tab earlier in the chapter in the "Basic Information tab" section.)

You may already have a fairly strong idea about which keywords are relevant to your business, product, or service and how you can use them on your Facebook Fan Page Timeline. That's great! If you need some help, though, we suggest using the Google Keyword Tool (`http://bit.ly/GoogleKeywordsTool`). This tool, shown in Figure 1-10, allows you to type in keywords to see how many people are actually searching for those terms.

If you're not sure which keywords or search terms you should be using, consider how someone who doesn't know about your business, service, or product would find you. What words or phrases would she type into the search engine to find you? Make a list of those terms and phrases; this will give you a base list to start with. Armed with your list, use your browser to navigate to `http://bit.ly/GoogleKeywordsTool`. This website is the Google Keyword Tool, and it helps generate a list of keywords relevant to your needs. To get started, follow these instructions:

1. **Type your list of keywords inside the Word or Phrase text box.**

Type each phrase or individual keyword on its own line.

2. **Select the Only Show Ideas Closely Related to My Search Terms check box if you want to restrict the type of results returned.**

We suggest trying your search first without selecting this check box, then with selecting the check box. That will give you an idea of how the tool works and whether the ideas returned need to be restricted.

Figure 1-10: The Google Keywords Tool allows you to see which terms people are using to find specific information.

3. **Click the Advanced Options and Filters link if you'd like to search specific countries, include adult ideas, show ideas and statistics for specific devices, or want to filter your keywords.**

   The default options are United States, English, and Devices: Desktops and Laptops. These options are usually sufficient for basic searches.

4. **Click inside the CAPTCHA text box and type the two words you see.**

5. **Click the Search button.**

   The results appear in two sections:

   • *Search terms* shows how often the terms you typed in are being searched (if at all).

   • *Keyword ideas* are terms and phrases Google thinks may be similar to what you asked for and may be good terms or phrases to consider, depending on how often they're being searched for.

Figure 1-11 shows a sample results page.

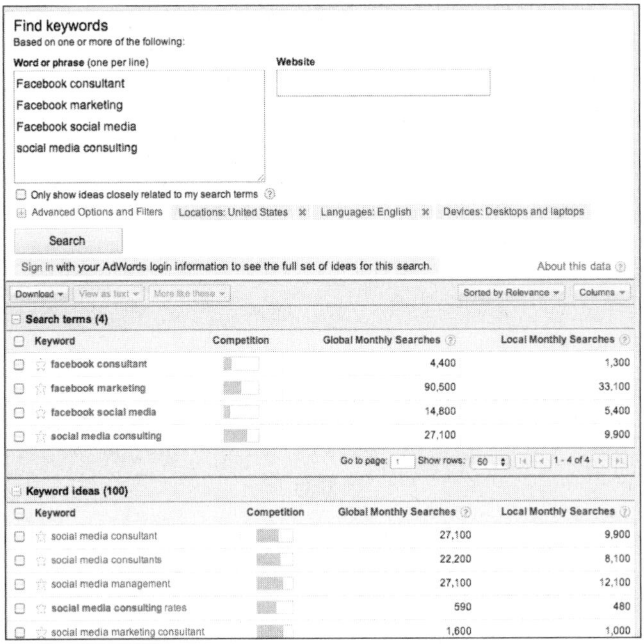

Figure 1-11:
Google
Keyword
Tool results
show how
often a term
or phrased
is searched.

The results of your search are displayed by the following:

✦ **Competition:** This bar shows you how many people are bidding for these keywords to use with Google AdSense (an advertising feature Google offers). The Competition result shows you whether this is a desirable keyword.

✦ **Global Monthly Searches:** This column displays how many times a specific keyword or phrase was searched for all over the world in the last 12 months.

✦ **Local Monthly Searches:** The word *local* here means searches that happened in the country you specified when you began your search. The default country is United States, but you can change that via the Advanced Options and Filters link under the Word or phrase box where you typed your search terms.

Figure 1-11 shows the search terms we used to see how people are searching for Facebook or social media consultants. The keywords we typed used to start the search were

✦ Facebook consultant

✦ Facebook marketing

✦ Facebook social media

✦ Social media consulting

The results show how many people are searching on those terms, but also gives us some ideas of related terms we hadn't considered (and how many people are searching on those terms).

It appears more people are searching for social media related help rather than Facebook-specific help. That tells us if we want to be found, we shouldn't pigeon-hole ourselves as just a Facebook marketing consultant if we want to have the widest reach with the search terms.

The following list provides a few more tips for choosing and using your keywords and phrases:

✦ Any search terms that are searched under 10,000 times are a good choice to use. You won't have as much competition from other sites because most people opt to use terms and phrases that have 50,000 searches or more. The thought is that more searches may bring more visits. Unfortunately, it also means much more competition, and it's hard to appear high on the SERPs (*search engine results pages*) when you're competing with thousands of other sites using the same keywords and phrases.

✦ It's best to use a combination of terms and phrases. You can choose a few high-volume phrases, but focus mostly on your niche phrases that have around 10,000 (or fewer) searches.

✦ Most people don't search for a single keyword, they use a phrase (usually in the form of a question). Try including a question when you do your initial search for terms related to your needs.

✦ Use your keywords and phrases on your Facebook Fan Page Timeline in these key places:

  • Fan Page Timeline title

  • About box

  • Company Overview

  • Description

  • Products

  • Status updates

Choosing a Vanity URL

When you initially create your Facebook Fan Page Timeline, it has a fairly long, ugly URL (or address), for example, `https://www.facebook.com/pages/Blogging-Basics-101/92244347970`. An address like that makes it hard for people to remember how to find you on Facebook. Luckily, as soon as you have 25 fans, you can create a vanity URL. A *vanity URL* is a custom address for your Facebook Fan Page, such as `http://facebook.com/BloggingBasics101`. Although most people refer to these customized URLs as vanity URLs, Facebook calls them *usernames*. Don't let that throw you. The terms are interchangeable. We should point out that you don't always need 25 fans to secure your vanity URL; sometimes you have that option as soon as you create your Fan Page Timeline.

You can also create a vanity URL for your personal Timeline; see Book I, Chapter 2 for more information on how to do that.

We have a few tips to share with you about vanity URLs:

✦ When you create your vanity URL, it's set. If you make a typo or change your mind, you're out of luck. Carefully check your spelling before you click the Save button!

✦ Try to match your vanity URL to your Fan Page Timeline title. People will remember the address much easier if it matches your Fan Page title. However, if the vanity URL you want is taken, it's okay if the title of your Fan Page is a little different from your vanity URL. When people search for your Fan Page Timeline on Facebook, your title is what will count.

✦ Think of at least three vanity URLs for your Fan Page. You may not be able to claim your first choice if someone else is already using that vanity URL.

✦ Facebook does not allow you to use the word *Facebook* in your vanity URL. The company doesn't want you to infringe on any Facebook trademark or imply that you're affiliated with it in any way.

✦ Vanity URLs can only use alphanumeric characters or periods, and can't contain spaces, hyphens, or other special characters — and if you use a period, it can't come at the end of the name.

✦ When a vanity URL is used, no one else can use it. This is true even if the vanity URL is abandoned. The only way to claim a used vanity URL is to prove you own the trademark.

✦ If you have trademarked your company name, but the vanity URL is not available, you can contact Facebook to help you obtain the correct vanity URL. Point your browser to `http://on.fb.me/InfringingUsername` and complete the form. Facebook usually helps you within 48 hours.

You can follow these instructions to create a vanity URL for your Fan Page Timeline:

1. **In your browser, go to** `http://facebook.com/username`.

The Username page appears with two boxes. The top box allows you to create a username (vanity URL) for your personal Timeline; the bottom box allows you to create a username for your Fan Page Timeline.

2. In the bottom box, use the drop-down list to choose the Fan Page Timeline you want to set the vanity URL for.

If you're the admin for more than one Fan Page Timeline, you see each of those Fan Pages listed in the drop-down list. If you are admin for a single Fan Page Timeline, that Fan Page Timeline will be the only one listed.

A text box appears.

3. Type the name you'd like to use for your vanity URL in the text box and click the link to see if it's available.

If the name is available, you can set it; if it's not, you'll need to try another name.

4. When you have a vanity URL you want to use, click the Save button.

You can shorten any Facebook URL even more by replacing `facebook.com` with `fb.com`. For example, `http://facebook.com/BloggingBasics101` becomes `http://fb.com/BloggingBasics101`. This trick comes in handy when you're including your Facebook URL on a business card or other small space!

It may be tempting to link to your website and try to convert your readers into customers when they arrive over there. Our experience is that people interacting within Facebook don't want to leave Facebook and are less likely to click links that take them away. If you think about it, you don't really want your visitors to leave Facebook either. Isn't one of your goals to convince new visitors to Like your Fan Page Timeline? If you're sending them away from Facebook, they may not Like your Fan Page Timeline before they click away. After they've clicked away, it's less likely they'll return to Facebook in the same flow as before, which means they won't be on your Fan Page Timeline, they'll be wherever they want to be on Facebook (probably their own News Feed). You've missed your opportunity for a Like because you pushed the new visitor away from your Fan Page Timeline. Instead of linking away from your Fan Page Timeline, give a specific call to action (such as "Like our Fan Page and receive a free chapter of our book!").

**Book IV
Chapter 1**

Creating a Fan Page Timeline for Your Business

Chapter 2: Touring the Fan Page Timeline Interface

In This Chapter

✔ Understanding how a Fan Page Timeline is laid out

✔ Familiarizing yourself with Fan Page Timeline tools and options

✔ Using Facebook as personal Timeline or Fan Page Timeline

*A*fter you set up your Fan Page Timeline, one of the first things you may notice is that Fan Page Timelines are set up similarly to personal Timelines. The general layout of the page is the same, but the information is geared toward your business. Several of the features of personal Timelines are missing (list of friends, summary of personal information, and so on) but have been replaced with features related to interacting with your fans, your business, tracking your fans (a link to Insights — Facebook's analytics program), and more.

This chapter explains how a Fan Page Timeline differs from a personal Timeline, what each Fan Page Timeline feature does, and how you can use it to manage your Fan Page presence on Facebook.

Reviewing the Parts of a Fan Page Timeline

Your Fan Page Timeline is laid out in sections: the blue Facebook navigation bar at the top of the page, the Admin panel, your cover photo, basic page info, apps, and your Timeline. The following sections explain what is included in each area of the page and how you can use the links and information to manage your Fan Page Timeline. Figure 2-1 shows the important parts of your Fan Page Timeline.

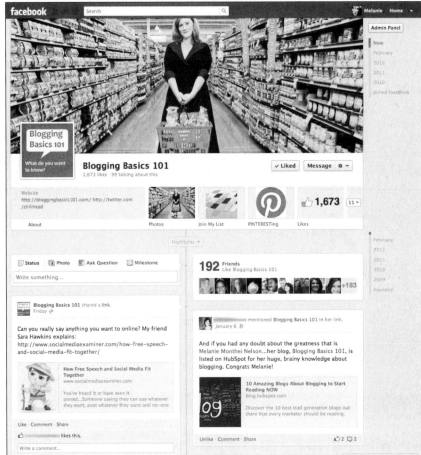

Figure 2-1:
The important parts of your Fan Page Timeline.

Using the Admin Panel

At the top of your Fan Page Timeline, as the Admin, you will see an overview of your Fan Page's admin features (it's not visible to non-admins) as shown in Figure 2-2. This overview is your Admin Panel and allows you to see at a glance what's happening with your Fan Page Timeline.

If you don't automatically see your Admin Panel, click the Admin Panel button to the right of your cover photo. The Admin Panel includes five boxes:

✦ **Notifications:** Shows you a list of the most recent interactions on your Fan Page Timeline. Click See All to see more interactions by date.

✦ **Messages:** Shows you if any of your fans have sent you a private message (and whether you or another admin have replied). Click See All to go to your Messages page, where you can see all the messages your Fan Page Timeline has received.

✦ **New Likes:** Shows you the last four people who have Liked your Fan Page. You can click the See All link to see a list of everyone who currently Likes your Fan Page.

✦ **Insights:** Shows you a glimpse of how your Fan Page Timeline is performing. You can click See All to go to your complete Insights data.

✦ **Page Tips:** Shows tips for using Facebook Fan Page Timelines efficiently. If your Fan Page is new, you may see the Create Username option here (see Book IV, Chapter 1 to find out more about usernames). Click the Next link to see additional tips.

In addition to the five boxes described in the preceding list, you see a toolbar at the top of the Admin Panel with four options: Manage, Build Audience, Help, and Hide. Click each one to manage different aspects of your Fan Page Timeline.

Figure 2-2: The Admin Panel provides an overview of how fans are interacting with your Fan Page.

When you click Manage, a drop-down list appears with options for the following:

✦ **Edit Page:** Click this option to go to your dashboard. We explain the dashboard and its functionality in Book IV, Chapter 1.

✦ **Use Activity Log:** Click this option to go to your Activity Log page, where you can see a list of all the activity on your Fan Page Timeline. The Activity Log for your Fan Page Timeline functions very similarly to the Activity Log for your personal Timeline. This is where you can control how content shows on your Fan Page Timeline — you can choose to allow, highlight, hide, or delete content. You can also report or mark content as spam. To control content, click the circle beside the update you want to manage. Choose how you want to manage the content from the menu, as shown in Figure 2-3.

Figure 2-3:
Use the Activity Log to manage your Fan Page Timeline content.

TIP

You can manage content from the past via your Fan Page Timeline Activity Log. Click the Year button at the top of the page and choose the year you want to see posts from. You can also filter your Activity Log by clicking the All button in the top right corner. Choose your filter from the drop-down list.

✦ **See Banned Users:** Click this option to see a list of the fans you've banned for one reason or another. You can click the Unban button to reinstate a fan's privileges. You can also click the Banned button in the top left of the dialog box to see a list of people who Like your Fan Page, other Fan Pages that have Liked your Fan Page, and people who have administrative rights for your Fan Page Timeline. When you're done, click the Close button.

✦ **Use Facebook as *[Your Fan Page Timeline Name]*:** As we mention earlier in this chapter, you can use Facebook as yourself (your personal Timeline) or as your Fan Page Timeline. We explain that more thoroughly later in this chapter in the section, "Using Facebook as Your Fan Page Timeline or Personal Timeline."

When you click Build Audience, a drop-down list appears with options for the following:

✦ **Invite Email Contacts:** Allows you to find friends and contacts via various e-mail clients (such as Yahoo! and Hotmail), as well as Skype and other tools. Just click the Find Friends link next to the software client you want to use and follow the directions.

✦ **Invite Friends:** Lets you invite specific people to Like your Fan Page. When you click Invite Friends, the Suggest *[Your Page Name]* dialog box appears. Use the drop-down list in the top-left corner to target specific people for invitation. You can also type a name in the text box. Click Submit when you're done.

✦ **Share Page:** Allows you to share your Fan Page Timeline on your personal Timeline, a friend's Timeline, in a group, another Fan Page you admin, or via private message. Type a quick status update introducing your Fan Page Timeline or giving context about why you're sharing the page (a call to action — Like our Fan Page so you never miss another sale! — works well here) and click the Share Page button.

✦ **Create an Ad:** Allows you to create a Facebook ad that may help introduce your Fan Page Timeline to more fans. We explain how to craft a Facebook Ad in Book V, Chapter 5.

When you click Help, a drop-down list appears with options for the following:

✦ **Visit Help Center:** Takes you to the Facebook Help files. We explain how to use these files to find the answers you're looking for in Book I, Chapter 5.

✦ **Take the Tour:** Uses your own Fan Page to help you understand the features of Fan Page Timelines. It's a quick way to familiarize yourself with the options you have for sharing, viewing, and managing your Fan Page Timeline content.

✦ **Pages Product Guide:** Shows a PDF that explains the features of Fan Page Timelines. The guide includes a getting started checklist and tips for using Timeline to optimize community engagement.

✦ **Learning Video:** Takes you to a video tutorial about the features of your new Fan Page Timeline and how it differs from previous Fan Page designs. This video is helpful if you're just getting started.

✦ **Send Feedback:** Allows you to tell Facebook your thoughts about Fan Page Timelines. When you click the Send Feedback link, the Your Feedback about Pages page appears. Answer the questions and type your feedback as required. You even have the option to attach a screenshot to further explain your feedback or issue. Click the Send button when you're done.

Click the Hide button to hide your Admin Panel and bring your cover photo to the top of the page. Remember that only admins can see the Admin Panel, so you don't have to hide it unless you just like a less cluttered look.

Understanding the importance of your cover photo and profile picture

Just like on your personal Timeline, your Fan Page Timeline also has a profile picture and a cover photo. These two images should work together to reinforce your brand, product, or business to your audience. We love the way HubSpot (`http://fb.com/Hubspot`) uses its cover photo and profile picture, as shown in Figure 2-4.

Figure 2-4:
HubSpot uses both the cover photo and the profile picture to reinforce its brand.

Both pictures work together to convey the HubSpot brand. The cover photo makes use of the large space, is visually appealing, and highlights HubSpot's logo (which is repeated in the profile picture). The profile picture is easily recognizable in the News Feed and uses the HubSpot logo so fans can quickly scan and find updates from HubSpot.

We recommend using a strongly branded image as your profile image (the smaller image) because this image is attached to all updates and comments you make while using your Fan Page Timeline. Don't change your profile picture regularly, unless that's part of your business's image. Your fans will appreciate having a standard picture to associate with your business. In social media outlets such as Facebook and even Twitter, your fans' streams move quickly, and they often scan that stream rather than read it word for word. A static, strong profile image becomes familiar to your fans and helps them quickly find your updates.

Your cover photo, on the other hand, can change as needed. In fact, Facebook encourages you to change it regularly and use it as a means of engaging your fans and bringing them back to your Fan Page Timeline. Remember, though, there are restrictions on what you can show in your cover photo. Facebook doesn't want you to use your cover photo space for promotions, discounts, or ads. We advise you on creating and choosing your cover photo in Book IV, Chapter 1.

The actual dimensions for a cover photo are 851 pixels wide x 315 pixels high. You can upload a picture with a minimum width of 399 pixels, but your image will be stretched to fill the 851-pixel space and will likely be distorted.

Utilizing the basic page info section

Under the cover photo, you see some basic information about your Fan Page (see Figure 2-4). This basic information serves as an overview of your Fan Page Timeline, as well as provides basic navigation to sending private messages, your installed apps, and more.

The basic page information includes the following:

✦ **The title of your Fan Page Timeline.** You determined the title when you created your Fan Page.

✦ **Your Number of Likes** is a public display of how many fans, or *Likes*, your Fan Page has. This number only counts individuals (that is, personal Timelines) that have Liked your Fan Page. If another Fan Page Likes yours, that Like doesn't count toward your total number of Likes. We explain how to create community and grow your fan base throughout Book IV, but particularly in Book IV, Chapter 3.

✦ **The Number of People Talking about This** is the number of interactions your Fan Page Timeline content has had within the last seven days. These interactions include Likes, comments, shares, poll/question answers, mentions in other status updates, tags, venue check ins, and so on. You won't see a Talking about This number if you haven't had any interactions on your Fan Page Timeline within the last week.

✦ **The Like button** allows you to become a fan of a Fan Page. You see the Like button only if you aren't currently a fan of the Fan Page you're viewing (if you're already a fan, the button says Liked). If you want to see the Fan Page Timeline's updates in your News Feed and support the brand, click the Like button and become a fan of the Fan Page.

✦ **The Message button** allows fans and nonfans to send the admin(s) of a Fan Page Timeline a private message. If you turned off this option in your dashboard, you (and your fans) won't see this button. See Book IV, Chapter 1 for instructions on how to implement the Message button. We encourage you to keep this feature turned on because it allows customers to contact you directly if they have an issue rather than sharing their comments publicly on the Timeline.

In order to answer your Messages, you must be using Facebook as your Fan Page Timeline or have your dashboard settings so that you always post as your Fan Page Timeline on your Fan Page Timeline. To do that, go to your dashboard (Admin Panel⇨Manage⇨Edit Page), choose Your Settings from the left navigation, and select Always Comment and Post on Your Fan Page as *[Your Fan Page Name]*, Even When Using Facebook as *[Your Timeline]*. When you reply to fan and nonfan private messages, your response appears to be from your Fan Page Timeline, not you personally.

✦ **The Quick Settings icon** (it looks like a gear) provides a drop-down list with items dependent on your relationship to the page. For instance, if you're the admin for the page, you see options fans and nonfans won't. When you visit someone else's Fan Page Timeline, whether as a fan or nonfan, you see a different set of options. The options include quick access to the following:

• *Promote with an Ad:* Only admins can see this option. Click this option to set up a Facebook ad. We explain the process of creating ads in Book V, Chapter 5.

• *Send Feedback:* Everyone can see this option. You can contact Facebook about an issue you're having or suggestions you have.

• *Visit Help Center:* Only admins can see this option. If you have a question about how to use Facebook (either for your personal Timeline or your Fan Page Timeline), the Help Center is the place to start. You can find more information about the Help Center in Book I, Chapter 5.

• *Share:* Both fans and admins see this option. Any time you come across a Page that shares interesting content, it's easy to let your friends know about it. Click Share to post an update on your personal Timeline, on a friend's Timeline, to a group, or directly to your Fan Page Timeline, depending on which audience you want to share with. You can also share the link via private message.

• *Unlike:* You see this option if you already Like a Fan Page. Sometimes you think a Fan Page is a fit and it isn't. No problem. You can click Unlike, and you'll stop receiving updates from the Fan Page Timeline. The Fan Page admin can't tell who Unliked the Fan Page.

• *View Insights:* Only admins see this option. Insights is Facebook's analytics program. A quick glance at your Insights page shows you how many active users you have and whether your interactions are up, down, or holding steady. Flip to Book V, Chapter 3 for information about how to use Insights and interpret your Facebook analytics.

• *Add to My Page's Favorites:* Everyone sees this option and it does just what it says it will. When you click this link, you can add the current Fan Page to your own Fan Page's favorites, and it will appear under Likes on the right side of your Timeline. This may be a Facebook glitch, but you can add a Fan Page to your favorites without Liking the Fan Page. If this link doesn't show up for you, then you've probably already added the Fan Page as a favorite. See Book IV, Chapter 1 for instructions on how to feature specific Fan Page Timelines in your Like section.

• *Remove from My Page's Favorites:* Everyone can see this option. Not feeling the love anymore? No problem. Go to the Fan Page Timeline you want to remove from your favorites and click this link. The Fan Page no longer appears in your list of Likes in your Timeline.

- *Report Page:* This link is visible only if you are not the admin of a Fan Page (because you wouldn't report your own Fan Page, would you?). If you aren't the admin of the Fan Page, you can see this link whether you Like the Fan Page or not. Click this link if you want to report a Fan Page as sharing inappropriate content. When you click the link, a dialog box appears with a list of violations. Select the radio button next to the Fan Page's infraction. You can choose from Spam or Scam, Hate Speech or Personal Attack, Violence or Harmful Behavior, Sexually Explicit Content, or Duplicate or Miscategorized Page.

  The options for reporting a Fan Page change, depending on the type of Fan Page it is. For example, a Fan Page Timeline for a business with a physical location has options to mark the Fan Page as not a public place, event at another place, permanently closed, or other/abusive content, yet you don't have the options to report the Fan Page Timeline for violence, hate speech, or sexually explicit content.

  You also have the option of reporting theft of your intellectual property. To do that, click the Is This Your Intellectual Property? link in the bottom-left corner of the dialog box. The Facebook instructions for reporting infringement claims appear.

✦ **An information box** that pulls relevant information from the Basic Information tab on your dashboard (this information is dependent on the categories you chose when you set up your Fan Page Timeline). We suggest providing a link to your website and your Twitter page if you have one. Doing so allows your fans to quickly see where else they can connect with you.

  To create a usable link, be sure to include http:// with any URLs you share in this box. For example, if you type **Shop our online store at happyfirst.com**, that link won't be clickable. You can fix that by typing **Shop our online store at** `http://happyfirst.com`.

✦ **The About link** takes you to the About page, which displays the information you shared in the Basic Information tab on your dashboard (see Book IV, Chapter 1 for more information). Your fans will generally click this link if they are looking for store hours, directions, or more information about your company. Be sure you've provided the information your fans are looking for.

  In Book IV, Chapter 1, we explain each tab of your Fan Page Timeline dashboard. One of those tabs is the Featured tab. From there you can choose to feature the admins of your Fan Page. If you do so, the featured admins appear on the About page for your Fan Page Timeline.

  When you feature admins, their personal Timelines are listed as links on your Fan Page Timeline's About page. In addition, the Fan Page Timeline that lists the featured admins also appears on that person's personal Timeline in the About section.

✦ **A list of apps installed** on your Fan Page Timeline (we discuss apps more thoroughly in the next section).

Understanding the apps navigation

Apps aren't actually labeled as such. If you refer to Figure 2-1, you see four pictures under the cover photo. These pictures depict apps installed on the page to enhance its functionality.

You can have many, many apps installed on your Fan Page Timeline: a newsletter sign-up, a contact form, links to downloadable content, custom applications . . . the options are endless. Facebook displays apps in rows of four, and by default only the first row is displayed. Users can click the small number at the end of the row (the number at the end of the row indicates how many more apps are hidden) to expand the apps box to show more rows of apps (up to 12), as shown in Figure 2-5.

As the admin of a Fan Page Timeline, you can see all your apps when you expand the apps box — you aren't limited to seeing the top 12. It's also worth noting that just because your audience can't see an app doesn't mean it isn't live. You can install more than 12 apps and they'll still work; your audience just won't see them.

You can choose the order in which your apps are displayed. The only exception is that the Photos app must always appear first; you can't move it. That means you really only have space to showcase three apps on the first row of apps under your cover photo. We suggest showcasing your most important apps (such as your newsletter sign up) in the first row of displayed apps so they aren't overlooked.

The Photos app is populated by the images you upload to your Fan Page Timeline and photo albums. For more information on how to add and delete photos to your Timeline, flip to Book II, Chapter 3.

You can display up to 12 apps to your audience. However, two of those apps are dictated by Facebook: Photos and Likes. The Photos app will always appear as the first app in the first row. The Likes app, on the other hand, can be moved around to any position in the 12 displayed apps.

Figure 2-5:
You can showcase up to 12 apps on your Fan Page Timeline.

To change the order of your displayed apps, follow these instructions:

1. **Navigate to your Fan Page Timeline and click the arrow to expose a full list of your apps.**

2. **Move your mouse over the app you want to edit and click the pencil icon.**

   A drop-down list appears. At the top of the list you see Swap Positions With and the apps available to swap positions.

3. **Choose the app to swap positions with.**

   The apps swap positions and you're done. You can continue to tweak the order of your apps until you're satisfied.

You can create and display your own images for each app. To do that, you need to create an image that is 111 pixels wide x 74 pixels tall. Although you're restricted from having specific calls to action in your cover photos (see Book IV, Chapter 1 for a list of cover photo rules), you can have them in your app images. For example, if you want people to sign up for your newsletter, create an image that reads Join Our Newsletter! We're sure you can come up with many creative ideas for customized application images.

When you have your image ready to install, follow these steps:

1. **Navigate to your Fan Page Timeline and click the arrow to expose a full list of your apps.**

2. **Move your mouse over the app you want to edit and click the pencil icon.**

   A drop-down list appears.

3. **Choose Edit Settings from the list.**

   A dialog box appears with several options.

4. **Click the Change link next to Custom Tab Image.**

   The Upload a Custom Image page appears.

5. **Click the Change link and upload your new image.**

   Facebook takes you back to the Upload a Custom Image page. This may be a little confusing because there's no Save button and no button to click to get back to your Fan Page Timeline. Don't worry, your changes were saved and implemented.

6. **Navigate back to your Fan Page Timeline and check out your new app image.**

Each application tab link has its own URL. That's a great feature because you can write a status update with a call to action and provide a link to complete the action. For example, if you want to remind fans to sign up for your e-newsletter, you can share a status update like this:

> Sign up for our monthly newsletter to receive exclusive discounts and coupons! `https://www.facebook.com/BloggingBasics101?sk=app_197602066931325`

Note that the link above takes the reader directly to the newsletter sign up tab on the Fan Page Timeline.

When you click any app, you go to a new page with that app's functionality. For example, if you click the newsletter sign-up app or the link from the previous example, you leave the Fan Page Timeline and end up on a page with the newsletter sign-up form. As you plan to design your application landing page, it's helpful to know that the page is 810 pixels wide. That's a lot of screen real estate, and you can create some pretty snazzy stuff with third-party application builders such as ShortStack, North Social, Offerpop, Lujure, and WizeHive.

Using Your Timeline

The Timeline portion of your Fan Page houses the main functionality — status updates and community interaction. This is where you interact with your fans and they interact with you.

Just like on your personal Timeline, your Fan Page Timeline has a line down the middle and information on the right and left sides. On your Fan Page Timeline, though, the top of the right side shows what other people are saying about your Fan Page Timeline, Friend Activity, and Likes (the other Fan Pages you've Liked as your Fan Page Timeline).

Timeline is an opportunity for you to tell the story behind your business. Since you can add new updates and assign them to a specific year, you're able to start with your first product sold and mark each milestone throughout your business history. Two companies that take advantage this opportunity nicely are Red Bull (`https://www.facebook.com/redbull`) and Fanta (`https://www.facebook.com/fanta`). Each gives a complete history of their growth with fun pictures and interesting facts.

You (and your fans) can filter the content on the Timeline by clicking the drop-down list under Basic Fan Page info, as shown in Figure 2-6.

Figure 2-6:
Filter the
content
on any
Fan Page
Timeline
using the
Filter list.

The list choices are self-explanatory. When you click a choice, the Timeline shows only posts highlighted by the Fan Page Timeline owners (these are usually milestones, but can be any highlighted content), activity by friends (those users on Facebook who are connected to both you and the Fan Page), posts by the Fan Page Timeline (these are usually general status updates), or posts by others (anyone who has interacted with the Fan Page Timeline — whether as a fan or not).

The following sections explain each Timeline component.

Status Update text box

At the top left of your Timeline, you see the Status Update text box. Just like with your personal Timeline, the Status Update text box is where you type and share your status updates for your Fan Page Timeline. Your Fan Page Timeline status update options include:

✦ **Status:** This option allows you to type a status update.

✦ **Photo:** Click this option to upload a photo from your computer, take a photo with your webcam, or create an album. See Book II, Chapter 3 for instructions and advice about using photos on Facebook. You can also use this option to upload or take video. See Book II, Chapter 4 for instructions and advice about using video with Facebook.

✦ **Ask Question:** This option only appears if you're using Facebook as your Fan Page Timeline (which we talk about later in this chapter) or if you've customized your Fan Page Timeline dashboard settings to always post as the Page (see Book IV, Chapter 1 for more information). Ask Question is a polling feature that allows you to ask your fans a question and choose an answer. To create a Question, follow these instructions:

1. *Click the Question option.*

   A text box appears.

2. *Type your question in the text box.*

3. *Click the Add Poll Options link in the bottom-left corner.*

   Text boxes appear under the heading Poll Options.

4. *Type the choices (answers) you want your fans to choose from.*

   Type one choice per text box.

5. *Select or deselect the Allow Anyone to Add Options check box.*

   Selecting this option allows anyone to add an answer to the poll; deselecting this option ensures your poll is limited to the choices you originally provided in Step 4.

6. *Click the Ask Question button to share your Question publicly.*

✦ **Milestone:** This option only appears if you are using Facebook as your Fan Page Timeline (which we talk about later in this chapter) or if you've customized your Fan Page Timeline dashboard settings to always post as the Page (see Book IV, Chapter 1 for more information). The milestone option allows you to create date-specific updates relating to major milestones for your business. When you click Milestone the first time, you see the When Did Your Page Begin dialog box, and you must create a milestone for when your business or product was founded (see Figure 2-7).

You can't create a milestone if you're trying to post to your Fan Page Timeline as your personal Timeline. The easiest way to get around that is to visit the Your Settings tab on your Fan Page Timeline dashboard (we talk about it extensively in Book IV, Chapter 1) and select Always Comment and Post on Your Fan Page as *[Your Fan Page Name]*, Even when Using Facebook as *[Your Timeline]*.

Figure 2-7:
Create a
Milestone
for when
your
business,
product,
or service
began.

Targeting your updates

You may find that some updates aren't relevant to your entire audience. In those cases, you can customize who sees your updates. To do that, follow these instructions:

1. **Type your status update as you normally do.**

2. **Click the Public button under the Status Updates text box, as shown in Figure 2-8, and choose Location/Language.**

The Choose Your Audience window appears.

3. **Type a country name into the Location text box.**

   New choices appear below the Location text box. The choices are dependent on which country you enter and may include Everywhere, By State/Province, and By City.

4. **Select the radio button next to the option you'd like to target.**

   If you select By State/Province or By City, a new text box appears. Enter the state, province, or city here.

5. **(Optional) Type a language in the Language text box.**

   You can target a specific country, state/province, or city without specifying a language. You can also target a specific language without specifying a specific country, state/province, or city.

6. **Click OK.**

   You're returned to your original status update.

7. **Click the Share button.**

   Your post is shared only with fans who meet the criteria of your customization.

Creating a milestone update

With the When Did Your Page Begin dialog box open, follow these instructions to create your first Milestone:

1. **Use the Date drop-down list to choose the year your business, product, or service was founded.**

2. **Click the Start Type drop-down list and choose the best options for your Fan Page Timeline.**

You can choose from *[Your Fan Page Name]* was born, founded, started, or opened.

3. **Click Save, and your Timeline is updated with your new milestone.**

If you'd like to add another milestone (either now or later), click the Milestone option in the Status Update text box, and this time, you see the Milestone dialog box shown in Figure 2-9.

Figure 2-9:
Use the
Milestone
box to create
and highlight
important
updates
to your
Fan Page
Timeline.

With the Milestone dialog box open, follow these steps to create a new milestone:

1. **Type the name of the milestone in the Event text box.**

2. **(Optional) Type the location of the event into the Location text box.**

3. **Use the When drop-down list to choose a year for your milestone.**

4. **(Optional) Click the +Add month link if you want to include the month.**

If you choose to add a month, Facebook then gives you the option to add a specific date to your milestone.

5. **(Optional) Click the +Add Day link to include a specific date for your milestone.**

6. **(Optional) Select the Hide from News Feed check box if you don't want this milestone to be public.**

7. **(Optional) Click Upload Photo to add a photo to your milestone.**

You can either choose from photos you've uploaded to your Fan Page Timeline's photo albums or you can upload a new photo from your computer.

8. **Click Save to complete your milestone.**

When you create a milestone, it spans both the left and right columns of the Timeline, as shown in Figure 2-10.

Figure 2-10: A milestone is larger than a regular update.

Because milestones take up more screen real estate, they are fairly obvious to your audience. You can really make milestones pop by including relevant and interesting images with them.

Editing updates and milestones

You can edit a milestone or status update by moving your cursor over the story until the star and pencil icons appear. Click the pencil icon to the story. From here you can choose from the following:

✦ **Pin to Top:** Pin a story to the top of your Timeline for seven days. Facebook limits the time to seven days to encourage Fan Page Timelines to create new content at least each week. After seven days, the story returns to its dated place on the Timeline. Pinning a story to the top of your Timeline helps draw attention to it and ensures that it's not buried as you create new updates throughout the week. For example, if you're hosting a giveaway on Facebook or offering a special discount to new fans, you may want to pin the post with that special information to the top of your Timeline so it's easily viewed by everyone who visits. If you don't pin the story to the top of your Timeline, it will move down the Timeline each time you post a new story.

One of the best ways to get the most out of a pinned post is to use a strong call to action in your update, and then provide the means to complete that action (such as including the link to a specific page).

✦ **Change Date:** This option appears only for regular status updates, not milestones. When you click this option, the Change Date dialog box appears, and you can change the year, month, and date of the story.

✦ **Edit:** This option appears if you're editing a milestone. When you choose this option, you can change the milestone's event title, location, date, or story text. You can also add or delete an image.

✦ **Hide from Page:** Hide your story or milestone from the Timeline.

✦ **Delete:** Delete your story or milestone from the Timeline.

✦ **Report Story/Mark as Spam:** The title of this option depends on whether you're editing a regular story or a milestone. Use this option to tell Facebook if a story is violating the Facebook Terms of Service (TOS) or if your intellectual property is being used by someone else. We think it's odd that this would be an option for your own stories, because you're unlikely to report your own milestone for a TOS infringement. It's possible that by the time you see this book, this option will have disappeared.

If you want to make a regular update into a milestone, you can highlight it. To highlight a story, move your cursor over the story and click the star icon. The story is now a milestone and appears larger on the Timeline. If you want to unhighlight a milestone, click the star icon again, and the story becomes a regular update. If you choose to unhighlight a story (milestone), it doesn't disappear, but it shrinks to the size of a regular update.

Finding Friends who Like this Page

When you visit a Fan Page Timeline, at the top right of the Timeline is a list of your friends that also Like that Fan Page Timeline. The purpose of this is to provide *social proof.* In other words, the hope is that if you see that your friends Like a brand, then you'll take that as an endorsement and also Like the brand. We discuss the idea of social proof and how it works with Facebook throughout this book as a whole. Facebook and businesses both realize the power of word-of-mouth, and they take full advantage of it by reminding you that your friends are on board — and encourage you to come on board too.

Finding Friend Activity

Just under the Friends who Like this Page box is Friend Activity, as shown in Figure 2-11. Any time you visit a Fan Page Timeline that one of your friends has talked about or tagged in an update, that activity shows here. It's a form of social proof — when you see that your friends are talking about the product, you're more likely to take it as a recommendation and also Like the Fan Page.

Figure 2-11:
Friend
Activity
shows
how your
friends have
interacted
with a
Fan Page
Timeline.

The Friend Activity you see is specific to you and is seen by fans and nonfans alike. What's interesting is that the updates that appear in Friend Activity don't have to have actually tagged the Fan Page Timeline in the update — simply mentioning the name of the product is enough to have the update show on the Fan Page Timeline. If you notice in Figure 2-11, Melanie's friend didn't tag the Fanta Fan Page Timeline, he just mentioned the company in the context of a video he was sharing. When Melanie clicked over to the Fanta Fan Page Timeline, she saw his update in the Friend Activity section. As the Page admin, you can't control this portion of your Fan Page Timeline.

Finding Recent Posts by Others

When a fan or nonfan posts on a Fan Page Timeline, those posts show up in the Recent Posts by Others box. Since these comments don't show up in the main Timeline as individual updates, it can be difficult for Page admins to see at a glance who has posted a question or comment directly to the Timeline. We suggest using your Admin Panel to see new interactions. To address those interactions, click on the action and you go directly to that update so you can respond.

Use your Fan Page Timeline dashboard to control whether the Recent Post by Others box appears on your Fan Page Timeline.

Reviewing Liked Pages

Just as you can Like a Fan Page as yourself (your personal Timeline), you can also like other Fan Page Timelines as your Fan Page Timeline. Any Pages you Like when you're using Facebook with your Fan Page Timeline will show up in the Likes area. If you Like more than five Fan Page Timelines, the pages displayed will rotate each time the page is refreshed. You can control which Pages are displayed by going to your Admin Panel at the top of your Fan Page Timeline and clicking Manage, and then choosing Edit Page. When your dashboard appears, click Featured in the left navigation, and then click the Edit Featured Likes button. Use the list to choose the five Pages you want to feature. When you assign featured Pages, those five Pages are displayed in a random order each time the page is refreshed. Other Pages you've Liked do not show up.

Managing third-party posts

Most Fan Page Timelines allow their fans and other Pages to share information on the Timeline. The idea is that an open community is an inviting community. Usually people are respectful and are truly interested in engaging with your brand. Sometimes, though, you'll find a spammy or otherwise inappropriate update or comment. You can manage third-party Timeline updates by moving your cursor over the update or comment you want to address and clicking the X to the right of it. When you click the X, you see the following options (which are dependent on whether you're looking at a comment or post):

✦ **Delete Comment:** This option is available for comments. When you choose to delete a comment, the Delete Comment dialog box appears with three options: Delete, Delete and Ban User, and Cancel. If you choose to Delete and Ban User, the person who posted the comment won't be able to interact with your Fan Page Timeline again. When you choose this option, a warning appears, asking if you're sure you want to delete the post and permanently block the person or Fan Page Timeline from posting to your Timeline. If you're sure, click Remove Post and Ban Page (User).

✦ **Hidden from Page/Hide Post:** The title for hiding a story depends on whether you're hiding a comment (Hidden from Page) or post (Hide Post). When you choose to hide a comment or post, you are marking it as spam, and it will no longer appear on your Fan Page Timeline. However, because you are the admin for the Fan Page Timeline, you can still see the comment or post as grayed out (see Figure 2-12).

If you want to reinstate a comment or update, you can move your cursor over the story and click the X next to it. Choose Unhide Post from the list. The comment or update re-appears on your Timeline. Or you can go to your Activity Log and use the filter in the top right corner to show either Comments or Posts by Others. On the page that appears, find the post or comment you want to reinstate and click the icon at the far right. Choose the option you want from the list.

Figure 2-12:
An example of a hidden comment on a Fan Page Timeline.

Hidden comment

✦ **Report as Abuse:** This option is available for comments. When you choose this option you can report a comment to Facebook as being harassment of you or a friend, or as a violation of the Facebook Terms of Service (you need to select which item the comment relates to). Choosing this option brings up a menu with the following types of reports:

- Spam or Scam

- Hate Speech or Personal Attack

- Violence or Harmful Behavior

- Sexually Explicit Content

Select the radio button next to the correct violation and click Submit. The person or page you reported is not told they were reported or who reported them.

When you report an item as abuse, you alert Facebook that you don't agree with the content. However, Facebook doesn't always take action because the content may not violate the Facebook Community Standards (https://fb.com/communitystandards).

✦ **Default (Allowed):** This option is available for posts. Facebook allows anyone to write on your Timeline, whether they are a fan or nonfan. The default for these posts is Allowed.

✦ **Highlighted on Page:** This option is available for posts. If you want to highlight a post by a fan or nonfan, choose this option. The post will appear as a milestone (spanning both the right and left columns of your Timeline). You may want to highlight a post if it's a particularly glowing accolade of your business, product, or service.

✦ **Allowed on Page:** This option is for Timeline posts by a fan (or nonfan).

✦ **Delete Post:** This option is for Timeline posts by a fan (or nonfan). This option allows you to remove the post from your Timeline completely. The post isn't hidden, it's completely removed and you cannot reinstate it.

✦ **Report/Mark as Spam:** This option is for Timeline posts by a fan (or nonfan). When you mark a post as spam, you remove it from your Timeline. To reinstate a post (unmark it as spam), visit your Activity Log and use the filter in the top-right corner to show your spam. Click the icon to the far right of the post and choose either Delete Post or Unmark as Spam from the list. If you want to completely delete the post, click the icon and choose Delete Post. The Delete Post dialog box appears and you have three choices: Delete, Delete and Ban User, and Cancel. If you choose to Delete and Ban User, the person who posted can't interact with your Fan Page Timeline again. When you choose this option, a warning appears, asking if you're sure you want to delete the post and permanently block the person or Fan Page Timeline from posting to your Timeline. If you're sure, click Remove Post and Ban Page (User).

To make it easier on you and your fans, create a set of posting guidelines for your Page. Explain exactly what is and isn't appropriate for others to post to your Timeline and what the consequence will be if the guidelines are ignored. Remember, you want to build community and encourage others to share and discuss, but this is still your Page and you can set the expectations here. If you have clear guidelines available and occasionally remind your fans where to find them, you may be able to stem some uncomfortable situations. PETCO shares rules on their Info tab about what is and isn't appropriate to post. You can see it in action at `https://www.facebook.com/PETCO?sk=info`.

Reviewing the Right Column Navigation

The right side of your Fan Page Timeline has two items: a navigation button and a clickable list of years. At the top right of any Fan Page Timeline is a button that changes depending on whether you're an admin or not. If you're an admin, you see an Admin Panel button that unhides your Admin Panel. If you're not an admin, you see the Create a Page button that takes you to the main page for creating your own Fan Page Timeline.

Below the button is a list of years associated with posts from the Fan Page Timeline. The number of years (and which years) listed will depend entirely on how the Fan Page Timeline has updated its Timeline. As we discuss earlier in this chapter, it's possible (and encouraged) to create stories associated with years that predate Facebook (again, see the Fanta page at `http://fb.com/Fanta` and see how it updated its Timeline to reach as far back as the 1950s).

Using Facebook as Your Fan Page Timeline or Personal Timeline

Many times in real life, people have both personal and professional relationships. Sometimes those relationships overlap; sometimes they are unrelated. The same is true on Facebook. You may choose to keep your personal Timeline focused on friends, family, and a few colleagues, and use your Fan Page Timeline to connect with other businesses and interact with your customers as your business.

Because your personal Timeline and your Fan Page Timeline are separate but connected, the Facebook folks thought it would be a good idea to give you the choice of how you'd like to interact on Facebook and your Fan Page Timeline — either as yourself (your personal Timeline) or as your brand (your Fan Page Timeline). That means you have the option to post comments to other Fan Page Timelines either as yourself or as your Fan Page Timeline! The idea of switching back and forth between Timelines may be confusing at first, but after you get the hang of it, you'll see how useful this feature can be.

Both your personal and Fan Page Timelines are connected to you. When you use Facebook as your personal Timeline, the people and Pages you interact with see the image and name associated with your personal Timeline (such as Melanie Nelson). When you use Facebook as your Fan Page Timeline, the people and pages you interact with see the image and name associated with your Fan Page Timeline (such as Blogging Basics 101).

You can use Facebook as either your personal Timeline or your Fan Page Timeline, depending on what you want to accomplish. Table 2-1 shows how your personal and Fan Page Timelines differ.

Table 2-1   Personal Timeline versus Fan Page Timeline

As a Personal Timeline, You Can . . .	As a Fan Page, You Can . . .
Interact with friends on your Timeline, groups, chat, and so on.	Only interact with individuals within the confines of your Fan Page Timeline. Your Fan Page Timeline can't post to an individual's personal Timeline.
Make new friend requests.	Not allowed to make friend requests.
Like a Fan Page Timeline. This Like counts toward the total number of Likes for a Fan Page.	Like a Fan Page Timeline. This Like does not count toward the total number of Likes for a Fan Page.
Tag individuals in status updates, photos, video, and so on.	Tag individuals associated with admins in status updates, photos, video, and so on. In other words, if an admin is Facebook friends with a fan, the admin can tag that friend in status updates, photos, video, and so on.

You can't post comments to someone's personal Timeline while using Facebook as your Fan Page Timeline. Allowing businesses to post on personal Timelines could get spammy pretty quickly, as you can imagine.

To use your Facebook account as yourself (meaning as your personal Timeline), just log in to Facebook as you normally do. When you'd like to switch to your business account, follow these steps:

1. **Click the Account down arrow in the top-right corner of the blue toolbar.**

2. **From the menu, choose Use Facebook as Page.**

   The Use Facebook as Page window appears and lists all the Pages you are associated with as an admin.

3. **Click the Switch button next to the page you want to use.**

   The main Timeline for that page appears.

You can easily switch back to using your personal Timeline by clicking the Account down arrow and choosing Switch Back to *[Your Name]*.

When you switch to using Facebook as your Fan Page Timeline, you notice that your Facebook experience is similar to when you're using your personal Timeline, but everything is now focused on your Fan Page Timeline instead of your personal Timeline page:

+ You still have a News Feed. However, now your News Feed shows the updates of other Fan Pages you've Liked, not updates from friends.

+ You still have notifications. These notifications, though, tell you who has interacted with the content on your Fan Page Timeline, not your personal Timeline or other Pages, groups, or Timelines you've interacted with.

+ Instead of your name, you see the name of your Page in the top-right corner. Clicking that link brings you to your Fan Page Timeline, not your personal Timeline.

+ Clicking Facebook in the top-left corner or Home in the top-right corner brings you to your Fan Page Timeline News Feed, where you see updates from other Fan Page Timelines, not your personal friends.

+ Your left navigation reflects your Fan Page Timeline needs. For example, instead of listing messages, groups, and apps you use, your left navigation now shows links to Events, Insights, and Facebook apps that are useful to pages such as Questions, Photos, Notes, and Links.

Being able to switch between appearing as your brand (Fan Page Timeline) or yourself (personal Timeline) allows you to do a few things:

✦ **You can post as yourself on your own Fan Page Timeline.** On your Fan Page Timeline, click Edit Page➪Your Settings, and then select (or deselect) the Always Comment and Post on Your Page as *[Fan Page Name]* Even when Using Facebook as *[Personal Profile Name]*.

✦ **Your Fan Page can Like other Fan Pages.** You have to Like a Fan Page before you can tag it in an update. When you're using Facebook as your Fan Page Timeline (not your personal Timeline), you can go to a Fan Page Timeline and Like it, but that action won't clutter up your personal news stream.

When you Like a Fan Page while using Facebook as your Fan Page Timeline, that Like does not count toward that page's overall Likes. Facebook only counts Likes received from a personal Timeline. In other words, if Melanie uses her Blogging Basics 101 Fan Page Timeline and Likes the Fan Page Timeline for redwallLIVE (`https://www.facebook.com/ redwallLIVE`), that Like is not recorded as part of the overall number of Likes for the redwallLIVE Page. But if she switches back to using her personal Timeline (Melanie Nelson), and heads over to the redwallLive Fan Page Timeline and clicks Like, then that Like is recorded in the overall number of Likes for that Fan Page Timeline.

✦ **You can interact with other Fan Page Timelines as your brand instead of as yourself.** If you want to comment on another Fan Page Timeline as your business instead of as yourself, just be sure you're using Facebook as the Timeline for your Fan Page.

✦ **When using Facebook as your Fan Page Timeline, your Fan Page Timeline has its own News Feed.** While using Facebook as one of your Pages, click the Home link (top-right corner), and you see the News Feed for your Business Page. Your News Feed lists the activity of all the other Fan Pages you've Liked with your Fan Page.

If you just want to switch over to view your Fan Page Timeline (but don't want to interact on Facebook as your Page), click the Account down arrow and choose Use Facebook as Page, and then click the name of the page (instead of the Switch button).

Using the Facebook Navigation Bar as Your Page

The Facebook navigation bar includes the main Facebook logo link and icons for friend requests, personal message alerts, and notifications. You still have the option to search. And you also see links for your personal Timeline, Home, and Account (denoted by a down arrow). Each of these options is identical to those shown on your personal Timeline page (see Book I, Chapter 4). However, each of these links has a flip side as well. Facebook offers Fan Page Timeline owners the option to use Facebook as either themselves (as a personal Timeline) or as their brand (as Fan Page Timeline). We cover this in detail earlier in this chapter in the "Using Facebook as Your Fan Page

Timeline or Personal Timeline" section. The following sections explain how each item differs, depending on whether you're using Facebook as yourself or as your brand.

Facebook link

When using Facebook as your personal Timeline, the Facebook link takes you to your main News Feed, where you see Top Stories, Recent Updates, and updates from your Facebook friends, Fan Pages you've Liked, and groups you belong to.

When using Facebook as your Fan Page Timeline, the Facebook link takes you to a News Feed for your Fan Page Timeline. Because a Fan Page Timeline can't connect with individuals and is restricted to Liking other Fan Pages, this News Feed only displays updates from the Fan Pages you have Liked while using Facebook as your Fan Page.

Fan Pages you Like with your personal Timeline do not show up in this News Feed unless you have also Liked the page as your Fan Page Timeline. Please see the "Using Facebook as Your Fan Page Timeline or Personal Timeline" section, earlier in this chapter, for an explanation of how to switch from one Timeline to another.

Friend requests

When using Facebook as your personal Timeline, the Friend Requests icon shows a list of people who have requested to become Facebook friends.

When using Facebook as your Fan Page Timeline, instead of friend requests, this icon now displays a list of new fans. These are Facebook users who have recently Liked your Fan Page Timeline. You may click their names to see their personal Timelines, but depending on their personal privacy settings, you may see limited information.

Facebook Fan Page Timelines can't be friends with individuals. If you want to friend someone, you'll need to switch back to using Facebook as yourself, and then make a friend request. We don't suggest friending your fans unless you know them in real life. Respect that your fans have connected with you on your Fan Page Timeline because they support your brand.

If you'd like to see a list of all your fans, click the Friend icon, and then click See All at the bottom of the list. The People Who Like *[Your Page Name]* dialog box appears. Unfortunately, Facebook does not make it easy to find specific fans — you have to scroll through the list one by one to find a specific fan. If you have more than a few hundred fans, finding just one could be a little tedious.

The People Who Like *[Your Page Name]* dialog box also shows you which other Fan Page Timelines have Liked your Fan Page, who you've made an admin of your Fan Page, and who you've banned from your Fan Page. Just click the down arrow next to People in the top-left corner, as shown in Figure 2-13, and choose which list you want to see.

You can grant administrative privileges to any fan by clicking the Make Admin button next to her name (see Book IV, Chapter 1 for instructions on how to grant admin privileges via your dashboard). Alternatively, you can also ban a specific fan from your Fan Page Timeline by clicking the X next to his name.

Personal messages

When using Facebook as your personal Timeline, the Messages icon displays a list of personal messages various people have sent to you. Depending on your privacy settings, you may also receive personal messages from people you are not directly connected with (such as friends of friends). You can read more about managing your privacy settings in Book I, Chapter 3.

When using Facebook as your Fan Page Timeline, the Messages icon shows a list of personal messages fans have sent. Facebook allows fans to send you private messages as a way to handle communication away from the public Timeline. While fans can send a private message to a Page, a Page cannot initiate private messages to fans.

Figure 2-13:
See who has Liked your Fan Page, who is an admin, and who you've banned.

The Message feature for Pages is automatically turned on. You can turn it off by going to the Manage Permissions tab of your Fan Page Timeline dashboard (Admin Panel⇨Manage⇨Edit Page) and deselecting the box next to Show "Message" Button on *[Your Fan Page Name]*.

Notifications

When using Facebook as your personal Timeline, the Notification icon displays a running list of people who have posted new updates related to your actions (for instance, Liking a photo you shared or commenting on a status update you already commented on), mentioned you in status updates, and so on.

When using Facebook as your Fan Page Timeline, the Notifications icon displays a list of your fans who have recently interacted with your Page either by Liking a status update or link, tagging your Fan Page Timeline in an update, or commenting on a status update or link.

Search text box

When using Facebook as your personal Timeline, type in search terms in the Search text box to find people, Pages, groups, apps, and events. You can also find basic web results, posts from friends, posts published publicly, and posts to public groups.

When using Facebook as your Fan Page Timeline, you can still use the Search tool. However, your results are limited to people, Pages, Events, general web results, posts by everyone, and posts by open groups. Because a Fan Page Timeline can't join a group, you don't see results for groups.

Profile link

When using Facebook as your personal Timeline, the Profile link goes to your personal Timeline.

When using Facebook as your Fan Page Timeline, the Profile link goes to your Fan Page Timeline.

Home link

When using Facebook as your personal Timeline, the Home link sends you back to your main News Feed.

When using Facebook as your Fan Page Timeline, the Home link sends you back to your Fan Page Timeline's News Feed. Remember, your Fan Page Timeline News Feed displays updates by other pages, not friends associated with your personal Timeline.

Account menu

When using Facebook as your personal Timeline, the Account menu (the down arrow) provides links to use Facebook as your Fan Page Timeline, Account Settings, Privacy Settings, Log Out, and the Facebook Help Center.

When using Facebook as your Fan Page Timeline, the Account menu (the down arrow) provides links to Switch to using Facebook as your personal profile, Use Facebook as Page (this could be another Page you're admin for), Help Center, and Log Out.

Chapter 3: Building Your Facebook Fan Page Community

In This Chapter

✔ Understanding how your fans use Facebook

✔ Knowing your goals (so you know when you've met them)

✔ Using different kinds of updates to appeal to your fans

✔ Taking care of customer service on your Timeline

*U*sing social media as an extension of your marketing strategy is mandatory these days. If you don't use Facebook or Twitter or at least a blog, you're missing out on key engagement with your customers and potential customers. Your Fan Page Timeline can be an important part of your marketing strategy and must fit with other efforts to attract fans. When people become fans and are welcomed into your community, they are more likely to convert to paying customers.

By setting up your Fan Page Timeline, you recognize that you need to market where your audience is . . . and they're on Facebook. Your Fan Page Timeline can reinforce your brand and bring an entirely new level of interaction to your customer relations. In fact, some businesses are so excited about using Facebook that they only see the potential for broadcasting their message. After all, your business and its products are phenomenal, and now you can tell everyone in the world! One of the key things to remember about Facebook is that although you own your Fan Page, your fans own the space. You control what you share, but your fans control how they consume it. If a fan decides you're sharing too often or not sharing content she's interested in, she can hide your status updates from her News Feed (or, worse, Unlike your Fan Page completely).

In Book IV, Chapters 1 and 2, we show you how to create your Fan Page Timeline. What you do when you have your Fan Page Timeline set up matters, and it's not a "set it and forget it" deal. One mistake some marketers make when including Facebook in their strategy is expecting a fast ROI. Social media (whether it's Facebook, Twitter, a blog, LinkedIn, or another tool) requires time to develop a community — it's a long-term effort. Any time you use social media, your space needs attention and interaction or it loses its value. In this chapter, we show you a few tips and tricks to interact with your fans so you both see value. We give you some advice about keeping your audience engaged and some things to think about for the future of your Fan Page Timeline.

The marketing advice we offer throughout this book is solid, but it's just an overview. If you really want to delve into Facebook marketing tactics, we suggest you check out *Facebook Marketing All-in-One For Dummies* by Amy Porterfield, Phyllis Khare, and Andrea Vahl (John Wiley & Sons, Inc.). It's a comprehensive guide to building a business presence on Facebook. We're confident you can use this minibook to get a running start, but if you want to delve even deeper into Facebook marketing, *Facebook Marketing All-in-One For Dummies* is a good resource.

Determining Your Goals and Objectives

You shouldn't assume your Fan Page Timeline isn't as important as your other advertising or marketing venues. You're building community and loyal followers here; in some cases, Facebook allows you to introduce your product to a much wider audience than you may have had access to previously. Before you interact with these existing and potential fans, you need to have a plan — just as you have a plan for your other advertising and marketing efforts.

Your plan should include a set of specific goals, a means to achieve those goals, a deadline for the goals, and a measurement for how well your efforts worked. Goals are useful when they are specific. Here is an example of a vague goal versus specific goals:

> **Vague Goal:** Get more fans to Like our Fan Page.
>
> **Specific Goal:** Gain 25 Likes in one week.
>
> **Specific Goal:** Have 50 new fans on our Fan Page by the end of the month.
>
> **Specific Goal:** Have five comments on posted status updates this week.

The goal of wanting more fans is too broad. How do you know when you've achieved your goal? When you've had one more person Like your Fan Page? By being more specific, you make one vague goal into several specific goals that allow you to build on your successes. With specific goals in mind, you know exactly what you're working toward and how long you have to achieve the goal.

The next step is defining a strategy for reaching the goal in the allotted time. That strategy is what the rest of this chapter is about.

As you determine your goals, consider the following questions:

✦ How do you or your company want to use your Fan Page Timeline?

✦ What are you hoping to achieve by using Facebook? For example, do you want to become an authority in your niche? Increase sales? Introduce yourself to a new market?

✦ How do you want to engage with fans?

✦ How do you want fans to engage with you?

✦ Will you share industry-specific information from many sources?

✦ Will you promote your products or services?

You want quality, not necessarily quantity, when it comes to fans. It's better to reach 10 people who really want to buy than 1,200 who just don't care. As well, you need to define *why* you want fans. You can have thousands, but if they aren't interacting or buying, what's the point? Marketing goals generally equal sales, but people using Facebook (and social media in general) don't like to be bombarded with sales pitches. Facebook is an open but private space. That means that while Facebook is a public forum, users consider it their private space. Users choose who they interact with and how. If those interactions become uncomfortable (for a Fan Page Timeline, that means spammy or intrusive), the user can Hide, Unfriend, or Unlike the person making them uncomfortable.

Does that mean you shouldn't market or sell your products or services on Facebook? No. You can sell, but make your pitches relevant and don't make every status update a pitch. When you do pitch, provide a call to action and provide a link that allows the reader to complete the action. In some cases, you may also want to include a picture, and provide context within your status update of how to use the product or show why it's relevant to your fans.

Establishing Your Authority

In order to build your community, you need to give people a reason to come to you. One way to do that is to establish yourself as an authority in your niche. To build authority, you need to fulfill a need for your audience: Solve a problem for them, entertain them, or educate them.

When users trust you to give them relevant information, they begin to look to you regularly for that information. As you share the information, they interact with it by clicking the Like button or commenting. If the information is particularly relevant, the reader will also share the information with his own network — essentially giving the content his stamp of approval. When a fan does that, his friends see that he's endorsing your content, and they may be more likely to engage with (and possibly share) your content too.

Growing a large, loyal community takes time, but it's not necessarily hard. The bottom line is respect. If you respect your fans and their needs, they'll appreciate you. As you nurture your community, consider the following advice:

+ **Build trust.** As you build your community, keep in mind that you are building trust. You can gain your readers' trust by making your interactions primarily about them. Before you start any marketing campaign, you should know who your target audience is, what they want, how you can help them, and how you can use that interaction to further your own goals as well. Use that information to craft status updates that address your audience's needs, include a call to action, and then provide a way to complete the action.

+ **Pitch genuinely.** Share useful information more than you're selling a product or service. Use the 80/20 rule: Spend 80 percent of your time listening and 20 percent talking, or 80 percent sharing information that is relevant to your audience and 20 percent asking them to buy. It isn't a problem to ask your readers to buy. In fact, your fans are probably coming to you because they like your product or service. Selling is a problem when you *only* ask your fans to buy and don't give anything in return. When you do sell, not giving your fans a way to complete a transaction is also a problem. Take advantage of the fans who are interested in your product. Give them a chance to purchase your goods or services by providing a Facebook shopping cart or linking directly to a product in your online store or website.

+ **Listen.** Ask for your fans' opinions and pay attention to what they reference when they comment on your Timeline. Listen to your audience in other venues such as Twitter or your blog as well, and introduce interesting conversations from those venues to your fans on Facebook.

Establishing Social Proof

When your fans come to rely on you for a specific purpose, you've gained authority. When you have authority, you have earned your fans' trust and they're likely to offer social proof of acceptance to their friends and others. *Social proof* occurs when members of a community see others engaging with content and sharing it, decide to check it out for themselves, and if they like the content, share it with other communities they're part of. If people are consistently commenting or sharing on your Fan Page Timeline, that's proof that other people like your product or service. When a new fan arrives, that social proof reinforces their decision to be there and interact with you.

When people visit your Fan Page Timeline, one of the first things they look at is the interaction there. If people only see posts from the page admin and no interaction (Likes or comments), it appears that the Fan Page Timeline is one-way. On the other hand, if people see conversation (even limited inter-action with a few Likes or comments spread out), that tells the visitor that people are indeed reading what's being shared and are investing their time in the community. One of the best ways to increase your social proof is to provide shareable content, which we go over in the next section. (See Book IV, Chapter 1 for directions on how to set your Timeline to show posts from everyone, not just your Fan Page Timeline updates.)

Creating Shareable Content

An unattended Fan Page Timeline leaves a negative impression on your visitors — and they are less likely to Like it — because they assume it's not relevant or cared for. Instead, it's important to update your Fan Page Timeline status regularly. How often you update your Fan Page Timeline depends on your audience and your niche. You don't want to litter people's streams with irrelevant information multiple times a day. Instead, focus your updates on topics relevant to your niche (and your audience's needs) and post them as needed. Some days may see more updates; other days will see fewer updates. We find that one or two posts per day seem to be ideal, but small businesses can sometimes get away with three or four updates a day. (Melanie has a client who posts up to ten times per day, but she's a special case. See the sidebar, "How one small business increased sales using Facebook," elsewhere in this chapter.)

To figure out when your fans are most likely to interact with your updates, check your Facebook Insights (Book V, Chapter 3 explains how to use Insights) to see which updates are garnering the most engagement. Experiment with posting in the mornings, afternoons, evenings, and on weekends, and then check your Insights again. Did you see a difference in how or when your fans engaged with your content? Consider when your audience is most likely to be on Facebook. They're probably on Facebook before work, possibly during their lunch hour if Facebook is allowed through their work firewall, and again in the evenings after dinner. We've found that Sunday evenings can be inter-active as well, but not all companies are willing to work on Sunday night.

Studies have shown that most people Like or follow a brand because they want exclusive deals, discounts, and promotions. When you're thinking about ways to interact with your fans, consider rewarding customers for being fans by giving them periodic perks.

Sharing instead of broadcasting

When visitors Like your Fan Page, they almost never go back to your actual Fan Page Timeline (unless you provide a specific link or call to action in a status update; we cover that later in the chapter). Instead, your fans rely on their News Feed to see status updates from friends as well as Fan Page

Timelines. You can imagine how important those News Feeds are and why you don't want to be hidden from anyone's stream. Every individual has his own idea about how Facebook should work for his personal needs. Most users agree that they don't see Facebook as a place for businesses to market to them. Rather, they see Facebook as a place to connect with a business they enjoy. What that means in a nutshell is that your fans don't want you broadcasting your message to them all the time, and that can be hard for a marketer to hear. Your main goal as a marketer is to share a message with others, and broadcasting is an efficient way to achieve that goal. Social media is changing the way you reach that goal by putting the power in the audience's hands instead of yours. As you share content, remember to make it relevant to your audience. Put the information in context as it relates to them. Present the information in such a way that your readers feel like you found this information specifically for them. As you consistently share this level of trust, your audience will look to you as an authority in your niche.

If you're posting about a popular topic (such as Pinterest) or sharing a popular link, be aware that your content may not be as visible in the News Feed. In the latter part of 2011, Facebook started grouping updates together based on topic (see Figure 3-1).

How one small business increased sales using Facebook

One of Melanie's clients, Purse-a-nality (http://fb.com/Purseanality), is a small local business in Tulsa, OK. The owner, Tammy Houghton, gets new products into her store every day. Her audience is largely stay-at-home moms with disposable income. These moms love their Facebook and like to interact there. Tammy takes advantage of that and posts pictures and updates about new products up to ten times per day. Rather than losing her community because of too many updates, she has built her community around those updates, and her fans expect her to notify them when new items are available. Within two months of creating her Fan Page Timeline, she tripled her daily sales during the Christmas season. Sales declined a bit (as is normal) after the holidays, but held steady. When she hit 2,000 fans, her business doubled again and she had to rent the space next to her shop and expand. When Purse-a-nality hit 3,000 fans, Tammy hired help to take care of the extra business Facebook drives to her bricks-and-mortar store. How did she expand her business so quickly and completely? She knew her audience. She understood what her audience wanted from her, and she gave it to them. Each of her status updates provides a picture, a call to action, and a way to complete the action.

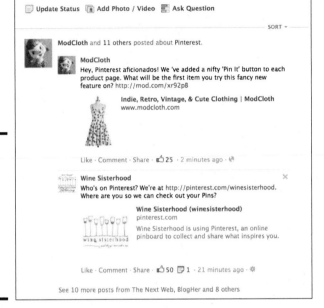

Figure 3-1:
Fans may
miss your
updates if
you post
about
the same
popular
topics as
others.

As you can see in Figure 3-1, only the most recent update is visible. If you click the See *[#] More Posts from [Name]* link, you can see the other posts. The issue is that your fans may not click the See More link and will miss your updates.

In order to build a loyal community, you must offer quality content relevant to your audience's needs. If your content is really good and truly meets the needs of your audience, you'll find that they share it with their friends sometimes. As you consider what to include in your status updates, think about sharing the following:

+ Links

+ Photos and video

+ Questions

+ Calls to action

Sharing links

RSS feeds have been popular for the last ten years. *RSS* stands for Real Simple Syndication and is a way for people to be alerted when new content is published on a blog, for example. In the past year or two, people have come to rely less on RSS feeds and more on links to content shared by their friends and colleagues via platforms such as Facebook and Twitter. Links shared by people you trust provide social proof — you believe the link has worth because someone you trust shared it with you. When you establish your Fan Page Timeline as an authority in your niche, your fans come to believe the links you share have worth. If they also see colleagues or friends sharing or commenting on those same links, the social proof intensifies.

Here are a few best practices for sharing links on your Fan Page Timeline:

✦ **Take the time to provide context.** Give your readers a reason to click the link by explaining how they can benefit from the information shared in the linked article. Without context or a short note from you, you're just posting a link — and that appears spammy. With so much questionable content floating around, links by themselves are suspect and your readers are less likely to click them for fear of spam.

✦ **Remember your goals.** If your goal is to encourage your fans to interact with your content, don't send them away from your Fan Page Timeline. A link takes people away from Facebook, and they may or may not return after they've read the article. If they do return to Facebook, they may not return to your update to Like it or comment. On the other hand, if your goal is to share information to gain authority as the go-to page for your niche, it's not as important if fans don't come back to comment or Like. Your job in this instance is to provide the tools for your audience to stay updated on niche-specific information.

✦ **Use a link shortening and tracking tool.** This point dovetails with the previous point. If your goal is to educate or disseminate or curate information for your fans, you may find yourself sharing many links that take fans away from your Fan Page Timeline. When you send people away from your Fan Page Timeline to read an article, they may not return to your Fan Page Timeline. If they don't return, they won't comment or Like the link, and it's hard to tell if anyone interacted with your content. You can check your Insights (see Book V, Chapter 3) to track how many clicks a link received. However, Melanie has found that she can't always get to her Insights page for Blogging Basics 101. That means she can't tell if her links are working or not. By using a link tracking service such as bit.ly (`http://bit.ly`), she can see how many people click her links. Many times, we've seen zero comments or Likes on a status update with a link only to check the bit.ly dashboard and find that link got 30 clicks. That tells us that fans are using the content and interacting with it, even though we can't see that on Facebook.

Figures 3-2 and 3-3 show a Fan Page Timeline and a bit.ly dashboard, respectively. The link shared on the Fan Page Timeline doesn't appear to have any interaction at all. But if you look at the bit.ly dashboard, you see that actually, that link has had ten click-throughs. That means ten fans have interacted with that content.

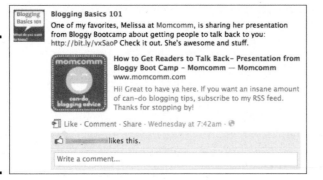

Figure 3-2:
A Fan Page Timeline doesn't show whether people click your links.

Figure 3-3:
Link-tracking tools like bit. ly show how many people clicked on a link.

Using photos and video to encourage sharing

If you think about how you interact on Facebook, which posts are the ones that inspire you to click most often? Many people click most often on the updates that include video or pictures. It's just so easy! Facebook displays photos nice and big so fans can see product pictures easily. Or you click and the video is *right there* in your news stream. You don't have to click around, and try to resume your place in the stream — everything is at your fingertips.

And it's so easy to share visual content with your friends! If you share interesting photos and video your fans love, they can just click the Share link and their friends will see the content as well. For more information on how to use photos and video with Facebook, flip to Book II, Chapters 3 and 4, respectively.

Asking questions

When people use Facebook, they scan and click quickly. Anything that takes more than a few seconds to consider may be lost in the shuffle. The result is that there are fairly specific ways to interact on Facebook to ensure you have a higher rate of engagement. Asking questions is an excellent way to engage fans, but only if done correctly. Because Facebook readers move from one update to the next very quickly, you have to make your questions scannable and easy to answer. Here are some tried and true options:

✦ **Yes/No questions:** These short questions just require a one-word answer, but leave room for your fans to expound on their point of view if they desire. Consider these two questions:

Question 1: Do your kids earn an allowance?

Question 2: What do you think about kids earning an allowance?

The first question is a simple yes/no answer. It's easy and it's fast. Fans can choose to expand on their answers, but yes or no will suffice. The second question requires a little more thought. If fans see that question in their stream, they may answer it in their heads, but probably won't take the step of crafting a response because many people have more complex thoughts on allowances in general.

✦ **Either/Or questions:** Similar to Yes/No questions, your fans still just need to leave their preference as an answer, but don't have to explain if they don't want to.

✦ **Fill-in-the-blank questions:** Give your fans a little prompt and ask them to share a word or two to complete a sentence. Add your own answer as well! Your fans will appreciate that you're interacting with them.

✦ **Polls with limited answers:** You can use Facebook Questions to pose a question to your fans and provide specific answers for their feedback. It doesn't get any easier than that. If you keep your choices limited to around three, your fans can scan the question and answer and quickly click their preference before they move on to the next status update.

A very popular Fan Page Timeline that Melanie follows has several good policies in place for their Fan Page, but they don't quite have their status updates nailed down for maximum engagement. The page admin regularly asks questions, hoping to hit on a topic that resonates with the audience, but the updates rarely have more than a few responses. Now, having only a few responses can be fine, but if you have over 5,000 fans (as this Fan Page Timeline does), you'd probably expect more interaction from fans. One problem is that the questions are a bit poorly formed. The page admins routinely ask several questions about a hot-button issue that can't be answered quickly. For example, this Fan Page Timeline may ask the following questions in a status update:

> Do your kids earn an allowance? How old should kids be when they start helping out around the house? What chores should be paid and which ones should be unpaid? How do you teach your kids about money?

As a mom, Melanie gets overwhelmed just reading that. She has so many thoughts, she doesn't know where to start. She has a personal philosophy on kids and money, but it's fairly complex and has caveats. Does she have time to try to distill her thoughts into a short comment? Does she want to share her point of view on this complex issue in front of 5,000 other fans, and potentially have others point out why she's right or wrong? Does she have time to be part of a larger discussion and continue to check what others are saying here? Sometimes the answer is yes, but most of the time, it's no. The status update simply wants too much information, so as a fan, Melanie skips it and moves on to the next one.

A more effective question might have been:

> Do you give your kid(s) allowance?

At this point, you're simply asking your readers to share a yes or no answer with you. If they choose to share the reasoning behind their answer, even better, but that extra effort is their decision. As the answers come in, the page admin can interact by asking more questions within the comment stream to keep the conversation going. For instance, if it's determined that most families do provide an allowance for their children, the page admin can ask about which chores are paid or not paid, and a little later, offer advice on age-specific chores parents can assign or a link to an article on the blog where a larger conversation is taking place. The key is to start an easy conversation, and then go with the flow. Follow your readers' lead and contribute where you can. Your job as the Fan Page Timeline admin is to facilitate the discussion, not dictate it or make it uncomfortable.

Don't be afraid to stray from your normal topics or to use humor in your questions. Melanie's audience on the Blogging Basics 101 Facebook Fan Page Timeline is currently primarily women between 30–50 years old. Being in that demographic herself, and knowing many of her fans personally, Melanie is aware that her fans also appreciate romantic classic literature (for example, Jane Austen and Charlotte Bronte). Sometimes just to engage on a different level, she throws out a yes/no or either/or question of the day, such as "Mr. Darcy or Mr. Rochester?" While she has perfectly acceptable interactions throughout the week as she shares articles about blogging and social media, her fans appreciate connecting on a different level with these off-topic questions (as evidenced by the number of responses shown in Figure 3-4).

Figure 3-4:
Don't be afraid to stray off-topic to encourage new interaction.

Sometimes the best way to know what your audience wants is to ask them. Knowing what your audience expects, needs, or wants can help you determine what type of information to share or which products to promote. Use the Facebook Questions app (click the Question link above the Status Update text box) to create questions with specific answers fans can choose from, or just ask your question as a status update and encourage fans to comment with their own answers. To begin, you may want to ask your fans questions such as:

✦ Which social media networks do they use?

✦ How do they use your product or service?

✦ What information would they like to see?

✦ What other Fan Pages do they Like and/or interact on frequently?

Make note of how your fans respond, and use that information to help establish an editorial calendar for your updates and blog articles (if you keep a blog).

Using calls to action

As we state earlier, Facebook users move quickly from one update to the next, skimming and clicking and occasionally commenting. If you want to bring attention to your status update and have your fans complete a specific task, place a strong call to action within the update and provide the means to carry out the action. That task could be buying a product or service, in which case, you need to provide a link to your online store. Or you may just want to increase engagement on your Fan Page Timeline for this update, in which case, you can ask fans to comment or click the Like button for your status update. For instance, if you've added or changed something (like a product's functionality), ask your fans to click the Like button if they think the change is a good one.

As you create strong calls to action for various campaigns, consider using a version of this workflow:

✦ Provide a call to action.

✦ Provide a path to action (such as a link created with a trackable bit.ly link).

✦ Measure the performance (record the number of click-throughs for your link, how many sales you made, and so on).

✦ If necessary, figure out where the campaign broke down and fix it.

Part of giving fans what they want is showing them where to find it. As you create status updates, consider how you can help your fans complete an action that not only helps them, but helps you reach your goals as well. Say you own a successful knitting shop, and you have a website with a shopping cart and a fairly active Fan Page Timeline. Most of your business is done within your bricks-and-mortar store, but one of your goals is to increase online sales at your website by 10 percent this month. Our first suggestion is to create strong calls to action for your fans. If you want to sell more, you need to tell your fans you want them to buy something, and then give them the means to buy it. For example, the next time you post a picture of a finished project, provide direct links to your website's store where fans can buy the pattern, needles, and yarn needed to complete the project. Consider the following status updates (imagine both accompanied by a picture of someone showing off the scarf they just knitted):

> Update 1: Melanie is modeling her latest knitting project, The Beginner's Scarf!

> Update 2: Melanie is modeling her latest knitting project, The Beginner's Scarf. Are you looking for a quick project? Buy the pattern from our shop (`http://bit.ly/patternlink`) – it takes 2 skeins of Irish Lass cotton (`http://bit.ly/yarnlink`) and size 9 needles (`http://bit.ly/needlelink`).

The first update explains the picture, but doesn't really offer any actionable information for fans. If someone really loves that scarf and is considering starting a quick project, they're left to their own devices to find the pattern, the yarn, and the needles. If the store happens to be nearby, they can hop in the car and head over, but that's a pretty big step to expect a Facebook fan to take. (What if your store isn't close by, but another craft store is? You may have lost a sale to another store.) Instead, the second update provides a subtle call to action, and provides several options (links) for completing the action. The update makes it easy for the fan to buy everything she needs to start a new project.

If you want to involve your fans even more, ask them to upload pictures of them modeling their own projects and tell you what pattern and yarn they used. Then, when you comment on the photo, provide links to your online store so fans can purchase the supplies.

 You can install a Facebook shopping cart app on your Fan Page Timeline to allow fans to purchase goods right from your Fan Page Timeline! Or, if your webmaster is really handy, ask her if she can pull in your online store with the help of iframes (see Book VI, Chapter 1).

Handling Customer Service

If you're monitoring your Fan Page Timeline and interacting regularly with your fans, you're probably building a community where people feel comfortable asking questions, praising your brand, and, yes, sometimes airing a grievance or two. The way you handle your customer interactions — both good and bad — will have an immediate and lasting effect on how people talk about your company.

Integrate your Facebook efforts with your entire marketing strategy

Remember that Facebook is just one part of your marketing initiative. Facebook pretty much owns your content and can decide at any time to take down your Fan Page Timeline if it's judged to violate the Facebook TOS (terms of service). You should not get rid of your website or blog. Instead, integrate everything into a social media strategy. Recognize that different parts of your audience will find you on different platforms. And recognize that each audience on each platform may have different expectations. How do you know what those expectations are? You ask your audience.

You can do a poll in your e-newsletter or ask your fans on Facebook. Not getting a great response? Narrow the choices. Sometimes people can't come up with an answer because there are too many options. Instead, ask whether they'd like to see Option 1 or Option 2 on the Fan Page Timeline next week.

Another way to build your community is to include a Facebook plug-in on your website or blog. You can find several to choose from. Visit `http://developers.facebook.com/docs/plugins` to see your options.

Interacting regularly with fans

The more you engage, the more likely people are to comment. Why? Because if they see that you're on the Fan Page Timeline regularly, they feel like they're more likely to be heard. You wouldn't walk into an empty room and start talking to yourself, would you? You'd be more likely to go into a room with several people who are welcoming and ready to converse. Taking the time to respond to comments or questions from your fans reinforces the fact that you take your Facebook community seriously and value your fans' opinions. On our own Fan Page Timelines, not only do we respond to fan comments, but we click Like on comments as well so they know we've seen it.

If you're looking for a way to grow your community, establish your authority, and interact regularly with your fans, try setting up a specific time to interact with them. On many Fridays, Social Media Examiner (`http://fb.com/smexaminer`) invites an industry expert to host a Q&A session on their Facebook Timeline. This works well because fans show up not only to ask questions, but to offer answers to questions as well because the host can't always get to everyone.

Addressing negative comments and reviews

Engaging doesn't mean controlling the conversation or the message. Your role as a community manager is to give your fans a way to express themselves; let the conversation flow. Only step in if there's a specific question directed to you or if you need to delete an inappropriate or rude comment. If you do see a negative comment, address it professionally and let it stand. Consider how you can turn the negative into a positive with your response. Acknowledge the fan's frustration, address the specific issue (or find out what the issue is), and apologize. Many times people just want their frustration to be recognized and acknowledged. You can't always fix the issue, but you can give the fan your attention, let them know they've been heard, and tell them that you're sorry they're upset. You may occasionally run into a *troll* (someone whose sole purpose is to cause trouble), but usually people just want to know that their concerns are being heard.

If you're managing your community effectively, you're probably visiting your Fan Page Timeline several times a day to address comments and share content. Invariably, you'll come across some spam. While it's perfectly okay to delete spammy content, you can curb spam and inappropriate comments by establishing some guidelines for what is and isn't acceptable content to share on your Fan Page Timeline. You can share these rules on your Info page. Every month or so, depending on how much spam you're seeing, you can remind your fans what the rules are by linking directly to the Info page or Note where you have your community guidelines. Or, if you have to delete a comment or status update or block a user, you can justify your decision based on your existing community guidelines.

Chapter 4: Using Your Fan Page Timeline for Check Ins and Deals

In This Chapter

✔ Ensuring your fans can check in to your venue

✔ Claiming unofficial check-in pages

✔ Setting up, promoting, and honoring a Facebook Deal

Social media tools such as Facebook have made people's lives open books. People can connect with each other anytime, anywhere. In the past few years, geolocation services such as Facebook's check-in option have played an important role in connecting people even further. Check-in tools allow you to tell people where you are, what you're doing, who's with you, and much more. Facebook's geolocation option allows members to check into a venue they're visiting, see what's going on nearby, tag friends who are with them, share photos, and share thoughts about what's going on where they are. Facebook members can do all this with the Facebook app or by going to `http://m.facebook.com` on their smartphones. These check ins appear in users' Facebook News Feeds.

As you can imagine, allowing customers to check into your venue can be an excellent marketing tool. When people check into a venue nearby, your business comes up as a Nearby Place. If a visitor checks in to your Place's venue, it shows up in his News Feed so that his friends can see he's frequenting your business.

And if you want to encourage even *more* traffic, you can take advantage of Facebook Deals. Facebook Deals is a way for businesses to interact with their customers via the Facebook Places application. You can reward customers for frequent check ins, offer discounts for services, or even donate to charities. Customers can redeem Deals by checking in to a venue with Facebook Places.

In this chapter, we explain how the check-in process works, how to create a check-in page for your business, and how to claim any unofficial check-in pages. Then you find out how you can ramp up sales for your business by using Facebook Deals in conjunction with check ins.

Exploring Facebook Check Ins

Geolocation tools (such as the Check In option on your smartphone's Facebook app) use the GPS capabilities included in your smartphone to determine your location and list the names of possible venues you may be visiting. You choose the relevant business from the list and *presto,* you're all checked-in. If you don't see your venue, you can type the name of the venue into the Search text box at the top of the screen to find the place. The venue might not be on Facebook or have enabled check ins yet. If that's the case, you can create a place, as described in the later section, "Ensuring your fans can check in via your Fan Page Timeline."

When you check in, you can tag friends who are with you, include photos from your visit, make suggestions for things to try, write a review, and automatically share your check in to your Facebook News Feed. Sometimes, you even find Facebook Deals at some businesses. *Facebook Deals* are coupons or specials available to people who check into a venue. For specific directions on checking in to a venue with your phone, see Book II, Chapter 5.

When you use the check-in feature, your Facebook News Feed updates, and your friends can see where you are. If you tag friends who are with you, your friends' Facebook News Feeds also update.

Protecting Your Privacy

Any time you or a friend check into a venue, you can tag others with you (or be tagged by others). If you don't want others to be able to tag you in their check ins, be sure you've turned off the Friends Can Check You into Places options. To do that, follow these steps:

1. **Click the down arrow in the top-right corner of any Facebook page and choose Privacy Settings.**

The Privacy Settings page appears.

2. **Click the Edit Settings link next to How Tags Work.**

The How Tags Work dialog box appears.

3. **Click the row that says Friends Can Check You into Places Using the Mobile Places App.**

The Friends Can Check You Into Places dialog box appears.

4. **Use the drop-down list to choose either Enabled (others can check you into places) or Disabled (others can't check you into places).**

5. **Click the Okay button.**

You return to the How Tags Work dialog box.

6. **Click the Done button.**

If you disable the Friends Can Check You into Places option, people can try to tag you, but those tags will not appear in their News Feed or yours. Instead, you have the option to approve individual tags. To do that, go to your Timeline and click the Activity Log link (under your cover photo), where you have a notification to review recent tags. You can click the Okay button, and then click the Needs Review link under the Timeline link in your left navigation list to view new tags. Click either the check mark (to approve) or the X (to ignore) the tags.

Using Facebook Check Ins with Your Fan Page Timeline

Facebook changed the way it handles check ins in mid-2011. Until then, businesses needed to create a Fan Page Timeline and a Facebook Places page. The Places page allowed people to check into a venue. Anyone could create a Places page, but a business could claim a page and restrict the ability to edit the Places page. For instance, if a customer created a Places page for a business, but put the wrong address, that could be a problem. Facebook encouraged business owners to claim any existing "unofficial" Places pages, choose one to edit and keep as the official Places page for the business, and delete the others. Doing so helped Facebook keep Places up to date and helped businesses ensure the information about their venue was accurate and not editable by the masses (though customers could still write reviews and other updates via the Places' Timeline for that business).

Businesses didn't care much for having to watch two separate pages for customer interaction, though. Having both a Fan Page Timeline and a Places page was confusing to customers, as well as the businesses. So, in mid-2011, Facebook merged Places pages with existing Fan Page Timelines. To take advantage of this feature, Fan Page Timelines must ensure they have chosen a category that allows them to share their physical address via the Info tab on the Fan Page Timeline.

Ensuring your fans can check in via your Fan Page Timeline

Many Fan Page categories allow you to include your venue's address on the Information tab. If you share your address, city, and postal code, your Fan Page Timeline will include the option to check in via Facebook's smartphone app. Not sure if you have the option to share your address? Go to your Fan Page Timeline and click the Edit Page button in the top-right corner. From the left navigation menu, choose Basic Information. If you don't see the Address, City/Town, and Postal Code text boxes, change your category or sub-category until you find one that both fits the description of your business or venue and provides the address fields. After you update your address, when people use their smartphone's Facebook app to check into your business, those check ins are recorded on your Fan Page Timeline.

It can take several days for your Fan Page Timeline to appear in the check in list. If you've waited and your venue still isn't showing up, you may need to kick it old school and create a Places page for your venue, claim that Place as the official representative, and then merge it with your Fan Page Timeline in order for check ins to work properly. To start that process and create a new Places page for your venue, follow these steps:

1. **Open your phone's Facebook app to your personal Timeline.**

   Alternatively, point your phone's browser to `http://m.facebook.com`.

   It's best to be at or near your place of business when you create your Places page. That way, your phone's GPS has an accurate idea of where your business is located, and your Places page has the correct information.

2. **Tap the Check-In button in the top-right corner.**

   The Where Are You? screen appears with a list of nearby venues.

3. **Tap the Search text box and type your business name.**

   We searched for local business *Purse-a-nality* (as shown in Figure 4-1), but no results were found. Instead, we were given the option to add Purse-a-nality to Places so that the business will appear in future searches.

Figure 4-1: Do a search for your business to create a Places page.

4. **Tap the Add *Company Name* link (where "company name" is the name you searched for).**

   The Add a Place screen appears with a map, the name of your venue, and a place for a description. You can edit the business name by tapping the text box for the business name and typing the new name. You can add a description of the business by tapping the Description (Optional) text box and typing a short description of the venue.

5. **When you're finished typing, either tap the Done button on the keyboard or tap the Add button in the top-right corner.**

   You're taken to the check-in page for this venue so you can complete your check in. From here, you can tag people, share photos, write an update related to your check in, and customize whom you share this update with.

6. **Tap the Post button to publish your new check in.**

Claiming official and unofficial Places pages

When you check to see if your venue is appearing in the check-in options, you may notice several options for check ins for your business. Figure 4-2 shows three difference check-in options for a local restaurant. Note that each one gives a different version of the restaurant name (Senior Tequlia, Senor Tequila, and Señor Tequila Mexican Grill & Cantina).

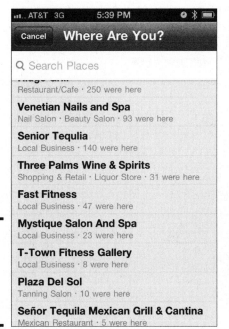

Figure 4-2: Multiple check-in options for a single restaurant.

Book IV Chapter 4

Using Your Fan Page Timeline for Check Ins and Deals

When you find multiple check-in pages for a business, it's a good bet that customers created the pages because the business didn't have its Fan Page Timeline set up to share its physical address. When the customers tried to check in, the restaurant didn't show up in their list, so they added it to the list. The result is different check-in options that the Fan Page Timeline can't track. If you're a business owner, what can you do? First, you need to check your Fan Page Timeline settings to ensure you're sharing your venue's address. Second, you need to claim each of the pages created by a customer. If you created the Places page so you could merge it with your existing Fan Page Timeline, you still need to claim it. Claiming your business on Facebook Places requires that you're the owner or official representative of the venue. You have to jump through a few hoops to prove you are who you say you are, but that's a good thing. You don't want just anyone claiming your business, right?

When you're ready to claim your business on Facebook Places, follow these steps:

1. **Log in to Facebook with your personal account**

   In this case, you want to use your computer, not your smartphone.

2. **Use the Search text box at the top to search for your business's name.**

3. **Click the See More Results link at the bottom of the list.**

   The search results page appears and lists options that match your search.

4. **Click each entry you think is related to your business to confirm that it is a rogue entry for your business.**

   You're taken to your business's Places page on Facebook, as shown in Figure 4-3.

   If the entry is not related to your business, leave it alone. Don't claim a page that isn't yours or Facebook will penalize you. If the entry is related to your business and you'd like to claim it, continue to Step 5.

Figure 4-3: A sample Places page for a business.

5. **Click the Is This Your Business link in the left navigation list.**

   A dialog box opens, explaining that claiming the business will turn it into a Fan Page Timeline if you haven't already created one. If you already have a Fan Page Timeline, don't worry, you won't have two. Instead, you'll have the opportunity to merge the check-in page with your Fan Page Timeline.

   While the dialog box says you'll do this when you claim the page, it actually won't be an option until Facebook has confirmed your claim. (As of this writing, this is an error in the Facebook documentation.) This dialog box also reminds you that only official representatives of the business can claim a Facebook place.

6. **Select the I Certify That I Am an Official Representative of *Company Name* check box.**

7. **Click the Proceed with Verification button and complete the process as instructed.**

   You need the following information:

   The information you share here should exactly match what you've shared on your Fan Page Timeline. However, not all the fields below are part of Fan Page Timeline information. In those cases (for example, Third Party Listing), go ahead and complete the field with the relevant information.

   • *Official Name of Business:* This is your business's official name. It will likely be the same as the name you type the Place Name box.

   • *Business Address:* Be sure this is your business's correct address so the Places map can provide accurate directions to your venue.

   • *Business Phone Number (If Available):* Share the ten-digit phone number you want customers to use in case they need to reach you about directions, store hours, or product availability.

   • *Business Website (If Available):* This is the URL of your actual website or blog, not your Fan Page Timeline. If you don't have a website or blog for your business, you can leave this text box blank.

   • *Third Party Listing:* If you have links to any reviews or endorsements of your business, list them here. Some examples are Yelp reviews, BBB endorsements, or Citysearch reviews.

   • *Your Relationship to This Place:* Type your title here. For instance, if you own the business, type **owner.**

8. **Click Continue and complete the verification process by providing a company e-mail address or document verification and click Submit.**

It usually takes about eight to ten hours for Facebook to verify your claim. When it does, you receive another e-mail explaining how to complete the claim process and merge your new Place page with your existing Fan Page Timeline.

Getting the Nitty-Gritty on Facebook Deals

Facebook Deals is a way to connect with your customers or the companies you do business with. With Facebook Deals, businesses who have included their physical address in their Fan Page Timeline information and/or claimed their venues (as described in the preceding section) can promote their business with discounts and Deals for customers. In addition, Facebook members who use the Facebook Check-In tool can see Deals related to businesses that are close to their current location.

Why should you consider creating a Facebook Deal? Simply put, it's free, and it's a great way to promote a relationship with existing and potential customers. You can reward frequent customers with specific discounts and Deals, or you can encourage groups to come in together. Keep in mind that each time someone checks in to your venue, her Facebook News Feed updates with a link to your business. If she tags people with her, the update appears in those extra feeds as well (unless the tagged person has his privacy settings adjusted, as explained earlier in the chapter in the "Protecting Your Privacy" section).

Why do updates in Facebook News Feeds matter? When something appears in a Facebook News Feed, all the friends connected to that person see the update. Facebook estimates that each user has an average of 130 friends (some have more, some have fewer). If you're a business owner and just one of your customers shares a Deal she liked via Places, that update reaches a potential audience of 130 *more* people than just that one person who took advantage of your Deal. The more reasons you can give people to share your business with their friends, the more exposure you get. If one of their friends chimes in and shares the Places update or the Facebook Deal, you've reached *two* sets of Facebook friends. Even if they have only 130 friends each, that's potentially 260 people who now know about your Place and Deals. And the endorsement that the users already like your business or the Deal encourages their friends to also take advantage of it.

In the following sections, we explain more about how to create and promote Deals for your business, and how to train your employees to honor them.

Exploring the types of Facebook Deals

Here are the current kinds of Facebook Deals:

✦ **Individual Deal:** These Deals are for both established and new customers, and they're for individuals instead of groups. Individual Deals are a great way to get rid of extra inventory or bring attention to a new product, and they work well to get foot traffic into your store.

✦ **Friend Deal:** These Deals are for groups (up to eight people per group) who check in together via Places. As you can imagine, this works well if you want to get maximum exposure for your Deal. All the people who check in will share the check in and Facebook Deal on their Facebook News Feeds. You're essentially advertising to all the friends of each person in the group.

Everyone in the group has to be checked in to the venue to redeem the Deal. So if a member tags eight friends in her check in, but all those friends aren't with her or don't also check in, she won't get the Deal.

✦ **Loyalty Deal:** Want to reward your tried-and-true customers? Set them up with a Loyalty Deal. These Deals are similar to a punch card and provide a reward after a certain number of check ins. When you create this type of Deal, the reward has to be redeemable after at least two check ins, but no more than 20 check ins.

✦ **Charity Deal:** Do you have a favorite charity? You can choose to create a Charity Deal so that part of your proceeds are donated to the charity of your choice. You have to manage the actual donation to charity on your own, so this option requires a bit of planning on your part (for example, how will you keep track of check ins and convert those into money for the charity?).

Facebook members can search for Facebook Deals via their smartphone's Facebook app or by pointing their phone's browser to http://m.facebook.com. Then they tap Check In to see a list of nearby places. If any businesses in their vicinity offer a Facebook Deal, they see a Deals icon next to the listing, as shown next to Purse-a-nality and Fuji Sushi Bar in Figure 4-4.

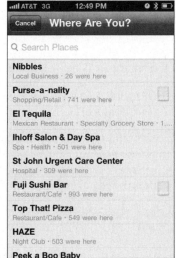

Figure 4-4: Facebook Deals are marked with a special icon.

To view a Facebook Deal, the Facebook member simply taps the name of the business offering the Deal. A page for that business appears that provides more information about the business and gives a description of the Deal. For example, in Figure 4-5, Purse-a-nality offers a discount to customers who check in.

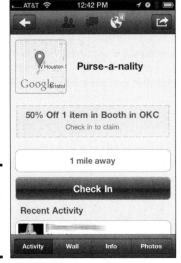

Figure 4-5:
An example of a Facebook Deal.

If members want to claim the Deal, they simply tap the Claim Deal! button and show the Deal to the cashier to claim their discount.

Creating a Facebook Deal

To create a successful Facebook Deal, consider your goals. Do you want to reward loyal customers? Do you want to entice new customers? Do you want more sales regardless of whether the customer is new? Do you want to promote a specific product? There are infinite possibilities, but knowing your specific goals allows you to tailor your Facebook Deal to achieve those goals more efficiently and track how well your Deal works.

Think ahead: Your Deal must be approved before it goes live. Facebook takes two days to approve your ad and then sends an e-mail letting you know your status. To help ensure your ad is approved, make sure it follows Facebook's formatting guidelines found at www.facebook.com/help/?page=18855.

When you're ready to create a Facebook Deal and associate it with your Facebook Place, follow these steps:

1. **Using your computer's browser, go to your business's Fan Page Timeline on Facebook and click the Edit Page button to find your dashboard.**

If you've included your venue's physical address in your Fan Page Timeline's information (Edit Page➪Basic Information), you see the Deals link in the left navigation of your Fan Page Timeline dashboard (see Figure 4-6).

Figure 4-6: The Deals link is at the bottom of your dashboard's left navigation.

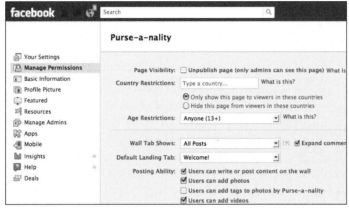

2. **Click the Deals link.**

3. **Click the Create Check-In Deal for This Page button.**

If you're using Facebook as your Fan Page Timeline instead of as your personal Timeline, Facebook asks you to switch over to your personal Timeline before continuing. See Book IV, Chapter 2 for information about switching between Timelines.

4. **Select the radio button next to the type of Deal you want to create.**

See the preceding section for the lowdown on the different Deals you can create.

5. **Define your offer by completing the Deal Summary and How to Claim options.**

Be concise with your Deal summary. Phones have small screens and limited space. Instead of writing a paragraph welcoming new customers and explaining your company philosophy, keep it simple with something like "50% Off Lunch Special."

In the How to Claim text box, tell your customers exactly what they ne to do to claim the Deal. For example, you could type something like **Show cashier this Deal** or **Show cashier your screen.**

6. **Add offer details and restrictions.**

    This option defines how customers can use your Deal. You can set the following:

    - *Start and End Dates:* Choose when you want your Deal to run. You can even include specific times of day for the start and end dates.

    - *Max Redemptions:* Decide how many Deals you want to give away with this promotion. You can choose to stop the Deal after *X* number of redemptions or let the Deal be redeemed an unlimited number of times.

    - *Repeat Claims:* Choose whether customers can claim the Deal only once or once per 24 hours.

7. **Click the Create Deal button.**

    You see a message with your Deal's start and end dates and some additional information about your Deal.

You can run only one Facebook Deal at a time.

Promoting your Facebook Deal

After you set up a Deal, create some buzz behind it. The easiest way to tell people about your Deal is to post a status update to your Fan Page Timeline as well as your personal Timeline (if that's a fit). Make sure your Fan Page Timeline has the correct business hours, address, and phone number.

Just because this is a Facebook Deal doesn't mean you shouldn't utilize your other social media channels. Tweet about your Facebook Deal, write a blog post explaining the Deal, and post the Deal on your website — all with a link back to your Fan Page Timeline on Facebook. And why not promote the Deal in the store as well? Have employees remind your customers to check into your venue via their smartphones so they can claim special coupons. Regardless of where you promote your Deal, be clear that the Deal is redeemable only if customers check in via their phone's Facebook app so there isn't confusion later.

nt more exposure targeted to specific demographics, consider running Facebook (see Book V, Chapter 5 for more information on how to . When you place your ad for the Deal, be sure to link it back to your Timeline.

ng on the purpose of your Deal (such as introducing your product ustomers), you may want to consider how you target specific demo- s when setting up your Facebook ad. If you want to reward existing customers, be sure to target people who already Like your Fan Page e on Facebook. Alternatively, if you want to target new customers, want to consider running the ad specifically for people who have Liked your Fan Page Timeline.

Honoring your Facebook Deal

A few companies have learned the hard way that it's important to plan your Deal before you run it. Some companies have had a bad experience because employees didn't know about the Deal, stores ran out of promotional products, and/or customers didn't know how to redeem the Deal successfully. As you can imagine, both sides of the transaction were unsatisfied. This section gives you some advice on how to plan your Deal so it's a good experience for you *and* your customer.

Facebook is a social place where people share their experiences. If customers have a poor experience or a Deal is denied, they can and will update their statuses associated with your business to let their friends know how they were treated and whether the Deal was a dud.

If, on the other hand, employees are friendly, understand the Deal and how to redeem it, and the transaction goes smoothly, customers are likely to share that positive experience as well.

As the manager or owner of a store, when you develop a Facebook Deal, you can do a few things to ensure the Deal runs smoothly and customers are satisfied:

✦ **Try the Deal.** After you know what Deal you want to offer and how you want it to work, give it a try. Staff meetings are a great time to make sure everyone knows what's coming and practice redeeming the Deal. If you find a glitch, fix it before the Deal goes live.

✦ **Think ahead.** When your Deal expires or all products have been claimed, how will you handle customers who come in and ask for the Deal? Your employees need to have a clear plan of action to address these requests or complaints.

✦ **Communicate with your customers on your Fan Page Timeline.** It's likely that many of your customers follow you on Facebook. Let them know about upcoming and current Deals, but also let them know when a Deal is expired so they don't make a wasted trip.

✦ **Prepare for the rush.** If you think your Deal is going to encourage an influx of customers, be sure you have enough people working to cover the added business. Ensure that each person working understands what the Deal includes, how it should be redeemed, and what their role is. In addition, make sure you have enough products to fulfill the Deal you create. If you offer an insulated bag with the purchase of a watch, know how many bags you have to give away and set your Deal to expire when those bags are gone. To do that, you need to consider how you'll track Deal redemptions and how many bags you've already given away.

✦ **Make a plan.** If you create a Facebook Deal that will be honored in multiple stores, you need to have a very specific plan in place. You have to create the Deal for each Places page for each store, communicate to employees across the board on how to promote and redeem the Deal, and let them know how to handle customer requests after the Deal is over.

If you have more than one store, Facebook suggests you contact a Facebook account manager to have that person help you set up your Facebook Deal.

After you have your plan in place, it's important to convey that plan to your employees. It's very frustrating to customers if they try to redeem a Deal and an employee doesn't know how to redeem it, or worse, refuses to redeem it because he wasn't aware of the Deal. For your Deal to run smoothly, be sure to tell employees what to expect. Take the time to explain the following:

✦ **Exactly what the Deal covers:** Also, figure out whether substitutions can be made.

✦ **How long the Deal will run:** Know the dates and times, as applicable.

✦ **The terms of the Deal, including any limitations:** These limitations should also be part of the Deal as users see it; customers aren't fond of the bait and switch!

✦ **How to process the Deal:** For instance, do cashiers have to key in a special code? Will that code be on the customer's smartphone screen, or will the employee need to know it? How will employees keep track of how many Deals are redeemed?

Facebook check-in Deals are excellent tools for customers to share what they're doing, find fun venues nearby, and save a few bucks while they're at it. With a little planning, check-in Deals can also be important tools to grow your business.

Introducing Offers

On February 29, 2012, Facebook unveiled several new changes to its platform, including a new version of Check-In Deals called *Offers*. At the writing of this book, Offers hasn't been rolled out to the masses. Instead, it's only being offered to a handful of very large businesses (such as Macy's and Old Navy) who are managed advertising clients (in other words, they spend more than $10,000 per month on Facebook advertising and have a dedicated account manager).

We understand that by the time you have this book in your hands, the information in this particular chapter may have changed significantly, and we wish we had a little more control over that. Facebook is an ever-changing platform (we actually think that's a good thing!), and we've done our best to incorporate the many changes that occurred while writing this book. Facebook has incorporated Offers into its Help Center; you can find more information about Offers at `https://www.facebook.com/help/offers`.

A few key things to know about Offers are

✦ Offers are like coupons for your customers (much like Check-In Deals) and are free to create.

✦ If your Fan Page Timeline is eligible to use Offers, you can go to the Sharing tool at the top of your Timeline (we don't see this as an option yet) and click the Offer link to start creating your offer. The advice we share about creating a strong Check-In Deal still applies to creating a strong Offer.

✦ When users claim an Offer, they receive an e-mail message with the Offer details that they can redeem at the store by showing the clerk.

Chapter 5: Customizing Your Fan Page Timeline

In This Chapter

✓ Creating a first impression

✓ Apps to create custom Application Pages

✓ Creating a Static HTML Application Page

✓ Content for fans and nonfans

A s you market your business through your Facebook Fan Page Timeline, you'll discover that there is more to setting up your Fan Page Timeline than simply creating it and filling out the basic information. Every marketer should be aware of a few elements in the Fan Page Timeline makeup. Knowing the flexibility of Fan Page Timelines and how you can manipulate each aspect can open up some ways to get better marketing traction out of your Fan Page.

Marketing starts with good branding, and these days your Fan Page is an important part of communicating that brand. The look of your Fan Page Timeline has a great impact on how effective it is as a marketing tool. Facebook empowers you to customize certain areas of your Fan Page Timeline; however, it comes with limits as well. While Facebook limits how much you can customize your Fan Page Timeline, it ultimately is for the better of the site.

Because Facebook is sure to control the content on its site, you can be certain that content will load quickly and not get hung up from customizations. With those restrictions, you also have a lot of freedoms, too. Custom Application Pages, for example, are always hosted outside of the Facebook servers and are viewed via iframes. An *iframe* is basically a window that displays content from another site. This means that you can do whatever you want with your Facebook custom tabs without affecting Facebook.

Why Looks Matter

In the most general sense, the overall look of a Fan Page Timeline and personal Timeline is very simple and consistent. As we dig in a little bit deeper into the capabilities of a Fan Page Timeline, we show you how to leverage some of Facebook's Fan Page Timeline customizations. Taking advantage of the options sends a stronger message and make a greater first impression when you market your business.

When someone visits your Fan Page Timeline, you have a matter of seconds to capture her interest. Some studies say that within four seconds, visitors judge your company, and over 75 percent of visitors are judging your company by the look of your site alone. Your Fan Page Timeline is an extension of your web presence, and a well-designed web presence is representative of a better company.

One important consideration is what outcome you're looking for. The appearance of your Fan Page Timeline plays a big role in the ultimate results. For example, say you want to get people to take a customer survey. This survey helps you get information about your customer base so that you know what items they're interested in, and you can collect customer data such as address and e-mail. A simple, clean design with a clear call to action (like a button that says Take Survey) will have better results than a messy design with only text links.

To put it simply, if your design is aesthetically pleasing and your message is clear and simple, you're sure to get better results!

Creating a first impression with a cover photo

When someone clicks a link or searches Facebook to land on your Fan Page Timeline, what he sees first is the most important thing. Creating your first impression is all about capturing visitors' attention with what they see in the first moment on your Fan Page Timeline. Your cover photo in most cases allows you to create this first impression with a branded look.

Your *cover photo* is an image that is displayed on the top of your Fan Page Timeline, the full width of the Timeline. You can choose any image or photograph that you upload to your Fan Page Timeline's photos; however, customizing it is a great idea for shaping visitors' first impressions. Figure 5-1 shows the Timeline view of a Fan Page from Involver software. This allows Involver to present a custom branded look to all visitors, as well as present a message to them.

Facebook has certain limitations to what you can show in your cover photo. Facebook prohibits administrators from including the following elements in a cover photo:

✦ **Calls to action** (asking visitors to do something) such as "Sign up Now" or "Tell Your Friends"

✦ **Pricing or purchasing information** such as the announcement of a sale or percentage off

✦ **Reference to user interface elements** such as Like or Share

✦ **Contact information** including phone numbers and web addresses

Figure 5-1:
A customized
Fan Page
Timeline.

Creating fans-only content

When someone visits your Fan Page Timeline, and he hasn't yet Liked it, he sees the same view as any fan, including all of your updates. You have to give him a compelling reason to want to Like your Fan Page. One great way to do this is to provide interesting content that's available to fans only, something he can get right at that moment. Application Pages (also called *tabs*) allow you to create separate content for fans and nonfans. Use this method to encourage new visitors to Like your Fan Page instantly for access to special information. When you build this tab, you can create it with two versions: One for fans and another for nonfans. Most visitors arrive at your Fan Page Timeline from a direct link outside of Facebook, such as a link in an e-mail message or on your website. When placing this link for marketing, consider using the URL that leads to your application tab.

Anything that can be built into a website can be built into an Application Page. This allows Facebook marketers to create exciting additions to make their Fan Page Timelines more engaging and branded to the company. For example, a common use of an Application Page is to hold contests, as shown in Figure 5-2. Figures 5-3 and 5-4 show examples of what a nonfan sees versus what a fan sees.

Figure 5-2:
Facebook contests embedded into a Fan Page.

Figure 5-3:
A tab for nonfans.

Choosing a profile picture

The next area to consider when making a first impression is the profile picture. This profile picture might be a logo of your company or picture of you (especially if you have a Fan Page Timeline for you as a public figure). By no means are you limited in what sort of image you can put within the profile picture area. However, the image area that can be seen is 125 pixels wide by 135 pixels tall. Regardless of what image you upload, you need to select a thumbnail segment of the image. You can use this area to get some attention and capture the interest of your visitors, or represent your brand with a logo or face. (See Figure 5-5 for an example.)

Figure 5-4:
A tab for
fans.

The profile picture is one of the first things that anyone who visits your Fan Page Timeline sees, even fans. All of your updates display the profile picture as well. You can use this area to highlight a special campaign or contest, but keep it real simple because this area is small. Too much detail won't stand out in the News Feed. Unlike tabs, no additional functionality is allowed in profile pictures. This area is limited to a simple image only.

Figure 5-5:
First
impressions
with profile
pictures.

The following steps describe how to choose or change your profile picture:

1. **From your Fan Page Timeline home screen, hover your mouse over the profile picture space.**

   An Edit Profile Picture link appears.

2. **Click the Change Cover link and choose from the following options:**

   - *Choose from Photos:* Select an image from photos currently uploaded to your Fan Page Timeline.

   - *Upload Photo:* Select a photo from your computer and upload it to your Fan Page Timeline.

   - *Reposition:* Use your mouse to center the portion of the image you want to display.

   - *Remove:* Remove the current profile picture.

   After you select a photo, you're prompted drag the image into the desired position. After doing so, click Save Changes. Your cover image will display in the cover image area.

Choosing Highlighted Apps

Highlighted Apps are the top three Application Pages that you select to display directly below the cover photo on the right side. These apps include a few that are built in to all Fan Pages by Facebook, such as a map to your location or the number of Likes your Fan Page has. You can also put all your custom Application Pages in this area. To do so, click the down arrow to the right of the Highlighted Apps area (the row containing Photos, Likes, Map, and so on) to reveal other applications or available spaces. (See Figure 5-6.) Click the plus sign at the top right of any of the blank areas to add a new application to your list. Only the top three appear at first glance on your Fan Page Timeline. Users have to click the down arrow to reveal all the other applications you have installed in your Fan Page.

Photos is always the first app on your Highlighted Apps. You can't move this one. All your latest photo uploads show here (the most recent one shows). This also looks like a button as well, so upload great photos that people will want to click!

When you have all the applications revealed on your Fan Page Timeline, the small button at the top right of the application is a pencil, indicating that you can edit the application. Click the pencil icon to edit the settings as follows:

+ **Remove** the app from your favorites.

+ **Swap** its position with another application (the top three are visible on landing on your Fan Page Timeline).

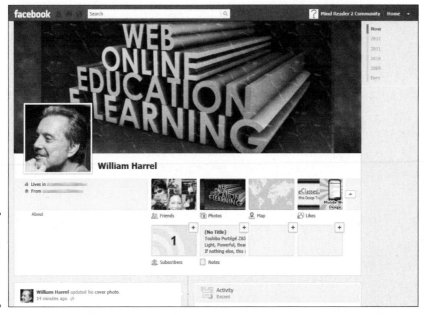

Figure 5-6:
Applications installed in your Fan Page.

+ **Reveal** the direct link to the Application Page.

+ **Uninstall** the application.

+ **Edit** the application's settings.

Editing the settings allows you to change the name of the application, as well as change the image that displays on your Fan Page Timeline. This image acts as a button leading to the application page from your Fan Page Timeline.

Adding Highlighted updates

Highlighted updates are a great way of highlighting certain status updates. A Highlighted update makes an update the full width of the Timeline, and as time moves along and you add more status updates, the Featured update retains the full width of the Timeline. This is great for milestones or important events. Another way to use a Featured update is to highlight calls to action for your visitors.

To make a status update a Highlighted update, hover the mouse over the status update in the Fan Page Timeline and click the Highlight (star) icon.

Using the Fan Page Timeline real estate

Facebook has a limited area that you can customize, and that customization is valuable when you're trying to get a branding or marketing message across to your Facebook audience. When space is limited, it's important that your use of the space is meaningful and effective. You want to be sure that you use every bit of the space available, yet use it in a tasteful way that doesn't leave a cluttered appearance. A well-designed Fan Page Timeline can attract more traffic simply because people may share it, especially if the design is particularly innovative. On the other hand, if you have a poorly designed Fan Page Timeline, there may be very little reason why someone would even consider returning to the Fan Page or recommending it to others.

Function is important too. Giving people a compelling reason to visit your Fan Page Timeline is going to bring more traffic than a cool design. For example, if you regularly post new videos, visitors may return to see the latest, while if your Fan Page Timeline merely shows a static graphic, one visit may be all you get from a fan.

To make the most of your Fan Page Timeline design, think about the restrictions and use them to your advantage. Here are some ways that you can do this and make the best use of the real estate that Facebook allows you:

+ Make the application images shown directly below the cover photo intriguing. Entice people to click to see more.

+ Consider the use of white space (blank space) to make images in a tab or profile pic stand out more.

+ Use the barriers in a creative way to make designs look like they were meant to be that way.

If you're not a designer, some of these ideas may be challenging. We recommend a simple design rather than something that isn't really well executed. If you can, it's well worth spending a few dollars to have a good designer put together some professional graphics for your Fan Page Timeline.

Creating Custom Application Pages

Facebook Application Pages are areas that can be completely customized to fit your brand and the look or functions that you want. Facebook permits an image that is 810 pixels wide, and there are no major limits of what web features you can apply here. Facebook's Application Pages are often referred to as *tabs* as well.

The Application Pages are rendered in iframes, which is an HTML structure that allows an HTML document to be displayed inside of another. In short, what you're viewing inside the frame (the tab) is a web page that's on another web destination not hosted on Facebook. You can literally iframe a portion of any website and display it inside of a Facebook tab.

Don't forget the little things

Customizing your Fan Page Timeline with graphics, and even applications, is great, but there are a couple little things we want you to keep in mind that have an impact on the appearance of your Fan Page Timeline. Perhaps the simplest thing you can do to ensure that your Fan Page has a nice dynamic look is to post good content. Here are a few tips to have a nice-looking Fan Page:

✔ **Include links in your posts often.** Links pull in thumbnails images, which are more catchy to the eye than text alone.

✔ **Look for a good thumbnail.** When posting a link, Facebook allows you to select from images available on the site you're sharing. Selecting one that tells the reader what the

site is about is more effective than something that means very little to the reader who just happened to be on that page.

✔ **Don't post too much content.** Sometimes you need to post frequently, but when you post too much text, people may be less likely to absorb your post when they're skimming their News Feeds. Save the longer posts for elsewhere and share short tidbits that will whet their appetite.

✔ **Select an image for your profile picture that can be seen well when it's small.** You want to make sure that people know what they're looking at when they see your posts in their News Feeds.

Because of this flexible format, your tab can show anything that's 810 pixels wide (or less), such as an image, video game, photo gallery, or video player.

Creating a custom Application Page doesn't require you to be a web developer. You can create a tab from scratch, or you can use one of the many apps that are available on Facebook that allow you to create a variety of types of Application Pages. Some popular apps for custom Application Pages are listed here:

✦ **Involver** (www.involver.com) includes several apps for tab designs, including both free and paid types. Some of the best free apps allow you to do many of the things that many Facebook marketers want to do, whether they're marketing for a small organization or a large company. Here is a partial list:

- *RSS feed:* Add an RSS feed to a Facebook tab to feature a blog or other information through RSS.

- *YouTube:* Feature the videos from your YouTube channel right on your Fan Page.

- *Twitter:* Show all of your updates from your Twitter feed on a tab.

- *Coupons:* Share coupons with your Facebook fans and add a social sharing aspect to coupons.

- *Static HTML:* Create a simple page with a static image that visitors can click through to view another site or page.

✦ **Wildfire** (www.wildfireapp.com) is known most commonly as a contest platform or promotion builder. They have a variety of applications that differ based on the type of contest you want to do. They are predominantly paid apps that start at as little at $5. Some promotions types that Wildfire supports are

- *Contests:* Build unique contests that include video, voting, or sharing.

- *Coupons:* Use coupons to monetize your fans and drive customers to your store or site.

- *Trivia and quizzes:* Use trivia and quiz apps to increase engagement with your fan base.

✦ **TabSite** (www.tabsite.com) allows you to create multiple tabs within a single tab, kind of like creating a full website within your Fan Page Timeline. TabSite has free options for the starter as well as paid options for more serious marketers. TabSite has a wide variety of features that can be built into tabs with its simple WYSIWYG (what you see is what you get) editor. TabSite offers the following to marketers:

- *Content text editor:* A WYSIWYG (what you see is what you get) editor that enables you to create and edit content of the application.

- *Image widget:* Enables you to upload images to a tab using drag and drop.

- *E-mail sign-up form:* Gives you the ability to easily embed an e-mail sign-up for popular e-mail marketing clients such as MailChimp or Constant Contact.

- *Google Maps:* Gives you the ability to add a Google map to your tab.

- *Facebook social plugins:* Enables you to add Like buttons, Share buttons, and so on.

- *HotLink:* Enables you to add a see-through layer that can link to any URL (for example, showing a portion of a larger image).

Most of the examples described in the preceding list have a simple, user-friendly interface. There is seemingly an endless list of Facebook customizing tools. Some of these options will hopefully help you open your imagination to all the things that are possible with your Fan Page Timeline, even if you aren't ready to jump to the expert level. If you're ready, we help you get started building your own Application Pages in Book VI, Chapter 2.

Book V

Marketing Your Business on Facebook

The 5th Wave   By Rich Tennant

"I'd respond to this person's comment on Twitter, but I'm a former Marine, Bernard, and a Marine never retweets."

Contents at a Glance

Chapter 1: Building a Network of Influence with Your Fan Page Timeline

In This Chapter

✔ Building a fanbase for your business

✔ Connecting with fans

✔ Adding Facebook into marketing campaigns

✔ Getting more Timeline posts from fans

Social media is about connecting with friends, fans, and followers. When marketing a business in the Facebook world, it's not uncommon for people to focus on how many fans they have. The fact is, if you have fans, but you have no influence over them, then you might be wasting your time and perhaps marketing dollars. Success on Facebook isn't just about building an audience, but about building an audience that is listening. Better yet, it's about building a network of influence — by that we mean you're not only influencing your own audience, but their friends and connections as well. That's what this chapter is about. In the following sections, we give you practical advice on how to increase engagement with your current customers and how to attract new customers.

While this chapter focuses on growing your business using your Fan Page Timeline, much of our advice is useful for individuals who are just looking to up their game on Facebook and have a more popular personal Timeline. We want to be clear, though, that if you're promoting your business or branding your business on Facebook, you should abide by the Facebook terms of service and create a Fan Page Timeline instead of using your personal Timeline for your business.

The Importance of Engagement

When people Like your Fan Page Timeline, they value a connection with your company, at least to some degree. That connection has to have some meaning, and no matter how small or large your company is, the more you can humanize your brand, the more value you will get out of your marketing efforts. This is done through engagement. You can't build engagement without some human effort behind your Facebook marketing. You can automate at lot, but at the end of the day, people are looking to connect with other people. When customers feel that your company values the personal connection to them, they are more likely to do business with you.

Don't forget about being top of mind. If customers have several choices when buying a product or service, all things being equal, whoever they remember is who gets the business. This is one big reason why engagement on your Fan Page Timeline is so important. Consumers tend to have a higher level of trust for a brand if they're more familiar with it by name or experience. This certainly presents a good case for having a presence on Facebook, but all the more for having an active presence where you engage with your consumers. Figure 1-1 shows an example of how a local restaurant chain reached out to its customers to meet a need. Customers commented and felt connected to the brand.

Figure 1-1:
Creating
meaningful
connections.

Facebook and other social media sites have fostered a social media–driven world where people expect to be able to interact with their favorite brands. Some of this will happen automatically if you have a wide enough name recognition. Some will happen only as you nurture your customer connections. What you'll find is that when you nurture those customer connections, they become better customers and they recommend you to their friends.

Building fans for your business

We're sorry to tell you that you won't have a successful experience with Facebook for your business if you don't make the effort to build an audience. Building an audience starts with inviting people to Like your Fan Page. The next step is to get some interaction from the people that like your Fan Page and turn them into loyal fans that will tell their friends about you.

Here are a few ways to start building fans for your business:

✦ **Start in house:** When you first launch your Fan Page Timeline, one of the most important things to do is get the ball rolling. People like to be where the party is, and having a starting group really helps! The best way to do this is to look to the people already involved with your company. Start by inviting everyone within your company to Like the Fan Page. From there, each employee or partner can ask their personal friends to Like the Fan Page as well.

✦ **Ask and invite:** No one is going to find your Fan Page Timeline if they don't know to look for it, so it's a good idea to take every opportunity to share Facebook with your customers. It seems too easy, but a simple "Please Like our Fan Page" really does work. Incorporate a link to your Fan Page Timeline into your e-newsletter reminding your customers to Like your Fan Page on Facebook. You'll get a good number of people that would be happy to click the Like button and be the first among your Facebook audience. If you hand customers a receipt, put your Facebook address on the receipt, or hand them a card with your Facebook address. At the very least, remind them verbally to find you on Facebook and be sure to Like the Fan Page.

Keep the News Ticker in the back of your mind, too. When you have several people Liking your Fan Page at the same time, the News Ticker is going to show more Facebook Like activity, and increase the chance that a friend of a fan will Like your Fan Page.

✦ **Use custom tabs:** When you create a custom Static HTML: iframe tab, you have the opportunity to create more incentives around becoming a fan (find out more about creating custom tabs in Book IV, Chapter 5). Because iframes allow you to have content that is only for fans (this is called *Like-gating* or *fan-gating*), you can create a tab that delivers something really compelling only through Facebook, and only to fans. For example, you can create a tab that invites potential fans to Like your Fan Page in order to download coupons, a white paper related to your niche, or even a short e-book. Giving potential fans a reason to Like your Fan Page is easy with a custom tab.

✦ **Use contests and sweepstakes:** Daniel loves to use contests to promote Fan Pages. Recently, he conducted a contest on a client's Fan Page Timeline that asked fans to upload a photo to a third-party app and have their friends vote for their photo. Because Daniel Like-gated the application, their friends had to Like the Fan Page to access the voting app within the tab. This led to a 430 percent growth in Likes!

Facebook has strict guidelines for hosting contests and sweepstakes on its platform. Be sure and read Book V, Chapter 4 to familiarize yourself with the guidelines. Breaking the rules could mean losing your Fan Page Timeline!

✦ **Make a difference:** About a year ago, one of Daniel's customers was launching a Fan Page Timeline for the first time. In an effort to create some buzz and get a burst of new followers, the customer launched a campaign to donate a dollar to a local charity for every Like on its Fan Page within a certain time. The charity was promoting the campaign, and so were all the company's employees. The customer grew his Facebook audience by giving potential fans a compelling reason to Like his Fan Page Timeline.

Connecting with your fans

You need to connect with your fans, but how do you keep up if you have a large audience? You can connect with your Facebook fans in many ways; you're not just limited to making comments and posts.

The following list provides a few ideas that you can use to connect with your fans:

✦ **Ask questions:** It's not about you, it's about your audience. The best thing you can do for your Facebook engagement is to ask questions of your Facebook fans. When you give them a chance to talk, not only do they actually take a step into engaging with you, but their activity shows up in their friend's News Ticker. When their friends see that activity, they may be more likely to come check out your Fan Page Timeline and become a fan.

✦ **Encourage them to check back later:** You want your fans to be repeat visitors. Sometimes it's just a matter of letting your fans know that more is coming tomorrow. How about posing a riddle of the day, and offering the answer the next day, along with a new riddle? This leaves people wanting more and wanting to come back to find out the answer. With Timeline's Pin feature, you can pin the daily riddle, question, or discussion to the top of your Fan Page Timeline. Or you could create a new cover photo each week with a new question. If your fans come to expect a new cover photo on a certain day each week, you encourage them to visit your Fan Page Timeline regularly.

✦ **Comment on other Fan Pages as your Fan Page:** It's not much fun to have a one-sided conversation, is it? It's important to remember that if you want people to interact with you, you also need to interact with them. You can even comment as your Fan Page Timeline (your business) rather than your personal Timeline (yourself). See Book IV, Chapter 2 for an explanation of how to do that.

Figure 1-2 shows how Daniel commented on another Fan Page's status update as his company redwallLIVE. By commenting as his Fan Page instead of himself, he's introducing his brand to potential fans.

Figure 1-2:
Commenting
as a Fan
Page.

You can't comment on personal Timelines when you're using Facebook as your Fan Page Timeline, you can only interact on another Fan Page Timeline. (We know it sounds confusing, but once you see it in action, you'll get it! Book IV, Chapter 2 explains this feature in detail.)

The value of commenting as your Fan Page is making mutual connections by connecting with other businesses and building connections with some of their fans. This may lead to some of their fans choosing to check out your Fan Page Timeline to find out more about your business.

✦ **Be a real person:** It's okay to let your personality shine through on your Fan Page Timeline. Be funny, be serious, be professional. We're sure you know your goals and your audience and you know what they can handle. We just wanted to encourage you to bring a little of yourself to the Fan Page Timeline!

If you have multiple people in your office who update the Fan Page Timeline, have them sign their updates with their name. Your fans will start to recognize your employees (and their personalities) and will feel a stronger connection with your entire company.

If you have a large audience, you can't always talk one on one with them all. Daniel suggests focusing on the influencers and those that are most engaging. You will still project a human brand to your audience, even to those who aren't commenting directly with you.

Integrating Facebook in Marketing Campaigns

If you own a business, you know finding and growing your audience is essential for long-term success because those connections are the ones that lead to repeat business and referrals. As your Facebook audience grows, take advantage of the opportunity to build loyalty with those that connect with your company. With a successful Facebook marketing strategy, you still use traditional marketing tactics. If Facebook proves to be a strong platform for your company, then use outside marketing campaigns as a tool to drive new connections to Facebook. Do this by making Facebook the ultimate call to action. If your primary goal is to build an audience for long-term sales and customer loyalty, then a call to action that leads them to Facebook is ideal.

Promoting Facebook via traditional advertising

You can advertise your company or product in many ways. With traditional advertising, your goal is to be seen by potential customers so that they know who you are and will choose to buy your product. Advertising is always more memorable if the person you reach takes some kind of action.

 In addition to creating a memory, creating a database is important too. Advertising can be expensive. Not only do you want a customer to buy your product today, you want her to buy again tomorrow. For example, after a car dealership sells a car to a customer, the next challenge is to get the customer to refer new customers to you. Continuing on, the next challenge is to get the customer back for service on his vehicle. If you can convince this loyal customer to connect with your Fan Page Timeline, he becomes part of your database from which you can ask for repeat business or encourage referrals. This is why promoting your Fan Page within your traditional marketing is so valuable.

The following list gives tips to promote your Fan Page Timeline using traditional marketing (and you can find more in Book V, Chapter 6):

+ **Billboard ads:** If your marketing campaign is going to reach a broad audience in a concentrated city (or several cities), a billboard may be part of your marketing strategy. Driving people to your Fan Page Timeline from a billboard is challenging. Billboards only allow for a very simple message, and a long URL might be difficult. If your company name is unique, it might be most effective to invite people to find people by searching your company name. Do this by telling people, "Search for us by name on Facebook." A more common name may make that difficult through. For example, redwallLIVE might be fairly unique and therefore easy to find in a search. On the other hand, something like Bob's Car Care may be the name of several places and it may be difficult to find the correct one in a Facebook search.

 Keep in mind that Facebook search is literal. If you search for *red wall LIVE* instead of *redwalLIVE,* you won't find Daniel's Fan Page Timeline. The capitalization isn't important, but the spaces between the words are. This is important to note as a Fan Page owner because you want to be sure to title your Fan Page Timeline as you think people will search for it. It's important to know as a customer so when you're searching for a company you know to pay attention to how the name is commonly spelled (and spaced) so you can find what you're looking for.

✦ **Print ads and handouts:** Someone who discovers your company in a favorite magazine or receives a handout has a little more time to read your message. Print ads and handouts are perhaps the easiest ways to get a message across because you can provide ample information. Often times, incorporating the Facebook logo and colors helps to make it more clear that your Fan Page Timeline can be found on Facebook.

✦ **Get your free sample:** People love getting free samples before they decide to make a purchase. One really powerful way to build a database is by offering a free sample to anyone who requests it. You can create an iframe tab that hosts a contact form where people submit their contact information to receive a free sample.

Makes sure that the actual form is just in the fans-only section, so that people have to Like your Fan Page to access it. (You can find out how to do this in Book IV, Chapter 5.)

✦ **The secret password:** If you've found a website that makes sense for you to advertise on, driving people with a good call to action is critical. You don't just want them to see the ad, you want them to click and take action. Imagine your company is a credit counseling service, and you're offering a free initial credit evaluation session. Your advertisement could say, "Click to go to our Fan Page Timeline and get the secret password to redeem your free initial session." With this, you have the opportunity use a fans-only iframe tab that gives the password. Not only are you sure to get people that are interested in your services, they become Facebook fans at the same time.

Having a memorable URL

When you share your Facebook URL as a call to action, it needs to be memorable. For example, if you are advertising on a billboard, then your audience has a matter of a couple seconds to read your ad. If the URL is a long destination, you may not get any traffic.

Make sure that you have custom Facebook username (also called a vanity URL) for your Fan Page Timeline. Book IV, Chapter 1 shows you how to create your own vanity URL.

After you have a vanity URL for your Fan Page Timeline, it's a lot easier to tell people where to find you. You may find that your company name is fine for a username, but not for an easy-to-remember ad, especially if it's long or hard to spell. If you have a company name that is not conducive to being memorable in the form of a Facebook URL, then try a typical web URL and redirect it to your Fan Page Timeline. If you do it this way, you can even redirect the URL to a specific tab, because Facebook tabs each have a unique URL.

You can buy a URL from NameCheap (`www.namecheap.com`), among other places. These services always have a simple function to allow you to direct your web address to any other page.

When creating your marketing materials, be sure you use the proper URL address. Make sure it's the URL you see when looking at your Fan Page Timeline the way your fans view it, not your home screen where you look at your News Feed.

Using apps to build influence

Using third-party apps can help to strengthen your engagement with your fan base because you can customize specific functions and characteristics into your Fan Page Timeline. Apps can provide a variety of functions if you have the resources to develop them. (You can discover the basics of developing apps in Book VI.) For example, if you provide efficient heating and air equipment, you could build a home efficiency calculator app that allows users to find out how they can lower their heating bills. The idea with this is to generate more influence with your fans by providing value.

Apps should, of course, be relevant to your business and the people you want to attract. For example, if your business is an arcade, how about having a game that fans can play right on your Fan Page Timeline? If you aren't ready to invest in developing (or even repurposing) a customized app, you can use several simpler apps to customize your Fan Page Timeline and provide value. You can find out about some of the ways to customize your Fan Page Timeline in Book IV, Chapter 5.

Outsourcing your Facebook management

When running a business (especially as the owner), sometimes you have to balance all the many tasks and determine what is the best use of your time. The question comes up frequently, "Is it okay to outsource social media to an expert?" There are certainly arguments for both sides of this conversation. The fact of the matter is, you will always be best at serving your customers. Because your end goal is to build a network that you have influence over, consider the balance of both sides. Outsourcing technical details might be ideal, but it's worth taking a look at the pluses and minuses of both sides when it comes to the content and active engagement:

✦ **Outsourcing social media marketing:** When you outsource your social media (such as content creation and daily management), your biggest benefit is that you can hire someone who is familiar with the tools and how to effectively use them to the best advantage. Social media consultants usually end up in the business because they enjoy social media and are very natural at executing social networking and communications. The negative is that they are likely serving several other clients at the same time, and so can't spend all their time on your company. Another negative is that they may not be fully familiar with your company, its culture, and its goals. It may take an outside resource weeks or months to learn the nitty-gritty of your business and your audience the way you do. Finally, be sure you're working with a person or agency that truly understands the space. We've seen many agencies that say they can handle a social media campaign, but aren't aware of Facebook's basic terms of service or are aware, but ignore them because they've seen others ignore them. If you're building a reputation on Facebook, you definitely want to be sure the people helping you aren't hurting your brand's integrity.

✦ **In-house social media marketing:** In-house people often find that their jobs can call them to many different activities. It's rare that someone can direct her full attention to just social media engagement, especially if the responsible party is the owner of the business. A business owner almost always has more immediate "fires" to put out, so social media management gets put on the back burner. For this reason, in-house Facebook management needs to come with discipline. The connections and influence you build yield great long-term value. The biggest benefit of managing social media in-house is that it is your voice. You're always going to be your best advocate and the best person to connect with your customers.

Chapter 2: Social Marketing Campaigns

In This Chapter

✔ Implementing Facebook campaigns

✔ Marketing a campaign

✔ Crowdsourcing to promote your contest

✔ Building your Fan Page Timeline for the campaign

✔ Understanding the Facebook promotion rules

*W*hen starting out your Facebook marketing, you're likely starting off finding out how to build your audience, make connections with your audience, and nurture those connections to become loyal fans. After you have built a foundation with your Fan Page audience, you likely need to give it a boost to get things to a higher level. It takes a little shaking of the trees to let people know that it's worth connecting with your company on Facebook. Social marketing campaigns are a great way to do this. A social campaign can allow you to reach people that you will not likely capture the attention of through daily interaction.

Campaigns tap into crowdsourcing. *Crowdsourcing* means using the resources that the public (the *crowd*) can provide to accomplish more than what you or your team can do with the resources you have. The word is a play on the word *outsource,* which is to look for a service provider outside of your organization to deliver a service.

In this chapter, we show you how to get a social marketing campaign started. We also show you how to build your Fan Page Timeline to best show off your campaign and draw in fans to enter your promotion.

Understanding What Makes Social Marketing Campaigns Work

The goal of a social marketing campaign is to increase your Fan Page Timeline engagement, fans, and awareness. The most successful campaigns are interesting enough to your fans that they're willing to do more than just read your status updates in their News Feeds. Both Fanta (`https://www.facebook.com/fanta/posts/285086828227700`) and Red Bull (`http://www.redbull.com/cs/Satellite/en_INT/Red-Bull.com/001243170444524`) took advantage of the new Timeline design in early 2012 to create complicated, but fun scavenger hunts that rewarded interaction. We want to point out, though, that the rewards weren't always physical prizes. Often just completing a task — if it's interesting or challenging enough — is enough. In the case of Fanta, fans worked together to help a cartoon character find her way through the Timeline time warp. Red Bull fans had to follow intricate clues in order to win prizes. Both companies were promoting awareness about their brand by enticing fans to explore their Fan Page Timelines, but the tasks kept fans' attention.

Another type of campaign businesses often use on Facebook is a *promotion* (this is what Facebook calls contests and giveaways). We want to point out that Facebook has specific guidelines in place for promotions. You can find them at `https://www.facebook.com/promotions_guidelines.php`. We also explain them in detail in Book V, Chapter 4.

Regardless of the type of campaign you choose to run, we want to share some of the defining characteristics that make a social marketing campaign work:

✦ **Interactivity:** In many instances, the audience you want to reach isn't the audience you already have, it's their friends. To reach that audience, you need to entice your current fans to share your content with their friends. Most Facebook users only share content that is funny, useful, or interesting. Regardless of the type of campaign you intend to implement, the content associated with it must be worth sharing. Another interactive option is to include a voting component within a promotion. For instance, if you host a contest that requires each contestant to get votes to win, they are incentivized to invite people to your Fan Page Timeline to help them win. You should note that contests should always be hosted on a third-party application (we talk more about this in Book IV, Chapter 5).

✦ **Incentive:** Giving people an incentive to take action is a must. As we said earlier, if your campaign is engaging enough, the act of completing a task or solving a problem may be enough. On the other hand, your fans will likely be motivated if they have the opportunity to win something exciting. The nature of the prize can depend on the type of campaign, your goals for the campaign, and your desired reach. For example, invite your fans to submit video of them interacting with your product. You aren't likely to get people to create their own dramatic video (and edit it) if there is only a chance that they could receive a prize worth $250. However, people would certainly upload a simple picture for such a prize. As with everything, it's important to know your audience. The value of the prize varies with different types of product industries and people.

✦ **Fans only content**: When you offer fan-only content, you require that the visitor Like your Fan Page Timeline before they can access the content. This is also called Like-gating or fan-gating. The example shown in Figure 2-1 is a landing page seen by nonfans visiting a Fan Page Timeline hosting a contest. The contest asked entrants to share a photo (via the application) and then reach out to their friends to get the most votes. To access the contest page to submit a photo or vote, users had to Like the Fan Page. After they Liked the Page, the landing page changed to show the entry form and voting mechanism. Using fan-only content increased this Fan Page Timelines Likes by 500 percent.

✦ **Data capture:** One of the most important goals from a business perspective is to capture data. That data may simply be Likes, or you may want to capture more specific information like a name, an e-mail address, or specific demographics. The purpose of acquiring this information is to understand your current audience and build a larger audience that you can continue to connect with. When you know your audience and can cater to their needs and interests, you can build the brand to consumer relationship.

Figure 2-1:
Increasing fans by inviting them to Like the Fan Page and vote.

Types of Facebook Campaigns

When you decide that you want to conduct a Facebook campaign, the next step is to determine what sort of campaign structure you want to have. This might be based on your ultimate goal. If your sole goal is to earn space in the mind of your current and potential customers, then just about any form of campaign might work. A more specific goal may help to uncover what a good campaign concept should be to achieve your end goal.

All the different forms of Facebook campaigns share several common features. We explain some of the most common features of Facebook campaigns in the following list:

+ **Voting contests:** A contest based around people entering the contest and getting votes for their entry. This usually means that they have produced something that can be voted for. Photo contests are a common, time-tested concept for voting contests. You always need a third-party app to conduct this contest, because Facebook requires this in their Promotions guidelines. Facebook's terms of service state that users can't require anyone to take a specific Facebook action to participate in the contest. This means that you can't define Liking a post as a form of voting. This doesn't mean that you can't benefit from these features, however. It just means that you can't require it as a condition of eligibility for the contest.

+ **Sweepstakes:** Participants enter the sweepstakes, and a winner is determined by random drawing. The downside is that the sharing component is not as strong in this format. With other sorts of contests (especially voting contests), you often rule some participants out simply because they aren't confident that they have a chance to win. In a sweepstakes, each one of your contestants has equal of a chance of winning in most cases. For this reason, you could attract more entries, even if you don't get as much voting traffic to your Fan Page Timeline.

+ **Fundraisers:** Fundraising campaigns are not necessarily a competition. This is using a Facebook campaign to promote the opportunity to do good by giving to a charity, and invite others to do the same. For example, offering to donate $1.00 for every Like your Fan Page Timeline receives in a certain period of time. Fundraising through Facebook campaigns help you spread the word in a lot of the same ways that contests do. Sometimes charities will form teams to encourage a little friendly competition in raising funds for your charity.

+ **Facebook as a landing page:** Almost any marketing campaign benefits from having a landing page. A *landing page* is where you direct people with your call to action. For instance, you could direct visitors to a page where they can request free samples, sign up for your e-mail newsletter, and so on. Today, as the web is such a critical part of marketing, a landing page should be part of any campaign. E-mail marketing messages often have a corresponding landing page (or several, depending on the content of the message).

Using Facebook as a landing page simply puts the leads or customers you attract with your advertising in the path of your Fan Page Timeline. This could be highly valuable as a simple way to increase your Facebook audience while targeting another goal. The best way to execute this is by directing a customized web address directly to your Facebook Application Page. Create a unique URL that you place in your advertising message (something like "Find out more at `www.ourlandingpage.com`"), and then direct that URL to your Application Page. All Application Pages have their own specific web address (something like `www.facebook.com/mypagename?sk=app_7146470129`). You can find out how to do in Book IV, Chapter 5.

Implementing Sharing Contests

Facebook contests have many variations, but one thing they all have in common is an *ask* or a call to action. This is the whole concept of the campaign, or what you ask people to do. It might be complete the form to enter, upload a picture, nominate a charity, and so on. If your ask is only to complete an entry form for the contest, then implementation of the campaign might be very easy. If your ask is to create a video, complete the form as you upload, then promote the contest to your friends and ask them to vote, then your ask is clearly more complicated. If the latter is the case, you face the potential of *abandonment,* when people begin to enter your contest, but then abandon the process, presumably because the effort to enter outweighed the potential reward.

Photo and video contests are popular forms of contests. People often love to share their photos and videos, especially when there is the opportunity to win something for it. Here are some of the things you need to know to have a photo or video contest:

✦ **A third-party app to host the contest:** Facebook has strict rules about not using any Facebook features as means of an entry (such as clicking Like or commenting as a means of entering the contest). Third-party apps allow you to manage the entry and hosting of the contest. Some great and well-known third-party apps that follow the Facebook rules are Wildfire App and Offerpop. Both of these allow you to implement a video or photo contest for your Fan Page Timeline.

Because Facebook requires that promotions be run within third-party applications, promotions can only be run on Fan Page Timelines and not on your personal Timeline. All third-party applications are installed in an Application page (also called a tab). Application pages display content through iframes, which means that the content itself (like the contest app and images) is actually hosted on a separate site, and your Application page displays that content. You can find out more about creating applications for your Fan Page Timeline in Book VI.

✦ **Clear instructions for how to participate:** It always helps to demonstrate visually, so use some visual aids. You could even make a video describing how easy it is to enter.

✦ **Market to the right crowd:** Video contests are more complicated than photo contests, and it takes more work to put together a video. Be sure that the people you market to are likely to have a video camera and are comfortable producing a video. Many can shoot some video with a smartphone; however, some people still are intimidated by the idea of shooting a video. Video contests also work best when participants are clear on what they should make a video of. You don't want people to be overwhelmed with the challenge of scripting.

Photo contests, although simpler by nature, require the same clear concept as video contests. A cutest puppy contest is a simple concept. Make sure that your concept is something that people can easily understand.

✦ **Decide if you want people to vote or if you'll have a panel of judges select the winner:** Gathering votes is a great way to incentivize fans to invite new fans to see the entries and select their favorite. This is a great way to attract new fans; however, in some cases, it may not be the ideal method. Do you want people to vote by clicking a button or by entering information? If you ask for information (such as a nomination or an e-mail address) you're likely to get less traffic, but more engaged traffic. This is something that you need to determine based on the goals of your contest.

Both Wildfire and Offerpop support all of the preceding features. Several other services can help you run contests, but we don't have room to list them all. If you're really interested in getting custom, you can even build your own application. Book VI talks about how to build your own custom apps.

Getting a good response

One of the biggest fears you may have at the beginning of every Facebook contest is if you will get a good response. When you've invested a lot of time and effort (and sometimes money) into a Facebook campaign, it would be a big letdown if it falls flat. You never know what is going to be a bang-up success and what isn't, but if you follow some best practices, you can certainly start off with confidence in what you're doing to reach out to your audience.

Consider the balance of effort versus reward. More appropriately, consider the *perceived* effort versus *perceived* reward: It doesn't matter how easy it is to enter your contest, or how exciting you believe it is, if it appears too difficult, you won't have a successful response. If the incentive or reward doesn't interest the people that you reach, you may not have the success you desire.

The following tips help you find the right balance so you can be sure to get a great response for your contest:

✦ **Private information:** People are often willing to give their home address, phone number, e-mail address, and so on, if there is context for doing so. For example, if you ask people to enter your promotion to have their profile pictures featured as the face of your company, and you also ask for a home address, you may have a lower response because people feel that the information you're asking for isn't relative to the need (and you don't need it at all). If capturing home addresses is important, offer a prize that must be sent in the mail.

✦ **Prize versus effort:** When it comes to video contests, contestants have to get equipment together (video), capture their footage, edit the video, upload it, and then complete a form. Video contests are often unsuccessful because of the level of difficulty. It's common for people to be intimidated by video, and perhaps concerned that it's a lot of work or difficult to do well.

If you run a video contest, make sure that the people that you ask to put together a video are among those more likely to do so.

The next thing to consider is, if the prize is $500, it may not be enticing enough to inspire the effort you want from contestants.

✦ **Relevant messaging:** When determining your contest concept, be sure that your contest message and your businesses message align. By this we mean that if your company prides itself on providing the highest quality to discriminating buyers, then any message that enforces discounts or free products is inconsistent with your business message.

Contests can be a great way to reinforce a brand message. The components of that message are often embedded throughout the entire contest and its marketing materials. Use contests to enforce a message you want to get across to your customers. For example, if you make paper products and you want to position yourself as a company committed to green products, consider a contest that asks people to show how they too are green. If it is a photo contest, it may be "upload of a picture of you wearing all green" or it may be "show us your best tips on being green."

✦ **Easy to enter:** It should be very clear how to enter the contest. Use a simple call to action and limit what activities you ask participants to perform. Every barrier you put in place has a potential of eliminating entries. For example, if you host your contest through some third-party Facebook contest application that requires users to allow the app access to their Facebook accounts, and then they have to complete an entry form, you inevitably have fewer participants than you would if you eliminate one of those steps.

As a general rule, the best first action (other than clicking to your contest landing tab) should be the basic information form. On this form, only include fields for the minimum amount of information that you need. Even if it's optional, some might abandon it if it seems like too much.

If additional steps are necessary, make it something participants can do after they've submitted the form. If you give participants a percentage of completion, people are often achievement-oriented and are more likely to complete it because it feels unfinished.

✦ **Simple messaging:** Share a clear message that leaves nothing to conjecture. The longer your contest description is, the fewer people will bother to read it. Be aware that some of your audience is going to find out about the contest through someone sharing it on a Facebook status update or other channel (like Twitter, maybe). Make sure that your concept is something that can be summed up in as few words as possible.

Avoiding a flopped contest

Sometimes, no matter what you do, you just don't get people to participate as quickly as you would like. One of the best ways to avoid this is to make sure that you don't launch a contest without a strong network to invite to participate. Sometimes personally asking your customers to enter is a great way to get the ball rolling. Not long ago, an HVAC service company asked every one of their technicians to invite their customers to enter their Facebook contest after each appointment. Putting a little extra attention on promoting your contest at the beginning makes a big difference. It helps to get momentum to encourage others to participate as well.

Some people feel that it's okay to ask a favor of a few customers or friends that you know personally to enter a contest to get things started. Others feel that this gives people an unfair advantage or otherwise less genuine entries. Regardless of your feelings on the matter, be sure that you never seed a contest with falsified entries to make it seem like there's lots of interest if there isn't. You wouldn't want your contestants to do that either.

Marketing a Facebook Contest

Initially, you might think that posting status updates telling people about your Facebook contest is enough. It isn't. The primary reason to conduct a Facebook contest is to increase the interaction that you get from your fans, not to mention grow your audience by attracting new fans. A Facebook marketing campaign in most cases involves more than just Facebook to make it happen.

Facebook works well with other forms of digital marketing. Sure, sometimes if you have a strongly engaged and interested audience, you might be able to post one status update and see it turn into a major success. Most times, however, you have to use other resources as well.

The following list provides advice on how to market your campaign and make it a success:

✦ **Announce it to your e-mail list.** If you have a holistic digital marketing approach, then you definitely have other tools in place, including an e-mail list. Say you send out a monthly newsletter. The content of that newsletter should highlight your Facebook contest and drive people directly to it. The cross-promotion of e-mail to Facebook and Facebook to e-mail makes your connection to your audience so much stronger and more effective.

Some best practices include putting a graphic right at the top of the e-mail and linking it to the desired landing page. Note that you can link directly to the page with its unique URL. Find this in your browser address bar when you view the tab that your contest is hosted on. You may have made it your default landing page, but that only applies for nonfans.

✦ **Pass out cards at the counter.** If your business is in retail or any other business where you see customers' faces, make sure to give them a small card that promotes the contest. Make sure there is an exciting hook that gets them interested in checking out the contest. They have to be interested enough to remember to check it out later after you give them the flier.

Alternatively, you can place a QR code by the register so customers can scan it with their smartphones. See Book III, Chapter 2 for more on QR codes.

✦ **Post it on your website.** Make sure an invitation to join the contest obviously stands out on the home page of your site, and remember to link directly to the contest page on Facebook. If anyone visits your website, you want the first thing he sees to be an announcement about your contest. This way, you can convert some of your web traffic into engaged Facebook fans.

✦ **Find a partner.** Finding a partner (also called *co-marketing*) is perhaps the most powerful method in promoting a Facebook contest. If you sell custom wheels and another company sells customized car parts, you can be pretty certain that you have nearly the same type of people in your target audience; presumably people that take pride in their cars and may want to make their cars ready for show. You're lucky, because this audience is already interested in sharing with friends.

This partnership might look like a contest where the winner gets his car fully outfitted with the two companies' products. By doing this, you promote the contest on both of your Fan Page Timelines, both of your e-mail lists, and so on. This means that you will likely expand each company's fan base just by cross-promoting with one another.

The Power of Crowdsourcing

One of the greatest reasons to conduct social media campaigns is because of the power of crowdsourcing. Crowdsourcing can yield great ideas, and help to expand your reach.

Using crowdsourcing to create a new product

A few months back, a client who sold T-shirts with clever puns wanted to introduce a new design. The only problem is, the company didn't have a new design to announce. Working with Daniel, they put together a Facebook contest that had two stages:

1. Invite Facebook fans to help determine the new slogan for the T-shirt.

2. Invite the Facebook fans to help create a concept for the new shirt's graphic.

The new T-shirt was released within a couple weeks at a big event that many customers attended. The contest was a grand success for a number of reasons:

✦ The company uncovered many new ideas for the new T-shirt design. Ultimately, the company was able to simultaneously test its popularity before printing the T-shirts.

✦ The company grew its Facebook following because it gave people a compelling reason to visit the Fan Page Timeline.

✦ The new T-shirt design sold better because Facebook fans already had a vested (no pun intended) interest in the shirt. The new product raised specific awareness and attracted new buyers.

✦ The crowd felt like they were part of the creation of a new product — and they were. This sends the message that the company values its customers.

Using crowdsourcing to determine your Facebook content

One of the greatest challenges is always keeping your Facebook fans interested and engaged in the topic of content that you provide on a daily basis on Facebook. You'll discover that discussion is what keeps people interested. Let your Facebook fans tell you what they're interested in, and allow them to lead the conversation. This is where crowdsourcing comes in. A contest or campaign can help you attract the interaction that will launch that sort of activity with your Facebook fans.

People like to be valued, and people tend to like the idea of being featured or recognized. One way to do this is to ask your Facebook fans to start a conversation about your company on your Fan Page Timeline. Maybe you would ask your fans for a new slogan for your company, or maybe you ask what they like best about your business. This invitation to engage in conversation might prompt participation from your audience without necessarily giving out a prize.

Preparing Your Fan Page Timeline for the Campaign

How well your Fan Page Timeline is built and prepared for the campaign can have a definite effect on the end results. That's why it's important to know how to get your Fan Page Timeline ready for any contest or campaign that you implement. Campaigns can be extremely simple or they can be very structured. Regardless, the most important thing is being sure that people know that you have a campaign. The following sections describe how you can prepare for your campaign. (To find out more about customizing your Fan Page Timeline, see Book IV, Chapter 5.)

Your cover photo

It's always good to have the theme of your Fan Page Timeline match your branding. When you conduct a campaign, you may want to tweak the cover photo design to highlight a theme, but you'll still want to keep your branding. For example, a Christmas fan photo of the week contest might feature holiday colors or other images to give the campaign a holiday theme, but you'd want to keep your brand's logo or other defining characteristic on the photo as well. The cover photo is a great way to highlight your campaign while still branding the look of your Fan Page Timeline. For example, you might include bells and holiday colors for a holiday campaign, or pictures of dogs and cats for a cutest pet photo contest. Your cover photo is 851 pixels wide by 315 pixels tall. (Remember that Facebook prohibits calls to action on the cover photo such as "Enter Now," so be sure to simply use it for branding and design aspects only.)

Setting up a custom tab

Custom Application Pages are very important. Application Pages are where you host your contest. When you prepare your custom Application Page, it's best to have a custom landing page for the contest that shows only a preview to nonfans and the full version to fans, as shown in Figure 2-1. This means that visitors who haven't Liked your Fan Page will see a different version of the Facebook tab. When someone clicks Like, she then sees another view of the tab. You can utilize this setting when you create a custom Facebook tab.

By setting up a separate tab for fans and another for nonfans, you save some content for fans, therefore giving them one more reason to become one. More importantly, when your campaign attracts tons of traffic, you can gain more of those visitors as fans. It's important to note again that you can't have the entry come by way of visitors Liking your Fan Page, the entry must happen within your third-party app. You can find out more about promotions in Book V, Chapter 4.

Contact forms

Using a contact form extends your lead capture beyond only people Liking your Fan Page. Facebook contests are a great way to grow your e-mail list as well. Embedding a contact form into your Facebook tab can be done the same way you would do it in HTML on most websites. Using the Static HTML app (see Book IV, Chapter 5), you can simply place your code in the fields. You don't have to know how to create a form — several services offer easily built forms. We recommend Formstack (`www.formstack.com`), specifically because its service has a lot of functions that allow you create lead capture forms, including database storage for the data, and the capability to connect it to your favorite e-mail marketing services.

Canvas pages

Canvas pages are different than the common Application Pages that are part of your Fan Page Timeline. (To discover how to set up your own Canvas page, see Book VI, Chapter 2.) A Canvas page allows you occupy the whole screen within the context of the application. This screen includes the Ticker, which updates with activity from the application, as well as other similar applications. Canvas pages are 760 pixels wide, which allows for a reasonable amount of content; however, it's just shy of the 810 pixel width of the Application pages within your Fan Page Timeline. Setting up a Canvas page might allow for a very interactive experience between users. This is most useful when your contest involves a game or something that can display activity within the app in real time. One distinct disadvantage is that Canvas pages redirect your fans to an alternate URL such as `http://apps.facebook.com/wordswith friends` instead of `www.facebook.com/wordswithfriends`. This means that your visitors may have a few seconds of wait time as it loads.

Canvas pages are great when space is necessary (or when it just enhances the quality of your campaign). Offerpop (`http://offerpop.com`) is a great third-party tool for setting up Canvas page–based campaigns. Offerpop has a variety of tools that allow you to create ready-made campaigns. Figure 2-2 shows the Offerpop Canvas page. (Most games are hosted on a Canvas page.) The News Ticker to the right only displays activity from apps, meaning the activity of your friends that are using apps or playing games.

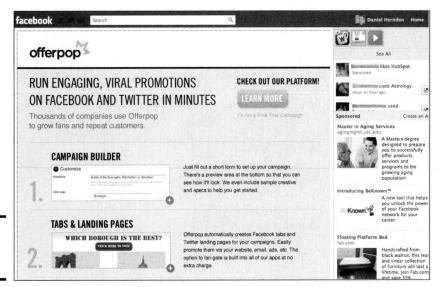

Figure 2-2:
A Canvas page.

The News Ticker

One big benefit of a Facebook campaign is the additional visibility that is created through the activity feed. Specifically, the Facebook News Ticker, shown in Figure 2-3, displays your friends' activity on the top-right side of your home screen. Here is a little bit of what to expect from the activity that shows up in the Facebook News Ticker:

✦ **Status updates:** If your contest encourages people to post a status update, people will see it in their News Feed, but it also appears in the Ticker.

✦ **New Fan Page Likes:** Often, contests result in new Likes for your Fan Page. This appears in the News Ticker as well.

✦ **Likes and Comments:** When people Like or comment on a post within your contest, the Ticker displays it.

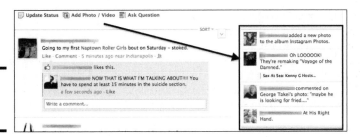

Figure 2-3:
The News Ticker.

✦ **Real time data:** All the data you see in the News Ticker can be seen elsewhere on Facebook. The News Ticker just displays the data as it happens in real time. This factor might be encouragement to launch campaigns in a carefully timed manner. When you launch a Facebook campaign, and everything goes live (your Facebook tab and profile picture) at the same time as your e-mail announcement and Facebook status posts, you may attract more activity through the action showing up in people's News Feeds.

Chapter 3: Using Insights to Track Your Facebook Success

In This Chapter

↳ **Using Facebook Insights to track your success**

↳ **Discovering EdgeRank**

↳ **Improving your EdgeRank**

*I*f you have a Fan Page Timeline, you're probably interested in how the page is performing with your audience. You want to know if you're reaching as many people as possible and how you can encourage them to interact with your content more. Facebook offers a stat-tracking program called Insights that's available for Fan Page Timelines (but not personal Timelines). Insights offers information about who your users are, when they visit your Fan Page Timeline most often, which of your posts have had the most response, and much more. This chapter explains how Insights works and how you can use the metrics you find on Insights to improve the effectiveness of your Fan Page Timeline.

This chapter also explains *EdgeRank,* which is Facebook's algorithm that determines what content is most relevant to each Facebook user. EdgeRank is important because it decides whether content shows up on a user's Top Stories or not (and remember, Top Stories is what most Facebook users have as their default News Feed). EdgeRank considers how an individual interacts (or doesn't) with different kinds of content and weighs those interactions. The result is Facebook's best guess at what someone is interested in. In the latter part of this chapter, we explain the elements that EdgeRank considers and how you can try to use those elements to your advantage on your Fan Page Timeline.

Tracking Your Facebook Stats with Insights

Insights is Facebook's analytics software and is available for Fan Page(s) that have at least 30 Likes. Insights allows you to see how people interact with the content on your Fan Page Timeline. You can track the demographics of your audience, which posts receive the most engagement, and even how people are finding and Liking your Fan Page. Throughout the following sections, we explain the details of what you can expect to find in Insights.

First, though, you need to open Insights. To do that, go to your Fan Page Timeline and open your Admin panel, then click the See All link in the Insights box. From your main Insights page, you can see an overview of how your Fan Page Timeline is performing.

Reviewing the main Insights page

Your main Insights page looks similar to the one shown in Figure 3-1 and provides an overview of your Fan Page's Likes, friends of fans, people talking about your Fan Page Timeline, and weekly total reach. (We go into more depth about each of those a little later in the chapter.) You can also see how your posts have been performing, export your data, and use the Settings icon (it looks like a gear) to get more information about how Insights works.

Figure 3-1:
Insights
provides an
overview
of the main
data points
for your
Fan Page
Timeline.

The main graph on the Insights page shows the following data for one month at a time:

✦ **Posts:** Circles at the base of the main graph indicate posts. The more posts or content you share, the bigger the circle for that day. If you move your mouse over a circle, you can see how many posts you made on a certain day.

✦ **People Talking About This:** This stat refers to the number of people who have Liked, commented on, or shared posts from your Fan Page Timeline over the last seven days. This stat also includes any mentions of your Fan Page Timeline by others, Event responses, or poll answers. Basically, any sort of interaction on your Fan Page Timeline is part of the People Talking about This data. You can compare the number of times you posted to how many people were talking about your Fan Page to get an idea of what content was working and what wasn't.

✦ **Weekly Total Reach:** This is how many unique Facebook users saw your content. Keep in mind that your total reach includes any Facebook ads or sponsored stories that point to your Fan Page Timeline. (See Book V, Chapter 5 for more information on Facebook advertising options.)

The graph on your main Insights page shows the last month or so of data, but People Talking About This and Weekly Total Reach show data for seven days within the timeframe. For example, in Figure 3-1, the dates of the graph are February 11, 2012 through March 9, 2012. If you mouse over a specific dot — for example, the Weekly Total Reach for March 2, 2012— then you see data that considers seven days total, not just the data for March 2. See Figure 3-2.

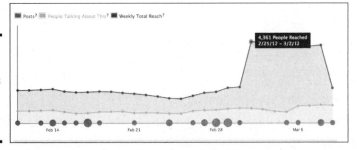

Figure 3-2:
Each data point covers more than just a single day.

Finding what you posted

Under your main graph, you can see a table listing the content you shared for the same dates displayed in the graph (in this case, February 11, 2012 through March 9, 2012). This table shows the date you posted, an excerpt of your post, a post's reach (or how many people saw it in their News Feeds), engaged users (those that clicked your content from the News Feed), talking about this (people who interacted with your content in some way), and virality (friends of fans who saw the post).

You can sort the table by different values by clicking any of the main tabs (except Post). For example, if you want to sort the table by number of engaged users, click the Engaged Users tab, and the table sorts itself based on how many users interacted with your content (with the highest engagements listed at the top; you can click Engaged Users again to sort with the least engagements at the top).

You can also use the All Post Types drop-down list to choose what posts are listed in the table. So if you just want to see how your posts with links did, click All Post Types and choose Link from the list.

If you want to see more information about a specific set of data, click the data, and you see an expanded explanation. Figure 3-3, for example, shows how you can click the Reach data and see how much of the reach was organic (basic Facebook functions like commenting on a post), paid ads, or viral (a friend of a fan saw your content).

Figure 3-3:
Insights
offers
general and
specific
data for
your Fan
Pages.

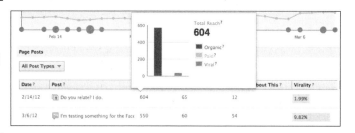

Exporting your data

If you want to back up your data or just keep a copy on hand, you can export your Insights data and download it to your computer. To do that, navigate to your Insights page, and then follow these steps:

1. **Click the Export Data button.**

   The Export Insights Data dialog box appears, as shown in Figure 3-4.

2. **Select the radio button next to the following options:**

   - *Select Data Type:* You can choose either page-level data or post-level data. Page-level data just gives you numbers based on your Fan Page Timeline's overall interactions (for example, overall Likes, Unlikes, friends of fans, and so on). Post-level data includes numbers directly related to individual posts (for example, name of post, date posted, total number of fans the post reached, and so on).

   - *Select File Format:* You can save your export file as either and Excel spreadsheet (`.xls`) or a Comma-separated values (`.csv`) file.

3. **Click the calendar to choose the start and end date range to export.**

4. **Click the Download button.**

Melanie likes to export Insights data periodically because she likes to have a backup of everything. This came in handy when in December 2010, Facebook changed the way it displays Insights. When it made the change, you couldn't access any data from before July 19, 2010. If you hadn't exported it, you couldn't access it. Because Facebook periodically changes things, and it owns everything on the platform, we recommend keeping your own backups to reference, just in case.

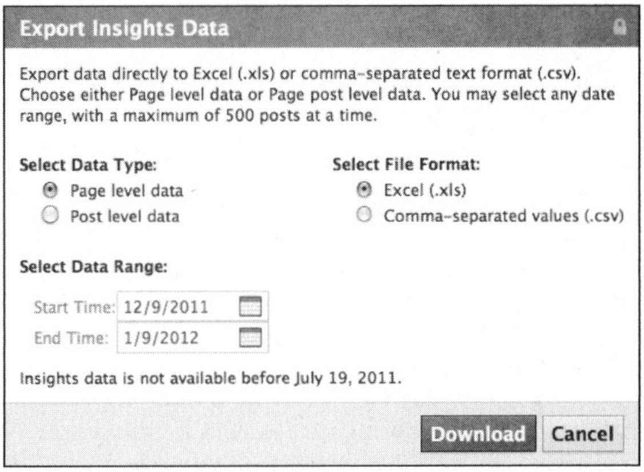

Figure 3-4:
The Export Insights Data dialog box allows you to choose which data to export.

> **Export Insights Data**
>
> Export data directly to Excel (.xls) or comma-separated text format (.csv). Choose either Page level data or Page post level data. You may select any date range, with a maximum of 500 posts at a time.
>
> **Select Data Type:**
> ⦿ Page level data
> ○ Post level data
>
> **Select File Format:**
> ⦿ Excel (.xls)
> ○ Comma-separated values (.csv)
>
> **Select Data Range:**
> Start Time: 12/9/2011
> End Time: 1/9/2012
>
> Insights data is not available before July 19, 2011.
>
> **Download** **Cancel**

Checking out your settings

The Settings button looks like a gear. When you click the gear icon, a menu appears with the following options:

✦ **Take the Tour:** Choose this option if you want to see what each part of your Insights page can show you. If you're a visual learner and want to see it on the page itself, this is a great option.

✦ **Page Insights Guide (PDF):** This option allows you to download a PDF copy of the Insights Product Guide.

✦ **Visit Help Center:** This option takes you directly to the Facebook Help Center files related to Insights.

✦ **Send Feedback:** You can send feedback about something that isn't working, questions you have, or suggestions to improve the data.

Diving Deeper into Your Insights

At the top of your Insights page you have more options: Likes, Reach, Talking About This, and Check-Ins. (Note that the Check-Ins option only appears if you've enabled your Places page. We talk about that in the "Tracking Check-Ins" section.) Each of these options allows you to choose a date range and also includes demographic information for age, gender, country, city, and language.

When you switch from tab to tab, be sure to check your dates and reset them as necessary. For example, if you're looking at Likes for June 18–24, then switch to looking at Reach, the dates may reset themselves instead of staying the same as the ones you were looking at on Likes.

Touring the Likes page

The main Insights page shows you how many Likes your Fan Page has, but if you want to know more about your fans, click the Like link on the left navigation list under Insights. A new set of data appears, as shown in Figure 3-5, that provides more specific information about gender, age, location, and even where your Likes came from.

Want to see who Likes your Fan Page? You can click the See Likes link in the gray bar labeled People Who Like Your Page, and a dialog box appears with a list of your fans (see Figure 3-6). You can use the drop-down list in the top-left corner to sort the list by people who Like your Fan Page, other Fan Pages that Like yours, admins for your Fan Page, or people you've banned from your Fan Page Timeline.

An important part of your marketing strategy is simply knowing who your audience is. The more you can find out about who your readers and fans are, the more you can customize your interactions with them. Facebook Insights doesn't give you specific data for individuals, but it gives you a helpful overview of who your audience is, where they're coming from, and what content they're interacting with the most. On your Insights Like page, you find the following data:

✦ **Gender and Age:** Facebook shows you how your audience breaks down, based on the information each Timeline shares. Any Timelines that don't specify gender aren't included in this metric (which is why your percentages may not quite add up to 100%).

✦ **Countries, Cities, and Languages:** You can see which countries and cities your fans reside in and which language they are using to view Facebook. You may be surprised at what you see here. The data shared for countries and cities is based on a fan's IP address, not what she lists in her Timeline.

✦ **Like sources:** As a marketer, you're interested in where your leads are coming from. You can tell whether your Likes are coming from your Fan Page itself on the Timeline, or if those Likes are coming from mobile devices (for example, a cellphone or tablet) or a third-party app (for example, a Like button on a website). You can also keep track of how many other Fan Pages Like yours. Finally, you can see how many fans have Unliked your Fan Page and when.

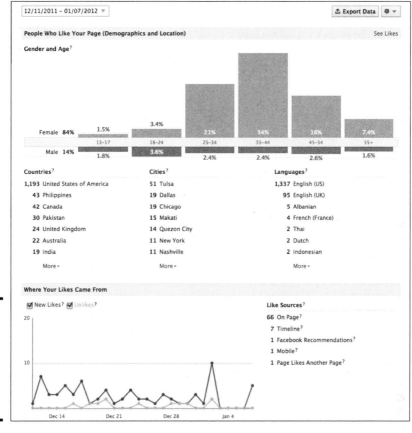

Figure 3-5:
Find out
more about
your fans
in the Like
section of
Insights.

Don't worry if you have a few Unlikes here and there. It happens, and it's part of Facebook. *Do* pay attention if you see a large number of Unlikes and try to determine the reason. Was it after a specific post? Have you checked your Timeline to be sure there isn't any offensive spam to delete? Even though you can't tell which individual fan(s) Unliked your Fan Page, Unlikes is an important metric to watch. Facebook gives you the date of the Unlike, which allows you to go back to your posts for that day and see if you shared something controversial that may have made someone Unlike your Fan Page. Or maybe you posted too many times that day. You won't be able to know for certain what made the fan Unlike your Fan Page, but you can use your data to help you draw a conclusion. Similarly, if you have an influx of Likes on a specific day, you'll want to see what you posted that was so popular and try to re-create that.

Figure 3-6:
Use the People Who Like *Your Fan Page* dialog box to find out who your fans are.

Understanding the Reach data

Facebook defines *reach* as the number of Facebook users who saw your content. Some users may have seen your content show up in their News Feed because they're fans of your Fan Page Timeline, while others saw the content in their News Feed because one of their friends Liked, commented, or shared your content.

A Facebook user has an average of 130 friends (most have many more in our experience). Any time a user interacts with content, the interaction is shared with their friends via the News Feed and those friends can also interact with the content if they want to. When you share compelling content, it has the potential to be seen by many, many more people than just your fans, thus increasing your reach.

The Insights Reach page is similar to the Insights Like page because it shows you data about gender and age, countries, cities, and languages. But on the Reach page, these metrics include not just fans, but anyone who saw your content.

The Reach page is where you find some of the most valuable data about how your Fan Page Timeline is performing and whether you're meeting the goals you set. You can track the following information:

✦ How you reached people

✦ Visits to your Fan Page Timeline

Diving Deeper into Your Insights **431**

Book V
Chapter 3

Using Insights
to Track Your
Facebook Success

✦ Tab views

✦ External referrers

The next few sections explain those metrics further.

How you reached people (reach and frequency)

The graph you see in Figure 3-7 includes data for how people found your content during a given time period. You can discover whether people found your content organically (that is, via News Feed, Ticker, or on your actual Fan Page Timeline), via paid ads, or virally (that is, via friend who Liked, commented, or shared your content), and also what the total reach was during that period. You can deselect any of those options to remove it from the graph. For instance, if you aren't using paid ads, you can remove that data from the graph by deselecting the Paid check box.

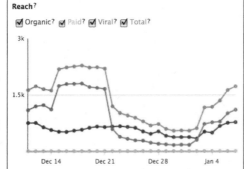

Figure 3-7:
See how
your content
reached
people.

Use the drop-down list to view specific data for All Page Content (any stories posted to or about your Fan Page Timeline), Your Posts (any content you posted, whether original or curated), or Stories by Others (content others shared about your Fan Page Timeline). Both the All Page Content and Your Posts options show you how those people were reached (organically, paid ads, and so on). Stories by Others only shows you viral data because *viral* in this case means that someone other than you as the Page admin was promoting or sharing the Page in some way.

The Unique Users by Frequency bar graph shows how many people saw content from your Fan Page Timeline and how many times they viewed it. This metric shows you your overall Facebook exposure. It takes into consideration every possible aspect of how someone could see your content. Watch how this data fluctuates and compare it to your increases and decreases in fans to see if there's a correlation. And, of course, compare this data to your post and engagement and try to recreate the successes you find.

Visits to your Fan Page Timeline

For the most part, after a Facebook user Likes your Fan Page, he doesn't come back to your Fan Page Timeline. Instead, fans rely on your content to show up in their News Feeds. However, if you want to see just how many people are actually visiting your Fan Page Timeline, look at the Page Views graph. Page Views include every single time your Fan Page Timeline was viewed for a given time period — even if it was the same person viewing the Page multiple times. For example, if one person visits your Fan Page Timeline five times, and three other people visit one time each, the total page views would be eight. You can also see how many unique page views your Fan Page Timeline had. Using the previous example, your unique page views would be four (the first person plus the three others who viewed your Fan Page Timeline).

If you scroll a little further down the page, you see columns for Total Tab Views and External Referrers. The Total Tab Views keeps track of how many times people view each of your Fan Page Timeline tabs. The list goes in order from the most views to the least, so it may change from time to time. This data is useful because there may be times when you run a campaign where you want people to visit a customized tab associated with your Fan Page Timeline, and you need to see how effective that campaign is. Or you may just want to see how many people are viewing and interacting with that custom Welcome page you paid to have designed.

If you've ever wondered where your traffic is coming from, check your External Referrers column. Not everyone is finding you from stories in their News Feeds. Your blog, search engines, and other websites may be important lead generators for your Fan Page Timeline. For that reason, we encourage you to include a link to your Fan Page Timeline on your blog or website, and even promote your Fan Page Timeline on your business cards and in-store marketing.

Finding out how others are Talking About This

If you scroll back to the top of your Insights page, you see the Talking About This link. This feature documents the number of people who are interacting with your content. It includes all types of engagement on content:

✦ Likes

✦ Comments

✦ Tagging (in posts as well as photos)

✦ RSVPs to event invitations

✦ Check ins

◆ Fan posts to your Fan Page Timeline

◆ Sharing content

◆ Answering poll questions

◆ Taking advantage of a check-in Deal

Like the other Insights pages, the Talking About This page breaks down your interactive users generically by gender and age, as well as country and language.

The demographic data for people talking about your Fan Page Timeline requires that 30 people interact with your data within seven days of the dates you're looking at. If you can't see your demographic data, that means fewer than 30 people were interacting with your content. Try changing your date range to see if that helps. If it doesn't, it's time to integrate some new content-sharing tactics to promote more interaction. See Book IV, Chapter 3 for tips on building your Facebook community.

Scroll down the page to see the How People Are Talking about Your Page section. Here, you can see more detailed information (though not much more detailed) about how people interacted with your Fan Page Timeline. You see two graphs, similar to the ones shown in Figure 3-8: one for Talking About This and one for Viral Reach.

Figure 3-8:
Discover
how
people are
interacting
with your
Fan Page
Timeline.

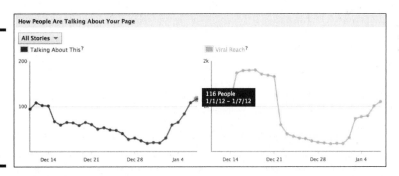

The Talking About This graph shows how many unique people collectively Liked, commented, shared, or somehow interacted with your posts. Each point on the graph represents a week and how many people interacted that week. The Viral Reach graph shows how many individuals saw your Fan Page Timeline via a story (comment, Like, or share) from a friend in their News Feeds.

Use the drop-down list to change the data the graphs show. You can choose from the following:

✦ All Stories

✦ Page Likes

✦ Stories from Your Posts

✦ Mentions and Photo Tags

✦ Posts by Others

Each option changes the graph to show the number of unique fans that interacted with your content. You can note the dates for the interactions, and then check your posts for those dates to see what did and didn't work the way you expected.

Tracking check ins

The Insights Check-Ins page is only available to Fan Pages that have claimed a Places page and enabled the check-in options (see Book IV, Chapter 4 for instructions on how to do that). If you've enabled check ins for your Fan Page Timeline and you have had more than 30 check ins during the dates you're looking at, then you can track your success on this page. (You can change the date range using the drop-down list at the top of the page.)

Just like on the other Insights pages, you can see your check ins broken down by gender, age, countries, cities, and languages. If you scroll down the page a bit further, you see a graph that shows how many people checked in via a mobile device or via the Facebook website. The *mobile device* line tracks how many people used their cellphones (or other mobile device) to check into your Place while they were physically there. The *Facebook website* line shows how many people tagged your place when they posted (see Book II, Chapter 2).

Getting to Know EdgeRank

You may have noticed that your News Feed doesn't display items chronologically. This is because an algorithm called EdgeRank ranks that content. Facebook uses EdgeRank to determine whether specific content will be of interest to you. Facebook looks at how you interact with others and with content on Facebook and makes assumptions based on those actions. Those assumptions determine what content is filtered to your News Feed in the Highlighted Stories.

Facebook is pretty closed-lipped about its EdgeRank algorithm, but as we researched, we found that Facebook appears to rank actions based on the level of effort it takes to interact and content based on the number of interactions. For instance, Likes are fairly easy to give and require very little effort on the reader's part. If a reader decides to leave a comment on your post, then that takes more effort and is rewarded accordingly. Likewise, Facebook tends to reward certain content more than others. Facebook users are usually more likely to engage with photos or video than text updates. Facebook's goal is to have people share interesting content that elicits a response, so Facebook gives higher EdgeRank value to video or photos. Facebook tends to rank content in this order (most EdgeRank juice to least):

✦ Photos

✦ Video

✦ Links

✦ Text

Understanding how EdgeRank works

Every single Facebook user has her own EdgeRank for each bit of content she consumes. As you can imagine, that can make it hard for your content to show up in everyone's News Feed (especially if you're trying to have your Fan Page updates show). Each person interacts with content, Pages, and people differently, and therefore, has her own version of EdgeRank based on those actions.

EdgeRank has five variables:

✦ **Object:** Any item that shows up in a News Feed is an object. This can be a status update, a video, or even an image.

✦ **Edge:** Any interaction with an object creates an edge (objects have an edge whether the content has interaction or not). Likes, comments, and clicks are all interactions and contribute to an object's overall edge score. If the content doesn't have any interaction, the score is low. The higher the score (that is, the more interaction), the more likely it is to show up in the News Feed's Highlighted Stories.

✦ **Affinity:** The relationship between a content creator and a content consumer. The affinity factor changes over time, depending on how a user interacts (or doesn't) with content. Affinity is determined by many things, such as how often a user

• Logs into Facebook

• Interacts with content from another user or Fan Page Timeline

• Clicks Like on content

• Types comments on content

• Clicks the Share option for content

Facebook keeps track of how a user interacts with content. When a user is consistently engaged with content from another Facebook user or Fan Page Timeline, the affinity is high. If the user ignores content, the affinity begins to wane and can become low. When affinity is low, it's less likely that content from the ignored user or page shows up in the user's News Feed as a Highlighted Story.

✦ **Weight:** Objects and edge (that is, interactions) both have weight. As stated earlier, Facebook determines the weight of each depending on how much effort it takes to complete. For example, it takes the most effort for a user to share a post created by someone else with his own audience, so Shares weigh more than a Like. It takes a little more effort to post a video than a text update (and video is more likely to garner interaction), so video weighs more than a straight status update. The following table shows how Facebook weighs Objects and Edge from most weight to least.

Objects	*Edge*
1. Photos	1. Shares
2. Video	2. Comment
3. Link	3. Like
4. Status	4. Click

EdgeRank Checker (`http://EdgeRankchecker.com`) is a website devoted to researching Facebook's EdgeRank algorithm. It found that comments appear to have four times the weight of Likes. What that means is that when a user took the time to leave a comment, the content had four times as many clicks than when the user just Liked the content. Of course, that helps a Page's EdgeRank, but it also helps you see why it's important to try to engage your audience beyond a simple Like. If your audience is commenting, it's social proof to their friends that your article was worthwhile and they're more likely to click your content (and maybe also respond, thus widening your audience even further).

✦ **Decay:** How long an object has been out there. The older your post, the more decayed it is. Facebook moves fast. Each time you check your News Feed, you see something new. Posts that are old lose their edge and weight and count less toward EdgeRank. That means you need to post more than once a day or your posts (that is, objects) won't seen by everyone, therefore not everyone can interact with your content and improve your EdgeRank. Don't re-post the same information multiple times a day. Instead, post varied, relevant content throughout the day, especially at the peak times the majority of your audience is online.

Check your Insights (discussed earlier in this chapter) to determine how time of day is affecting interaction on your posts. If you're posting at 6:00 am and not seeing a lot of interaction, try posting later in the morning. Or, if you're posting at 4:00 pm and seeing many comments or Likes, try to post more around that time. You will likely need to experiment with several times of day to find the sweet spot for your audience.

Using EdgeRank to improve your News Feed position

Facebook uses each of the five variables discussed in the previous section to ascribe a rank (or EdgeRank) for each user. To make the most of your EdgeRank, you need to do three things:

✦ **Determine who your audience is.** When you know whom you're talking to, you can customize your updates to meet their needs. By sharing content your audience wants, you increase your affinity with them.

✦ **Create and post content that encourages feedback and engagement.** The kind of content you post is directly related to knowing your audience. When you know whom your audience is and what they want from you, find new ways to give that content to them. If you usually post text status updates, try sharing video or photos. Regardless of the type of content you share, provide a specific call to action. If you tell your readers what you'd like from them, they're more likely to follow through for you.

✦ **Post when your audience is looking.** As we mentioned earlier, it doesn't do you much good if you're posting great content at times when people don't see it. You may have a great idea at 2:00 am, but if you post it then, few fans will see it. Instead, write it down and post it later in the day when more of your audience is on Facebook. Use your Insights to see if you can find a pattern of when your audience is most active on your Fan Page Timeline. What you find may surprise you! Keep in mind that not everyone has access to Facebook during the day because of firewalls or other restrictions at work.

If you want to use EdgeRank to improve your audience engagement, you need to post content people want to interact with. In Book IV, Chapter 3, we explain exactly how to build your Facebook community. The keys to a loyal and interactive community are solving a problem, educating your audience, and/or entertaining your audience. You need to have clear goals in mind and know how you're going to achieve those goals. Use calls to action, post links that promote sales, and tag other Pages in your status updates if it makes sense. When you tell your audience what you want them to do and provide a way for them to do it, they're more likely to follow through. And if you're sharing a link to a post by another brand, tag its Fan Page Timeline in your status update. Your update will be seen by that Fan Page Timeline's fans as well — which enhances your overall reach. The bottom line for using EdgeRank to your advantage is to know your audience and what they expect from you. If you give your audience what they want, you establish yourself as an authority and your audience comes back to you for answers and comes to appreciate the community you're building (and they're part of).

Chapter 4: Facebook Promotions

In This Chapter

✓ Running a Facebook promotion by the book

✓ Setting up best practices for a successful promotion

✓ Finding the best apps to run your giveaway or contest

✓ Understanding Like-gating and how it fits with your promotions

As a Fan Page admin, you'll be interested in creating ways to encourage new visitors to become fans. One way to convert potential fans into actual fans is to offer them the chance to win something.

In this chapter, we explain why you may want to host a Facebook promotion and how to interpret the Facebook Promotions Guidelines (`http://fb.com/promotions_guidelines.php`) so you don't run the risk of losing your Fan Page Timeline and its community. We also explain the concept of Like-gating content and help you find some great tools to administer your promotions.

Using Facebook Promotions to Market Your Business

Running a Facebook promotion is an excellent way to promote your Fan Page Timeline, bring attention to a specific product or service (especially a new launch), and possibly garner more Likes for your Fan Page. Facebook defines a *promotion* as either a contest or giveaway. A *contest* is a promotion in which users are asked to submit something that will be voted on, either by the public, the Fan Page owner, or a panel of judges. The winner of a contest is whoever receives the most votes. A *giveaway* (also called sweepstakes), on the other hand, is a promotion of chance. Users are asked to complete an entry form and a winner is chosen at random. It's okay to use the words *giveaway* and *sweepstakes* interchangeably, but you wouldn't use *giveaway* and *contest* interchangeably because they are different beasts.

Giveaways and contests are fun and easy ways to drive traffic to your Fan Page Timeline. They aren't expensive to run (depending on what you're giving away), and your fans love to win something! The benefits for you as a company could include:

+ Bringing more people to your Fan Page Timeline

+ Increasing your Fan Page Likes by Like-gating the entry form (we discuss this later in the chapter)

+ Growing your e-mail list by collecting e-mail addresses on the entry form (needed to contact the winner anyway)

+ Recording important demographic information or product feedback by incorporating a short survey as part of the entry form

+ Inspiring fans and customers to share their own experiences related to your brand via story, photo, or video contests

You must be clear about what information you're gathering and how you'll use the information. For example, if you're collecting e-mail addresses, let fans know if you're going to automatically subscribe them to your newsletter — and give them an opt-out option.

Getting the word out

When you create your Facebook promotion, remember that you need to get the word out. It stands to reason that you'll tell your Facebook fans about your promotion, but you may be interested reaching beyond your current fans. In order to reach a wider audience, you need to integrate your Facebook promotions with all your other outlets: Twitter, blog or website, e-mail newsletter, and even offline in your store! People won't know about the promotion unless you tell them. Write status updates on Facebook and Twitter that include a link directly to your Facebook promotion entry form, publish a blog post explaining the promotion and its purpose (and the prize, of course). Take advantage of your e-newsletter list and send out an alert that you're having a promotion on Facebook, and then suggest they forward your newsletter to their friends so they can enter as well. If you have a bricks-and-mortar venue, ask employees to remind your customers to find your Fan Page Timeline online and enter to win.

Using a strong call to action

Of course, when you're hosting a Facebook promotion, you'll probably be posting status updates telling people about it. Unfortunately, many people do this half-heartedly, so they don't see a great response. You should use a strong call to action in all your marketing efforts, but on Facebook, it's even more important. Facebook visitors move fast. They skim their News Feeds for video, pictures, and links. In other words, they're looking for action. Consider this sample status update:

One day left to enter our giveaway! Win a full pass to our conference!

The previous status update looks interesting, but has a weak call to action and doesn't offer a way to complete the action. Instead, try a status update like this one:

> Enter to win a full pass to the International Marketing Conference! Just complete the entry form at `http://bitly./link`! Good luck!

Notice that this status update tells you exactly what you can win (a conference pass), has a clear call to action (complete the entry form), and way to complete the task (a link to the form).

When you include a link in your status update, don't send your fans to your Timeline! Every navigation tab on your Fan Page Timeline has its own URL. Send fans directly to the entry form tab. If you send them to your Timeline, they may not know how to find the entry form; even if they can find the entry form, it's an extra step. Sending fans directly to the entry form is much more efficient (and you'll have a higher rate of completion). To find the URL for any custom tab on your Fan Page Timeline, follow these instructions:

1. **Use your browser to navigate to your Fan Page Timeline.**

   Under your cover photo, you see your apps.

2. **Click the app you want to send fans to (in this case, the app for your giveaway).**

   The new page opens.

   If you can't see the app you want to use, click the More next to the fourth application box to reveal the rest of your apps.

3. **Copy the new URL from your browser's address bar.**

4. **Click the** *(Your Page Name)* **link next to your profile picture at the top left of the page to return to your Fan Page Timeline.**

5. **Paste the URL into your status update text box and type a status update with a strong call to action.**

6. **Click the Share button to share your update with your fans.**

If you want to track how many people click the link in your status update, use a link-shortening and tracking tool such as bitly. Visit `http://bitly.com` and create an account, and then return to your Facebook Fan Page Timeline and follow these instructions:

1. **Copy the URL of the destination tab (see Step 3 in the previous set of instructions).**

2. **Navigate your browser to** `http://bitly.com` **and log in.**

3. **Paste the URL into the text box and click the Shorten button.**

4. **Copy the resulting shortened link.**

5. **Return to your Fan Page Timeline and copy the bitly link into your new status update.**

When you want to see how many people have clicked your link, return to bitly and check your dashboard. You may be surprised how many times fans clicked your link!

You can also see how many people have clicked your links via your Fan Page Insights.

Understanding the Facebook Promotions Guidelines

Many businesses and bloggers running Facebook promotions don't realize that Facebook has guidelines regarding how you can (and can't) administer a promotion on Facebook. The result is that many businesses run the risk of losing their Fan Page Timelines because they run improper giveaways or contests. You can find the guidelines at `http://facebook.com/promotions_guidelines.php`.

Before you create a Facebook promotion, it's important to understand the federal and state laws that govern sweepstakes, contests, and lotteries. It's a good idea to talk to a lawyer before you start your promotion (and that goes for promotions on your website, blog, Facebook, or anywhere else you're holding one) to ensure you're in compliance with the law. "Everyone else was doing it" won't help you should someone bring a lawsuit against you. For starters, we suggest reading "Blog Law — Is Your Giveaway Legal?" by Sarah Hawkins at the Saving for Someday blog: `www.savingforsomeday.com/blog-law-is-your-giveaway-legal`. That article provides an overview of the United States federal laws governing promotions and gives you an idea of what to consider as you create your own promotion.

For the most part, the Facebook Promotions Guidelines are pretty self-explanatory, but there are a few parts that can be confusing. The result is that even if you think you understand the guidelines, you may not. To help clarify the guidelines and ensure your Facebook promotions are on the up-and-up, we quote the rules and explain what you need to know.

> *1. Promotions on Facebook must be administered within Apps on Facebook.com, either on a Canvas Page or an app on a Page Tab.*

This means that you can't run a giveaway or contest on your Timeline (that is, neither your personal Timeline nor your Fan Page Timeline). You must use a third-party application to build and administer your promotion. Later in this chapter, we show several online tools that will help you create a promotion within a third-party application.

You've probably seen many people or businesses post a status update similar to this: "Like our Fan Page and leave us a comment to enter to win a free pizza!" Or "Comment on your favorite widget color, then have your friends come vote! The comment with the most Likes and responses will win a widget!" The problem with these ideas is that they're implemented on the Timeline and require the user to take a specific action with a Facebook tool (that is, Liking or commenting; see guidelines 4 and 5, which prohibit the use of using Facebook functionality as a means of entry). Bottom line: You simply can't run a Facebook giveaway on your Timeline.

Because you can't install third-party apps on your Personal Timeline, you won't be able to run a giveaway or contest on your Personal Timeline.

> *2. Promotions on Facebook must include the following:*
> *a. A complete release of Facebook by each entrant or participant.*
> *b. Acknowledgment that the promotion is in no way sponsored, endorsed or administered by, or associated with, Facebook.*
> *c. Disclosure that the participant is providing information to* [disclose recipient(s) of information] *and not to Facebook.*

This means that Facebook wants it to be clear to you and your entrants that Facebook is in no way part of your promotion. Facebook simply wants you to clarify that it isn't liable for your actions. Sometimes bad things happen with promotions: someone defaults on the prize, an entrant doesn't think the winner was chosen fairly, and so on. Facebook doesn't want anyone contacting its admins about those issues — those issues are yours and yours alone to handle.

One of the applications we discuss later in this chapter (in the "ShortStack" section) is ShortStack. If you use ShortStack to create your promotion, it provides some nice verbiage you can include in your giveaway that adheres to this rule. The text is placed clearly on the promotion and ensures you're adhering to this promotion guideline. Figure 4-1 shows how your giveaway may look using ShortStack's verbiage.

> *3. You must not use Facebook features or functionality as a promotion's registration or entry mechanism. For example, the act of Liking a Page or checking in to a Place cannot automatically register or enter a promotion participant.*

This guideline means that just because a user Likes your Fan Page or uses Facebook Places to check into your venue, doesn't mean you can automatically enter her in your promotion. Every once in a while, you may see a Fan Page Timeline announce that it's going to pick a random fan to win a prize. This is prohibited under Section 3 because those fans haven't opted in (via an entry form) to the promotion. You must use the third-party application to provide an entry form. Section 3 ensures that the entrant actually *wants* to enter your promotion.

Figure 4-1:
Be sure
to include
a notice
releasing
Facebook
of liability
related
to your
promotion.

4. You must not condition registration or entry upon the user taking any action using any Facebook features or functionality other than Liking a Page, checking in to a Place, or connecting to your app. For example, you must not condition registration or entry upon the user Liking a Wall post, or commenting or uploading a photo on a Wall.

This rule refers to the act of *Like-gating* content. When you create a custom Facebook tab, it's possible to hide specific content from nonfans until they click the Like button. Upon clicking Like, the new fan can then access the hidden content. This is called Like-gating; you may also hear it referred to as fan-gating or fan-only content — it's all the same.

For promotions, this means that you can hide your entry form until a user clicks Like. After she clicks Like, she can then complete the entry form to be part of the promotion. It's important to note that the initial Like of the Fan Page did not enter the user into your promotion. She only entered the promotion when she completed the entry form. Section 4 states that Like-gating of your promotional content is completely acceptable as long as you don't make the Like an entry. Figure 4-2 shows a promotion that has been Like-gated. Notice that the "gate" page asks the user to Like the Fan Page in order to reveal the entry form. Figure 4-3 shows what the user sees after she clicks Like and reveals the entry form. From here, she can enter the promotion and hope for a win!

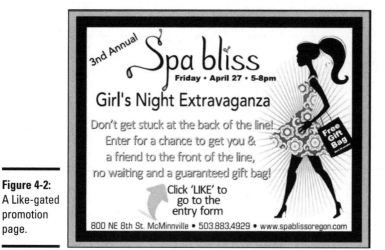

Figure 4-2: A Like-gated promotion page.

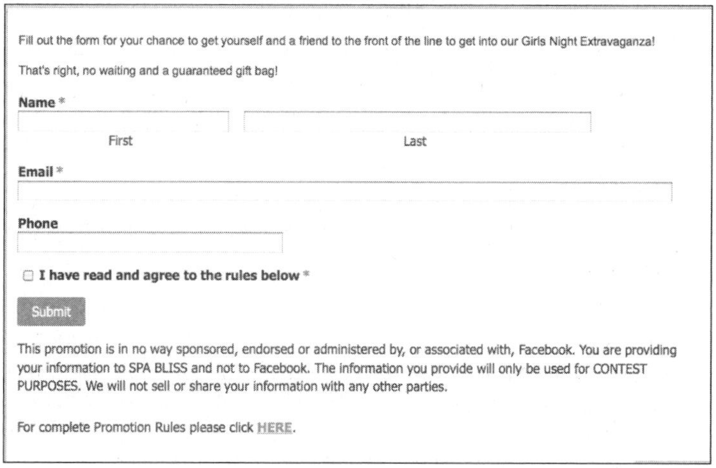

Fill out the form for your chance to get yourself and a friend to the front of the line to get into our Girls Night Extravaganza!

That's right, no waiting and a guaranteed gift bag!

Name *

First Last

Email *

Phone

☐ **I have read and agree to the rules below** *

Submit

This promotion is in no way sponsored, endorsed or administered by, or associated with, Facebook. You are providing your information to SPA BLISS and not to Facebook. The information you provide will only be used for CONTEST PURPOSES. We will not sell or share your information with any other parties.

For complete Promotion Rules please click HERE.

Figure 4-3: The entry form is revealed after the user clicks the Like button.

> *5. You must not use Facebook features or functionality, such as the Like button, as a voting mechanism for a promotion.*

This means you can't ask people to Like your Fan Page, comment on your Timeline, write a status update, or check-in to a Place as an entry to your promotion. (Refer to the example under Section 1 about asking your fans to leave a comment or vote/Like a comment or image to win a prize.) Sections 1 and 5 work together to ensure that you aren't using your Timeline or any Facebook feature to enter a giveaway or contest.

WARNING!

If you disregard the Facebook Promotions Guidelines . . .

So what happens if you don't follow the rules? You could lose your Fan Page Timeline. Think about that. If you lose your Fan Page Timeline, you lose your

- ✔ Content (images, video, notes, status updates . . . *everything*)
- ✔ Community (all your fans)
- ✔ Credibility (trust is what social media is built on)

The applications we describe in the "Using Apps to Create Customized Giveaways and Contests" section all have point-and-click interfaces that are easy to use. Those tools were built with a firm understanding of the Facebook Promotional Guidelines and have a few features built in to make it easy for you to

adhere to the rules. It doesn't make sense to risk losing your hard-earned Facebook community when it's easy to create a promotion that adheres to the Facebook Promotions Guidelines.

If you do lose your Fan Page Timeline, you can head over to My Facebook Page was Disabled at `https://www.facebook.com/help/contact.php?show_form=page_disabled` and complete that form to try to reinstate your Fan Page Timeline. We warn you, though, that it's very difficult to reinstate your Fan Page Timeline after it's been deleted. Most companies who have lost a Fan Page Timeline have had to start it from scratch and rebuild their community.

Some businesses and bloggers choose to host a promotion on their own website or blog rather than Facebook. These off-site promotions usually ask the entrant to Like a specific Fan Page on Facebook as an extra entry. This, too, is against the Facebook Promotions Guidelines. We understand the reasoning: If the giveaway isn't hosted on Facebook, you should be able to do as you like. Unfortunately, the minute you bring Facebook into the equation, Facebook's rules apply.

Many of the promotions run outside of Facebook at a business website or blog ask entrants to Like a Fan Page on Facebook, and then return to the website or blog to leave a comment saying the entrant completed the task. Therefore, the comment on the website or blog is the entry, not the Like. The flaw is that, if the comment were really the entry, the entrant wouldn't have to do anything other than leave the comment. Because you ask the entrant to complete a task on Facebook before commenting, you use Facebook functionality as a means of entry. Section 3 states this is not allowed.

The bottom line? You can't use Facebook functionality as a primary or additional entry to a promotion.

If you want to invite people to contribute images or video or ideas to garner votes in order to win a prize, you still have to use a third-party app (see Section 1 of the Facebook Promotions Guidelines) to create and administer the promotion. Most of the third-party apps have options for voting promotions and are fairly easy to implement. We discuss those tools a little later in this chapter.

> *6. You must not notify winners through Facebook, such as through Facebook messages, chat, or posts on profiles or Pages.*

This means you can't use Facebook chat, private messaging, or Timeline posts to notify someone that he won your promotion. You can notify your winners via private e-mail (not Facebook messaging) or via your website or blog. We suggest stating how you'll notify winners within the promotional rules you share as part of your contest or giveaway. When you've notified the winner privately and he has confirmed his win, you can announce it on your Fan Page Timeline.

Facebook doesn't require you to have promotional rules, but it's a good idea to put some together before you run your promotion. You want to be sure you're adhering to any local, state, or national laws. Need some tips? Check out this Quora discussion on creating rules for promotions (don't forget to read the comments too): www.quora.com/What-legal-issues-come-up-when-running-a-contest-or-giveaway/answer/Antone-Johnson?srid=3DA.

> *7. Ads may not imply a Facebook endorsement or partnership of any kind. Ads linking to Facebook branded content (including Pages, groups, events, or Connect sites) may make limited reference to "Facebook" in ad text for the purpose of (1) fulfilling your obligations under Section 2 and (2) clarifying the destination of the ad. All other ads and landing pages may not use our copyrights or trademarks (including Facebook, the Facebook and F Logos, FB, Face, Poke, Book, and Wall) or any confusingly similar marks, except as expressly permitted by our Brand Usage Guidelines (https://www.facebook.com/brandpermissions/) or with our prior written permission.*

This section means that Facebook doesn't want to be affiliated (implied or otherwise) with any promotion you administer. The liability is simply too high. You must make it clear to your audience that this is your promotion and yours alone. Don't imply that Facebook has anything whatsoever to do with your promotion and be sure you're not using any copyrighted or trademarked elements in your ad or promotion.

> *8. Definitions:*
> *a. By "administration" we mean the operation of any element of the promotion, such as collecting entries, conducting a drawing, judging entries, or notifying winners.*

b. By "communication" we mean promoting, advertising or referencing a promotion in any way on Facebook, for example, in ads, on a Page, or in a Wall post.
c. By "contest" or "competition" we mean a promotion that includes a prize of monetary value and a winner determined on the basis of skill (that is, through judging based on specific criteria).
d. By "sweepstakes" we mean a promotion that includes a prize of monetary value and a winner selected on the basis of chance.

These definitions are self-explanatory, but it's important to note them. The first, *administration,* is particularly important. See how it refers to *collecting entries?* When you host a giveaway on your website or blog and ask people to Like your Fan Page as an additional entry, you're essentially collecting entries via Facebook and you can't do that unless you're using a third-party app on Facebook.

Using Apps to Create Customized Giveaways and Contests

The biggest complaint we hear about the Facebook Promotions Guidelines is, "But it's just so easy to do it on the Timeline! I don't want the hassle of setting up an application! That sucks the fun out of it."

We suspect what these complainants mean is that page admins think setting up a promotion via a Facebook application will be hard and they'd rather just post a status update because that's easy and they already know how to do it. We have very good news for you: The companies who create Facebook promotions applications understand the need for an easy way to set up promotions. In the following sections, we list a few of the most popular apps for you so you have a starting place. Most of these tools can have you up and running with a promotion in less than 15 minutes (or faster after you've used them a few times). It's true that setting up a promotion via an app is still not as fast as creating a simple status update, but this way, you don't risk losing your Fan Page Timeline!

ShortStack

ShortStack (http://shortstack.com) offers Facebook applications that allow you to create custom tabs for your Fan Page Timeline. The one that concerns you in this chapter is the app that allows you to create a Facebook promotion (including Like-gating if you want; note that ShortStack calls it "fan only" content). (You could also create a printable coupon or a contact form. Or you could share images and video from an external site or pull in PDF documents using www.scribd.com and a ShortStack app.)

A few things to know about ShortStack:

✦ You can use ShortStack for free if your Fan Page Timeline has fewer than 2,000 Likes.

✦ You can Like-gate content on a custom tab with the click of a button.

✦ You can schedule your promotion to auto-publish in the future, and ShortStack takes care of everything.

✦ You can include custom CSS or templates featuring your logo or design in ShortStack widgets to reinforce your brand.

✦ You can manage multiple client sites with a single account.

Wildfire

Wildfire (`http://wildfireapp.com`) has a robust cache of applications to help you customize your Fan Page Timeline, including creating a contest or giveaway. Running a Facebook promotion is not free, but it's not expensive, either. Wildfire's Basic plan will set you back a $5 set up fee and $0.99 per day. So if your promotion lasts five days, your total would be $9.95. If you use the Standard level, you can customize you promotion to reflect your brand. Besides promotions, you can use Wildfire's tools to create group deals, coupons, and sign-up forms.

A few things to know about Wildfire:

✦ You can use Wildfire for as little as $5 per campaign, but they offer different pricing levels based on your needs (from $5 up to $250).

✦ Wildfire achieves Like-gating via iframes (iframes are discussed in Book VI). You need to work with a little code to get this up and running, but Wildfire offers tutorials to help you.

✦ You can publish your campaign to multiple outlets at the same time.

✦ Wildfire's tool chooses your winner for you.

Strutta

Strutta (`http://www.strutta.com`) allows you to create promotions that can stand alone or live on Facebook. It's a premium tool and pricing starts at $199 for giveaways and $299 for contests. If you want to customize your promotion, you need to upgrade to the Pro version that jumps to $1,999. The interface is very user friendly, which makes creating your promotion a breeze.

A few things to know about Strutta:

✦ You can optimize your promotion for mobile devices.

✦ Strutta offers analytics or you can use your Google Analytics tracking code to track your promotion's success.

✦ You can use Strutta's promotions tools outside of Facebook. Embed your contest or giveaway on your blog or website.

✦ The basic templates are clean and attractive.

TabPress

If you're comfortable coding your own promotions page, you can use HyperArts' TabPress Facebook app (`http://on.fb.me/TabPress`) to create your own iframe application to host your giveaway. You need to be comfortable using HTML, CSS, Javascript, or any other code you want to include because you have total control of the look and feel of the end product. To use TabPress, go to `http://on.fb.me/TabPress` and install the app on your Fan Page Timeline (see Book VI, Chapter 3 for instructions on installing an app to your Fan Page Timeline). Then return to your Fan Page Timeline and click the new Welcome icon in your left sidebar navigation (it will be an orange, green, and white square) to reveal your TabPress Dashboard. From there, start coding. Yes, it's that easy!

A few things to know about TabPress:

✦ TabPress is free for Fan Page Timelines with up to 2,500 fans.

✦ TabPress is fully customizable because you're coding everything yourself.

✦ Like-gating is a free feature.

HyperArts is one of our favorite companies because it shares information freely and has great tutorials on its blog (`www.hyperarts.com/blog`) to help you create Fan Page customizations yourself.

When using iframes, keep in mind that your canvas is 810 pixels wide, so you need to size your images accordingly. Any links you share should be coded to open a new tab or window, or they will automatically open within the iframe. That can be a problem if you're linking to content that isn't optimized for an 810-pixel canvas. If you want to build your own iframe app, flip to Book VI, Chapter 1.

Creating Best Practices for Your Facebook Promotion

Following the Facebook Promotions Guidelines is the first step to hosting your contest or giveaway. Beyond adhering to Facebook's rules, though, you need to make sure your promotion is fulfilling your own goals. Do you want to grow your e-mail list? Do you want to draw attention to a specific product or service? Are you interested in growing your fan base? Do you want your Facebook community to participate more? Whatever your goals are, be sure you know how you're going to reach them. To that end, it makes sense to create your own set of best practices. Here are some ideas to get you started:

✦ **Know the goal(s) of each promotion you administer.** How can you determine whether a promotion is a success if you don't know what you want to achieve? Write down measureable goals (for example, "Our Fan Page Timeline will garner 150 new Likes" is better than "grow number of Likes"), and then decide two things:

- What do you need to offer your audience (the prize) to entice them to share information (via the entry form)?

- What information do you need to collect from your entrants to meet your goals?

The more valuable the prize, the more participants are willing to share their information. If you're offering a $25 gift card, don't expect your entrants to complete a lengthy survey. If you're offering a vacation, though, people are more willing to answer some questions for you or jump through some hoops.

✦ **Keep the hoops to a minimum.** Our experience with running promotions is that people want free stuff, and they don't want to put a lot of work into entering your promotion. On the other hand, as the business owner, you have certain goals you're trying to reach. The key to balancing both is keeping the barrier to entry commiserate with what you're offering for a prize. If you're offering something small as a prize, your fans are less likely to do more than Like your Fan Page Timeline. However, if you're offering an iPad or a trip as a prize, your fans will be more forgiving of the hoops you make them jump through for entry. In general, the barrier to entry as it relates to likelihood of entry is as follows:

- Completing an entry form is the easiest form of entry and will probably result in the most entries and traffic. People are most interested in promotions where they don't have to exert a lot of effort, but have a reasonable expectation of payoff.

- Liking a Fan Page to access an entry form (that is, like-gating your entry form) is the next highest barrier to entry and may or may not decrease the traffic to your promotion. However, be aware that you may see a drop in Likes after the promotion ends because those who didn't win may Unlike your Fan Page.

- User-generated content is the highest barrier to entry. Though you may have fewer entries in this type of promotion, those entering are usually brand enthusiasts or serious about sharing their own information to enhance their visibility to your audience. Examples of user-generated content for a promotion could be inviting entrants to share original recipes or a story about your product, or submitting photos or video based on specific criteria.

✦ **Tell entrants what information you require, why you require it, and how you'll use it in the future.** If you need both an e-mail address and a street address, tell your entrants why. Are you going to add those addresses to your database and send them periodic notifications via e-mail and snail-mail? Or will you add their e-mail address to your newsletter or e-mail list, but only use their street address for shipping purposes and then delete it from your database? These are important things your audience needs to know in order to decide whether to participate in your giveaway. The way you plan to keep and/or use their information may determine whether they choose to enter the giveaway.

✦ **Go beyond your current fans.** If you're running a Facebook promotion on your Fan Page Timeline, it stands to reason you'll tell your fans about it. But if the purpose of your promotion is to spread the word about a specific product or service, create buzz around an idea, or even increase your Fan Page Likes, you need to garner attention beyond your existing fan base. You can do that by

- *Using a Facebook ad in conjunction with your Facebook promotion.* You can target Facebook ads to very specific audiences based on interests, location, or even friends. Be sure to create your Facebook ad with a strong call to action and include a direct link to your Facebook promotion. See Book V, Chapter 5 for more information about creating an enticing Facebook ad.

- *Promoting your contest or giveaway on your other social channels.* Facebook shouldn't be your only social media outlet. More likely than not, Facebook is just one of the ways you're creating community. Use your Twitter, website, and blog outlets to spread the word. Use QR codes or signs in your bricks-and-mortar store to link your in-person customers to your promotion.

Chapter 5: Facebook Advertising

In This Chapter

- ✓ Discovering what Facebook ads are (and aren't)
- ✓ Setting up your own Facebook ad
- ✓ Using your Facebook Ads Manager
- ✓ Sharing administrative privileges
- ✓ Closing your Facebook ads account

*O*ne of the things Facebook does well is collecting specific demographic information about users. Facebook members share their likes and dislikes, brand loyalties, where they live, and so many other personal interests just by filling out their Timelines, Liking Fan Pages, and updating their status. Facebook doesn't sell this information, and each user controls what she shares or doesn't share with others. (Admittedly, though, it can be hard to *not* share on a platform like Facebook.) What Facebook does do with that information is use it to allow advertisers to specifically target users with their marketing. Because Facebook is and always will be a free platform, it makes money from advertisements.

If you run a business and are looking to get the biggest bang for your buck, Facebook ads aren't a bad way to go because you can reach a very targeted audience. This chapter explains the considerations of setting up a Facebook ad and how to track your ad's success rate. We give you a pretty broad overview, but if you really want to get into the nitty gritty of Facebook advertising, we suggest getting a copy of *Facebook Marketing All-In-One For Dummies* by Amy Porterfield, Phyllis Khare, and Andrea Vahl (John Wiley & Sons, Inc.). Those ladies explain every nook and cranny of social media marketing you can imagine.

Finding Facebook Ads

Although Facebook isn't overrun with ads, it's unlikely you've missed seeing them. They're in your right sidebar under your Ticker (see Figure 5-1).

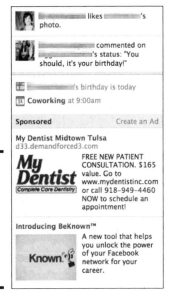

Figure 5-1: Facebook Ads and Sponsored Posts appear in your right sidebar.

The ads you see are usually not too invasive and actually may have some interest for you. That's because Facebook and advertisers are trying to target the most useful ads for *you* based on the information you've shared in your personal Timeline, or how you've interacted with other pages within Facebook, or even who your friends are (and how they've interacted on Facebook). You may see ads for external websites or Facebook pages such as Fan Page Timelines, Events, and apps. Ads for Facebook-related items may also show which of your friends have Liked a Fan Page or RSVP'd to an event. Seeing those connections with people you know provides *social proof* — reinforcement that your friends endorse something — and you may be more likely to complete an action (for example, Liking a Fan Page).

Sometimes ads miss their mark. If you're seeing an ad you don't like or if an ad keeps coming up in your sidebar and you're tired of seeing it, you can remove it. Just move your mouse over the ad and click the X at the top when it appears. You have the option to hide the ad itself or hide all ads from the same advertiser. When you hide the ad, you have the opportunity to have a say in what kinds of ads you receive in the future. Unfortunately, no, you can't opt out of all advertisements. If you're interested in seeing the types of ads Facebook think you personally would be interested in, go to `https://www.facebook.com/ads/adboard`.

Deciding if Facebook Ads Are Right for You

If you're looking to get the most bang for your advertising buck, Facebook ads may just be what you're looking for. Of course, that will largely depend on whether your audience is using Facebook, but with more than 800 million active users, we know at least some of them are. Plus, with that many users, just think of the new customers you can find!

Why is Facebook such a great place to advertise? Well, Facebook is in a unique position. It has access to very specific demographic information for each user. Facebook allows advertisers to target ads to exact specifications regarding location (down to the ZIP code), gender, age, interests, education, and even employment. And, of course, you can use keywords as well. Heck, you can even target people whose birthdays are today! That kind of precise audience targeting means you should enjoy a healthy return on your investment. Other benefits of using Facebook advertising include the ability to

✦ Choose to buy your ads based on either cost per click (CPC) or cost per impression (CPM)

✦ See if people complete an action within 24 hours of seeing your ad

✦ Set your own daily or lifetime budget and only pay for what you use

✦ Change any aspect of your ad (image, content, link, budget, and so on) during the ad's run

✦ Stop the ad completely — even if the time isn't up yet

If you've ever used other methods of advertising (online or offline), you know you don't always have that kind of flexibility.

Although you can advertise just about anything — Fan Page Timelines, Groups, Events, apps, and external websites — Facebook gives you two choices of ads: Facebook Ads or Sponsored Stories.

Choosing an ad: Facebook Ads

You can use a Facebook ad to attract interest for any page within Facebook (for example, Fan Page Timeline, Group, Event, or app), or you can promote an external website. Any time you promote something within Facebook, it's called an *Engagement Ad,* and it includes two important parts:

✦ An opportunity to complete an action within the ad (instead of interrupting the user's flow by having to click over to your Fan Page Timeline)

✦ Relevant actions by users connected to the viewer to help build awareness through social proof

For example, if a user sees your ad for your Fan Page Timeline, the ad will include a Like button so he can Like the Fan Page right from the ad and can see if any of his Facebook friends Liked your Fan Page as well. Figure 5-2 shows an example of an Engagement Ad for Facebook Live at CES.

Figure 5-2:
Engagement
Ads provide
social proof
and an
opportunity
to complete
an action.

If you are using cost per click (CPC) for your ad, you're charged each time someone clicks Like or clicks through to your destination page.

You can do a few other things with Facebook ads, and we cover those in the later section, "Designing your Facebook ad."

Choosing an ad: Sponsored Stories

Sponsored Stories (also called *Featured Stories*) are stories about a Fan Page Timeline, Place, or app that are already available in your News Feed. A Sponsored Story may show a friend who Likes a Fan Page, or checks into a Place, or Likes or Shares a status update from a Fan Page Timeline. The interactions you see within a sponsored story (for example, Likes or Shares) are interactions that already show up in your News Feed or Ticker. The difference is that a business or individual is paying for the Sponsored Story to be more prominent and less likely to be lost in the constant flow of information. Figure 5-3 shows an example of a Sponsored Story ad.

Figure 5-3:
A Sponsored
Story may
show when
someone
Likes your
Fan Page.

Should you create an ad just to get Likes?

If you want to create an ad just to garner more Likes to your Fan Page, you may do just that. But what use is it if you have a lot of fans, but no one is converting to a customer? It's more important to have fans who want to engage with your business, tell their friends about you, and eventually buy from you. To find those people, create your ad accordingly.

If you promote an ad that says you're giving away an iPad, you'll get a lot of traffic and Likes — but how many of those people are interested in your product(s) and how many just want to win an iPad? You may say, "But I just want to get as many eyes on my updates as possible!" We know, we know. Remember, just because someone Likes your Fan Page, doesn't mean she sees your update. Users can hide your Fan Page updates from their News Feeds, stop interacting with your Fan Page Timeline so they don't see it as often in the Top Stories on their News Feeds, or even Unlike your Fan Page after they don't win the iPad.

Consider this: Having a bunch of fans who don't care about your brand could actually hurt you in the long run. In Book V, Chapter 3, we explain how Facebook uses an algorithm called EdgeRank to determine how your Fan Page Timeline performs in individual News Feeds. We also explain an important metric in Insights (Facebook's analytics program) called People Talking about This. Both EdgeRank and People Talking about This rely on your fans interacting

with your shared content. If you have a hundred fans and many of them Like, comment on, and share your content, then your EdgeRank for your fans is probably pretty high (meaning you're showing up in their News Feeds regularly) and your People Talking about This number is pretty high. If your People Talking about This number is high, then it's likely you have a wider reach because the friends of your fans see those interactions as well. That's all pretty good, right?

Now, say you have 100 Likes, and you run an ad that promises an iPad giveaway. You end up getting 1,000 total Likes. You just increased your fan base by 1,000%. But what if only the original 100 fans are still talking about you and the new fans are just ignoring you because they were only interested in the giveaway? Facebook looks at your overall fan base and the number of people interacting with your content, so it looks like you've had a huge drop in engagement. Consequently, your overall EdgeRank drops, and you aren't showing up as much in people's News Feeds — especially the new fans who didn't really care about your brand or product and so aren't Liking, commenting, or sharing. Which would you rather have? A smaller number of fans who are more likely to help you spread the word about your product(s) and buy from you, or a large number of fans who do nothing at all?

 At the time we're writing this book, Sponsored Stories are still relegated to the sidebar with other Facebook ads, but we expect them to start showing up in your News Feed soon (possibly before this book hits the shelves). You'll know you're seeing sponsored content in your News Feed if you see a link that says *Sponsored* below the post.

Knowing the no-noes — what you can't do with ads

Facebook has guidelines for everything. It has terms of service for your personal Timeline and your Fan Page Timeline, guidelines for giveaways and contests, and yes, guidelines for advertisements. Facebook must approve each ad you create, so it makes sense to know what you can and can't do with your ads. If you don't comply, Facebook rejects your ad. You can read the guidelines in their entirety at `https://www.facebook.com/ad_guidelines.php`. Here are a few examples of what you not allowed to advertise (again, read the guidelines for a full list):

✦ Pornography

✦ Alcohol, drugs, or tobacco

✦ Gambling or lotteries

✦ Any site that uses domain forwarding (that is, you think you're going to one website and end up on another)

✦ Any site that contains spyware or malware

Facebook won't double-check your ad to be sure it's legal — that's completely up to you. If your ad doesn't comply with the law, you're liable, not Facebook.

Creating Your Facebook Ad

There are about eleventy billion ways you can start the ad creation process. Okay, we're exaggerating. But Facebook does give you several opportunities to click and create an ad on just about every page you browse. We show you one of the ways, but suffice to say, if you want to create an ad and you see a Create Ad link, you can click it wherever you see it and the steps will be largely the same.

To get started with a Facebook ad, go to `https://www.facebook.com/business/ads/create/index.php`, and you see the Advertise on Facebook page. This page offers all the options you need to create a Facebook advertisement. There are three general steps:

1. Design your ad.

2. Target your audience.

3. Set your campaign, pricing, and schedule.

We explain each of those steps more thoroughly in the next few sections.

Designing your Facebook ad

The first section of the Advertise on Facebook page, Design Your Ad, looks similar to the screen shown in Figure 5-4.

Figure 5-4:
Options for
designing
your
Facebook ad.

You have four settings to determine as part of your ad's design:

✦ Destination

✦ Type

✦ Story Type

✦ Page Post Selection

Some of these options will change, depending on choices you make. For
example, if your ad is leading users to your Fan Page, you'll see the options
in the previous list. If your ad leads users to your website or other URL outside of Facebook, your options will be a bit different.

Destination

Where do you want people to end up when they click your ad? Do you want
to send them to your Fan Page Timeline or your Place page? Or would you
rather send them to your website outside of Facebook? Use the Destination
drop-down list to make your choice. If you want the ad to link to a website
outside of Facebook, choose External URL from the top of the list. Otherwise,
you can choose a Fan Page Timeline, a Place, or even an application as the
click-through destination.

If you choose External URL, new choices appear. You need to type the URL
in the text box, fill out the Title and Body text boxes with marketing copy,
and upload an image for your ad. Alternatively, you can click the Suggest an
Ad button and Facebook will pull some information from the website and get
you started. You can edit as necessary.

If you create an ad for an external website, you can create a customized title. Facebook has a few limitations though:

+ You can only use 25 characters.

+ You can't use all capital letters.

+ You can't use multiple exclamation points.

If you ignore those guidelines, Facebook won't approve your ad.

Type

You won't see the Type option if you're creating an ad that links to an external website, but if you're creating an Engagement Ad (that is, an ad that links to a destination page within Facebook), you see two options: Sponsored Stories and Facebook Ads (both are defined earlier in this chapter). Select the type of ad you want to create.

Story Type

The options listed under Story Type change based on the type of ad you chose to run (that is, either a Sponsored Story or a Facebook Ad). If you chose Sponsored Story under Type, your choices for Story Type are as follows:

+ **Page Like Story:** When someone Likes your Fan Page, that user's friends see a Sponsored Story in their sidebars.

+ **Check-In Story:** When someone uses Facebook's check-in tool to check into your Place, that user's friends see a Sponsored Story in their sidebars. This choice only appears if your destination link is a Places page.

+ **Page Post Like Story:** When someone Likes one of your status updates, that user's friends see a Sponsored Story in their sidebars.

If you chose Facebook Ads under Type, then your choices for Story Type are as follows:

+ **Page Post Ad:** These include status updates you've already shared on your Fan Page Timeline and the activity associated with those posts (links, Likes, and so on). They do not include extra marketing messaging. When you select Page Post Ad, the Page Post Selection drop-down list appears. Use it to choose which status update you'd like to use in your ad. The ads have character limitations, so it's best to use a short update so the text isn't cut off. You can to preview the ad, so you can try out a few different posts before you settle on the one you like best.

Figure 5-5 shows an example of a Facebook ad that uses an existing status update from the Blogging Basics 101 Fan Page.

Figure 5-5:
A Facebook
ad can use
existing
Fan Page
Timeline
updates.

Page post ads are only visible to people you've already shared the information with. That means if you geo-targeted a status update and therefore limited the audience who could see that update, you can still use that update as a Sponsored Story, but only the original audience will see it. People outside of that limited initial target will not see it. However, if you share a status update publicly, the Sponsored Story is also public and is more likely to be seen by a wider audience. See Book IV, Chapter 3 for more about targeting Fan Page Timeline status updates.

✦ **Facebook Ads for Pages:** This option allows you to customize your marketing material for the ad and create a strong call to action. When you select the Facebook for Ads for Pages option, the page changes to look similar to Figure 5-6.

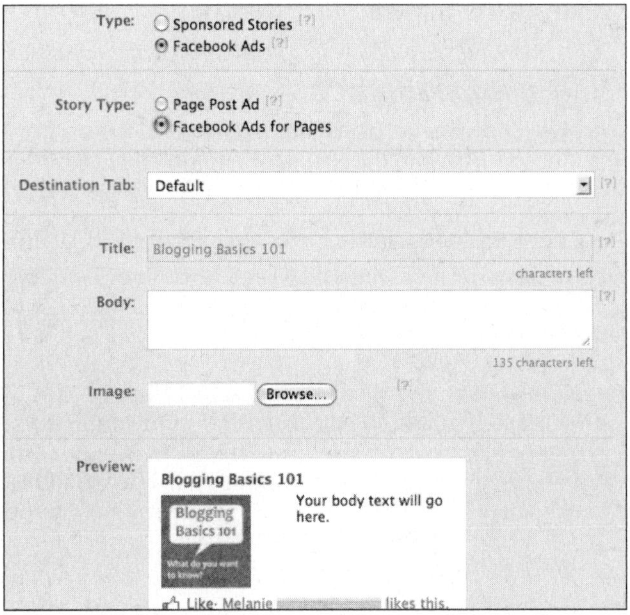

Figure 5-6:
The
Facebook
Ads for
Pages
options.

> Type: ○ Sponsored Stories [?]
> ⊙ Facebook Ads [?]
>
> Story Type: ○ Page Post Ad [?]
> ⊙ Facebook Ads for Pages
>
> Destination Tab: Default [?]
>
> Title: Blogging Basics 101 [?]
> characters left
>
> Body: [?]
> 135 characters left
>
> Image: Browse... [?]
>
> Preview: **Blogging Basics 101**
> Your body text will go
> here.
> Blogging Basics 101
> What do you want to know?
> Like · Melanie ▓▓▓▓▓▓ likes this.

If you want to make a Facebook Ad for Pages, you need to provide the following information:

- *Destination Tab:* Use the drop-down list to choose which tab on your Fan Page Timeline you want people to land on when they click your ad. You can send people to whichever tab will get you the best conversion for your goals. If you want people to sign up for a giveaway, send them to the custom tab for the entry form (see Book V, Chapter 4 for the lowdown on running giveaways on Facebook). Or you can send people to a custom Welcome tab — those are great because they have a 47% conversion rate. (See Book IV for more advice on Fan Pages.)

- *Title:* If you're placing an ad for a Fan Page Timeline, the title will automatically match that of your Fan Page Timeline. For instance, if Melanie creates an ad for her Fan Page Timeline, the title is automatically Blogging Basics 101 because that's the title of her Fan Page Timeline. You can't change the title for a Fan Page Timeline ad.

- *Body:* You have 135 characters to get your point across. This is where you want to hook readers and encourage them to complete an action. You can explain the benefits of your products, highlight a coupon or special deal, and so on.

- *Image:* Use the Browse to choose an image to upload for your ad. Most research has found that images of people do better than product images. And remember that the ads are fairly small, so choose a picture that is still legible when it's small.

Targeting your audience

One of the biggest draws for using Facebook ads is the ability to fine-tune who sees your ads. You can customize your audience right down to the ZIP code you want to reach, if you like. Figure 5-7 shows the Targeting information box.

Pay close attention to the Estimated Reach box in your sidebar (also shown in Figure 5-7). As you customize your targeted audience, you can watch your Estimated Reach become more targeted.

If you haven't looked at your Insights yet, now is a good time to check them out (Book V, Chapter 3 can tell you more about how to use your data). Insights is Facebook's analytics program that provides important demographic and engagement information about your current audience. You can use that data to determine who you want to target your current ad to.

Figure 5-7:
The Targeting information you choose determines your Estimated Reach.

You can start targeting your audience based on location, age, gender, interests, and even who they're connected to. You can go even further by including specific relationship status, language, education, and employment information. Each Facebook user has shared a certain amount of data pertaining to his life, and Facebook uses that information to help you reach the best audience for your business or product ads.

Setting campaigns, pricing, and scheduling

The final step in setting up your Facebook ad or Sponsored Story campaign is determining how much you want to spend, when you want to run your campaign, and whether you want to pay for clicks or impressions (and how much you're willing to pay for each). We explain each of these items in more detail in the following sections.

Campaign & Budget

Facebook allows you to group similar ads into *campaigns*. Each campaign can have multiple ads that are similar, but may be slightly different (for example, if you're doing A/B or split testing to see which ad works best). Each time you create an ad, you can put it in an existing campaign, or you can create a new campaign. We suggest naming your campaign something indicative of your goals, or if it's part of a split test, something that reminds you which ad it is. The intent, of course, is to make it as easy as possible to find your ad on your dashboard later when you want to edit it.

When setting your budget, you can choose to spend a specific amount per day or you can set a lifetime budget. When you set a daily budget, every day Facebook will promote your ad until the ad has met its budget for the day. The next day, it starts over. So if you have a budget of $50 per day, Facebook shows your ad until it meets that $50 parameter. Then, tomorrow, Facebook shows the ad again until it reaches its $50 limit. Facebook continues to show the ad until the end date you set.

Be careful! If you only want to spend $50 total, but want your ad to run for five days, you need to set your daily budget to $10 and your dates accordingly. Otherwise, you may end up paying quite a bit more than you intended for a campaign. Pay special attention to your end date. Facebook automatically sets the end date a month from the start date, so you may have to change it.

Schedule

By default, your campaign is set to run continuously. If you want to set specific dates for your campaign, just click the check box to deselect the option, and you can set begin and end dates. Click inside the box with the calendars to set your dates; click inside the time box to set the start and end times. You may note that the times are Pacific, so be sure to adjust for your own time zone!

Even if you have your campaign running for five days, if you've limited your daily budget, Facebook stops showing your ad when you've reached that daily budget. Facebook won't continue to show your ad, then charge you more later.

Pricing

Ad pricing is based on either cost per impression (CPM) or cost per click (CPC). *CPM* stands for cost per *mille* (which is French for 1,000; and M is the Roman numeral for one thousand — CPM seems to make sense in every language except English). When you choose the CPM model, you're choosing to pay for every thousand times the ad is seen. Choose this option if it's more important for your ad to be seen than for people to click on it. CPM works well when you're trying to build brand awareness. *CPC* stands for cost per click. You only pay when someone actually clicks your ad (this can include clicking the Like button, submitting an RSVP to an Event, clicking through the ad and landing on the destination page, and so on). Choose this option if it's more important for people to complete an action.

When you set your bid, you're determining what you're willing to pay for a click or an impression. The least amount you can pay for CPC is $0.01 and the least you can pay for CPM is $0.02. However, it's unlikely that ads with those bids would ever be seen. Facebook uses an auction-type system to determine which ads are shown. Basically, all ads and Sponsored Stories are competing for the same ad space. When you place your bid, it's wise to use the maximum amount you're willing to pay for CPM or CPC. Facebook will calculate the least you would have to pay to "win" your ad space. That price may be lower than the maximum price you submitted. For instance, if you say you'll pay $5 for each click, but the next lowest bid is $3, Facebook sees that you have a higher maximum and will sell the space to you for, say, $3.50 instead of the $5 you bid. On the other hand, if you're in a competitive niche, you may end up paying that full $5 (but not more than your bid; if you want to raise your bid later, you can).

Facebook gives you a suggested range for your bid based on your target audience, your keywords (that is, interests), and so on. You don't have to bid more than the minimum of a penny or two, but you'll have more success if you make a reasonable bid based on Facebook's suggestions.

After you've designed your ad, targeted your audience, and determined your budget, click the Review Ad button. The new page shows you what your ad will look like and gives you the opportunity to edit as needed. Or, if you're ready to go, click Place Order. You'll be taken to your Facebook Ads Manager.

It can take up to 24 hours for Facebook to approve your ad.

Finding and Using the Facebook Ads Manager

The Facebook Ads Manager is the command center for the ads and Sponsored Stories you're running on Facebook. From here, you can edit your ads and stories, as well as track how they're performing. You can find your Ads Manager by navigating to `https://www.facebook.com/ads/manage`. (See Figure 5-8.)

Figure 5-8:
The Ads
Manager
page gives
you an
overview of
how your
campaigns
are
performing.

Creating your Facebook ad

Creating a successful ad can be tricky. Even though you have access to a targeted audience, you still need to create an engaging ad. Here are a few tips for creating a successful Facebook ad:

✔ **Know who you want for a client.** We've said throughout this book that it's important to know your audience. Facebook allows you to target specific people based on basic demographics, as well as those who have Liked a specific Fan Page (such as a competitor's Fan Page Timeline) or have interests in specific activities or products. If you know who you want for a client, target them.

✔ **Use a clear, strong call to action.** Tell people what you want them to do (and give them the means to follow through), and they're more likely to do it. There's a character limit for your headline and ad content, so use it wisely.

✔ **Be sure to send people to a page that's relevant to the action you want them to complete.** If you want them to buy something, send them to your Facebook shopping cart or your online store. If you want them to Like your Fan Page, send them to a custom Welcome page that explains *why* they should Like your Fan Page or how they can get something for free by clicking Like. Sending new fans to a custom Welcome page has a 47% higher conversion rate than sending them to your Timeline. There's nothing special about your Timeline, but your custom Welcome page can share whatever marketing and message you want. (See Book IV, Chapter 1 for more advice on creating a custom Welcome page.)

✔ **Choose an image that works.** It's been shown time and again that Facebook users react better to ads with pictures of real people. We know you've spent a lot of time building your brand and probably paid a lot for your logo. And that time and money are worth it in other marketing areas. But on Facebook, people want to see people. Choose an image of a person (even you!) that conveys the message you're trying to get across.

Viewing campaign data

One of the benefits of using Facebook ads is that you can pause, change, or even stop your ad at any time. Click the pencil icon next to Campaign Name, Status, Budget, and Duration to edit those items. Yep, that's right. If you see that something's not working, change it.

The data shared in the Audience graph shows you how your ad is performing based on your targeted audience (Targeted) and who you're actually reaching (Reach). The Social Reach metric tells you how many people who saw the ad also saw their friend(s) mentioned within the ad (for example, Emily Likes this Fan Page or Ryan RSVP'd to this Event). Facebook says ads with that kind of social proof are twice as likely to work.

If you're not reaching enough of your target audience, tweak your campaign. You may need to raise your bid so your ads appear more frequently.

The Response graph gives you an overview of how many people are clicking your ad. If your ad is for a Fan Page Timeline, Event, or app, the Connections data refers to how many people in the last 28 days have connected with your Fan Page Timeline, Event, or app within 24 hours of seeing your ad. You won't see Connections data for ads that link outside of Facebook, though, so keep that in mind.

Below those two graphs are filtering options so you can look at data based on dates or campaigns. When you use the drop-down list to filter the data, the table below the lists changes. Refer to Figure 5-8 as you read the options. Using the buttons, you can filter data in the following ways:

✦ **General Date:** These aren't specific dates. Instead, you can choose Last 7 days, Today, Yesterday, Last 28 Days, or Custom. If you choose Custom, you can choose a custom date range.

✦ **Ad Status:** You can view all ads (except deleted), or those that are active, pending, paused, disapproved, completed, or deleted.

You also see two more buttons:

✦ **Select Rows to Edit:** This option is grayed out until you select the check box next to an ad campaign in the list. When a row is selected, the button becomes active, and when clicked, allows you to edit the checked rows.

✦ **Full Report:** Click this button if you want to run a single report with all the stats for all your campaigns. We cover this option more in depth in the "Generating a Report" section, later in the chapter.

Under the buttons are several numbers that reflect the following engagement metrics:

✦ **Campaign Reach:** How many unique people saw your campaign during the selected dates.

✦ **Frequency:** The average of times each person saw your ad or story during the selected dates.

✦ **Social Reach:** The number of people who saw their Facebook friends mentioned in your ad or story. You only see this number for ads or Sponsored Stories that link within Facebook.

✦ **Connections:** The number of people who took an action related to your ad or story (for example, Liking your Fan Page or responding to an Event invitation) within 24 hours of seeing it.

✦ **Clicks:** The number of people who clicked the ad or story. It includes all clicks (for example, clicking the Like button, clicking to install an application, and so on).

✦ **CTR:** The number of clicks divided by the number of times the ad or story was shown during the selected dates.

✦ **Spent:** How much you've spent on the campaign during the selected dates.

Below that is a table with similar headings showing data for a given ad or story. You can see data for Status, Reach, Frequency, Social Reach, Connections, Clicks, CTR, Bid, and Price.

Understanding the left navigation options

Your main Ads Manager page has links in the left column that allow you to quickly move from one page to another to manage various aspects of your account:

✦ **Campaign & Ads:** When you navigate directly to `https://www.facebook.com/ads/manage`, you see the page shown in Figure 5-8. If you click the Campaign & Ads link in the left navigation bar, though, you see a page similar to Figure 5-9, where you can see your Notifications and Daily Spend and a few other options. Notifications are updates on the status of ads (for example, whether they've been approved) or whether Facebook charged your credit card on file.

Below the Notifications and Daily Spend are the four buttons described in the "Viewing campaign data" section. They actually have different names here, but they serve the same purpose as described previously. For instance, Lifetime stats allows you to choose a date range for the data; All Except Deleted allows you to filter data based on status; and Select Rows to Edit and Full Report are the same.

Figure 5-9:
The
Campaign
& Ads page
shows your
Notifications
and Daily
Spend.

Just under the Campaigns & Ads link is the All Ads link. This link shows the table shown in Figure 5-9.

✦ **Pages:** Click this link to see a list of Fan Page Timelines you own or are an administrator of. This is a quick way to see how your Fan Page Timelines are doing at a glance. You can see page notifications, when you last updated, total page Likes, and weekly activity. If you click the name of a Fan Page Timeline, you navigate to that Fan Page Timeline. If you click the Switch link, you switch to using Facebook as that Fan Page Timeline (see Book IV, Chapter 2 for an explanation of how to use Facebook as a Fan Page Timeline instead of as yourself).

✦ **Reports:** You can run reports about how your ads, stories, and campaigns are performing so you can decide if they need to be tweaked or are fine as is. The reports include data such as impressions, clicks, connections, and spend. We explain more about reports later in this chapter in the "Generating a Report" section.

✦ **Settings:** Click this link to see your Ad Account Settings page. On this page, you can find your account ID, close your ad account, and set your business name and address. If you're located in in the European Union, you can enter your EU VAT number here as well. This is also where you can set your permissions and e-mail notifications.

✦ **Billing:** Your Billing page provides an overview of any outstanding balances, your daily spend limit, and your account spend limit. We want to point out that your daily and account spend limits are the maximum Facebook will allow you to spend — not necessarily the bid or limit you set when creating your ad or story. Facebook won't charge you more than the limit you set, but it lets you know what your limit is if you'd like to change your settings. For instance, if Melanie sets the daily spending limit at $25, her Facebook daily limit may be $250. Facebook knows Melanie set the limit at $25 and won't allow her to spend more than that in a given day. However, she can up the limit as high as necessary up to $250. In addition to monitoring your balance and spend limits, you can check your transactions by date and type (for example, Facebook coupons, PayPal, credit card, and so on).

The Funding Source link is below Billing. This page shows you which credit card(s) you have on file. You can also add a funding source by clicking the Add a Funding Source button in the top-right corner. Follow the directions to add a credit card, PayPal account, or use a Facebook Ad Coupon.

✦ **Creative Library:** Click this link to see the images you've used for various ads and stories. You can sort this page using the drop-down list and choosing All Campaigns, a specific campaign, any campaign without ads, or deleted campaigns. You can also edit, preview, or re-use your images.

Click the New Creative link if you'd like to add a new image to your library. The Add New Creative page appears, and you can upload a new image and assign it to a new ad or story.

✦ **Learn More:** While this chapter is an excellent resource, Facebook has an extensive library of help files for Facebook ads. Click the Learn More link to start finding the answers you need. Here are few additional resources you may want to check out:

• *Facebook's Business section:* `https://www.facebook.com/business`

• *Video tutorials for Facebook advertising tools:* `https://www.facebook.com/business/sessions`

• *Facebook Help files for Advertising:* `https://www.facebook.com/help/ads-and-business-solutions`

• *Facebook advertising Guidelines:* `https://www.facebook.com/ad_guidelines.php`

Generating a Report

The data Facebook collects for your ads, stories, and campaigns can be an invaluable resource for you as you gauge whether your ads are working. You see several ways to run a report. In fact, Facebook has a Full Report button on just about every page of your Ad Manager. When you click the Full Report button, the View Advertising Report page appears, as shown in Figure 5-10. And there's a Report link in your left navigation list as well.

Figure 5-10: Run a Full Report on ad performance from the View Advertising Report page.

Data for 01/13/2012 is through 6:27 am Pacific time only.
Certain statistics, such as unique impressions / clicks, are not available using custom or lifetime time aggregation.

View Advertising Report | Export Report (.csv) | Generate Another Report | Schedule this Report

Report Type	Summarize By	Time Summary	Date Range
Advertising Performance	Campaign	Custom	🗓 Lifetime

51,934 Impressions **22** Clicks **12** Connections **0.042%** CTR **$27.99** Spent **$0.54** CPM **$1.27** CPC

Date Range ?	Campaign ?	Impressions ?	Clicks ?	CTR ?	CPC ?	CPM ?	Spent ?	Connections ?
Lifetime	improve your blog	51,934	22	0.042%	1.27	0.54	27.99	12

✦ **Export Report (.csv):** Click this button to run a report and save it as a `.csv` (comma separated value) file that you can open in either Excel or Numbers.

✦ **Generate Another Report:** Click here to generate another report. It's the same as using the Report link in the left nav bar.

✦ **Schedule This Report:** Click this button if you want to run a weekly report and receive it via e-mail. To schedule reporting, following these steps:

1. *Go to* `https://www.facebook.com/ads/manage` *and click the Full Report button.*

   The View Advertising Report page appears.

2. *Click the Schedule this Report button in the top-right corner.*

   The Create a Recurring Schedule window appears.

3. *Complete the form using the drop-down lists.*

   You can run several different types of reports, including advertising performance, responder demographics, conversions by impression time, and inline interactions. Decide how often you want to receive the updates and which ads, stories, or campaigns you want to include.

4. *Type your e-mail address in the Subscribe via E-mail text box to ensure you receive the reports.*

5. *Click Save.*

When you click either the Reports link in the left navigation list or the Generate Another Report button on the View Advertising Report page (see Figure 5-10), you come to a slightly different reporting page, as shown in Figure 5-11.

Figure 5-11:
The Reports Page allows you to run reports with data you need.

Reports

These reports provide the insights you need to optimize and manage your advertising on Facebook. In addition to pro performance, Facebook Ad Reports help you learn much more about who is engaging with your ads.

Report Type:	Advertising Performance
Summarize By:	Campaign
Filter By:	No Filter
Time Summary:	Daily
Date Range:	1/5/2012 to 1/13/2012
Format:	Webpage (.html)

☐ Include Deleted Ads/Campaigns

Generate Report

Advertising Performance
This report includes statistics like impressions, clicks, click through rate (CTR), and spend. Although this information is available in your Ads Manager, you may find this a useful way to export and manage your Facebook performance.

On this page, you can run reports based on specific data you want to study. Use the drop-down lists to choose the data you want to include in the report, set the dates you want to include, choose the format for the file, and click Generate Report. If you chose Webpage .html from the Format drop-down list, a new page appears with your data. If you chose to save the file as a .csv, then a window appears asking you save the file to your computer. You can then open the file with your preferred software (usually Excel or Numbers).

Adding or Deleting an Administrator on Your Facebook Ads Account

It's always a good idea to have a back-up plan. Melanie likes to have at least one other trusted person as an admin on her Fan Page Timelines as well as Facebook ads account. That way, if she's locked out for some reason, she still has a spare key, so to speak.

When you add someone to your Facebook Ads account, he may have access to your credit card information. It's very important to only grant privileges to someone you trust.

To add an administrator to your Facebook ads account, follow these steps:

1. **Navigate to** https://www.facebook.com/ads/manage**.**

2. **Click the Settings link in the left navigation and scroll down the page until you see Permissions, as shown in Figure 5-12.**

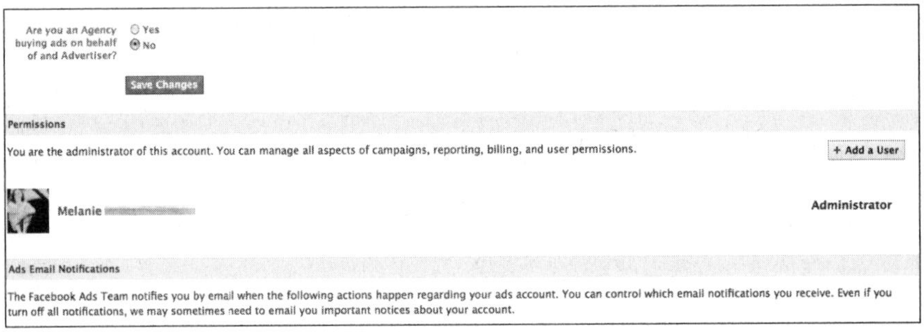

Figure 5-12: The Permissions section on the Settings page.

> Are you an Agency buying ads on behalf of and Advertiser? ○ Yes ● No
>
> Save Changes
>
> **Permissions**
>
> You are the administrator of this account. You can manage all aspects of campaigns, reporting, billing, and user permissions.   + Add a User
>
> Melanie ▓▓▓▓▓▓▓   Administrator
>
> **Ads Email Notifications**
>
> The Facebook Ads Team notifies you by email when the following actions happen regarding your ads account. You can control which email notifications you receive. Even if you turn off all notifications, we may sometimes need to email you important notices about your account.

3. **Click the Add User button.**

The Add a User to This Ads Account window appears.

4. **In the text box, type the name of the person you want to grant administrative permissions to.**

   You can type either the name of a Facebook friend or an e-mail address.

5. **Use the drop-down list to determine the new user's permissions (General User or Reports Only).**

6. **Click the Add button.**

   A window appears stating the person has been added to your account.

7. **Click Okay.**

   The new administrator appears under Permissions on your Settings page.

Of course, it's possible that you may need to delete an administrator as well. To delete an admin, follow these steps:

1. **Navigate to** `https://www.facebook.com/ads/manage.`

2. **Click the Settings link in the left navigation and scroll down the page until you see Permissions.**

3. **Click the X next to the user's permission status (for example, General User).**

   A window appears, asking if you want to remove this person from your account.

4. **Click Remove.**

   A window appears confirming that the person is removed from your account.

5. **Click Okay.**

   The person and her Timeline are removed from your account and no longer appear in your Permissions area.

Closing Your Facebook Ads Account

If you decide Facebook ads just aren't for you, no problem. When you close your Facebook ads account, any active ads, stories, and campaigns will cease and you won't be able to create any new ones. Facebook will charge any leftover balance to your credit card on file, and then will delete the card from your account.

If you think you may want to return to Facebook ads later, pause your account instead of closing it. To pause your account, click the Campaign & Ads link. From there, change the status of each ad, story, and campaign to Paused.

To close your Facebook Ads account, follow these steps:

1. **Navigate to** `https://www.facebook.com/ads/manage.`

2. **Click the Settings link in the left navigation pane.**

3. **Click the Close Ads Account link at the top of the page just under your Account ID.**

   The Close Ads Account window appears.

4. **Select the reason(s) you're closing your account (or type a reason in the text box labeled Other).**

5. **Click the Close Ads Account button.**

   It may take up to two days for Facebook to completely close out your account.

Introducing Two New Advertising Opportunities

February 29, 2012 was a huge day in the world of Facebook. At the first-ever fMC (Facebook Marketing Conference), Facebook unveiled the new Timeline for Fan Pages (see Book IV, Chapters 1 and 2), Offers (see Book IV, Chapter 4), updates to Insights (see Book V, Chapter 3), and more. Facebook also announced two new advertising opportunities: Reach Generator and Log-Out Ads. The following sections explain what those are.

At the time of writing this book, not all features announced at fMC had been rolled out to the public. We've done our best be up to date as this book goes to print. In the cases where features weren't available to the masses yet, we tried to update chapters (like this one) to let you know that by the time you have this book in your hands, you may have additional options, and we've tried to share as much information as we have about the features (which, in some cases, isn't a lot).

Reach Generator

Reach Generator is a new premium ad tool available to large Facebook clients. (It's unclear at the time of writing this if it's going to be available to individuals and small businesses — it seems cost prohibitive for those entities as yet.) Reach Generator allows you to reach a higher number of fans (and their friends) via sponsored activity.

As discussed throughout this chapter, you usually pay for ads via a cost per click (CPC) or cost per impression (CPM) structure. In other words, you can pre-pay a set amount, and your ad stops when you've reached that amount. If you only want to pay $25 for an ad, when your ad has reached the clicks or impressions that equal $25, your ad stops. With Reach Generator, you pay an ongoing fee. For this fee, you sponsor one Fan Page Timeline post every day and Facebook guarantees that post will reach 75% of your fans over the next 30 days. These Reach Generator ads appear more like content and will show up in the News Feed, in addition to appearing in the sidebar with other ads and sponsored content. Reach Generator sponsored content only appears in the News Feed of those users who have Liked the Fan Page already (so are already fans). Friends of people who have Liked, commented on, or shared content from a Fan Page Timeline will also see the ad.

Log-out ads

Leaving no ad opportunity untapped, Facebook also announced that they are offering log-out ads. When you log out of Facebook, the page you see will display a premium ad. These log-out ads will count toward the goal of reaching 75% of fans via Reach Generator sponsored posts. Any premium post ad may be shown as a log-out ad, including photos, video, offers, events, and more. And, unlike sponsored ads in the News Feed, users don't have to be associated with Fan Page Timeline to see these log-out ads.

Chapter 6: Identifying Your Target Audience for Successful Marketing

In This Chapter

✔ Using Facebook Insights to identify your audience

✔ Marketing Fan Page Timelines offline

✔ Why online and traditional marketing are important

✔ Other online marketing tools used for Facebook

You might be reading this book to get a better understanding of how you can use Facebook to market your business. If this is the case, we would be remiss if we didn't offer you balanced advice. There are a lot of strong reasons why Facebook is one of the most important places to market your business in the Internet age. The primary reason is its user base. The driving reason to use Facebook for marketing is not at all primarily because of how dynamic and interactive you can get with your market. It's not because of the two-way conversation and the ability to respond to your customers in real time. These are secondary reasons. The fact is that millions of potential customers are on Facebook. In this chapter, we discuss marketing your Facebook presence using a healthy mix of traditional and online tools.

Identifying Your Audience

To conduct any form of marketing or advertising, it's important to identify your target audience for the best results. To effectively market to the right audience, you need to identify who that appropriate audience is — that is, the people who will buy your product and are a good fit to be your customers. The way to determine this might be to identify who your customers are today. The best way to do this is with real data, by taking a look at who your currently engaged customers are. You can do this by taking a closer look at your company and customer list, but you can also use Facebook as a tool to help you. To identify your audience on Facebook, you have amazing analytics tools within your Fan Page called Insights, shown in Figure 6-1.

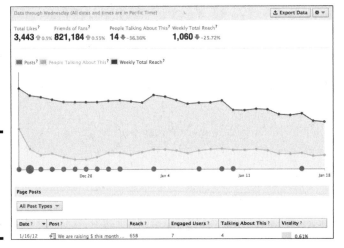

Figure 6-1:
Facebook
Insights
tells you
who your
audience is.

Facebook Insights tells you not just how many people you reach with your Fan Page Timeline, but the demographics of the people that Like your Fan Page. This way, you can know specifically your balance of male versus female, age range, and many more details. This data tells you who has shown an interest in your Fan Page Timeline, but you can dissect the information even more and see the demographics of people that are actually talking about your Fan Page Timeline. Insights is designed to give you a better understanding of what your Facebook audience is so that you can refine your marketing on and offline. You can read more about Insights and how to use the data in Book V, Chapter 3.

Using Insights enables you to clearly define who that audience is, and to put that information in your quiver for your next barrage. When it's time to promote your Pilates studio and build your Facebook following by advertising offline, you don't want to buy an offline ad in a men's magazine if your Facebook Insights shows that 70 percent of your existing Facebook audience are women. Furthermore, you might find that your fans on Facebook are 30 percent men, but 100 percent of those talking about your Fan Page Timeline are women. This would suggest that your true target audience is women. This is a simplistic example, but these principles can be applied across multiple demographic factors. If you get the right message to the right audience, you can attract the right kind of people to grow your business without wasting time and money on the wrong crowd.

Using the Insights Information

Take a look at your Insights for your Fan Page Timeline. To do so, visit your Fan Page Timeline and be sure you are logged into the account that you use to administer your Fan Page Timeline. Clink See All in the Insights section on the Admin Panel at the top of your Fan Page Timeline. (See Figure 6-2.)

Figure 6-2:
Click
Insights
on your
Fan Page
Timeline.

On your Insights page, you have the following content:

✦ General Insights about your Likes and activity

✦ Demographic information about your Fan Page Likes

✦ Demographics about your *reach* (the people who have seen your content in a given time frame)

✦ Demographics of people Talking about This (people commenting on posts, tagging, checking in, and other interactions)

✦ Demographics on check ins

Examine the following details to find out how you can better implement traditional and online marketing:

✦ **Gender, age, and city:** Find this information by clicking on any of the links at the top of the Insights page (Likes, Reach, Talking About This, or Check Ins). This data tells you the balance of male versus female by age, which narrows down the scope of people that your business is connecting with. Using this data you can determine where you should purchase advertising, as well as what sort of imaging and messaging will resonate most with your audience. (See Figure 6-3.)

If you have a national audience, you need to take a different route than if your audience is concentrated in one city. Don't just consider what you have now, but also consider where you would like to grow if you see opportunity in a particular area.

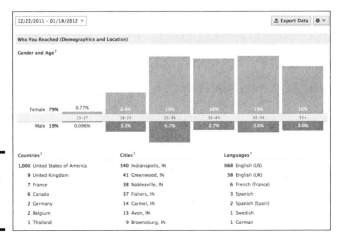

Figure 6-3:
Gender and
age demo-
graphics.

✦ **Reach and frequency:** Reach shows how you reached people. This data tells you how many people you reached through which method. The three represented reach data are *organic* (natural growth); *viral* (visited your Fan Page Timeline through others sharing or the Ticker); and *paid* (visited because of a Facebook ad campaign). This is usually best to measure Facebook campaigns online, but you may be able to examine traditional advertising's impact on these numbers. For instance, if you know you ran an ad in a local publication and you see a spike in your data, you can probably attribute that spike in traffic to your ad.

The Unique Viewers by Frequency graph is interesting because it tells you the frequency of those that you have reached. (See Figure 6-4.) In other words, you can get an idea of how many people looked at content more than once. This might give you an idea of the level of interest in your content. It does not typically give a strong picture of whether your content was good or bad in general.

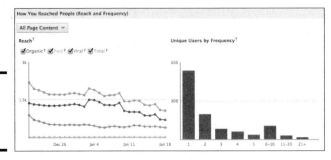

Figure 6-4:
Reach and
frequency
data.

✦ **Fan Page Timeline views and unique visitors:** This data tells you about your traffic in terms of date as well as the numbers of unique visitors. The graph (shown in Figure 6-5) gives you an idea of traffic by day. Page Views represents the total times your Fan Page Timeline was viewed in a given day. Unique Visits represents the number of individuals that visited your site, regardless of how many times the individuals visited. Use this data to relate it to an offline campaign date — for example, a lot of traffic on the day your print ad was published can be an indicator that it was a successful advertisement.

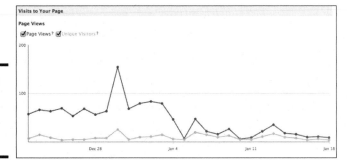

Figure 6-5:
Visits to
your Fan
Page
Timeline.

✦ **Total tab views:** This data tells you how many visitors you have had on a specific tab, as shown in Figure 6-6. Knowing these numbers is great if you create different tabs for different advertisements (each tab has its own unique URL). You can use this data to get an indication of which campaigns are bringing more traffic than others. This data is merely an indicator, because more people search for a Fan Page using the Search function, which would not bring them to a specific tab.

Figure 6-6:
Tab views
and
referring
links.

Total Tab Views[7]	External Referrers[7]
565 Wall	48 pspindy.com
433 Static FBML 3	5 offerpop.com
87 Html	4 google.com
64 Static HTML: iframe tabs	2 36ohk6dgmcd1n-c.c.yom.mail.yahoo.net
29 Information	1 coupons4indy.com
24 Photos	1 us1.campaign-archive1.com
14 Photo Contest	1 sz0130.ev.mail.comcast.net
More ▾	More ▾

✦ **External content referrers:** Here you find out what online sources are leading traffic to your Fan Page Timeline. (See Figure 6-6.) If you have banner ads, coupon sites, or URL redirects, then you can discover how people are finding your Fan Page Timeline. One great way to use this for offline marketing is to have unique URLs in ads such as www.ourfacebook page.com that redirects to your actual Fan Page Timeline. Insights shows that URL as the referring site.

If you understand how all the data is created, you can use it to your advantage when managing a full marketing campaign. The knowledge not only allows you to push out better marketing, but it helps tell you where and what kind to buy if you pay close attention.

Understanding Why Both Online and Traditional Marketing Are Necessary

According to a study at the University of Texas, people remember 10 percent of what they read, 20 percent of what they hear, but 90 percent of what they do and say. This means that when your advertising method is more of an experience, your results are much higher. And how can you offer a more interactive marketing experience? Online. Depending on your goals and campaigns, you can ask your audience to participate as you market to them (via polls, games, and other things). Of course, you can only get so many people to take that high level of action, but that's okay because in the end, you really only want to spend time reaching those customers that are right for your business and that are going to buy your product or service.

With all of this talk about reaching the right customers, it's important to remember that a healthy mix of marketing tactics will yield the greatest results. Traditional marketing (such as print, TV and radio advertising, and so on) is tried and true. It's never going away, though it's changing. Traditional marketing is the foundation of your messaging. Choosing which forms of traditional marketing are right for your business (and which forms are worthless) is easy when you know who your audience is and what their lifestyle is like. But remember this: No matter what their lifestyle, there is a good chance they are on Facebook!

Marketing Facebook Offline

Offline (or traditional) marketing has just as much room for innovation as online marketing. By including your Fan Page Timeline information on your traditional marketing materials, you may expand your reach to those you have not been able to connect with on Facebook. This integration also enables you to add an interactive element to the traditional advertising campaign.

Facebook plays the role of a lead capturing method when it's integrated in traditional marketing. This means that every Like is a lead that you now have subscribed to further marketing messages.

Several studies have shown that when Facebook users Like a Fan Page Timeline, they do not consider that action consent to be marketed to. Remember the advice we've given throughout this book, and don't overdo the hard sell. If your fans feel like you're invading their space with too much marketing, they stop listening — either by ignoring your updates, Unliking your Page, or hiding your updates.

Offline marketing comes in many forms, and they all have their respective strengths and limitations. The way that you effectively use them to market your Fan Page Timeline will vary with each example.

Direct mail marketing

Direct mail can be one of the most powerful or one of the weakest forms of marketing. The reason for the variation is that so much of mail today is a marketing message, people ignore messages that appear to be an advertisement. When a customer receives something from someone he trusts, the story is different. Direct mail is always more successful when it has some context, meaning the recipient has some reason to expect what is sent to them. Using direct mail with this principle in mind can lead to some powerful results.

The best use of a Facebook direct mail marketing campaign is giving people something worth responding to. Don't just direct people to a contest or ask for followers. Instead, consider that when people get their mail and look through it, they're at home. They may not be on the computer, but they likely have one close by. Getting someone to take a moment to log on to Facebook might be realistic if you give them a good enough reason. You may want to create fan-only discount codes via an application (see Book VI for more information about creating and using apps). Just remember to make the discount large enough to entice your customer to stop what they're doing and log on to Facebook to find your Page.

A permission-based marketing response always works best when you give the customer some value. For example, if the people you send a message to are already your customers, direct mail could be the contact they need to consider connecting with you another way (such as on your Fan Page Timeline).

 Always make sure that with any print campaign that you give customers an easy to remember URL. That way, you don't lose a potential opportunity because the web address is just too long to type in. You may want to use a custom URL that forwards to a custom tab on your Fan Page Timeline.

TV ads focused on Facebook

Some time ago, TGI Fridays created a campaign to increase its Facebook following. The restaurant did a series of TV commercials as well as other marketing tactics where a fictional character named Woody asks friends to join him for a free burger. In the commercials, Woody stated he was the restaurant's biggest fan. This character fronted the commercials and print ads to implore you to become a fan so that the restaurant could give everyone a free burger. The company offered a burger to the first half million fans. This allowed the restaurant to grow its Facebook Page fanbase to nearly one million. The restaurant realized the value of having a connection to its customers through Facebook and decided to invest time, money, and energy into growing its fan base.

What the restaurant did was more brilliant than the pieces of flair that the wait staff wears. The restaurant didn't hide the fact that it was trying to grow the number of Facebook fans: That was the topic of discussion. The approach was that if the restaurant's Fan Page Timeline hit 500,000 fans, every fan would get a coupon for a free signature burger.

The restaurant's fanbase is near 1 million fans at the time of this writing. Each fan (eligible for the free burger) gave his or her e-mail address (via a third-party app) so that the restaurant could send the coupon. This meant that the restaurant created a strong database to regularly connect with customers, and it used Facebook as way to strengthen customer loyalty. Those that Liked the Fan Page and shared their contact information considered it worth their time. (Even though Liking a Fan Page and providing contact information isn't a big step, it's just enough that you're more likely to get a response from people that are within your true market.)

With a campaign like this, the restaurant made the best of its investment in TV commercials. This is something you should do with every advertising investment: Make sure you get the most out of your investment by giving your audience a call to action with which you can bridge a sustained relationship with them. This philosophy also poses a significant argument for using both paid Facebook ads and your Fan Page Timeline in tandem with each other. This way, you're always building your audience but also sustaining it with a continued connection.

Radio ads focused on Facebook

Radio can be the hardest tool to use to promote Facebook for many companies because you don't have the benefit of visual aids or the option of click throughs. If you use the radio to promote your Fan Page Timeline, make sure that you know how easy or difficult it is to find your Fan Page Timeline for the first time, and prepare for that with your *copy* (the commercial's script). If your URL isn't easy to spell correctly, you should create a custom URL that's easier to spell and redirect that URL to your Fan Page Timeline. You might even want to be sure that you have a prominent ad on your own website that links to your Fan Page Timeline so that those people looking for you have several ways to find you on Facebook.

You should take note of the way people search for you within the Search text box on Facebook. For example, if your Fan Page Timeline name is A.B.C. Pilates Studio and people typically type ABC Pilates, they may have trouble finding you! If you haven't already set your name, change it to something that works well for search.

Radio works best when the ads are frequent. Make sure that the station and time you choose is consistent and targeted at the right kind of audience. Finally, make sure that your call to action is very clear on how to find you.

Online Marketing Resources

Facebook is not a standalone online spot for marketing your business. Facebook is indeed one of the most visited sites on the Internet, but for many, it's a place to connect with people, discover interesting news, blogs, and more. Facebook acts as a portal to the rest of the Internet.

Using other marketing tools on the web is something that you don't want to forget about. When people are on the Internet catching up on TV shows, checking e-mail, searching for products, or even visiting your website, they're only a click or two away from becoming a fan of your Fan Page Timeline. The following sections describe a few ways to use some of the most common tools for marketing your Fan Page Timeline on the rest of the web.

E-mail marketing

Of all marketing channels, e-mail marketing is credited with delivering the highest return on investment. From our experience, we've found that the most successful Facebook promotions are supported by a permission marketing e-mail distribution list. This tells us that e-mail marketing must be a strong way to build your social media audience and drive them to engagement.

One of the biggest benefits of e-mail marketing is that you can communicate with your Facebook fans directly, even if they miss your updates in the News Feed. Figure 6-7 shows an e-mail newsletter that reminds subscribers to enter a contest on a Fan Page Timeline.

Figure 6-7:
Pairing
e-mail
marketing
with
Facebook.

Your e-mail marketing software should allow you to efficiently track the success of your campaign. Tracking is what makes e-mail marketing so powerful; you can measure how many people opened your e-mail, as well as how many people clicked the links in it. E-mail marketing software is also generally required to deliver an e-mail in a full HTML formatting. This means that you can send an e-mail that has a fully designed layout, much like you see in Figure 6-7. E-mail marketing software also manages unsubscribes from people that do not want to receive your e-mails any longer. MailChimp (`http://mailchimp.com`), Constant Contact (`http://constantcontact.com`), Aweber (`http://aweber.com`) and ExactTarget (`http://exacttarget.com`) are some of the most popular options.

Although you can create e-mails in plain-text format, marketing e-mails tend to be more effective when they have images to help communicate your message in a simple manner. It's easy to create a template for your e-mail that resembles the design of a Fan Page tab. We suggest including a distinctive graphical button within your e-mail (also shown in Figure 6-7) that makes it easy to click directly to the destination.

E-mails typically have a short lifespan. Make sure that you follow two important tips in an e-mail marketing campaign:

✦ **Don't give away too much information in your e-mail.** Make sure you share just enough to get your reader interested. Make him visit your Fan Page Timeline to get the rest of the details. If you satisfy his interest in the e-mail, he may forget to click over to Facebook later.

✦ **Send your e-mail when you have something notable to share with customers.** You will get more traffic if you offer something particularly interesting, so it's always better to tie e-mails to a specific campaign (such as a special promotion or contest) rather than just an invitation to check out your Fan Page Timeline. With campaigns, it usually makes sense to send an e-mail at the beginning and another towards the end of the campaign as a reminder.

E-mail can be tied into your Facebook marketing in the reverse as well. We suggest installing an app on your Fan Page Timeline that allows your fans to sign up for your e-mail list (most e-mail marketing software has an app; check their website's FAQ section). When it's installed you can post a status update reminding your fans to sign up (be sure to provide the link to the sign up tab). Or, if fans are perusing your Fan Page Timeline, they may see your app and sign up on their own (but don't count on it; 90% of fans don't return to your Timeline unless you tell them to).

Search marketing with PPC

PPC (pay per click) ads typically appear at the top of search results in Google and other search engines. These ads are paid out based on how many times the ad is clicked. In other words, the advertiser is charged when someone clicks the ad, not based on how many times it's displayed. PPC is a great way to create advertising directed at the right audience (anyone who is searching for your product or service) and you can do it on almost any budget. With PPC ads, you define what you're willing to spend, and that amount is applied to ad appearances until the budget is exhausted.

Because all Facebook users are Internet users, it makes sense to use the Internet to promote your Fan Page Timeline. In this case, you use search results to draw relevant traffic to your Fan Page Timeline. (See Figure 6-8.) For example, if you are a Pilates instructor and people search for *Indianapolis Pilates studios* in a search engine, PPC allows them to see an ad at the top of their results page that links directly to whatever page is defined by the advertiser.

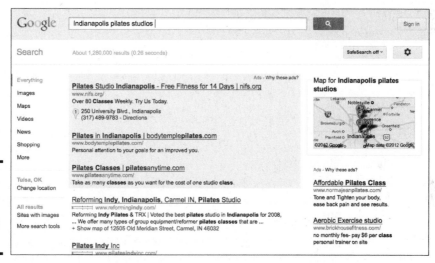

Figure 6-8:
Promoting Facebook with Google PPC.

When people search for a product you sell, you don't want to miss the opportunity to capture their purchase. Make sure that if you promote a Fan Page Timeline with a PPC ad that you have the ability to take orders within a custom tab, or direct people to where they can place an order.

Integrated Campaigns

Using a mix of tactics including both online and offline channels is the ideal situation. If your goal is to grow your Facebook audience by drawing your customers there, make sure that your call to action is clear in every portion of your campaign. It helps to use the Facebook logo and colors in your advertising. This is because the Facebook logo is easily recognizable, and you can be sure that people know the destination to respond to your ad is on Facebook.

Using custom Application Pages is the most important element of your Facebook promotions, even if your initial goal is simply to increase Likes on your Fan Page. All promotions are conducted on a Facebook Tab. It makes a big difference to give your audience something to see that is unique to them. For example, BMW customized its Fan Page Timeline with an interactive Application Page that allowed visitors to assemble a car with the custom options they like. Visitors had to Like the Fan Page to use the interactive Application Page, which encouraged many to do so.

Book VI

Developing Facebook Apps

The 5th Wave   By Rich Tennant

"Stop working on the Priority Parking Spot
Allocation app. They want to fast track the
Coffee Pot/Cubicle Proximity app."

Contents at a Glance

Chapter 1: Custom Apps for Fan Page Timelines

In This Chapter

- ✔ Using apps for Facebook marketing
- ✔ Extending the Facebook experience
- ✔ Discovering iframes, Application Pages, and Canvas Pages
- ✔ Finding out what apps can do to increase engagement

*I*f you're a Facebook marketer, you're likely always looking for ways to increase the engagement that you have with your customers. For many Facebook users, interesting status updates aren't enough to hold their attention. Facebook apps allow you to create a far more engaging Facebook presence. You're not just looking for more people to visit your Fan Page Timeline and Like it; you also want to give fans more of a reason to interact with your brand or find other value.

An app can be as simple as a means to host a custom image for Application Pages, or as complex as an interactive video game. Apps are designed to deliver all the interactive elements of Facebook to your fans in a custom way. Fans can Like, comment, post, and interact in countless ways with other sites, with games or within your Fan Page Timeline. Apps use some of the existing features of Facebook, but any web-enabled code can be used to develop custom apps for Facebook (such as PHP, JavaScript, and other web software languages).

Using Apps for Facebook Marketing

Companies that make apps for their Fan Page Timelines want to make Facebook a more engaging environment and extend the connection to their audience of fans. The most common appearance of an application on Facebook is the Application Page, also referred to as a *tab*. Within a Fan Page Timeline, you can create any app and install it into an Application Page, limited only by the capabilities of the web itself. Some apps are a simple element, such as an image to enhance your Fan Page Timeline, and some apps are more complex, such as interactive elements your fans can use. Building an app gives you the opportunity to integrate more deeply into the core Facebook experience. Your app can integrate with the News Feed as well as notifications and other features. Here are a few of the things that apps can add to your Facebook integration:

✦ **Share content in a new way.** Apps can use many, if not all, of the elements of the web by using iframes. This means that you can view anything that can be created on the web through any web browser. The only limitation is size — if you can write the code, you can do it. Facebook has been phasing out FBML, a custom code language specific to Facebook. The iframe model means that the content that you would host elsewhere (on another service or website) can be viewed within the tab or Canvas Page on Facebook. This means that whatever you would like to share can be shared on Facebook as well.

Apps can also interact with other elements of Facebook if you build the features into the apps. This includes participants within the app having the ability to post content on their Facebook Timeline and more.

✦ **Gain followers in a relatively short time.** Apps enable you to put together powerful promotions, which allow you to create an interactive experience for your fans. Doing so can empower you to create promotions, contests, and more, which enable you to grow your Facebook audience in a relatively short time.

Because apps can interact with Facebook features such as the News Feed and notifications, a successful promotion has sort of a viral effect and can draw other participants through friends. With these features, you can catapult your audience to a new level.

✦ **Provide a valuable service.** The longest lasting and most effective apps are those that provide some kind of value to the consumer, not just an interesting experience with your brand or Fan Page Timeline. Games that offer a desired value to users will be used more and uninstalled less. This sort of value leads to strong audience engagement, allowing a greater impact from a marketing standpoint. It's fine to have a Facebook app that allows you to virtually pour your favorite soda and share it with your friends, but if you can actually use a Facebook app to get weather updates or create customized birthday cards, then you can get so much more mileage out of the app.

Services may include games for some. Games are very addictive to certain players. Certain games might have a great success rate with players, and lead to in-game purchases for new levels and features. More than half of Facebook users log into games and at least 20 percent of them have purchased in-game features. Aside from generating revenue through in-game sales, apps of this sort can be an advertising opportunity as well.

Extending the Facebook Experience

Apps take connecting with an audience to new levels in several ways. Here are some of the ways that Facebook apps extend the capabilities of your Facebook marketing:

✦ **Screen real estate:** One of the simplest things that you gain with a Facebook app is more space. You have limited space for your content within Facebook, and it all has to fit into a format that is compatible for Facebook. Both tabs and Canvas Pages provide this to you.

Tab apps can use up to 810 pixels of screen width; Canvas Page apps by default are 760 pixels of screen width but can be set to a fluid width that allows it to take up the full width of the user's browser. A Canvas Page is literally a blank canvas where your content would be displayed. This is done by directing the app to a URL that you provide in the creation of the app.

This real estate means that you can include more pictures, videos, and other content into your Fan Page Timeline — content that isn't possible within the Timeline, without an app. Having that space is valuable to a marketer because you can offer more features or say more things with Canvas Pages and Application Pages. The extra screen width also makes games more enjoyable, such as the Canvas Page for the Words With Friends game, shown in Figure 1-1.

**Book VI
Chapter 1**

Figure 1-1:
More real estate with Canvas Page apps.

✦ **Social channels:** The reason why apps help provide a great avenue for growing fans is that they easily move through the key social channels that make Facebook interactive. Features include bookmarks, News Feed content, and more. Imagine a friend is participating in a new, fun game. While he plays, he may be prompted to share his story relative to his Facebook experience on his Timeline as a status update. (See Figure 1-2.) Perhaps he will be asked to invite other friends to enjoy the game. Inevitably, his activity within the app will also show within the News

Ticker to the right of the screen on each of his friends' home pages. This encourages his friends to also play the game. Some may simply check it out, but not play, while others will play and share it. Social channels allow Facebook apps to expand their coverage to a broader audience.

Figure 1-2:
Social
channels.

✦ **Analytics:** It isn't enough to only know how many fans you have. Marketers need to know what kind of people they are, what their interests are, and how they can market to them. Fan Page Timelines are all equipped with Insights, the Facebook analytics tool, as shown in Figure 1-3. Facebook Insights for apps tells you how users interact with your app, what sites refer traffic to your app, and what user actions contribute to active user count, as well as providing demographics on your authorized users and active users.

Knowing this information means that you can fine-tune your app, its content, and your marketing surrounding it to be sure that you get the most out of it as a marketing tool.

Figure 1-3:
Facebook
Insights
shows how
fans interact
with your
app.

Discovering iframes

To offer apps on your Fan Page Timeline, you will quite possibly need to do as much building off Facebook as you would on Facebook. Both Canvas Pages and Application Pages are blank spaces provided by Facebook in which you input an app URL that Facebook will then display through an iframe. This means that much or all of your content isn't on Facebook at all — it's simply viewed through a window.

In HTML elements, frames allow an HTML browser window to split into segments. To put it simply, it's basically like viewing two websites or portions of websites at the same time. iframes are simply that except that they're specifically within another page.

In terms of Canvas Pages, the page itself is built through Facebook's setup procedures, and then the content within the page is viewed by directing to the appropriate web location. To illustrate this, Daniel built an app on a Canvas Page that is directed to a URL not specifically designed for the space. Figure 1-4 shows a made-up company built to test a web concept. As you can see, once the foundation of your app is built within Facebook, an iframe allows you to display any content on the web of your choosing.

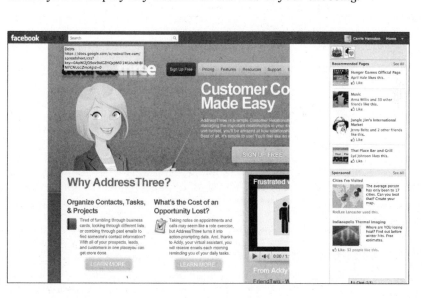

Figure 1-4:
Canvas apps can direct to any site.

Increasing Engagement with Apps

Apps have capabilities specifically designed to increase the engagement of a Facebook user. You can deploy mechanisms within the programming of your app to increase an individual's use of the app, as well as increase the number of people using the app.

Bookmarks

When someone starts using your app, Facebook creates a bookmark for that user. This bookmark appears within the user's home screen (as shown in Figure 1-5) so that she can quickly return to that app to use it again. If the user has several apps that she uses, she has several bookmarks. The bookmarks are ordered based on how often the user uses your app. If a user has several bookmarks, those bookmarks may not display at the same time in the default view.

To encourage reengagement, icons have numbers to the right of them, indicating that they have a new request from someone via that app or game. This encourages people to continue activity within the app.

Figure 1-5:
Bookmarks provide quick access to your app.

Social discovery

Real-time social app activity is one of the greatest drivers of increased engagement. Facebook calls this *social discovery* from the developer's perspective. People are more likely to interact with an app if their friends are also interacting at the moment, especially when it comes to entertainment apps such as games. To the right of each Canvas app screen is a real-time Ticker that shows a feed of what friend activity is currently happening.

When a user first enters an app, Facebook presents stories that are most relevant to that app. These stories are about that user and his friends interacting with that app. After the user uses the app for a while, the updates in the Ticker begin to broaden to include what friends are doing in other apps as well. This includes apps that the user currently uses and has installed on his Timeline, as well as apps that he hasn't installed but his friends have. The content of the Ticker is intended to be as relevant to the user as possible. For example, if the user is playing a game, the News Ticker displays stories related to other games.

Social discovery helps users find new games when Facebook generates stories about friends playing games. When an app is used, Facebook receives a ping indicating that a user is playing the game. Facebook apps ping Facebook five seconds after the user begins using the app and again every five minutes. The pings trigger stories that say something like "Bob Smith is playing Words With Friends." If Facebook doesn't receive that ping for 15 minutes, the story changes to something more like "Bob Smith Used Words With Friends."

App developers can turn off social discovery. This is most applicable if the app is for more personal information, such as weight management or dating. The development tools for games have other achievement story options that can be sent to the News Ticker (shown in Figure 1-6) using the achievements API. This is applicable if your app is a game that has score milestones or levels. Those achievements can show up on the News Ticker as "Bob Smith has won a new bicycle!" These achievement stories are also social discovery because they allow other players to see what their friends are doing and increase awareness or activity for other games through that social component.

**Book VI
Chapter 1**

Custom Apps for Fan Page Timelines

Figure 1-6:
The News Ticker shows game stories.

Draw people in with notifications

Notifications allow apps to stand out prominently without being intrusive. They do this by sending notifications to the notifications bar in the same way that you receive other notifications. Essentially, the user has to allow the app to send a notice to friends inviting them to the app. Notices can also deliver other features, such as giving a virtual gift to a friend. This creates another way to invite new users into the app experience through the friend network of the players. Notifications are triggered by requests within the app, of which there are two kinds:

✦ **User-generated requests:** These requests are confirmed by the user and can be sent by the user to friends, in the form of invitations or virtual gifts.

✦ **App-generated requests:** These sorts of requests can be sent only if the recipient specifically permits the application within his or her Timeline. These sorts of requests can be used for app reengagement such as "Jane Smith has completed her move; now it's your turn!"

Publishing stories

When using an app, a user can publish stories about what he's doing within the app, such as the foursquare check-in shown in Figure 1-7. Your app can prompt users to publish these stories within the app. If the user chooses to publish the story, it will publish to the user's Timeline and may appear in the News Feed of the user's friends. When stories are published from the app, they include a link to the app and can include an attachment such as an image. Images often represent an accomplishment such as a badge that the user earned. You use the Feed Dialog to publish content to your user's Timeline, which is a feature that prompts users to publish something to his or her Timeline. Every app requires the user to grant it permission to access his or her Facebook Timeline. This feature doesn't require any further permissions.

Figure 1-7:
Publishing
stories.

News Feed discovery stories

The discovery stories appear in the Ticker when someone begins using a new app, but they also appear in the News Feed of friends of the user, as shown in Figure 1-8. These stories are triggered when a user first installs a new game or starts using an app. Because the first thing a user sees when logging in to Facebook is the News Feed, these stories can be highly visible. However, because users have the ability to control (to some degree) what kind of content they see in their News Feed, depending on user's settings, they may not see updates in the News Feed about your app.

Users' permissions with apps

In most cases, apps access the user's Timeline to use the social features such as posting updates or displaying stories in the Ticker. All apps require that users permit the app to access their Timelines. To ensure that your app is a success, it's important to have a fair understanding of Facebook's authentication process. The permissions process typically contains more specific permissions for each part of the Timeline that can be accessed by that application. This all happens through one authentication process, but each item is displayed to the user asking to verify that he or she permits this. Figure 1-9 shows the screen a user sees when granting permissions.

Make sure you include the appropriate permissions within your app. Too few permissions might prevent your app from providing the necessary features it is intended to deliver for the user. For example, if the function of your app includes posting badges to the user's Timeline, you certainly need permission to access the user's Timeline. The downside is that requiring too many permissions can deter users. There is a direct correlation between the level of permissions required to use an app and the number of people using it. Too many may result in the user being uncomfortable granting those permissions. This certainly is also dependent on the trustworthiness of your brand or app and the quality as well. If the quality of your app and the demand to use it is high enough, the required permissions are less of a concern for most people.

Figure 1-8:
Discovery stories in the News Feed.

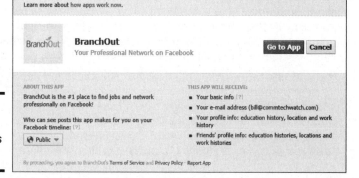

Figure 1-9:
Granting permissions for an app.

Facebook apps use OAuth 2.0 protocol to allow a user to authenticate an app and give your app permission to perform functions on the user's behalf. The OAuth 2.0 process has three steps that must be completed.

✦ **User authentication:** Verify that the user is who she claims to be (she is legitimately logged into her own Timeline). To authorize your app, users are asked to log into their accounts using their login credentials (username and password), as shown in Figure 1-10. If they're already logged in, Facebook validates the login cookie in their browsers to validate their identities.

Figure 1-10:
Users must log in to authenticate.

✦ **App authorization:** Your application needs certain access to the user's Timeline, such as the permission to post updates or invite friends through the app or access to personal data such as e-mail address or activities. App authorization ensures that users know what data and capabilities they grant the app access to. Permissions within an app cover any type of access to the user's Timeline. For example, if the user completes the post and clicks the button to post an update, the app needs to have permission to post updates to his or her Timeline. This process happens at the same time as the user authentication portion (refer to Figure 1-10). After the user allows the app, OAuth redirects the user to the destination site within the app and passes along an authorization code.

✦ **App authentication:** After the user has been authenticated and the app has been authorized by the user, app authentication occurs. (This happens behind the scenes, and the user doesn't see this process.) The authorization code gained in the prior steps is used to authenticate the app by sending this code and the *app secret* (a private code unique to your app) to the Graph API token endpoint. To put this in simple terms, app authentication verifies that the app has proper clearance by making sure the process has been followed. Essentially, Facebook collects a unique code from the individual giving the app permission and from the app itself to be sure that all things match and the right steps have been taken.

This process is more valuable than it is complicated. Since the rise of social media, spammers have managed to find more and more opportunities. This means that the only way that you could spam someone is by following the technical rules, and that makes it really difficult to do. This eliminates the majority of spam.

Apps that don't require user permissions

Apps that access data or features within someone's Timeline must have the OAuth authentication process followed. Many apps deliver only front-facing features such as playing a video or linking to a site. These apps still require a similar process to set up, but bypass the need for user authentication. Custom tabs are a great example. In most cases, tabs are more of a customized Fan Page Timeline, not a game or tool that requires any special access.

What you lose with an app that doesn't require permission is some of the features that often help the popularity of a Fan Page or app to grow virally. Depending on your goals, you may want to weigh this option. This works great for building your Fan Page Timeline into a customized website. The example shown in Figure 1-11 is an app that doesn't require OAuth from the Fan Page visitors. In this case, the tab provides information and a stronger brand representation to the visitors, and isn't intended to increase engagement or drive traffic on its own.

Figure 1-11: Apps that your users don't need to authenticate.

Static HTML apps do require an app secret. Any authorization with this form of app is done with the administrator of the Fan Page Timeline, who ultimately is the user of the app.

Features that encourage sharing with friends

Typically, there are two primary objectives for an app from a marketing standpoint. The first is to increase the engagement level with your current fans or users. The second is to build your audience by encouraging sharing.

The following sections describe some of the specific features that help to make your app more social and encourage users to share with friends. These can be separated into three segments: The News Feed, requests, and automatic channels.

The News Feed

The News Feed is the first thing that users see when they log into Facebook. This is where people find out what their friends are doing.

✦ **The Feed Dialog** prompts users to publish updates, and it's self-explanatory, as it's a dialog box that allows the user to post an update to her feed. You can see what users see in Figure 1-12. This is what Facebook recommends as the best way to ask users to publish stories about your app. It doesn't require that the user log into your app or grant it any special permission; it's essentially a shortcut to post a status update.

Figure 1-12:
The Feed
Dialog.

✦ **The Feed Graph Object** is for situations where certain app activities trigger a post to the user's Timeline. This requires that the app be given the authorization with posting privileges through the OAuth process. The end result is to post onto the user's Timeline, without the dialog box described in the Feed Dialog bullet. A Feed Graph Object is shown in Figure 1-13.

Figure 1-13:
The Feed
Graph posts
to a user's
Timeline.

+ **The Like button** allows users to share content from an app or a website (using Facebook social features) and post it on their Timelines. This action shows up as an activity update on users' Timelines and in their friends' News Feeds. Updates may say something like "Bob Smith Likes My Great Website."

Requests

When app users want to invite friends to take action, they do this with requests. Apps can generate requests as well if the app has been given the corresponding privileges. There are two types of requests:

+ **User-generated requests** are sent by explicit action from the user. In this case, a certain activity might trigger the request. Typically, you would create a feature in your app that says "invite your friends" or another similar request. A dialog box appears, enabling the user to send or cancel the request.

+ **App-generated requests** are sent by the app; however, this can happen only if the user has given the app permission to submit requests to her friends lists when she authorized the app. This request is related to an activity (such as completing a turn in a two-player game), and then a defined request is sent (such as indicating to the other player that it is his turn).

Automatic channels

The automatic channels are those that are enabled by default. These features encourage more use and traffic to apps and Facebook. You don't need to do anything additional for these channels to be in place because they are part of all apps.

✦ **Bookmarks,** described previously in this chapter, enable people to quickly return to your app.

✦ **Notifications** let app users know when they have a request, an update, or anything else to respond to. These appear to the right of the bookmark.

✦ **Dashboards** are screens that show the bookmarked links of the apps a user has used recently and those that friends have used.

✦ **Usage stories** are the activity updates that show up in the News Feed or in the Ticker. These are typically targeted at people who haven't used your app to attract new users.

✦ **App profiles** are similar to a Fan Page Timeline or a personal Timeline. App profiles include a Timeline, info tab, and configurable tabs as well.

Chapter 2: Building Canvas Pages and Application Pages

In This Chapter

✔ Seeing the difference between Canvas Pages and Application Pages

✔ Building your Dev App

✔ Defining roles for your app

✔ Facebook Credits and Insights

*I*f you're embarking into the app-driving marketing space, it's time to consider the format of your application. Facebook apps, like many other web apps, can be designed in a nearly unlimited number of formats. The sky is the limit. Facebook apps take on three major forms:

✦ Application Pages

✦ Canvas Pages

✦ Plugins to other sites

A myriad of Facebook features can be embedded into other websites and web tools known as Facebook Platform. With Facebook Platform, you can create an app that integrates with the Facebook API to use various Facebook features. This requires much of the same development functions, they are just applied in a different environment. You can find out more about Facebook Platform for Websites in Book VI, Chapters 3 and 4. In this chapter, we focus on Application Pages and Canvas Pages.

Finding the Differences between Canvas Pages and Application Pages

When you develop an application, you need to know from the start whether the app will appear on an Application Page or Canvas Page. Application Pages and Canvas Pages have similar functionality, but they have enough differences (display size, for one) that one or the other may be better suited to house your app. The following sections describe Application Pages and Canvas Pages to help you choose which is better for displaying your app.

Let us clarify the relationship among Application Pages, Canvas Pages, and apps. All Facebook apps are built using Facebook Platform, which allows you to take the application you build (using any common web code language) and connect it to Facebook's features. When someone uses your app within the context of Facebook, the app needs to be displayed somewhere. Canvas Pages and Application Pages are your two choices on Facebook.

✦ **App:** A broadly used term to refer to any software, site, or game built on the web that has functions that a user interacts with. We talk about two kinds of apps:

  • An app that you or a third party builds and displays on Facebook. This might be a photo contest, including features like uploading photos, displaying photos, and voting for photos.

  • Facebook's native apps, which connect to your app to allow you to use Facebook features such as displaying the app on a Fan Page Timeline or Canvas Page, inviting the users friends to vote, or posting updates for the user on her Timeline.

✦ **Application Page:** A page (sometimes called a *tab*) where your app can be displayed within the context of your Fan Page Timeline, as shown in Figure 2-1). An Application Page is simply an iframe space that's 810 pixels wide, in which your app is viewed.

✦ **Canvas Page:** A place where your app can be displayed within the context of its own space. Canvas Pages have a very different format, including bookmarks above the app, and the Ticker to the upper right.

Figure 2-1:
Application
Pages are
part of your
Fan Page
Timeline.

Application Page features

Application Pages appear in the center of a Fan Page Timeline and have a shortcut to the left of the Timeline of your Fan Page. (Application Pages used to be available to personal Timelines some time ago, but were discontinued due to limited use.) Application Pages take up a width of 810 pixels and display in the same relative area as the Timeline or News Feed on your Fan Page.

Within Application Pages, you can have a completely functional, interactive application, or you can simply display an image to enhance the look of your Fan Page Timeline. Companies often treat Application Pages as a way of personalizing their own social environment on the web. Facebook references Coca-Cola's Fan Page Timeline as an example of a great implementation of an Application Page application (shown in Figure 2-2).

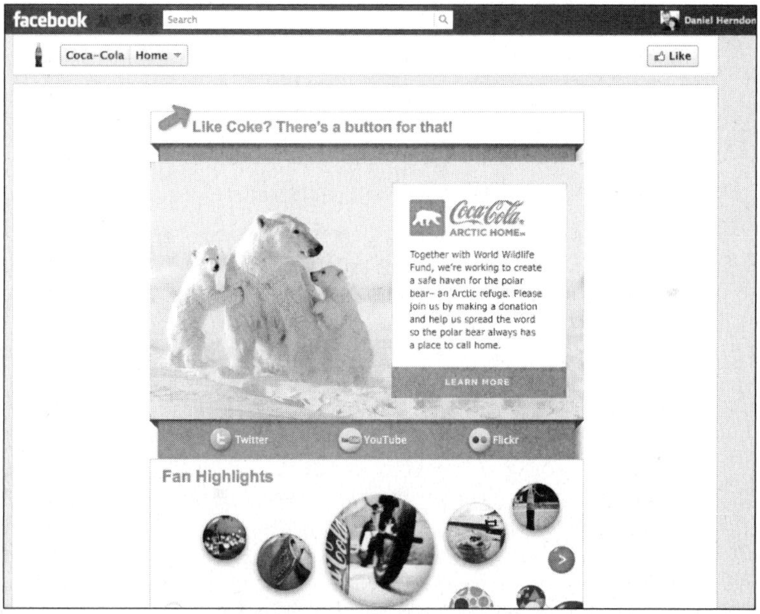

**Book VI
Chapter 2**

Building Canvas Pages and Application Pages

Figure 2-2:
A Facebook Application Page app.

Application Pages display within the context of your Fan Page Timeline. This means that people can quickly find your app and use it instantly. If you want to increase traffic to your Fan Page to grow your Facebook audience, use Application Pages to create a destination space. In this case, you may initially develop an app for short interactions (such as getting votes in a photo contest).

Canvas Page features

Canvas Pages are 760 pixels wide by default; however, they have optional settings to be *fluid width,* which means that the application can expand to the width of the user's browser. The additional space presents some definite benefits with Canvas Pages. When you create an app, the fluid width gives you the options to design apps that scroll or stretch to the size of the screen of the user.

Canvas Pages offer a couple additional interactive components for users that Application Pages lack. A defining characteristic of Canvas Pages is the Ticker at the top right of the screen, which displays activity of the user's friends on Facebook. These features can create a more interactive experience for users by showing them what their friends are doing within the same app (as well as other apps). Above the Ticker are bookmarks where users can quickly find the most recent apps they used. The purpose of the Ticker and bookmarks is to increase the interaction with fans by promoting their friends' activity within that app or other apps. This action encourages previous users to re-engage, as well as new users to discover your app if their friends are using it.

The app requires Open Graph actions to be published when your app invokes an Open Graph API call. Put simply, your app and Facebook's API have to be connected to each other, so that when someone takes an action within your app, Facebook captures that information and displays the activity within Ticker. We talk more about Open Graph later in this chapter.

Canvas Pages redirect users to a separate page, which means additional load time. Use a Canvas Page when you need a deeper experience for the user that will take a longer time (such as playing a game that takes several minutes).

Because a Canvas Page redirects users to another page, you may end up developing a custom Application Page as well to direct the user to your app. Your app will have a Fan Page Timeline of its own that can be customized just like any other Fan Page. If you create a canvas app as a promotional tool for your business, you'll want to build a link into your Fan Page Timeline to promote the app and its function. One retailer used an Application Page as a customized look for its Fan Page with a button linking to the Canvas Page that housed its catalog. This was a great use of these two options because the Fan Page presents the branding and information about the company. However, when someone decides to look at the catalog, they link to another area (the Canvas Page) that they may spend several minutes reviewing.

Choosing between an Application Page and a Canvas Page

Depending on the app, it may be obvious before you even touch a keyboard whether an Application Page or a Canvas Page is the better choice. Other times, it's not so simple to decide between the two. Table 2-1 gives you a rundown of the size and features of Application Pages and Canvas Pages to help you decide which to use.

A case for an Application Page

One time, Daniel and his team had a customer that wanted an app to conduct a contest. In the early stages of planning the app, it seemed obvious that they should build a Canvas Page rather than an Application Page for the app. They weighed the options of both. Ultimately, they arrived at the decision to build an app for an Application Page rather than a Canvas Page because the Application Page didn't redirect the user to a new location. In this case, building ongoing relationships with fans through the Fan Page Timeline was important. The simplicity of keeping the user on the Fan Page outweighed the benefits of having more space to display features.

Table 2-1	Application Pages versus Canvas Pages		
Type	*Width*	*Features*	*Downsides*
Application Page	810 pixels	Shortcut on your Fan Page Timeline	Offers limited display width and no Ticker to engage users
Canvas Page	760 pixels or fluid width	Flexible width, Ticker, bookmarks	Requires more load time and may require an Application Page so that existing fans can find it.

Creating Your Developer App

The first step to building your own app is to set up a Developer App (*dev app* for short). This is the step you need to take to become a developer on Facebook and have a place to find all of your apps. Yes, that's right — Facebook apps are stored in the developer app.

Follow these steps to set up the developer app:

1. **Point your browser to** `https://developers.facebook.com/apps`.

   An authorization screen appears, as shown in Figure 2-3. You need to allow the app to access basic information on your Timeline to use it. This is all that's required to have developer capabilities with Facebook.

2. **Click Allow.**

   After you complete the authentication, you see the Developer page. The first time you go to the Developer page, you see a blank screen and the Create New App button, as shown in Figure 2-4.

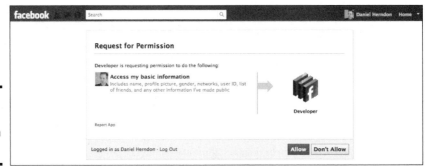

Figure 2-3:
Click Allow
to become a
developer.

Figure 2-4:
The
Developer
screen
before you
create apps.

3. Click the Create New App button.

The New App dialog box appears, asking you to name the app. See Figure 2-5.

4. Enter what you want the app to be called in the App Display Name text box; enter what you want to appear at the end of the app's URL in the App Namespace text box.

You can name your app whatever you wish, but note that the namespace can't have uppercase letters or symbols. For example, if you type **fordummies** in the App Namespace text box, your app's URL will be `http://apps.facebook.com/fordummies`.

Both of these text boxes need to be filled with names that haven't been taken by another app. If the name you chose is taken, Facebook will immediately indicate that it isn't available. (If you're having trouble finding a name that hasn't already been taken, you can always determine the namespace later.)

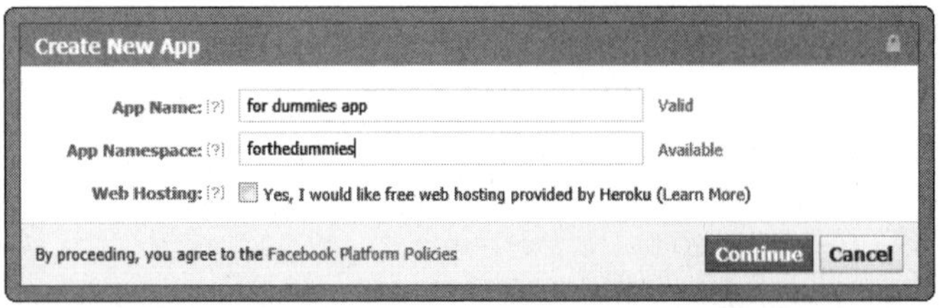

Figure 2-5:
Naming
your app.

After you've named your app, you may have to verify your account with a mobile phone number or a credit card. See Figure 2-6.

5. **Click either the Mobile Phone or Credit Card link and fill in the appropriate information to confirm your account.**

   This is simply a method to deter fraudulent developers. Clicking the Mobile Phone link brings up the Confirm Your Phone dialog box, as shown in Figure 2-7.

Figure 2-6: Confirm your account.

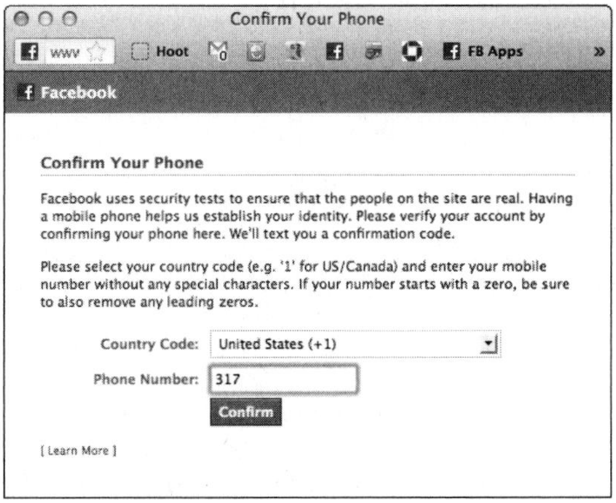

Figure 2-7: Verify your mobile phone number.

6. **Fill in the CAPTCHA security check by typing the words shown in the Text Box field.**

   This is a standard CAPTCHA designed to stop spammers and hackers.

   You just created your core app! You're now on the configuration screen of your brand-new app, as shown in Figure 2-8.

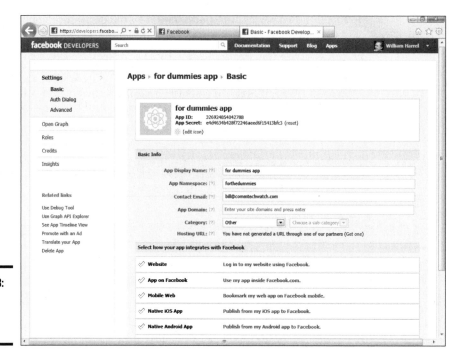

Figure 2-8:
The app
settings
page.

Getting to Know App Settings

After you create the app, you have a little bit more discovery to do to move on to the next step, where you integrate your app into Facebook. This app is the foundation that allows you to plug in any type of apps including those hosted on Application Pages, Canvas Pages, as well as all other Facebook integrations for websites.

Every app has a Timeline similar to a Fan Page Timeline. The first part of the App Settings page shows your app icon and profile picture that will display on the app Timeline page. Both of these can be set to a custom image very easily. You can upload a JPG, GIF, or PNG file for either, up to a file size limit of 5MB.

From the App Settings page, you can change the following options:

✦ **Profile image:** To change the profile image, click the default gear image to reveal the Update a Logo dialog box. You can upload any image you want, but keep in mind that this image typically displays at roughly 75 x 75 pixels. Be sure to consider the small display size when you design or choose your image. If you upload an image that is larger than 75 x 75 pixels, it will be resized. Remember that the file size is limited to 5MB.

✦ **Icon:** The small icon that appears below the app profile picture will be seen below posts coming from the app, as well as in bookmark form in the bookmarks section of the users' Timelines. Click the Edit Icon link to the right of the icon to upload an image. The icon is 16 x 16 pixels, so anything larger will be resized, and file sizes are limited to 5MB for this as well. If the image you upload doesn't work, it may be because it's too big. Try uploading a smaller image.

✦ **App ID and App Secret:** The App ID is a unique identifier of the app itself, sort of like a catalog number for the app. The App Secret is a (yes, you guessed it) secret code that you use to authenticate the application when conducting an API call with another app. (An *API call* is when your app is calling upon the application programming interface of Facebook to use its features.)

✦ **App Display Name and App Namespace:** This is the app name and namespace that you chose when you created the app.

✦ **Contact E-mail:** By default, the Contact E-mail is the e-mail address associated with your Facebook Timeline. You can change this if needed.

✦ **App Domain:** Use this field to enable authorization on domains and subdomains. This means that if your app is part of your website (and not necessarily on a Fan Page or Canvas Page), the core Facebook app will know to authorize that domain and subdomain, such as `example.com` or `anything.example.com`.

✦ **Category:** Selecting a category (and, optionally, a subcategory) for your app helps people who are searching for certain kinds of apps find your app.

In addition to server space, Facebook also partners in the same way with service providers to set up a URL for your app. This URL will be necessary to tell Facebook where to look for your app.

In the section of the App Settings Page shown in Figure 2-9, you need to select what kind of an app that you want to launch. Facebook has six different types of apps to deploy with the Facebook developer tools:

✦ **Website:** Facebook can be used to log into a website in place of your website's separate login credentials. Select this section, and enter your domain name (website URL) into the text box.

✦ **App on Facebook:** An app on Facebook is any of those that we refer to most frequently in this book. This means that the app will be accessed somewhere within Facebook, through a Canvas Page. To use this feature, you select the App on Facebook section and enter two URLs. Make sure that you include the entire URL, including the `http://` portion.

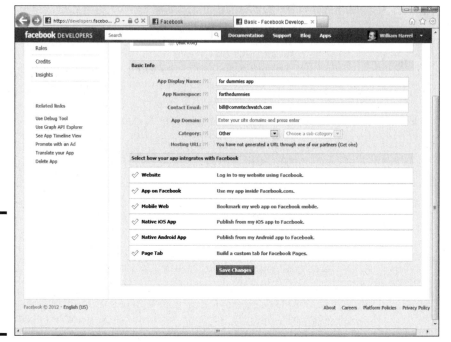

Figure 2-9:
Selecting how your app integrates with Facebook.

In the Canvas URL text box, enter the URL for the web page where your app is hosted. The secure URL text box typically takes the same URL, only with `https` in instead of `http`. Users have the option to enable secured browsing using HTTPS on their Account Settings page. To support these users, you need to set up your destination URL on a secured server using an SSL Certificate. This is the default destination for users viewing your app. If a secure URL isn't available, users will be warned that they're about to enter unsecured browsing. Facebook requires you to have an SSL Certificate, but doesn't completely block out the unsecured version.

✦ **Mobile Web:** If you redirect users to a mobile site, select this option and enter the URL. The Mobile Web option is applicable for games or other applications that are supported on both standard web and mobile web. When you use this feature, users can bookmark your app on Facebook Mobile.

✦ **Native iOS App:** Use this feature to publish an iPhone app to Facebook. For example, if you have a shopping app, your app could have a feature that allows users to post products they're interested in on their Timelines. To create an iPhone app, you need to fill in five fields. Refer to Apple's developer toolkit for further information about these fields:

 • iOS Bundle ID

 • iPhone App Store ID

- iPad App Store ID
- Configure for iOS SSO
- URL Scheme Suffix

✦ **Native Android App:** To publish a Facebook app on an Android phone, you have only the Android Key Hash field to fill in. For security reasons, Facebook checks the Android Key Hash before authorizing your app.

✦ **Page Tab:** The last option, Page Tab, is where you create a custom Facebook tab. Click this row and fill in the following text boxes:

- *Page Tab Name:* Enter the name of the tab that will appear on your Facebook Page.

- *Page Tab URL:* Enter the HTTP version of the URL you will be viewing in the tab.

- *Secure Page Tab URL:* Enter the HTTPS version of the destination web application.

- *Page Tab Edit URL:* Enter the administrator edit link (if you have one available) to access the editing of the app.

The Auth Dialog page

Go to the app's App Settings page and click the Auth Dialog link in the left navigation pane (refer to Figure 2-8). The Auth Dialog page, shown in Figure 2-10, is where you customize details provided to users, such as descriptions of the app and where to find your privacy policy. Users see an authorization dialog box when you use Open Graph for your app. (*Open Graph* is the integration feature that Facebook uses to share activity on your Timeline; see the following section for more.)

As you complete the text boxes within this app, you can click the Preview Dialog link to the top right of your screen to see how the dialog box will appear. Each of the URL text boxes just directs users to the page on your site that you enter as the source for that information. For example, if your privacy policy is at www.mycoolapp.com/privacy, enter that URL into the Privacy Policy URL text box.

Open Graph

Go to the app's App Settings page and click the Open Graph link in the left navigation pane (refer to Figure 2-8). Open Graph is the integration of Facebook that makes your app more engaging. Using Open Graph allows you to deeply interweave the social elements of Facebook with your app and create a more social experience. The foundation of Open Graph apps are Actions and Objects. This means that within your app, you have an action that people do in your app, and an object that people connect with by doing that action.

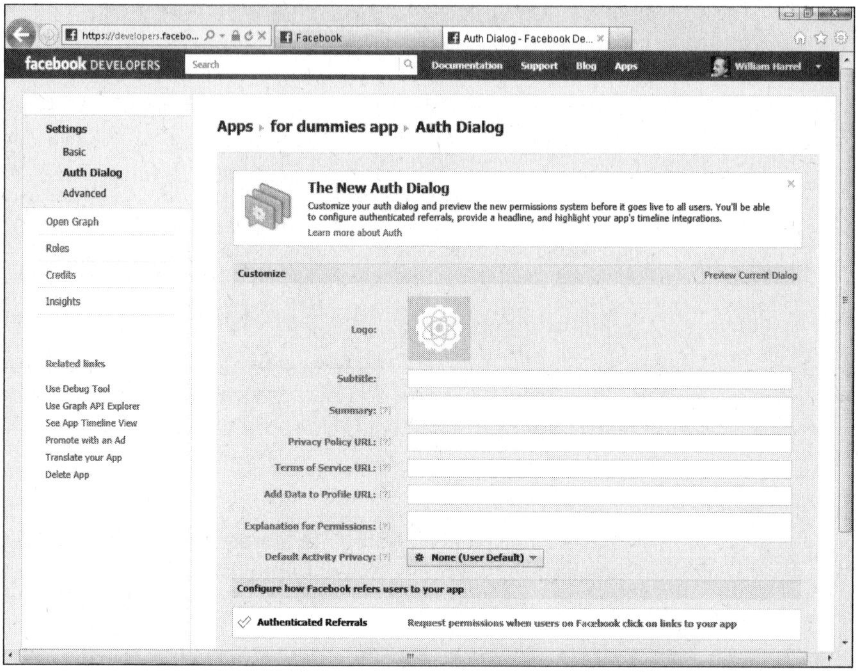

Figure 2-10:
Customize
the Auth
Dialog.

Facebook provides some example Open Graph actions and objects, as shown in Figure 2-11. For example, if your app allows users to track their movie experiences in real life, then the social activity the users are sharing is watching a movie. In this case, the action is Watch. That action has the corresponding object, Movie. An app like this would be targeted at making real-life experiences more social by sharing them with friends. These actions would be shared on the user's Timeline, in News Feeds, as well as in the Ticker. This takes the social act of Liking a Fan Page or article a step further by allowing a Facebook app to define more actions. You have complete freedom to define your actions and objects.

Figure 2-11:
The Open
Graph
actions and
objects.

When deciding how to implement an Open Graph app, don't think too much about the activities being done within the app itself. Think about building apps to make activities that people enjoy more social. Open Graph apps are all about stories being shared on the user's Timeline. For example, if your business is a gym and you want to engage people into your experience through Facebook, your app could contain tutorials giving people a routine to follow, of which they complete steps as they move through the routine. Your action might be Complete and your object might be Exercise.

Facebook has a light approval process for actions and objects. It wants to ensure that certain standards are followed, but it isn't terribly strict as these standards are pretty reasonable. The core of the matter is to create actions that make sense and protect the integrity of the Open Graph concept. Facebook wants to ensure that your app publishes actions that are simple, genuine, and not abusive. You can read these guidelines in the Facebook Developer help section at `http://developers.facebook.com/docs/opengraph/opengraph-approval`.

After you've determined your action and object, go to the next page in the Open Graph section. To the left, a link says Dashboard. This is where you build out the actions that people will do within your app.

For each action type, the Facebook dev app gives you a code that you use to build app functions around the action. You can add more actions and objects to your app.

The last section (shown in Figure 2-12) asks for *aggregations,* which are collections of actions that will be displayed within the app to summarize the user's activity over time. The app changes the action tense to fit the need.

You can change the way this displays by selecting from templates offered within the dev app. Follow these steps:

1. **Click the action shown in the Aggregations section.**

2. **In the Data to Display text box, enter what data you would like to aggregate, such as how many objects versus how many actions. (See Figure 2-13.)**

   Ultimately, this matters most within the context of the goals of your app. Do you want to highlight how many different exercises the user has done or how many times the user has exercised?

3. **Click the template icon to select the template you would like to use for the layout of the summary.**

4. **Choose how you would like the data sorted from the Sort By drop-down list.**

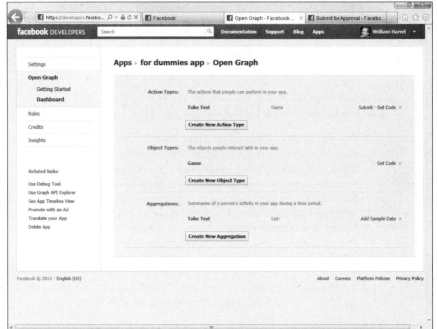

Figure 2-12:
Create
Open Graph
objects,
actions, and
aggrega-
tions.

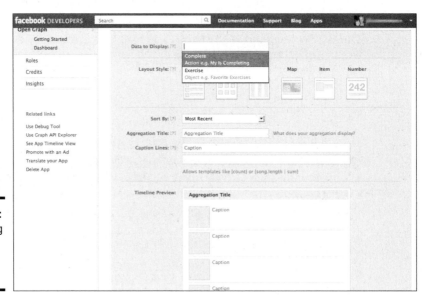

Figure 2-13:
Customizing
action
aggrega-
tions.

5. **In the Caption Lines text box(es), type a caption for your action.**

The caption area allows custom formatting. You can also enter a term such as {count}. (In this case, {count} is replaced with the number of actions or objects.) You can choose from several custom format options for captions, including place, time, and more. You can see what options are available by typing a curly bracket ({) into the text box, and the app displays the available options. This means that your captions can be different each time based on changing information (such as completing more actions or completing them in less time, in different places and other details).

6. **Click Save Changes to save the settings.**

Defining roles for your app

When developing an app, you may work in a team. Depending on the level of detail and the size of your team, you can add and remove team members from your dev app. Just like Fan Page Timelines, apps have administrators assigned to them who have rights to edit and manage the page. With a dev app, there are a few other roles. (See Figure 2-14.) The following list shows the roles assigned to a Facebook dev app:

✦ **Administrators:** Have complete access to the dev app. They can access all the app's settings.

✦ **Developers:** Can access all technical settings, but are restricted from changing the secret key, changing or adding additional users, and deleting the application.

✦ **Testers:** Can test the application in what is called *sandbox mode.* They can't make any changes to the app. (Sandbox mode is completely for testing the app.)

✦ **Insights Users:** Can access Insights for marketing purposes, but can't modify the application in any way.

✦ **Test Users:** Imaginary users that Facebook allows you to create to access the app to test its functionality. When you use the test user, Facebook creates a login URL that expires in two hours. You can access a user access token to take actions on behalf of the user and test API functions. You can create up to 500 test users for an app.

Credits

If your app has features in it that cost money (such as games with additional levels), you'll use the Credits section. *Credits* allow your users to buy digital goods and services from the app. Facebook credits provide a way for app developers to generate revenue within games and other types of apps on Facebook. What this provides is security; people trust the Facebook brand and they have a single consistent place to buy the credits they want, including across mobile apps.

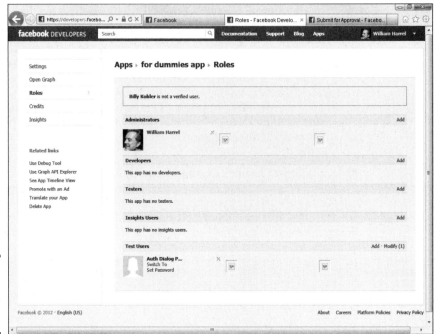

Figure 2-14:
Defining
roles in your
dev app.

To get started with credits, you need to register your company within the app. To the left on your dev app screen, click the Credits link. Here, you select your country and click the link to register a company. This link leads to a page that allows you to register your company, including entering your banking information where PayPal can directly deposit funds it collects on your behalf.

The Credits Callback URL text box on the Credits Settings page sends a ping to this location that is JSON-encoded (JavaScript Object Notation, which is part of the JavaScript markup language). If you aren't skilled in PHP and relative code languages, you'll need someone who is to help you complete this process.

You can assign credits testers, which are people who will test the app without having to be charged credits when they use the functions of the app. They can do anything that a user would do, only without having to pay for it.

Insights in Facebook Apps

Insights is designed to help you know the effectiveness of your app. (See Figure 2-15.) What Facebook Insights tells you is what users use your app and how they use it. While Insights provides limited data, the data is invaluable if you intend to use the app as a marketing tool. Insights comes with several segments that provide critical information to the app developer:

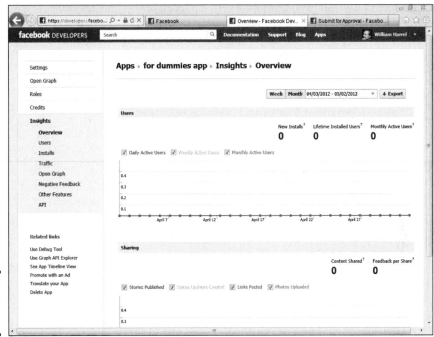

Figure 2-15:
Dev app
Insights.

✦ **Overview:** A snapshot of how much activity your app gets. This includes the number of users, data on sharing, and a measure of performance based on API requests (that is, how many times the app pulls data).

✦ **Users:** How many users use your app. It breaks it down into total active users, daily active users, new users by day, and demographic information. Lastly, the list shares how many users block your app.

✦ **Installs:** Statistics and information about users who have installed your app. This allows you to gauge the app's success.

✦ **Traffic:** Statistics showing how much and how often your app is used. This option also allows you to access your app's performance.

✦ **Open Graph:** Breaks into several smaller sections that relate to Open Graph details, such as how much activity the app gets (such as Likes and Comments), click-through rates of stories your app posts (meaning the percentage of viewers who actually clicked), and Ticker and News Feed impressions. The subcategories for Open Graph are

- Story CTR (Click Through Rate)

- Likes and Comments

- Aggregation Activity

- Ticker

- Demographics

- Action Lifecycle

- Object Lifecycle

✦ **Negative Feedback:** This information shows the negative feedback your app receives. You can use this feedback to improve your app.

✦ **Other Features:** There are two options here.

- *Requests:* Allows you to gauge how the requests for information your app asks for are received and processed — whether they're accepted, ignored, or sent.

- *Credits:* Tracks how much revenue your app brings in and any chargebacks or refunds that may have occurred.

✦ **API:** Allows you to measure the technical efficiency of your app, as well as see how much actual activity the app gets. This can be different from the number of users because some users may perform a lot of activities, while others may spend only a short time in your app. It also assesses any glitches in the app. It shows you API errors, restrictions, and warnings so you can be sure to keep your app working properly.

All the preceding items can be viewed by week or month, or narrowed to a specific date range. You also can export the data to an Excel spreadsheet or a `.csv` file (Comma Separated Value). The analytics are critical to measure the effectiveness of your app. You can also use this data for marketing purposes to measure against other efforts.

Chapter 3: Creating Your Own Apps

In This Chapter

✔ Understanding the Facebook core app

✔ Creating a Facebook app

✔ Installing a Facebook app

✔ Authenticating a Facebook app

*Y*ou can develop apps for all kinds of reasons. Some apps conduct surveys, other apps sell things. Some are marketing tools. Some collect charitable contributions. You're limited only by your ambition and imagination.

Facebook apps are, in effect, web applications that run inside the Facebook interface, and they can do most things non-Facebook web applications can do. The difference between standard web apps and Facebook apps is the latter also integrate with Facebook, allowing users to Like them, post comments inside them or about them — nearly everything Facebook users can do in Facebook, they can also do in your app, depending on which Facebook features you decide to exploit.

We should add that in many instances, when developing Facebook apps, you're often also limited by your programming skills. Before getting deeply into this discussion of creating Facebook apps, we should point out that highly sophisticated games, marketing, and revenue-generating apps are usually developed by professional programmers. (But that doesn't mean you can't do it, too.)

Creating and Deploying a Facebook App

Facebook apps are little programs that run inside the Facebook environment. A simple way to look at is that Facebook is your operating system, similar to Windows, Mac OS, or iOS. Apps use the core environment — the Facebook program and the capabilities the folks at Facebook have built into the core — to run in.

At Facebook's core

When developing apps for Facebook, it's helpful to look at the Facebook platform as a group of core technologies, and there are many. Depending on what your app does, it will integrate with one or more of these core technologies. The most commonly used core technologies are Social Plugins and Platform Dialogs.

Social plugins

Social plugins, discussed in Book VI, Chapter 4, are some of the common objects you use in your daily interaction with Facebook. They include the Like button, Send button, Subscribe button, Comments dialog boxes, and so on. When developing your Facebook apps, you can take advantage of these common objects and use them in your apps.

Platform dialogs

Facebook has lots of dialogs — boxes for posting to your Timeline, posting to your friends' Timelines, sending messages, and so on. Your apps can generate these dialog boxes and accept input from users. Platform dialogs are discussed in Book VI, Chapter 4.

A basic app

Creating and deploying apps on Facebook is a huge, deep subject. To help you appreciate the possibilities and familiarize yourself with the process, we delve into setting up and installing a simple app. While creating apps can get complicated, installing them on your Facebook account isn't very difficult, thanks to the great tools the folks at Facebook provide.

The little app we install in Facebook in this chapter really is quite basic. The purpose is to walk you through the process. This app doesn't exploit any of Facebook's objects, nor does it use social plugins or platform dialogs. We look at using these features in Book VI, Chapter 4.

Creating and deploying an app on Facebook consists of two procedures, one on a non-Facebook server and the other inside the Facebook interface, as follows:

✦ **Create the app and save it on a web server.** This is the hard part that usually requires, depending on the scope of your app, web page design and programming skills. This process entails designing the app and making it available on the Internet, so that Facebook can find it and load it into a Canvas Page. Designing and developing apps is beyond the scope of this book, but you can find several examples of Facebook apps on the web; another resource is *Facebook Application Development For Dummies* by Jesse Stay (John Wiley & Sons, Inc.).

✦ **Deploy the app on Facebook.** This process entails going to Facebook's app developments pages, installing the app, and making it available to Facebook users. Again, Facebook has several tools for making this part of the process fairly simple.

In this example, you take a simple mind-reading game app and install it into Facebook.

Before you can install apps on Facebook, you must first confirm your Facebook account.

App, app — who has the app?

Before you can install an app on Facebook, you need an app. Remember that an app is a separate file (or files, for more complex apps) located somewhere else on the Internet. The app itself is not installed and saved on Facebook's servers. A Facebook app is a web app that runs inside the Facebook interface. For this example, we created a simple app; if you're feeling adventurous, you can use your own app.

Because Facebook doesn't allow you to upload your apps to its servers, you need access to an Internet server. The following procedure to upload and save files on an external, non-Facebook server assumes basic knowledge of FTP and computer file directory structure. If you don't have this knowledge or access to an external server, Facebook partners with Heroku, an app-hosting service that integrates with the Facebook developers' pages. Get more info on Heroku at `https://developers.facebook.com/blog/post/558/`.

The following steps show you how to make an app available on a public web server:

1. **Using Dreamweaver, a source-code editor, text editor, or whatever you use for creating web pages, create a page consisting of the following code:**

```
<script type=text/javascript>
var iRandom;
function Restart()
{
iRandom = Math.floor(Math.random()*10)+1;
alert('Can You Read My Mind?');
}
function Go()
{
var read = document.getElementById('myRead').value;
if (read>iRandom)
    alert('Go Down!');
if (read<iRandom)
    alert('Go Up!');
if (read==iRandom)
    {
    alert('You Read My Mind!');
    Restart();
```

```
      }
   }
</script>
<h2>Can You Read My Mind?</h2>
<hr />
<h2><img src="images/mindread.png" alt="Mind Reader" width="300"
      height="232" hspace="10" align="left" />Are You Psychic?</h2>
<p>I'm thinking of a number between 1 and 10. To test your mind-reading
      skills, type a number in the field below and click Go. If you guess
      wrong, you can try again until you get it right. To start the game
      over, click the Play Again button.</p>
<p>Good Luck!</p>
<p>I'm thinking of a number between 1 and 10:
   <input name='MyRead' type=text id='myRead' size="5">
   <input type='button' onClick='Go()' value='go'>
</p>
<p>
   <input type='button' onClick='Restart()' value='Play Again'>
</p>
<p><em>If this took more than one guess, you're probably not psychic.
      Sorry.</em></p>
<hr />
<script type=text/javascript>
Restart();
</script>
```

This is a simple HTML form with one field and two buttons, some accompanying text, an image and some JavaScript. The user guesses a number between 1 and 10 and types it into the field. When the user clicks the Go button, the script matches the number to a number randomly chosen when the page loaded. If he or she guesses correctly, a dialog box confirms the correct guess. If the wrong answer is chosen, the dialog box tells the user if the number is higher or lower than the randomly generated one, allowing him or her to guess again.

2. **Name the file** `index.html`.

3. **Create a subdirectory named** `apps` **in the root (main) directory of your public web server, and then create a subdirectory of** `apps` **and name it** `images`.

The root directory is the main directory of the site. On the web, subfolders are typically accessed by tacking the directory name onto the back of the site's domain name, as follows:

   `http://www.MyWebSite.com/apps/`

4. **Upload** `index.html` **with an FTP client, such as Dreamweaver or whatever you have, to the** `apps` **subdirectory you created in Step 3.**

5. **Upload the image file (for example,** `mindread.png`**) to the** `images` **folder inside the** `apps` **folder.**

That's it! To test the app, navigate in your browser to the URL where you saved the page, for example:

`http://www.mysite.com/apps/`

You should get the mind reader app shown in Figure 3-1.

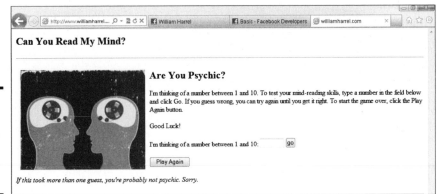

Figure 3-1:
Your web
app prior to
deploying
it on
Facebook.

Go ahead and try it if you want. If you guess wrong, a dialog box will let you know. Simply enter another number based on the feedback dialog box telling you to go up or down in the number value. When you get it right, the dialog box tells you that you're a mind reader.

Installing the Facebook app

Getting the app to work on Facebook is fairly simple, once you know where to start.

1. **Start your Web browser and log into Facebook.**

2. **In the browser's address bar, type the following URL:**

```
http://developers.facebook.com/
```

This takes you to the developers greeting page. From here, you can branch off to pages for building websites, building mobile websites, or building Facebook apps.

3. **Click the Apps link in the upper-right corner of the menu bar, and then click the Create New App button.**

This displays the New App dialog box, as shown in Figure 3-2. From here, you can name your new app and give it an app namespace. The app namespace is the directory where Facebook saves data about your app. The namespace needs to be different from other namespace names on Facebook. We named ours *mymindread*, so you can't use that name.

4. **Type a name for your app in the App Display Name text box.**

You can name the app whatever you want, we named ours *Mind Reader*. You can use that name, too. Facebook saves apps with unique ID numbers that generate when you save this dialog box.

Figure 3-2:
The New
App dialog
box for
starting
the app
installation
process.

5. **Type the App Namespace until you get one that works, and then click Continue.**

This field requires seven letters. The namespace can't be the same as any other namespace on Facebook. Also, the namespace can't have any spaces, uppercase, or non-alphabetic characters. After you type the namespace, a message beside the App Namespace text box displays either a green Available message or a red Failed, depending on whether you type a namespace already in use. Just keep trying until you get an Available. (Or, you can change it later in the process.)

After you click Continue, you see a security CAPTCHA.

6. **Type the security code and click Submit.**

This takes you to the Basic Settings page. The following describes each option on the page:

- *Edit Icon:* Use this link to upload a graphics file to use as an icon for your app. The icon should be 75 x 75 pixels. If yours is larger, Facebook will resize it, possibly distorting it.

- *App Display Name:* The name of your app.

- *App Namespace:* The app's namespace.

- *Contact Email:* This is the e-mail address for the app to send data to.

- *App Domain:* The domain name on the server where you saved you app earlier — just the domain name — such as `yourdomain.com`.

- *Category:* Pick a type of app from the drop-down list. Mind Reader is a Game. As you can see, there are several categories.

- *Choose a Sub-Category:* Some categories have subcategories. Choose a subcategory that suits your app.

7. **Scroll to the lower half of the page.**

This is where you set up your app's integration with your external app located on the other server, as shown in Figure 3-3.

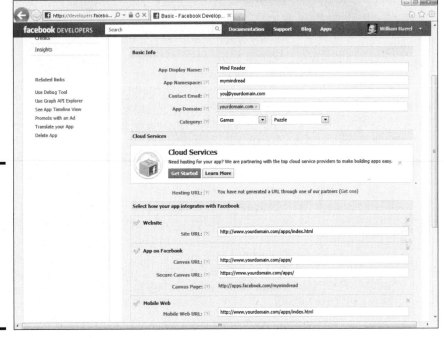

Figure 3-3:
Use these
fields to
associate
your
external
content
with the
Facebook
core.

- *Site URL:* The address for the app. Type the entire URL path, including page name.

- *Canvas URL:* The directory of the external app.

- *Secure Canvas URL:* This text box is for setting up apps that run on secure, encrypted servers that you access with the HTTPS protocol.

- *Canvas Page:* The Facebook URL for your app. Facebook generates it according to the data you entered in previous fields. This is how users get to your app.

- *Mobile Web URL:* If you developed a separate version of the app for mobile devices, put that URL here, or use the same Site URL, if the app will run on mobile devices as is.

Notice the Canvas Page URL text box that Facebook filled out automatically, based on the information you typed in the other text boxes. This is the URL to the app itself inside Facebook. You could place that URL in the address bar of your browser while logged into Facebook and go straight to your new app, as could anybody else logged into Facebook. This is one way to provide access to users, by posting the Canvas Page URL on your Timeline, in messages, on other web pages, and so on.

8. **Click the Save Changes button at the bottom of the page.**

Adding your app to a Fan Page tab

As discussed in Book IV, Chapter 1, you can create your own Fan Page Timelines on Facebook. One of the ways to make your app available is to publish it as a tab. Tabs show up in the left column of your Fan Page Timeline.

Creating a tab on one of your Fan Page Timelines is a three-step process, as follows:

1. **While filling out the Basic settings form when installing your app in Facebook, select the Page Tab check box to open that section of the form, shown in the following figure.**

2. **Fill in the Page Tab Name (the name of your app as you want it to display on the Fan Page Timeline), the Page Tab URL, and the Secure Page Tab URL.**

   These last two should match what you typed in Canvas URL and Secure Canvas

URL in the App on Facebook section of the form. Save the form.

3. **While logged into Facebook, go to the following URL (replace `your_app_id` with the Facebook ID for your app and `your_canvas_url` with the URL for your app on your web server:**

   ```
   http://www.facebook.com/dialog/
       pagetab?app_id=your_app_
       id&next=your_canvas_url
   ```

   The URL takes you to the Add Page Tab dialog box.

4. **Choose the page where you want to install the app from the Choose Facebook Pages drop-down list, and then click the Add Page Tab button.**

Facebook adds the tab to the requested page.

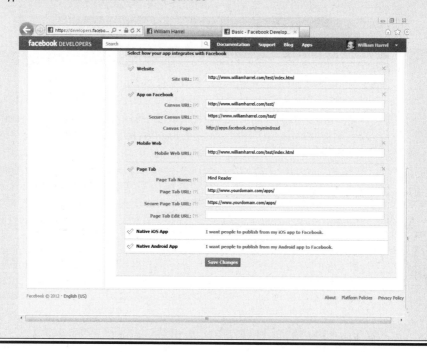

Facebook checks the data you entered as it saves the app info. If any entries are not in the correct format, you're prompted to change them.

That's it! While many apps require additional set up, the simple Mind Reader app does not. It doesn't require any permissions or other settings. As described in the preceding Tip, you can make your app available to users in many ways. You can also create a link on your Fan Page Timeline, as described in the "Adding your app to a Fan Page tab" sidebar in this chapter. For a description of the differences between tabs and Canvas Pages, see the Book VI, Chapter 2.

Once Facebook has successfully saved the data, the app ID displays at the top of the page. The app ID is critical to several aspects of promoting your app, such as described in the "Adding your app to a Fan Page tab" sidebar. The app ID can also be used in your app scripts, inside the app itself.

Authenticating Your App

The Auth Dialog, shown in Figure 3-4, allows the user to install your app on the user's Facebook Home page and authenticate the app. Authenticating an app grants it the permissions it needs to run properly. Permissions define which objects of a Facebook account the app needs. For example, if your app needs to post the user's Timeline, the Auth dialog box requests this permission from the user.

The Auth dialog form

The Auth dialog form, shown in Figure 3-5, allows you to configure the appearance and messages presented in the Auth dialog, as well as define which permissions the app needs to request from the user.

While installing your app from Facebook's developers' pages, you can get to the Auth dialog form by clicking the Auth Dialog link in the left column under Settings. Facebook displays the form shown in Figure 3-5. Here is a description of the options in this form and how they affect your Auth dialog:

✦ **Logo:** Use this option to place and upload a logo for your Auth dialog. Simply click the box and browse to the logo image file on your computer in the dialog box. The file uploads to the Facebook servers. The image should measure 75 x 75 pixels.

✦ **Headline:** The name of your app goes here. It displays across the top of the Auth dialog.

✦ **Description:** Enter a description of your app here — what it does, why, and so on.

✦ **Privacy Policy URL:** Creates a link in the Auth dialog that takes the user to a page on your web server that describes your privacy policy. (You know, "We will provide everything we know about you to the highest bidder as soon as their check clears," or something like that.) All kidding aside, because your app accesses personal information on Facebook, you can use this option to assure users their data is safe with you.

✦ **Terms of Service URL:** Creates a link in your Auth dialog box that takes the user to a page on your web server that describes the rules or terms of service (ToS) for your app.

✦ **Add Data to Profile URL:** Your Facebook app can provide many activities to your users. Some of these activities include Facebook Timelines, News Feeds, and Tickers through an advanced development feature called Open Graph, described briefly in Book VI, Chapter 2. For details on Open Graph, check out *Building Facebook Applications For Dummies*, by Richard Wagner (John Wiley & Sons).

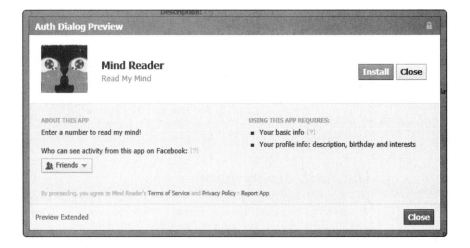

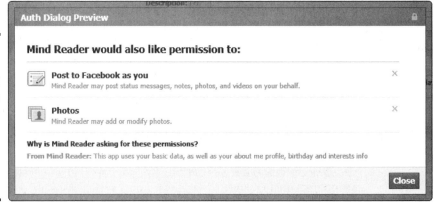

Figure 3-4: Auth dialog for installing an app (top), and what the app can manipulate on the account (bottom).

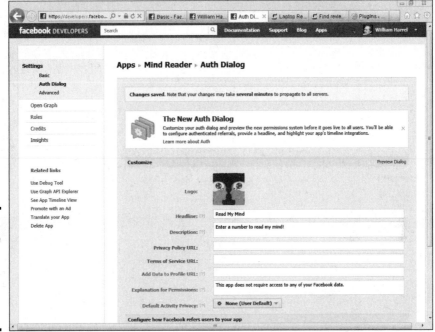

Figure 3-5:
Configure the
appearance
and
messages
in the Auth
dialog.

♦ **Explanation for Permissions:** Type the description of the types of permissions your app needs to get from the user's Facebook account. This helps the user decide whether to authenticate the app.

♦ **Default Activity Privacy:** Use this drop-down list to define which types of privacy settings the user can choose for your app on her site. In other words, can the user allow other users to see and use the app? Depending on what you choose here, the Auth dialog will display a similar drop-down list to the user. The choices are: None (User Default), which lets the user decide; Public, which allows anybody to see the app; Friends, which allows only the user's friends to see the app; and Only Me, which allows only the user to see the app.

Request permission

In addition to the preceding options, the Authenticated Referrals section of the Auth dialog form lets you define which permissions Facebook requests from the user. Their two options are: User & Friend Permissions and Extended Permissions. To enter permission in either of these text boxes, you simply start typing the permission string in the field, as shown in Figure 3-6. Facebook will then suggest available strings based on what you type.

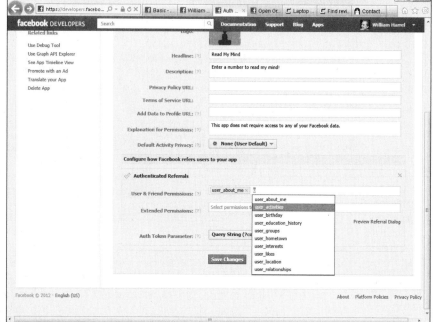

Figure 3-6:
Use these
fields to
request
permissions
from the
user's
Facebook
account.

✦ **User & Friend Permissions:** You include required permissions, permissions that typically just request information, rather than make changes to the user's Facebook objects, in the User & Friend Permissions text box. Note that you must request access to each specific type of data. To get the user's birthday, interests, location, relationship data, and so on, you'll need a string in this field for each one.

✦ **Extended Permissions:** Typically, the Extended Permissions allow you to make changes on the user's Facebook objects, such as posting, uploading photos and videos, and so on. The user can also revoke any of these permission after authenticating your app. In most instances, revoking permissions for an app will break it or change how the app works.

✦ **Auth Token Parameter:** Some apps interact with the Graph API. An Auth Token, or authorization token, is passed to the Graph API to allow the app to interact with it on behalf of Facebook users. This is a somewhat sophisticated concept designed for use with intricate apps. You can get a full description of app authentication at `http://developers.facebook.com/docs/authentication/`.

Chapter 4: Tour of the Facebook API

In This Chapter

✓ **Finding technical information**

✓ **Understanding the Facebook API core concepts**

✓ **Using Facebook SDKs**

✓ **Placing Facebook objects on your website with Social Plugins**

Developing apps for the Facebook platform requires a little knowledge on two fronts. The apps themselves often consist of HTML and CSS for creating and formatting websites, as well as JavaScript, PHP, Python, or Objective-C programming. To deploy an app on Facebook and take advantage of all the various objects, such as News Feeds and other Facebook features, you need to have an understanding of the basic Facebook application programming interface (API).

Facebook provides a rather well-developed API for creating apps, with plenty of tools to help you integrate your app into Facebook's social fabric, as well as extensive documentation. However, like most documentation (usually written by techno-geeks), finding information isn't always easy. Using it can be difficult, especially if you don't know what to look for.

In this chapter, we take a look at the API and its core concepts, the various development tools, and the documentation — where to look for each tool and where to find detailed instructions on how to use them. In many instances, the Facebook documentation includes detailed deployment information, as well as online tools that actually create some of your app code for you — the parts of the code that integrate your app with the API, anyway.

Consider this chapter the tourist guide for using the Facebook API, as well as a map for finding the documentation for developing and deploying your Facebook apps.

Finding Technical Information

No matter how you slice it, just like creating apps for any other platform, developing Facebook apps is an undertaking highly technical in nature — a expedition up Geek Creek. You know what they say about going up Geek Creek without a paddle. . . . Facebook's online developer's documentation, as well as a few other resources, is your paddle.

Like all aspects of information technology, Facebook changes frequently. Not only are the Facebook interface and features under constant development, so is the site's app technology. Books like this one are great for demystifying the documentation. However, sometimes the applications these books cover change between the writing of the material and when the books hit bookstores. It's almost inevitable that these technologies change within a year or two. In many cases, sometimes the only current documentation is the site's online manual, which usually gets updated with the site itself. But often, you just can't get by without the site's online documentation.

Facebook's online API documentation

Because Facebook apps can do so many things, and can run from the very simple to the highly complicated, writing a step-by-step, do this, and then do that, tutorial would not only be difficult, it probably wouldn't be all that useful. The Facebook API, depending on what you want your app to do, supports many options. Hence, the online documentation is divided by topics. In the following sections, we take a look at where to find technical information on some of the more important Facebook app development topics.

Where to start

In Book VI, Chapter 3, we provide a step-by-step exercise on installing a simple app in the Facebook API. That exercise really is very basic. You can get more detailed information at the following locations:

✦ **Getting Started, Canvas Tutorial:** Complete with code samples, this section, shown in Figure 4-1, provides information on creating your app, installing it in Facebook, authorizing it, and exploiting social channels (such as the News Feed and game stories). You can also find a link to a sample app that uses real-time updates as one of its Facebook integration features. You can get to this page at `https://developers.facebook.com/docs/appsonfacebook/tutorial/`.

✦ **Getting Started, Apps on Facebook:** This page provides an overview of the app creation process, describing the Canvas Page, Social Channels, and Analytics. Analytics allow you to gauge the performance of your app in terms of how often it gets used, who is using it, and so on. This page is located at `https://developers.facebook.com/docs/guides/canvas/`.

✦ **Getting Started, Sample How-Tos:** This page provides links to several prebuilt apps that show you how to exploit specific features of the API, including Social Plugins, Insights graphs for analytics, and Facebook's Credits feature for making and collecting payments. You can find this page at `https://developers.facebook.com/docs/samples/`.

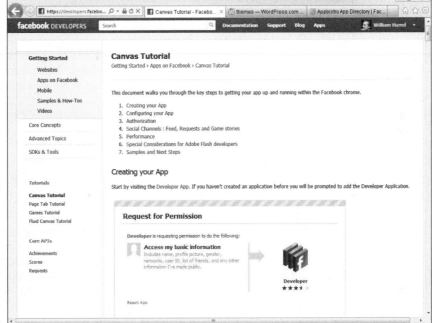

Figure 4-1:
Much of
Facebook's
app devel-
opment
documenta-
tion starts at
this page.

Advanced API documentation

The more sophisticated your apps become, the more you need to know about core concepts, Facebook's software development kits (SDKs), and other advanced topics, such as Dialogs, Credits, and ads. You can get detailed information on the following Facebook documentation pages:

✦ **Core concepts:** Core concepts include Social Plugins, social channels, and authentication, among others. We talk more about these later in this chapter in the "Social Channels" and "Authentication" sections. You can get detailed information about core concepts at `https://developers.facebook.com/docs/coreconcepts/`.

✦ **SDKs and other tools:** Facebook's SDKs enable you to add functionality through JavaScript and PHP, as well as write code specific to Apple iPads and iPhones and mobile devices that use Google's Android platform. Other Facebook API tools include the Developer App, debugging options, a JavaScript test console, and several others. You can find a gateway page to these tools located at `https://developers.facebook.com/tools/`.

✦ **Advanced Topics:** Advanced topics include Dialogs, Facebook Query Language (FQL), and Credits, among others. The gateway page to documentation on these features is located at `https://developers.facebook.com/docs/advancedtopics/`.

Helpful tutorials

In addition to the Canvas tutorial described in the earlier section, "Where to start," the folks at Facebook provide several other online tutorials, on topics such as creating page tabs and games. Here are a few that we found helpful:

✦ **Page Tab Tutorial:** You can get a more detailed description of this process in the tutorial located at `http://developers.facebook.com/docs/appsonfacebook/pagetabs/`.

✦ **Games Tutorial:** Game apps are very popular on Facebook. A well-designed game can drive traffic to your Facebook account. For a detailed explanation of creating game apps, go to `http://developers.facebook.com/docs/guides/games/`.

✦ **Fluid Canvas Tutorial:** A fluid canvas adjusts its size to the browser window and screen resolution. As you can imagine, for some apps this can be very helpful. For a detailed tutorial on making your canvases fluid, try `http://developers.facebook.com/docs/fluidcanvas/`.

Understanding Facebook's Core Concepts

Building Facebook apps requires an understanding of what Facebook calls its "core concepts," or what, in terms of app creation, makes the Facebook API tick — the building blocks upon which you develop your apps. To provide a broader understanding of app development, in this section, we take a quick look at the core concepts.

One of the core concepts is Social Plugins. However, these are Facebook apps of a different nature — you deploy them *on* your website with links back to Facebook, instead deploying them *from* your website *to* Facebook. Although Facebook lumps them in with the core concepts for app development, we discuss them in a separate section, "Placing Facebook Objects on Your Web Pages with Social Plugins," later in this chapter.

Third-party technical information

In addition to Facebook's extensive developers' manual, several other publications and websites are available to help you in creating and deploying apps. Here are a few we have found helpful:

✔ *Facebook Application Development For Dummies* by Jesse Stay (John Wiley & Sons) covers Facebook app development from start to finish. It includes such topics as which scripting languages to use, OAuth 2.0, real-time objects, and the Search API, as well as how to develop and sell business apps. We found this book quite helpful.

✔ *Building Facebook Applications For Dummies* by Richard Wagner (Wiley) is a must-have reference for the Facebook app developer. In addition to covering how to create and deploy Facebook apps, it also explains how to migrate existing web apps to Facebook, as well as creating mobile apps and how to promote your Facebook apps.

✔ **Top 10 Facebook Apps for Building Custom Pages and Tabs** on Social Media Examiner (`www.socialmediaexaminer.com/top-10-facebook-apps-for-building-custom-pages-tabs/`) showcases several apps that help you with creating page tabs and Facebook pages. These apps create fancy-looking pages, multiple tabs on pages, and write HTML and other code for you to help spruce up your Facebook pages. They install directly into your Facebook account and provide extensive help in these and several other processes.

✔ **AppBistro** provides many free apps, as well as several professionally designed apps that you can rent on a monthly basis, such as those shown in the following figure. If nothing else, you can get an untold number of ideas from this site, at `http://appbistro.com/t/top-picks/fan-builder-kit`.

**Book VI
Chapter 4**

**Tour of the
Facebook API**

Open Graph versus Graph API

Facebook's developer documentation starts the discussion of each of these two concepts with the following statement: "At Facebook's core is the social graph; people and the connections they have to everything they care about." This, and the word *graph* shared between these two concepts would lead you to believe they are the same. However, except for their reliance on something called the *social graph*, these two concepts are quite different.

According to Facebook cofounder Mark Zuckerberg, the social graph is the network of connections and relationships between the people on Facebook. The objects in the social graph are people, events, photos, pages, and so on. The network is the connection between these objects. Your apps exploit these objects from within and from outside Facebook.

Though highly simplistic, Figure 4-2 shows a visual representation of the social graph for one user's Facebook account.

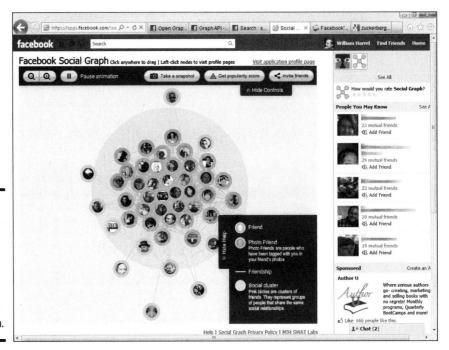

Figure 4-2:
This Facebook app shows a visual representation of Facebook's social graph.

Open Graph

Also called the *Open Graph protocol,* Open Graph started in 2010 allowing people to Like third-party, or non-Facebook websites and pages. Perhaps the most common use for this protocol is Like buttons on blog posts. Open graph has been expanded to allow third-party sites and pages to interact with several Facebook actions and objects, as well as non-Facebook actions and objects within the app. Put simply, Open Graph is the social graph open to access from websites outside of Facebook.

Graph API

Graph API differs from Open Graph in that it represents objects within the Facebook API, such as people, Events, pages, and so on. Every object in Facebook, each photo, each person, each Event, each app, is assigned a unique ID. Your apps can access and use these objects by referencing their IDs. Some objects have number IDs and are referenced like this: `"id":` `"19292868552"`, other objects have alpha, or word, IDs, and are referenced as follows: `"username":` `"dannyt"`. In very simple terms, the Graph API presents and represents objects on Facebook.

**Book VI
Chapter 4**

Tour of the
Facebook API

Requesting access to and accessing objects

Before your apps can access a user's information and other objects associated with an account, the app must be granted access to these objects. Your apps request access to objects through Authentication. Your app in turn accesses the objects and potentially shares them with the user's friends through Social Channels.

Authentication

The first time a user accesses your app, an Auth Dialog appears, as shown in Figure 4-3, asking the user for permission to actions and objects from their Facebook account. Which actions (writing to a Timeline, uploading photos, etc.) and objects (News Feeds, events, Pages, etc.) your app needs access to depends on what the app does inside the Facebook API — your app code dictates what permissions you need. You setup and deploy the Auth Dialog your users see through the Auth Dialog settings form, as demonstrated in the "Authenticating Your App" section in Book VI, Chapter 3.

Figure 4-3:
Example
of the Auth
Dialog
requesting
permissions
from a user.

Social Channels

Most Social Channels work in third-party websites, as well as in apps on Facebook. Note, though, that not all objects are Social Channels. A photo, for example, is an object, but because it isn't used as a vehicle for passing data from one user to another, it isn't a channel. The Like button, on the other hand, facilitates the flow of information from one user to another (or to many others), making it a Social Channel. Social Channels include the following objects:

+ Feed Dialog

+ Feed Graph object

+ Like button

+ Request Dialog

+ Bookmarks

+ Notifications

+ Dashboards

+ Usage stories

+ Search dialog

Cool core tools for creating advanced apps

While not exactly core concepts, Facebook provides several tools for creating highly sophisticated apps — apps that post to users' Timelines, add tabs to user pages, prompt users to add friends, query and display information from databases, collect funds, initiate chat sessions, and many other functions. The following list takes a look at some of the more commonly used tools and what features they can add to your apps:

+ **Ads API:** Part of the Graph API, the Ads API allows you to place advertisements in your apps or create apps that generate and manage ads on Facebook. To use this tool, you must apply and meet certain criteria. You can find out more about the Ads API at `http://developers.facebook.com/docs/reference/ads-api/`.

+ **Chat API:** You guessed it. This tool allows you to integrate Facebook Chat into other chat applications, such as instant messaging apps, web-based chat apps, and mobile instant messaging apps. You must use the Jabber/XMPP service to make the connection between Facebook Chat and your application. To find out more, check `https://developers.facebook.com/docs/chat/`.

+ **Credits:** Credits is Facebook's payment system, which allows you to create apps that sell things and otherwise collect funds through Facebook. To exchange funds in any fashion on Facebook requires using Credits. You can find additional information on implementing Credits for your apps at `http://developers.facebook.com/docs/credits/`.

✦ **Dialogs:** Dialogs are used for just about everything on Facebook, including apps that collect Credits. You can use Facebook dialogs in your apps, on third-party sites, and so on. There are, of course, several types of dialogs, including Friends, Feed, Pay, Request and Send, and you can display them as pages, pop ups, and in iframes. Find out more at `https://developers.facebook.com/docs/reference/dialogs/`.

✦ **Facebook Query Language (FQL):** If you're familiar database applications, then you know about SQL. FQL differs from SQL in that it queries Graph API data, instead of a SQL database. Most of the query language is similar to SQL, although it isn't nearly as robust in math and other functions. For a description of how queries are formatted and which Graph API tables you can query (and how), go to `http://developers.facebook.com/docs/reference/fql/`.

✦ **Internationalization API:** This API translates your app (or website) among the 70 languages Facebook supports. Pretty cool, right? Be forewarned, though: Even for apps built in Facebook Canvas Pages and iframes, the translation is not automatic, and must be set up for each language you want to use. Find that information at `http://developers.facebook.com/docs/internationalization/`.

Book VI
Chapter 4

**Tour of the
Facebook API**

XFBML — The Facebook markup language

Similar to HTML, XFBML (eXtended FaceBook Markup Language), allows you to integrate Facebook functions into your apps and web pages. XFBML contains special tags that call up Facebook actions and objects, such as Like buttons, Comment dialogs, and so on. These special tags provide a more robust integration with Facebook than iframes, which are discussed in Book VI, Chapter 1.

Why does XFBML provide a more robust integration with Facebook than do iframes? For example, when deploying a Like button, if you do it with XFBML, you can also include a Send button, which allows users to send messages to selected users about your Pages (or anything else they want). In other words, XFBML simply gives you more options than iframes.

To use XFBML, your apps and web pages must load the Facebook JavaScript SDK library (discussed in the "Developing Apps Easier with SDKs" section in this chapter). To use XFBML in your apps and pages, you place the XFBML tags in your page and enter the code that loads the required Facebook JavaScript SDK. The SDK interprets XFBML tags for the browser, thereby allowing the page to perform Facebook actions and exploit Facebook objects.

The good news is that for many objects, you don't have to learn XFBML to use it. As discussed in the "Placing Facebook Objects on Your Web Pages with Social Plugins" section in this chapter, Facebook provides many code generators for most of the more common objects, such as Like buttons, Comment dialogs, and so on.

Developing Apps Easier with SDKs

Facebook's SDKs perform two important functions. Depending on the SDK, they either load libraries of scripting functions that browsers can use to execute script code not otherwise available to the browser, or they provide programming environments that make writing code for a specific platform, such as Apple's iOS mobile platform, easier. Some SDKs perform both functions.

Facebook has four SDKs, two for writing code in popular web scripting languages (JavaScript and PHP), and two for writing platform-specific code for iOS (iPods, iPhones, and iPads), and Google's popular Android operating system (OS) used on many smartphones and tablets. For the sake of this discussion, we separate the SDKs into two categories, placing the web scripting language SDKs in one group and the OS SDKs in the other.

Typically, web scripting languages are used for web apps, and OS SDKs are used for creating standard apps that don't usually require a web page to run in. These are called *mobile apps*. You probably already have several mobile apps running on your smartphone or tablet.

Web scripting SDKs

The two most popular scripting languages on the web are JavaScript, a client-side language, and PHP, a server-side language. Client-side scripts are executed by the browser, and server-side scripts are run by the server. Each have their own pluses and minuses. PHP, for instance, is better at data manipulation, such as querying databases and displaying data, while JavaScript works better for visual and behavioral effects, such as simple animations, and displaying menus and buttons.

Another advantage to server-side scripts is that, because the server processes the code, this removes much of the stress from the browser and device resources, which can be very beneficial on mobile devices. In addition, not all mobile devices, especially older smartphones and feature phones, support JavaScript. Server-side scripts can help assure that your pages and apps display and work on a wider range of devices.

Facebook's JavaScript SDK

The JavaScript SDK supports client-side calls to Facebook's server-side API, allowing your apps and web pages to take advantage of most Facebook features, including the Graph API and Dialogs. It also processes XFBML for exploiting Social Plugins (discussed in the "Placing Facebook Objects on Your Web Pages with Social Plugins" section, later in this chapter), as well as providing a mechanism for your Canvas pages to communicate with Facebook.

To use the Facebook JavaScript SDK, all you have to do is load it at top of your webpages and Canvas Pages. This allows your app to then use XFBML to interact with the Facebook API. Although, depending what your app does inside Facebook, each application will require slightly different code to load the SDK, the basic script for loading it goes beneath the <body> tag in your pages and looks like Listing 1-1.

Listing 1-1:   Loading the JavaScript SDK

```
<div id="fb-root"></div>
<script>
  window.fbAsyncInit = function() {
    FB.init({
      appId      : 'YOUR_APP_ID', // App ID
      channelUrl : '//WWW.YOUR_DOMAIN.COM/channel.html', // Channel File
      status     : true, // check login status
      cookie     : true, // enable cookies to allow the server to access the
    session
      xfbml      : true  // parse XFBML
    });

    // Additional initialization code here
  };

  // Load the SDK Asynchronously
  (function(d){
    var js, id = 'facebook-jssdk'; if (d.getElementById(id)) {return;}
    js = d.createElement('script'); js.id = id; js.async = true;
    js.src = "//connect.facebook.net/en_US/all.js";
    d.getElementsByTagName('head')[0].appendChild(js);
  }(document));
</script>
```

Book VI Chapter 4

Tour of the Facebook API

You can get detailed information on the JavaScript SDK from `http://developers.facebook.com/docs/reference/javascript/`.

PHP SDK

Because the PHP SDK loads server-side scripts, it consists of several PHP pages that you download from github (`https://github.com`) and upload to your web server (the server that hosts your app or web pages on which you want to include Facebook objects). In order to use the PHP SDK, you need to acquire an app ID from Facebook's Developer App, which we show you how to use in Book VI, Chapter 3. You need a lot more info to set up and use this SDK, which you can find at `http://developers.facebook.com/docs/reference/php/`.

Mobile app scripting SDKs

Facebook also provides SDKs for popular mobile devices, such as Google's Android operating system (OS), found on many of today's popular smartphones and tablets, as well as Apple's iOS, used on iPhones, iPod touches, and iPads.

iOS SDK

The iOS SDK allows you to create apps for Apple's handheld devices: the iPod Touch, iPhone, and iPad. Like the PHP SDK, the iOS SDK must be downloaded from github (`https://github.com`). You must also register it with Facebook and install it, which requires an app ID you need to acquire from Facebook. Technically, the iOS SDK is a Facebook app itself. As shown in Figure 4-4, it contains dialogs and debugging tools to help you through the app development process, but it does not completely eliminate the need for programming skills. The URL for the iOS Getting Started page, which contains links to multiple other iOS SDK technical documents, is as follows: `https://developers.facebook.com/docs/mobile/ios/build/`.

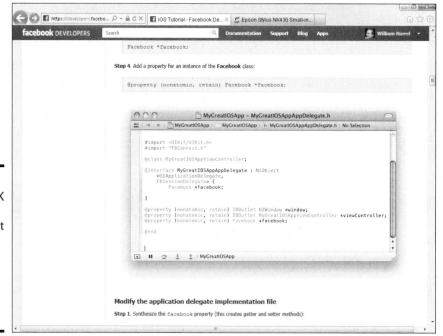

Figure 4-4:
The iOS SDK provides an environment for developing apps for Apple's mobile devices.

Android SDK

The Android SDK allows you to develop Facebook apps for mobile devices (smartphones and tablets), that run on Google's popular Android OS, which powers hundreds of devices. Like the iOS SDK, you must download this one from github (`https://github.com`), register it with Facebook, and install it. If you've used Google's Android SDK, you see some similarities in this one. As shown in Figure 4-5, the Android SDK provides several dialogs for walking you through the development process, including a code editor, a debugger, and a compiler. You can get full installation and usage details for the Android SDK at `https://developers.facebook.com/docs/mobile/android/build/`.

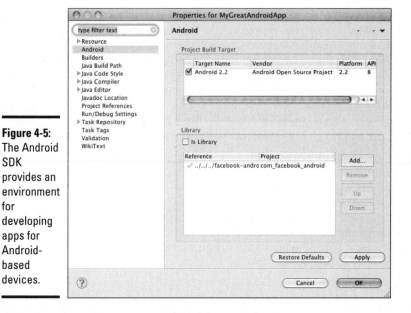

Figure 4-5:
The Android SDK provides an environment for developing apps for Android-based devices.

Placing Facebook Objects on Your Web Pages with Social Plugins

The Facebook API provides a platform for developing apps that integrate and interact with Facebook, both inside the Facebook API and from third-party websites. Social Plugins allow you to add Facebook objects to your web pages. A common application for Social Plugins is placing Like buttons on blog posts, but, of course, there are many other uses.

If you've used Facebook for more than a minute, you're familiar with most of the objects you can control with Social Plugins. They include the Like, Send, and Subscribe buttons, as well as Comments, Activity Feed, Recommendations, and a few others.

You can implement most plugins in one of two ways, with either the XFBML or iframe technologies. The latter, iframe, is discussed in Book VI, Chapter 1. Similar to HTML, XFBML (which requires the JavaScript SDK), formats your app web pages. For an explanation of XFBML, see this chapter's sidebar, "XFBML — The Facebook markup language." To find out more about the JavaScript SDK (and other Facebook SDKs), see the "Developing Apps Easier with SDKs" section, earlier in this chapter.

To implement Social Plugins in your pages, you need to write some code. Facebook provides code generators for most Social Plugins. All you have to do is provide some basic information in the code generator forms, click the Get Code button, and copy and paste your code into your page. Figure 4-6 shows the Like button code generator. The page located at `http://developers.facebook.com/docs/plugins/` provides links to pages containing social plugin code generators.

Activity Feed

The Activity Feed plugin displays recent Facebook activity on your site. The Activity Feed can contain information about users interacting with content in your site, such as Like, Read, Play, and so on. Comments also show up in the Activity Feed. What the user sees depends on whether she is logged into Facebook. When logged in, the user sees activities from her friends. When logged out, the user sees recommendations (discussed in the later "Recommendations" section) from your site, and provides the user an opportunity to log into Facebook.

Figure 4-6: Facebook's code generators automatically create the code for deploying Social Plugins in your pages.

Add to Timeline

The Add to Timeline plugin places a button on your site to create an ongoing connection between your page and the user's Timeline on Facebook. If designed to do so, the app can post app-specific information to the user's Timeline each time your users interact with the page or app! This keeps your app forefront on all of your users' Facebook Timelines, increasing awareness of the app between your current users and their friends.

Comments button

The Comments box allows users to, you guessed it, comment on your site, or, more specifically, your page. If, just as comments work on any other Facebook page, the user doesn't uncheck the Post to Facebook check box, the comment is posted to her friends' News Feeds — a terrific way to promote your site.

Facepile

The Facepile plugin displays profile pictures of Facebook users who have connected with your page in one way or another. You can configure it to display the pictures of people who have signed up for your site, people who have Liked your site, and so on. The images display tiled in your Like box.

Like box

The Like box, which displays on external web pages, differs from the Like button in that it provides information about your web page, such as how many users have Liked this web page, as well as which of their friends have Liked it. Users also see recent posts from the web page, and can Like the web page from within Facebook without having to go to it. You can include several options, such as Faces and profile Streams, as shown in Figure 4-7.

Like button

When the user clicks the Like button for your external web page, this creates a connection between your web page and the user. Your web page will appear in the user's Likes and Interest section of his or her Timeline. You can also target ads to the people who have Liked your web page.

Live Stream

Live Stream allows users of your website or application to exchange comments and activities with each other in real time. You would typically use Live Stream when hosting a real-time event, such as chats, live classes, and seminars. Put simplistically, Live Stream allows for real-time interactivity between you and your users and your users among themselves.

Login button

The Login button allows users to login to your pages through Facebook. It also shows pictures of the user's friends who previously signed up for your site.

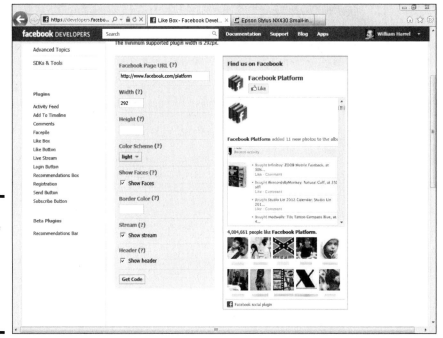

Figure 4-7:
An example of a Like box and the code generator used to create it.

Recommendations box

Recommendations shows personalized recommendations to your users. Recommendations are generated by all the social interactions with URLs from your site. A recommendation might look something like this: "Your App Name," with a link to the app. The next line might read, "1,000,000 people recommended this."

Note that recommendations are generated by domain, or by multiple domains, that must be specified within the plugin. You can get an explanation of this and how to implement it at `http://developers.facebook.com/docs/reference/plugins/recommendations/`.

Registration

This plugin allows visitors to your site to sign up for your pages with their Facebook accounts. You've probably seen this before. As shown in Figure 4-8, the plugin creates a form on your page and prefills it with information from the user's Facebook account. You can choose to use several Facebook object fields for information, or just a few. There's also an option to allow the user to sign up through *your* registration process, just in case she doesn't want to use Facebook credentials, eliminating the need for separate forms.

Send button

Including a Send button on your external web page allows users to send content to their friends. They can, for example, send the URL for your web page in a message or in an e-mail. The Send button differs from the Like button in that it allows users to send content to selected users, instead of all of their friends.

Subscribe button

Placing a Subscribe button in your web page lets users subscribe to your public updates. As part of the Subscribe button implementation (with JavaScript), you tell your app to listen in real time for clicks on the Subscribe button, which informs you immediately when a user subscribes.

Registration Bar

As we write this, the Registration Bar has not yet been implemented. In essence, it combines several plugins into a simple-to-use bar. Users will be able to Like content, share with friends, and get and make recommendations, all from the same location on your web page or from your app. When the page or app loads, the Registration Bar will load collapsed at the bottom of the web page, until the user nears the bottom of the page. At that time, it will expand, providing the user with the options listed here, as well as several others.

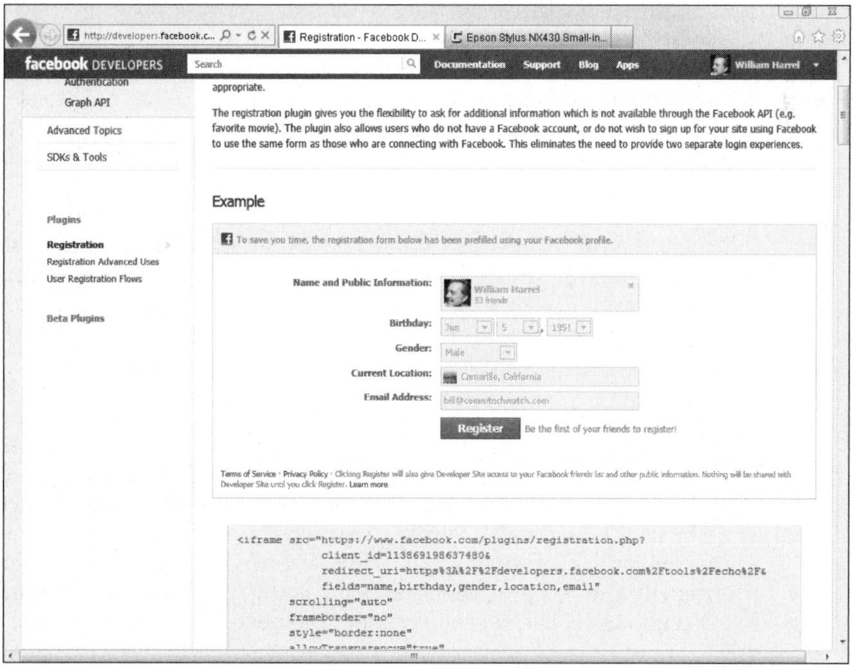

**Book VI
Chapter 4**

**Tour of the
Facebook API**

Figure 4-8:
An example of the Facebook registration form, which allows users to use Facebook credentials to register for your site.

Index

A

About Me section, 232
About Page, 82, 311, 312, 318, 333
abuse, reporting, 91, 345
account, ads, 472–474. *See also* ads
account, Facebook. *See also* Account Settings page; privacy settings
  ads, 43
  apps associated with, 37
  for business, 301
  deactivating, 34–35
  deleting, 44
  finding friends, 19–24
  overview, 17
  reinstating, 35
  starting, 17–19
  text messages, setting up to accept, 185–186
Account menu, 73, 353
Account Settings page
  apps settings, 37–39
  Facebook Ads option, 43
  Facebook e-mail account, 215
  General Settings, 25–30
  mobile settings, 39–40
  notifications, 35–37
  overview, 25
  password, changing, 253
  payments, 40–43
  Security tab, 30–35
Acquaintances list, 59
actions, Open Graph, 515–517
activating Facebook e-mail, 27

active sessions, 34
activity applications, 79
Activity Feed plugin, 274, 548
Activity Log, 82–83, 85, 327–328
Ad Account Settings page, 469
Add to Timeline plugin, 274, 549
Add/Remove Friends option, Manage List menu, 62
address, business, 311, 373
Admin Panel, 286, 305–306, 326–329
administrators (admins)
  on ads account, 472–473
  apps, 519
  Fan Page Timeline, 314, 315, 333
  Group, 160, 162, 169
  multiple, 35, 47
Adobe Flash, 126, 145–146
ads
  Account Settings page, 43
  administrators on ads account, 472–473
  Ads Manager page, 465–470
  benefits of using, 455
  budget, 464
  campaigns, 464
  closing ads account, 473–474
  creating to get Likes, 457
  designing, 458–462
  Engagement Ads, 455–456
  finding, 454
  generating report, 470–472

  guidelines for, 458
  log-out ads, 475
  overview, 453
  pricing, 464–465
  promotions, 452
  Reach Generator, 474–475
  schedule, 464
  Sponsored Stories, 456–457
  targeting audience, 462–463
  tips for creating, 466
Ads and Business Solutions category, Help Center, 92
Ads API, 542
Ads Manager page, 465–473
advanced API documentation, 537–538
advanced apps, 542–543
Advanced Chat settings, 212
Advanced Topics page, 538
Advertise on Facebook page, 458–465
advertising, 220, 264, 404–405. *See also* ads; marketing
affinity, in EdgeRank, 435–436
age, Insights data on, 428, 479
Age Restrictions option, 308
aggregations, Open Graph, 517, 518
albums
  creating, 129–132
  moving photos from one to another, 134–135

Notes